"Evola is one of the most inter
war generation. He has
knowledge at his disposal."
Mircea Eliade,
author of *The Sacred and the Profane*

"A dazzling and interesting, but very dangerous author . . ."
Hermann Hesse,
author of *Siddhartha*

"It is one of Evola's greatest merits that he combines a
prodigious wealth of erudite detail with the gift of isolating
from their local conditioning the ideas or
disciplines that are of value to us."
Marguerite Yourcenar,
author of *Memoirs of Hadrian*

"Fire in ice and ice in fire . . . the eagle's cry . . .
the demon of action."
René Guénon,
author of *The Crisis of the Modern World*

"But this at least one cannot take away from [Evola]: his
consistency, a universal education, and the courage to
make a daring, sovereign formulation."
Gerd-Klaus Kaltenbrunner,
in *Die Welt*

"One of the most difficult and ambiguous figures
in modern esotericism . . ."
Richard Smoley,
in *Parabola*

Other books by Julius Evola

The Doctrine of Awakening

Eros and the Mysteries of Love

The Hermetic Tradition

Introduction to Magic

Meditations on the Peaks

The Mystery of the Grail

Revolt Against the Modern World

The Yoga of Power

MEN AMONG THE RUINS

Postwar Reflections of a Radical Traditionalist

JULIUS EVOLA

Translated by Guido Stucco
Edited by Michael Moynihan

Inner Traditions
Rochester, Vermont

Inner Traditions International
One Park Street
Rochester, Vermont 05767
www.InnerTraditions.com

First U.S. edition published by Inner Traditions in 2002

Originally published in Italian under the title *Gli uomini e le rovine* by Edizioni Mediterranee

Library of Congress Cataloging-in-Publication Data

Evola, Julius, 1898–1974.
    [uomini e le rovino. English]
    Men among the ruins : post-war reflections of a radical traditionalist / Julius Evola ; translated by Guido Stucco ; edited by Michael Moynihan.
        p. cm.
    Includes bibliographical references.
    ISBN 0-89281-905-7
        1. Philosophy, Modern—20th century. I. Stucco, Guido. II. Moynihan, Michael. III. Title.
    B3614.E921 S7813 2002
    190—dc21   2001051516

Printed and bound in the United States

10 9 8 7 6 5 4 3 2 1

Text design and layout by Priscilla Baker
This book was typeset in Janson, with Schneidler Initials and Univers as display typefaces

Back cover photograph: passport photo of Julius Evola, circa 1940. Collection of Gaspare Cannizzo. Published in *Julius Evola: Scritti per Vie della Traditione 1971–1974*, Edizioni di Vie della Tradizione, Palermo, 1996.

A limited hardcover edition of this book is available from Dominion Press, P.O. Box 129, Waterbury Center, VT 05677.

CONTENTS

꘎⟞⟝⬤⟞⟝꘎

EDITOR'S NOTE

For the present English edition, we have endeavored to convey precisely Evola's own system of terminology. Thus the reader will note the capitalization of words like Tradition (when used by Evola to denote a transcendent spiritual tradition), Idea, Land, Leader, Mothers (Evola utilizes this term in a sense inspired by J. J. Bachofen), Orders (referring to Knightly Orders, *Männerbünde*, etc.), and the State. We have attempted to follow the precedent of the Italian edition (Rome: Volpe, 1972) as closely as possible in this respect. In addition, we have followed the now common scholarly practice of capitalizing the terms Fascism and Fascist only when they refer specifically to aspects of the historical Italian Fascism of the Mussolini regime. The terms are set in lower case when they refer to "generic" or less specific conceptions. The footnotes to the text are all from Evola, with the exception of occasional clarifications by the Editor, which are noted as such. We have also made a concerted effort to provide the bibliographical details of English translations (when these exist) for books cited by Evola.

Editor's Acknowledgments

Sincere gratitude is expressed to the following people for their efforts with regard to this edition: Dr. H. T. Hansen for his new preface and for the use of his excellent introductory essay, Jon Graham at Inner Traditions, Martin Schwarz, Markus Wolff, Phillip Luciani for his initial support of the project, Dr. Stephen Flowers for helpful suggestions, and above all to Joscelyn Godwin for his many generous contributions and insights.

FOREWORD

Joscelyn Godwin

Now that we have passed the end of Evola's century, his voice is being heard more widely than it ever was in his lifetime. This is the ninth of his books to appear in English translation; many more have appeared in French and German, while in Italy even his innumerable journalistic writings are seeing the light again, and several periodicals are dedicated solely to his ideas.

This revival of an obscure Italian thinker is a remarkable phenomenon. At the present rate, it will not be long before Evola begins to receive the tribute of doctoral dissertations, scholarly articles, and academic conferences, prior to being established in whatever place is eventually accorded to him in the history of ideas. But two things will always act like gravel in the cogs of the academic machine, which is usually able to reduce any historical subject to a pure and emotionally anodyne state. The present publication is an attempt to deal with, though not to remove, one of these obstacles.

Evola is a rare example of universality in an age of specialization. He was universal not only in the horizontal domain, as philosopher, engineering student, artillery officer, Dadaist poet and painter, journalist, alpinist, scholar, linguist, Orientalist, and political commentator—not a bad record of achievement before his fiftieth year—but in the vertical dimension as well.

It is this vertical dimension that constitutes one of the obstacles to the modern, agnostic approach, but which from Evola's own standpoint gave sense and value to what otherwise might appear as the thinly spread talents of a "renaissance man" or dilettante. One might call it a spiritual dimension, if that adjective were not so exhausted and if it did not carry connotations of a religiosity that Evola despised. His was not the spirituality of piety and mysticism, but the aspiration to what he understood to be the highest calling of man: the identity of Self and Absolute. His route to it led initially not through religion (he soon discarded his strict Catholic upbringing), but through philosophy, not just book-learned but also lived with a white-hot intensity comparable to that which left

Nietzsche a burnt-out wreck. Soon after this, Evola plunged into a particularly esoteric form of occultism, again not of the literary or armchair type, but one that entailed trials, asceticisms, and a mastery of terrors that most of us can barely imagine. As a consequence, his character and ideals were fully formed before he was out of his twenties, and he remained true to them for the rest of his life. All that changed was a gradual refinement and a tireless filling-in of the steps on the ladder, from the heights of the Absolute (so beautifully expressed in *The Doctrine of Awakening*, Evola's book on Buddhism) down through the mysterious intermediate realms treated in his essays "Magic as a Science of the Self," to the dirty world of politics, where Evola the journalist, as a fearless critic of the Fascist regime, seemed to lead a charmed life.

This brings us to the second and far more serious obstacle to the appreciation of Evola's thought in a social-democratic society: his extreme right-wing views. One might argue that his reputation would be best served by suppressing them, and especially by not publishing the present work in which they are given such blatant form. *Men among the Ruins* is, by any standard, far from being Evola's best work, and it should never be the gateway to his thought: that function belongs to his masterwork, *Revolt Against the Modern World.* However, if Evola is to be studied and understood even by those—and this is increasingly the case in the United States—who cannot read him in the original language, it is academically dishonest to suppress anything.

The virtue of the academic approach resembles that of a bomb-disposal unit. That is to say, it can handle explosive materials at arm's length, without harming either itself or others. It does this with the tools of rationality and scholarship, unsullied by emotionality or subjective references. At least, that is how it is supposed to work, and why there is such a concept as "academic freedom"—that is, the freedom to work on controversial topics and to come to one's own conclusions without political interference.

The bomb-disposal unit in the present publication consists of the exhaustive introductory study of Evola's politics by Dr. H. T. Hansen. This first appeared as a preface to the German language edition (*Menschen inmitten von Ruinen*, Tübingen, Zurich, Paris: Hohenrain-Verlag, 1991). It provides the factual and intellectual-historical basis that is essential for anyone who sets out in a serious spirit to criticize Evola's political ideas, because it will disabuse them of hearsay and prejudgments, and allow for the informed and open debate that such matters deserve—one can scarcely call them controversial, since there is virtually no controversy to be had about them. Those who react to Evola's text only on an emotional level are, unfortunately, beyond such assistance; it would be better for them to save their blood pressure by not reading him at all.

The value of such reading and debate lies, naturally, in their educative function, but also, in the present case, in the self-knowledge that one gains from the dispassionate handling of explosive material. Evola is a great teacher in this regard. If he were a mere right-wing fanatic, he would be as tiresome as any other person enslaved to an ideology. The difference between him and the fanatics, intelligence aside, is that he writes always with the vertical dimension in mind. Those who do not know his writings on esotericism must take this on trust until they have discovered them. They will then find in works such as *The Hermetic Tradition* and *The Yoga of Power* one of the keenest minds in the field, whose personal experience—and there is no other explanation for it—gave him the key to the mysteries of self-transformation and self-realization. The challenge to esotericists is that when Evola came down to earth, he was so "incorrect"—by the received standards of our society. He was no fool; and he cannot possibly have been right . . . so what is one to make of it? If one can cross the *pons asinorum* represented by these questions, then one has passed the first initiation, and can begin to learn the serious business that Evola has to teach.

PREFACE TO THE AMERICAN EDITION*

Dr. H. T. Hansen

More than ten years have passed since I wrote my introduction about Evola's political endeavors for the German edition of *Men among the Ruins*. In the meantime numerous books on Evola have appeared, along with an even greater number of essays and specialized studies. In addition, several anthologies have been published that make his extremely extensive production of newspaper and journal articles more readily accessible.[1] Probably because of the centenary of his birth in 1998, it became apparent that the public consideration of Evola is no longer taboo, especially in Italy. This is evident not only from the more or less objective reports in the popular print media, but also by the increasingly frequent scholarly writings on this Roman cultural philosopher, esotericist, and political thinker.

Nothing fundamentally new in regard to my overall assessment of Evola has ensued out of this, but particular aspects of his work can now be better explicated, and some things must also be revised in light of the documents that have surfaced in recent years. Above all, this concerns Evola's presumed relationship to Mussolini, and by no means should it be kept from English-speaking readers.

However, the introduction of new material into an old text is always difficult, because changes made to one part more often than not necessitate changes to other parts in order to round out the overall picture—thus entailing a complete revision of the text. Neither the time nor the inclination for this is at my disposal. This is the reason for my provisional solution, which may not be entirely adequate, of pointing out the passages that require corrections and explaining the new facts, but leaving any conclusions to the reader.

Before I move on to concrete matters, I would like to draw attention to a book that takes a comprehensive look at the philosophical foundations of Evola's political views. This was also the starting point of my original introduction.

---

*Translated from the German by Michael Moynihan.

Piero di Vona, a philosophy professor from Naples, has dealt with the subject very knowledgeably in his recent volume *Metafisica e politica in Julius Evola* (Metaphysics and Politics in Julius Evola).[2] Unlike the usual strictly political analyses, he does not treat the realms of metaphysics and politics as being separate, but instead views them in Evola's case as inevitably linked.

What follows are some new assessments and concrete additions to my original introduction.

Page 50: Here I have addressed the question of the forged passport, which Evola supposedly made use of in the 1940s in Vienna. Through research in the Roman official archives, the American scholar Dana Lloyd Thomas has discovered that in 1942 Evola in fact had his passport withdrawn by the Italian foreign ministry.[3] This was done to pressure Evola to return to Italy. The Department of Foreign Affairs was specifically alarmed over Evola's lectures in Germany and Austria, in which he had declared the concept of "Latinity"—a term highly upheld by fascist officials—to be unsuitable for the Italian people as a whole. Evola differentiated instead between a "Nordic" component of the people, classified as a higher element, and the "Mediterranean" component, which was deemed as lower. The Department of Foreign Affairs feared that this would drive a wedge between ethnic groups, undermining the unity of the Italian nation in the middle of the war. At a lecture in Vienna in 1941, Evola had even gone so far as to deny the Italians the right to their own nation, as he argued for the merging of his country in a "Holy Roman Empire of the German Nation." This led to an aggressive intervention on the part of the Italian general consul in Rome and, ultimately, to the withdrawal of Evola's passport. Evola was incensed and protested vehemently. Mussolini had to personally intervene and countermand the measure, but due to resistance on the part of the Roman bureaucracy, this took a protracted time to take effect.

This episode also shows that, as has been mentioned, the relationship between Evola and Mussolini was indeed different from the one I outlined in 1991. Just as I completed my introduction in 1990, the book *Taccuini Mussoliniani* (Mussolinian Diaries)[4] by Yvon de Begnac appeared, but I was no longer able to make use of it. This work comprises notes that Yvon de Begnac, who intended to write a comprehensive biography of Mussolini, took down between the years 1934 and 1943 during many long discussions with Il Duce. It was not until 1990 that the material was published, after having been edited by Francesco

Perfetti and graced with a positive foreword by Renzo de Felice, the renowned scholar of Mussolini's life. According to these notes, Evola must have already come into contact with Mussolini in 1922, through the Futurist Filippo Tommaso Marinetti. Incidentally, at that time Evola was apparently so enthused with Sigmund Freud that he said, "The world of Freud must become the true world of thought." According to statements by Mussolini, this was even how he himself first became acquainted with Freud's ideas.[5] De Begnac also reports that a meeting took place between Spengler and Evola. Because there is no further corroborating evidence for all this, however, certain doubts persist concerning the notes of de Begnac.

The direct intervention of Mussolini in the passport affair nevertheless seems to indicate that Evola was not just an ordinary Italian traveling lecturer, but was instead probably engaged in a more or less delicate mission on behalf of Mussolini to build a bridge of understanding between Italy and Germany. But as Dana Lloyd Thomas has expressed, if Mussolini's intentions were strategic, Evola's were eschatological. It is therefore likely that from a certain point on, Evola was deemed "politically unsuited" for missions of this sort because of his metaphysical dogmatism. Evola himself, however, never commented on anything in regard to this sphere of questions.

Thomas's research has also uncovered documents which show that in 1939 Evola submitted an application to become a member of the Partito Nazionale Fascista (the Italian Fascist Party).[6] Apparently he did so in order to be able to enlist as a volunteer in the war that was then breaking out. Evola wanted to serve as an officer, as he had in World War I, and this was possible only if he became a party member. His application was denied, however, for two reasons: first, in light of his numerous journalistic attacks against Fascism it was not believed that Evola, now at forty-two years of age, really wished to follow the party line; and second, because he had received a military demotion in 1934. The grounds for this lay in Evola's refusal to engage in a duel with a reporter whom he had sharply attacked in his journal La Torre. Apparently this did not have to do so much with an actual confrontation (which, incidentally, is forbidden by Italian law), but rather with the protocol over how two former officers should settle a conflict according to military rules of honor. But Evola appears to have been against the duel because he did not want to place himself at the same level with this man whom he later described, along with other journalists, as an "authentic gangster." The proceedings over this were finally brought before a military court, which ruled against Evola and demoted him.

Page 57ff: "Evola and National Socialism." Here, too, my fundamental assessment has not changed, although it appears now that Evola was more critical of National Socialism—above all in the character of its unofficial "ideologue" Alfred Rosenberg—than I had originally assumed. A book precisely on this theme has just appeared that analyzes the various essays from an antifascist position and on a broader textual basis.[7] Recent research has also addressed the connections between Evola and Edgar Julius Jung, the private secretary and speechwriter of Franz von Papen, chancellor of the German Reich, and these reveal the closeness and friendship between Evola and Jung.[8] Jung was an adherent of the concept of the *Ordensstaat*[9] and apparently wanted to build, together with Evola, a "Ghibelline Front" against the excesses of National Socialism. We know from the traditional philosopher Leopold Ziegler, who was very closely allied with him, that Jung had even formulated a plan to shoot Hitler.[10] By 1934, however, Jung had been murdered by the National Socialists.

The relationship between Evola and Raphael Spann, which is evident through correspondence, further indicates the existence of a loose, primarily Catholic, resistance movement against so-called "biological racism," to which Evola also belonged.[11] Thus, Evola's efforts to arrive at a racial theory of his own can be seen in another light, as can the later plans for his Italian-German journal of racial studies, *Sangue e Spirito–Blut und Geist* (Blood and Spirit), which at a certain point—despite previous approval—were suspended for no apparent reason. It is possible that there was something of a revolutionary conservative front against the racist beliefs of National Socialism, which were then provoking worldwide protest, and against Alfred Rosenberg, who was regarded as the movement's "spiritual representative." Rosenberg's book, *Der Mythus des 20. Jahrhunderts* (The Myth of the Twentieth Century), was referred to as "nonsense" in the intellectual circle around Spann.[12]

In regard to Evola's close connection to Edgar Jung and to the Spann circle—all of whom were definitely prepared to take covert or overt action against the National Socialist system—it is conceivable that he had an infiltration strategy in mind, such as the brothers Raphael and Adalbert Spann also wanted to put into practice. This is all the more likely considering that Evola, as the citizen of a nation allied with Germany, was allowed a much greater degree of political freedom than was accessible to the Germans themselves.[13]

There is no convincing proof, however, for such a conjecture, nor did Evola himself ever explicitly assert anything in this regard, although we do find a sentence in his autobiography that can be interpreted along these lines: "A secret front of the Right intended increasingly to orientate itself back to the original idea [i.e., the 'conservative revolution' in the sense of Moeller van den Bruck], and my contribution could have been useful, in a doctrinal sense, toward this purpose."[14]

In connection with this, the opinion of Christoph Boutin, who has written the most extensive work to date on Evola's political conceptions, should not go unmentioned.[15] Boutin thinks it can be discerned from the various remarks made by Evola that he was active as an agent for the German *Sicherheitsdienst* (Security Service, abbreviated SD) and procured political information.

Philippe Baillet, the great authority and outstanding French translator of Evola, disputes this, but due to the lack of available documents is also unable to clarify the situation.[16] However, he does point out a few sentences in Evola's later book on Fascism and National Socialism that offer one possible explanation.[17] There it says that "the SS strove to be a *'weltanschauliche Stoßtruppe'* (ideological storm troop).[18] The SD, which had at that time already set itself up within the SS, originally also was to carry out cultural activities and cultural supervision (according to Himmler's declaration of 1937). Even though the SD later developed in other directions—including counterespionage—its Office VII nevertheless did retain this former character, and serious researchers and professors were also members of the organization." Evola writes there also of the "honor service" of the SS, to which culture-creating personalities who made relevant contributions were appointed, and as examples he mentions Professor Franz Altheim and Professor O. Menghin from the University of Vienna.

Philippe Baillet has also drawn attention to one point in particular that further explains the fascination which the Roman cultural philosopher had for National Socialism.[19] Besides its voluntaristic aspect, Baillet points namely to the aesthetic components of National Socialism (the orchestrated and almost choreographed military deployments, Speer's "Cathedral of Light" displays, and so on), which in the case of the SS—with their uniforms and long, black coats, as well as their death's head insignia—were endowed with a character that was especially cold, impersonal, and reminiscent of glacial regions. The fact that Evola responded to aesthetic stimuli is evident in any case from his own personal style, with his monocle and impeccable suits. In Baillet's view, this also allowed Evola to overlook the "mythological patchwork" of National Socialism, where a sparkling outer appearance covered up the inadequate contents.

As for the National Socialist–era documents that speak against Evola's cooperation with the SD, I have already addressed these in my introduction.

Page 85, concerning Giovanni Preziosi: In my original introduction I portrayed this Catholic conspiracy theorist and friend of Evola's in too positive a light. His anti-Semitism actually appears to have been pathological and he apparently suffered from paranoia. As a result, in the final phase of his life he denounced one and all, so to speak.[20]

Page 89: In the meantime it has become evident that Evola's book *Cavalcare la tigre* (Riding the Tiger) had already been written before *Men among the Ruins*.[21]

There may certainly be other aspects to improve upon in my original introduction, but at the same time this new preface should not become overly long and detailed.

Introduction

JULIUS EVOLA'S POLITICAL ENDEAVORS*

Dr. H. T. Hansen

This essay can be traced back to the fact that as Julius Evola's works have achieved wider recognition, his relations to Fascism and National Socialism have prompted many to dismiss his body of ideas as a whole and without further inquiry. This has also affected his purely esoteric writings, which have nothing to do with political questions. Nevertheless, a portrayal of Evola's political activities unearths new, often unsuspected aspects that can contribute to a greater and better understanding of the complete oeuvre of this cultural philosopher.

In order to facilitate the reader's independent judgment of Evola's political work, it seems most fitting to let Evola speak for himself as much as possible and to be cautious with value judgments and interpretations. In doing this, we have placed special value on documents of the different epochs and the various creative phases. It was also our intention to include extensive quotations from the thinkers who most influenced Evola. However, this method unfortunately leads to a mounting number of references and bibliographical notes that can tire the reader. This road has already been traveled by Philippe Baillet on the occasion of the colloquium on René Guénon and Julius Evola at the Section of Religious Sciences at the Sorbonne in 1986 (see Actes du IIème colloque de Politica Hermetica: "Métaphysique et Politique: René Guénon – Julius Evola," Paris, 1987).

Above all, the purpose of our study is to show how Evola arrived at his frequently "scandalous"-seeming statements; what part of them can be attributed

---

*Translated from the German by Markus Wolff.

to the prevalent Zeitgeist; where the parallels to other thinkers can be found; and what part can be traced back to his own "personal equation" (one of Evola's favorite expressions for someone's nature and personality). Therefore, this study aims to hand an additional interpretive tool to the reader of Evola's writings to facilitate a clear judgment.

But from the beginning we want to emphasize a single point: to Evola, the center of all things is not man but rather the Transcendent. Regardless of the question that concerns him, he is always searching for the direct relationship to the Absolute—that is, that domain which lies beyond the merely human, because human affairs are one way today but tomorrow may be quite different. According to the view of Tradition, on the contrary, the principles that form the foundation of our world remain forever the same. He is not interested in what is bound to time, but instead in that which is above time, the "eternal." Therefore, one cannot expect from Evola the now prevalent Western "human-ist" values, but must reckon with a total inversion of the standpoints that one is used to. The question of whether such an altered viewpoint can serve to solve today's countless problems cannot be debated in this context. We are exclusively concerned here with the examination of Evolian lines of thought. (This abso-lute stress on the spiritual realm can also be found in other intellectuals of this time—for example, in Martin Heidegger.)

We will show, in the process, that even Evola, although very seldom found in the "lowly regions" of everyday politics, was subject to a development of his political views that related to different stages of his life, even though his under-lying principles always remained the same. The leap made from his 1928 book *Imperialismo pagano* (Pagan Imperialism; German edition: *Heidnischer Imperialismus*, Leipzig, 1933), written in youthful exuberance, to the *"apoliteia,"* an attitude totally removed from politics that he preached in his old age, is certainly immense.

The immediate occasion that inspired the present essay was the first Ger-man edition of Evola's only manual of political doctrine, *Men among the Ruins,* as well as the new edition of *Revolt Against the Modern World* (English edition: Rochester, Vt., 1995), and the anticipated reactions to them. The German reader has already been introduced to Evola's relationship to Fascism and National Socialism through various newspaper and magazine articles, by my earlier in-troduction to *Revolt Against the Modern World,* and by Eduard Gugenberger's and Roman Schweidlenka's book *Mutter Erde, Magie und Politik* (Vienna, 1987). The latter two authors devote an entire and generally fair chapter to Evola, although their many quotes from him could be misunderstood without their larger context. However, Umberto Eco has also taken aim at Evola several times, as he did at the Frankfurt Book Fair, and in a surprisingly spiteful manner that would not normally be expected of such an intelligent and humorous author. Does an author who feels the calling to "enlighten" have to resort to slander in order to elevate his own standpoint as the right one?

Every reader will have to judge for himself the amount of distance he wishes to keep from Evola after working through the materials offered here. We will add some comments on the structure of this study. A lot of space has been given to the influences of Evola's youth, because the intellectual foundations of his later far-reaching teachings (twenty-five books, around three hundred long essays, and well over one thousand newspaper and magazine articles) were already in place by the time he was twenty-five. When selecting quotes from his "teachers," we have consulted only those works of which we know, via his own statements, that he did indeed work through them in his youth. The identical tone of these quotes and Evola's core statements (especially in *Men among the Ruins*) will then be obvious to all his readers. This should not cast any doubts regarding Evola's uniqueness, but instead seeks to document a relatively recent intellectual climate that seems to belong to a whole other world in its incisive questioning of what we regard today see as self-evident "humanism": a different world, whose utterances seem barely publishable today. The difficulties that apparently obstructed the uncensored edition of Nietzsche's *Collected Works* by Colli and Montinari in recent years can be traced to exactly that. Next follows the treatment of the main theme: Evola and Fascism, as well as National Socialism, and then his views on racism and the Jews. Notes about Evola's effect on Italian neofascism as well as a short treatment of the "moral" question will conclude this study.

Decisive Influences on Evola's Thought

Although hesitant to repeat what we have already written in the introduction to the recent English edition of *Revolt Against the Modern World*, we will recapitulate briefly the most important dates of Evola's life.

Giulio Cesare Evola was born into a family of the Sicilian landed gentry in Rome on 19 May 1898, and was raised strictly Catholic. Given his rebellious spirit, this had the effect that Evola soon encountered the then ultraprogressive circles of poets around Filippo Tommaso Marinetti and Giovanni Papini, who, as founders of Futurism, demanded a total break with conventional forms of thought and style. Instead, Futurism wanted modern life to be understood as movement, dynamism, and ever-present speed that supersedes the categories of space and time. Also, Marinetti's famous exclamation of "war, the world's only hygiene" had its effect on Evola, since it was the time of World War I and Evola had enlisted as an artillery officer.

Evola himself writes about Papini in his autobiography *Il cammino del cinabro* (The Path of Cinnabar, named after a symbol in Chinese alchemy; Milan, 1972, p. 15f.): "Of course, that nihilism which preserves only the naked individual, that individual who despises any support and takes a stand against any evasions and subterfuge, has to make an impression upon youth." This passage already shows one of Evola's most important character traits, one that continues through his whole work: his unconditional and militant antipathy toward everything bourgeois. The fact that Evola never married, never wanted children, never had a middle-class job, and broke off his engineering studies before the last exam, in spite of his excellent record (so that he wouldn't be, as he writes, a "Doctor" or a "Professor" like the others) can be traced back to this sentiment. Thus, Evola is not even a "dropout," since he never dropped in to begin with. This is perhaps a symptom of his upbringing, about which next to nothing is known, as Evola himself hardly ever mentioned his personal life—not even in his autobiography, which is solely concerned with the development of his ideas. Only the "inner" life counts for him.

Futurism's lack of a truly inward-looking nature and its "loud, ostentatious" side were also the reasons that Evola turned away from the movement. But Papini had left a lasting impression, not only because of his fight against intellectual groveling, so ardently shared by Evola, but especially because he introduced him to many non-Italian streams of thought. Two of these must be emphasized: first Eastern religions, then Western mysticism, specifically Meister Eckhart and Jan van Ruysbroeck. These discoveries laid the groundwork for Evola's lifelong demand for crystalline clarity in all religious and esoteric questions, and for his simultaneous aversion to all sentimentalism and ecstatic fanaticism in this area.

However, before we treat esoteric influences, we should describe Evola's worldly philosophical foundation. Three thinkers exercised a special fascination on him in his youthful years, because he could also totally identify with them, being in the same age group. In addition, all three died at a very young age—two by suicide and one (Otto Braun) perished in World War I. Evola's own inclination toward suicide and toward death in general, which he called *cupio dissolvi*—the desire for self-disintegration—was mirrored in them. He himself evaded suicide only by reading a section from the Buddhist Pali Canon (see the introduction to *Revolt Against the Modern World*, p. xv).

First we look at Carlo Michelstaedter (1887–1910), whose influence Evola denoted as more positive and more important than Nietzsche's, that transvaluator of all values whose sharp polemics added so much to Evola's style. Michelstaedter came from a Jewish family in Görz, a town on the Isonzo in northern Italy. Initially he had studied mathematics in Vienna (see below as to the significance of Vienna in this context), but later delved into painting and Greek philosophy. After he had finished writing his work *La persuasione e la rettorica* (Conviction and Rhetoric; the edition used here: Milan, 1982) one evening, he shot himself the next day. His opinion that he had nothing of value to add to this work surely influenced his decision. Evola was an intimate friend of one of Michelstaedter's cousins and thus lived through these events at close range. Soon after, this cousin likewise ended his young life by committing suicide.

The fundamental point of Michelstaedter's book is the demand for *persuasione*—that is, conviction. By conviction, Michelstaedter means much more; he sees it as an absolute sufficiency of the Self, which he holds to be the only real principle in the individual. As long as the Self does not exist in itself, but only in the "other" that conditions its life through things and relationships, and thus retains elements of dependence and need, there is no conviction but rather a lack, which is the true death of value. "Value is found only in that which exists for itself, which demands the principle of inner life from nothing and nobody—autarchy." Thus Evola describes the essence of Michelstaedter's philosophy (in *Saggi sull'Idealismo Magico* [Essays on Magical Idealism], Todi, Rome, 1925, p. 136 ff.).

Let us hear Michelstaedter himself in *Persuasione e rettorica*: "*Fear*, which most people believe to be restricted to a certain danger, is in truth the terrible horror in the face of the infinite darkness of him who feels unconscious and powerless in a specific case because he has been carried beyond the realm of his power" (p. 60). "*He who fears death is already dead.* He who wants for a moment that his life should be his alone, who wants for a moment to be convinced of what he does, must seize the present; *he must see everything in the present as final,* as if death is certain to follow: *and he must create life out of himself in the darkness.*

Death can't take anything from him who has his life in the present; because nothing in this man demands continued existence, nothing in him comes from the fear of death. . . . And death only takes away that which *is born. It only takes away that which it already seized on the day one was born, which lives from fear of death for the very fact that it was born*" (p. 69). "Because in this final present he must possess everything and give up everything, be convinced and convince, possess himself by possessing the world—and *be one, he and the world*" (p. 82; emphasis original).

"The path of conviction is not taken by '*omnibus*' (all). This path has no road-signs or directions that one can share, study, or repeat. But everyone senses the need to find this path, and the measure of this need is one's own pain; everyone must open this path anew for themselves, because everyone is alone and can expect support only from oneself. There is only one suggestion for this Path of Conviction: do not surrender to contentment with what has been given to you (by others)" (p. 104).

The principle of autarchy, which Evola already knew from mystical and esoteric sources, found its philosophical justification here, and led to the authoritative self of his philosophical period.

As the second thinker should be mentioned Otto Braun, who had already tried to analyze Nietzsche's *Zarathustra* at the age of thirteen, and who said something that Evola himself could have uttered: "It is very curious that Nietzsche never conveyed to me the principle of enjoying life to the full, but only that of the *greatest* fulfillment of duty, however, not in the bourgeois sense of the phrase." (Otto Braun, *Aus den Nachgelassenen Schriften eines Frühvollendeten*, Berlin, 1921, p. 21, from his diary entry of September 14, 1910; English edition: *The Diary of Otto Braun, with Selections from His Letters and Poems*, London, 1924.)

Evola himself quotes the following verbatim in his *Saggi* (p. 144): "But I will endeavor to recreate *everything* that comes my way to suit *my* goal; for me, that is free will" (Otto Braun, p. 148).

Further passages likewise reveal the resonance between Evola's and Braun's thought. From a letter to his parents in October 1915 (Braun, p. 150): "Composure, here characterized as well-formed spiritual attitude, glowing inwardly with passion, but outwardly hard as hammered steel, gloriously concealing the measureless, seems necessary to me. When I look at my *state*, that symbol of infinity and all that is finite, but to me an especially *visible symbol* for others, which I always carry in my heart, as the saints carry the name of Christ, then it appears completely strong and great and perfectly formed, yet teeming within with a multitude of movements and the colorful play of forces."

One should keep these words in mind when we deal later with Evola's views of the State. This passage likewise is quoted in *Saggi* (p. 143 ff.).

Evola's abhorrence of Bolshevism and Americanism was influenced by his reading of Count Hermann von Keyserling, as well as the following passage from Braun (p. 151): "Should Germany perish, and the world be divided between America and Russia (which would mean the death of everything that we called our Gods), I believe that . . . all of us . . . who still love the Gods would do better to leave a world that would be so unsuited to us, as Cato did. This time and its events are so terrible in their scope and power that all thought must indeed despair, and only a deed of salvation can rescue us. I still believe that the ocean is again pregnant, as when they cut off Uranus's member with a scythe and threw it into Poseidon's lap, wherefrom sprang Zeus [*sic*] in waves and foam. Perhaps today, we should again wait for a God to arise in this way."

The following passage is a very clear expression of Evola's yearning and striving, and certainly an essential emotional key toward the understanding of what it was that Evola, in spite of his reservations, wanted to see in rising Fascism (Braun, p. 156): "The coming age must be one of unconditional synthesis, positive and constructive in its whole character, creating new forms and continuing to mold old forms in an organic manner. In this nothing is a greater danger and should be avoided more than the comfortable retreat into old existent patterns. The incredible will, the grand impetuosity of this rich, dynamic, urgent age . . . would be annihilated. I am deeply convinced that the womb of the coming years will give birth to fabulous things; it would be highly ruinous if we were to be robbed of receptiveness to these newly gestating forces through insipid talk, like that of reawakening religiosity. I hold the assumption to be sacrilegious, even devilish, that a time . . . of these immense economic, political, and cultural upheavals . . . could ever return to the placid waters of a Christianity consolidated by the state. I am as decidedly non-Christian as ever."

Now to the third of these thinkers who, together with Nietzsche, Evola calls the "holy damned ones," because none of them was equal to the strength of his thoughts. The spiritual current they bore within annihilated them, because they lacked a supra-normal self-realization centered on transcendence, at least in Evola's opinion. The third was Otto Weininger (1880–1903), who lived in Vienna, was of Jewish ancestry, and influenced Evola the most out of those we have spoken of so far. The culture of the fin-de-siècle—and not just in the German-speaking realm—bore the imprint of his influence. As early as 1912, the first Italian translation of his main work, *Sex and Character*, appeared and caused a furor, especially in Papini's circles. Papini himself had issued excerpts of the book, and spoke out vehemently against Jewry in his own work *Gog*, following Weininger's line of thought, which could not have failed to have had an effect on Evola. In 1956 Evola was commissioned by a major Italian publisher to make a new translation of *Sex and Character*, in order to correct the mistakes of the old edition and to add to Weininger's critical and bibliographical material. Detailed notes on this can be found in Alberto Cavaglion's interesting book *Otto Weininger in Italia* (Rome, 1982).

Weininger's influence on Evola ranges from ethics to the attitude toward women, and from his thoughts on statehood to the attitude toward Judaism and racial questions. Evola's late work *The Metaphysics of Sex* (first Italian edition published 1958; later released in the United States as *Eros and the Mysteries of Love*, Rochester, Vt., 1983) was originally planned as an introduction to, and correction of, *Sex and Character*, but subsequently grew to such a length that it became a book in its own right.

Here are some passages from Weininger's main work; we quote from the Viennese edition of 1904.

> Truth, purity, loyalty, uprightness toward oneself: these are the only imaginable Ethics. (p. 206)

This could be a quote from Evola himself. Add Hebbel's epigram that Weininger quotes (Otto Braun also studied Hebbel intensively):

> Which do you pay for more dearly, the lie or the truth?
> The first you pay with your Self, the second, at worst, with your happiness.

Further:

> Man is *alone* in the cosmos, in eternal, immense *loneliness*. He has no purpose except himself, nothing else he lives for—he is far beyond wanting-to-be-slave, ability-to-be-slave, having-to-be-slave: far below him human society has disappeared, social ethics have fallen away; he is alone, ALONE.
>
> But only now is he *one* and *all*; and that is why he has a *law* within himself, that is why he *is all* law, and not arbitrary desire. And *he* demands *from himself* that he follow this law within himself. . . . Nothing stands above him, the alone,

the all-one. But he must comply with the pitiless *categorical imperative within*, which tolerates no negotiations with itself. He calls for *Salvation* . . . (p. 210)

We also present a paragraph from the chapter entitled "The Problem of Self and Genius." It deals with a passage from Schelling, which Weininger quotes verbatim. Evola studied German Romanticism especially thoroughly, and Schelling in particular. His definition of Tradition also shows the influence of Schelling, in addition to Guénon (see my introduction to *The Hermetic Tradition*, Rochester, Vt., 1995, p. xii).

> We all possess a secret, wonderful ability to retreat from the vicissitudes of time into our innermost self, stripped of all outside influences, and there, in the shape of immutability, to contemplate the eternal in ourselves. *This contemplation is the innermost and most unique experience, on which all and everything that we know and believe about a supernatural world depends. Only this contemplation persuades us that something IS, while everything else to which we apply that term only APPEARS to be.* It is different from all other sensual contemplation in that it can only be produced by *freedom* and is alien and foreign to all those whose freedom, overwhelmed by the thronging power of objects, barely suffices to bring forth consciousness. . . . *In this moment of contemplation, time and duration melts away for us: WE are not in time, but rather time, or better yet, pure absolute eternity, is WITHIN US.*

Another passage in the same chapter is as follows: "*However, the Self-event is the root of all worldviews*" (p. 217).

Or: "*Moral action can therefore only consist in acting according to an idea*" (p. 228, Weininger's emphasis). "The idea is our fatherland," says Evola, to the chagrin of many nationalist circles, as we will see below. Another quote from this chapter: "A man becomes a genius through a supreme act of will, after affirming the whole universe within himself" (p. 236).

The constant recurrence of manliness, as opposed to mere masculinity, as a category in Evola's thought can certainly also be attributed to Weininger. Adriano Romualdi, in his *Julius Evola: L'uomo e l'opera* (Julius Evola: The Man and His Work, Rome, 1979), even called Weininger the "originator of the idea of manliness as a metaphysical essence" (p. 17). It is almost superfluous in this context to mention how closely Evola's attitude toward woman—as a metaphysical opposite of man and in the political sense—is based on Weininger, because this is more than obvious. But Evola was not the only one who thought of *Sex and Character* as an epochal work. For example, August Strindberg wrote the following words to Weininger on July 1, 1903: "To finally see the problem of woman solved (!) is a relief for me. . . . " In another letter, to Arthur Gerber, he says: "What Weininger has written are not opinions, they are *discoveries! Weininger was a discoverer!*" (quoted in the preface to the second edition of *Sex and Character*, p. vi).

Among the other personalities influenced by Weininger are Alfred Kubin, Ludwig Wittgenstein, Franz Kafka, Robert Musil, Georg Trakl, Arnold Schönberg, and Thomas Bernhard.

It would be just as hard to understand Evola's attitudes toward Jews (to be treated in detail later) without Weininger. Two definitive passages from *Sex and Character*, whose essence time and again forms the foundation for Evola's own pronouncements, will illustrate this. However, these do not concern themselves with the centuries-old prejudices, which both Weininger—despite his ancestry—and Evola fall prey to, but instead deal with "metaphysical categories."

But first I want to define exactly what I mean by Jewishness. One is *not* dealing with a *race* or a *people*, and even less with a legally acknowledged profession. *One can only define it as a spiritual attitude, a psychic constitution, which offers an OPPORTUNITY for ALL men and which merely found its most grandiose REALIZATION in historical Jewry. Nothing proves the veracity of this statement more than anti-Semitism.* The truest, most Aryan of Aryans, certain of their Aryanness, are no anti-Semites; they cannot even fathom *hostile* anti-Semitism; . . . on the other hand, one can always detect certain Jewish traits in the aggressive anti-Semites . . .

It would be impossible for this to be any other way. As one LOVES only those traits in the other which one would wholeheartedly embrace oneself, yet can never fully attain, so one HATES in the other only that which one never wants to be, yet which one partially retains. One does not hate something with which one has nothing in common . . . (p. 413f.) And then: *Indeed, when I speak of a Jew, I never mean the individual or the whole group, but man in general, as far as he shares the PLATONIC idea of Jewishness.* It is my sole intention to define the meaning of this *idea.* (p. 415; emphasis by Weininger himself)

Evola's racial thought is decisively marked by these views; hence his disapproving attitude toward Vacher de Lapouge, Gobineau, and Chamberlain, the men who are otherwise known as the fathers of modern racism.

The apparently negative characterization in Evola's *Men among the Ruins* of the leader who identifies with his people and who, spurred on by them, strides toward "great" deeds (like Napoleon, but of course also Mussolini and Hitler) must also be traced back to Weininger. Weininger compares these popular leaders and popular tribunes with his classification of the prostitute. A quote from *Sex and Character* will illustrate this:

> For the great politician is not only a speculator and millionaire, but also a pop singer; he is not only a great chess player, but also a great actor; he is not only a despot, but also a toady; he not only prostitutes others, but is himself a great prostitute. The politician, the warleader who never "lowered himself" does not exist. After all, his descents are famous; they are his sexual acts. *The proper tribune also belongs in the gutter.* The complementary relationship with the mob is a downright part of a politician's constitution. In fact, he can only use the rabble; with the others, the individuals, he makes a quick end, if he is unwise; or, if he is as smart as Napoleon, he pretends to value them, so as to render them harmless.

One feels these sentences slamming down like hammer blows, in a dogmatic manner of which virtually only youth is capable (Weininger wrote this when he was barely twenty years old), and they must have fascinated Evola in his quest for the Absolute.

One element that is finally decisive for Evola's hostile attitude toward Jews (in the ideal sense mentioned above) is the identification of modernity with the Jewish spirit by Weininger and himself (and certainly also by his followers). Weininger writes (p. 451f.): *"The spirit of the modern age is Jewish* wherever it is found" (emphasis by Weininger). Then he adds:

> Our age, which is not only the most Jewish, but also the most effeminate of all ages; the age in which the arts are only a rag for wiping its moods, and which attributes the artistic urge to animal games [Weininger is a opponent of Darwin's theory of evolution, like Evola and Spengler]; the age of the most gullible anarchism; the age without a sense for the state and justice; the age of sexual ethics; the age of the most shallow of all historical methods (historical materialism); the age of capitalism and Marxism; the age in which history, life, and science are reduced to economics and technology.

It is this modernity that Evola assaulted from his youth onward, and which he even metaphorically equated with metaphysical "evil." Himself influenced by the incisive critical method of modernity, he nevertheless fought against it (and the corresponding trait of his own character), and saw in this the justification for his anti-Jewish attitude.

We conclude this section on Weininger with a remark by the great sexologist Wilhelm Stekel. In the magazine *Waage* (1904, 44–45), he writes about Weininger: "Thus one should not pass judgment on genius, even when it shows pathological traits, because we have to prefer morbid genius to healthy inactivity" (quoted in Emil Lucka, *Otto Weininger: Sein Werk und seine Persönlichkeit*, Vienna, 1905).

The influences that originated from Fichte (Evola repeatedly quotes his *Sittenlehre*), Oscar Wilde, and Gabriele d'Annunzio can be mentioned only in passing. Those of Plato, Nietzsche, Spengler, and Gustave Le Bon must be looked at more closely.

First let us turn to Plato, whom Evola mentions in his philosophical works as well as in his "Self-Defense." Plato's dialogue *The Republic* must be counted among the politically most important books of the West. One should note what Plato says there about freedom, education, equality (VIII, 557–565) or about those (IX, 586) who "look down always with their heads bent to the ground like cattle; at the banquet tables they feed, fatten, and fornicate. To get their fill of such things they kick and butt each other with iron horns and hoofs and kill each other. They are insatiable as they do not fill the real and continent part of themselves with true realities" (trans. Grube). The antidemocratic tradition, to which Evola professes to belong, would be unthinkable without Plato (see Karl R. Popper, *The Open Society and Its Enemies*, London, 1957).

Next we turn to Nietzsche, that "earthquake of an era," as Gottfried Benn calls him. Evola's affinity to this thinker cannot be overlooked even in a cursory examination. The fight against Christianity, the bourgeoisie, and the prevalent moral prejudices on the one hand, and on the other the predilection for the grandiose, for that which exceeds man, the pitilessness, without caring about himself, and the caustic language without any concessions are clear signs of this. Again we provide some excerpts to illustrate this, the first being from *Beyond Good and Evil* (part 9: "What Is Noble?" aphorism 257, trans. R. J. Hollingdale, London, 1990):

Every elevation of the type "man" has hitherto been the work of an aristocratic society—and so it will always be: a society which believes in a long scale of orders of rank and differences of worth between man and man. . . . Without the *pathos of distance* such as develops from the incarnate differences of classes, from the ruling caste's constant looking out and looking down on subjects and instruments . . . that other, more mysterious pathos could not have developed either,

JULIUS EVOLA'S POLITICAL ENDEAVORS

that longing for an ever-increasing widening of distance within the soul itself, the formation of ever higher, rarer, more remote, tenser, more comprehensive states; in short precisely the elevation of the type "man," the continual "self-overcoming of man," to use a moral formula in a supra-moral sense . . .

The essential thing in a good and healthy aristocracy is, however, that it does *not* feel itself to be a function (of the monarchy or of the commonwealth), but as their *meaning* and supreme justification—that it therefore accepts with a good conscience the sacrifice of innumerable men who *for its sake* have to be suppressed and reduced to imperfect men, to slaves and instruments. Its fundamental faith must be that society should *not* exist for the sake of society but only as foundation and scaffolding upon which a select species of being is able to raise itself to its higher task and in general to a higher *existence*. (aphorism 258)

"In a tour of the many finer and coarser moralities which have ruled or still rule on earth I found certain traits regularly recurring together and bound up with one another: until at length two basic types were revealed and a basic distinction emerged. There is *master morality* and *slave morality*—I add at once that in all higher and mixed cultures attempts at mediation between the two are apparent and more frequently confusion and mutual misunderstanding between them, indeed sometimes their harsh juxtaposition—even within the same man, within *one* soul . . . [W]hen it is the rulers who determine the concept "good," it is the exalted, calm states of soul which are considered distinguishing and determine the order of rank. The noble human being separates from himself those natures in which the opposite of such exalted proud states find expression: he despises them. It should be noted at once that in this first type of morality the antithesis "good" and "bad" means the same thing as "noble" and "despicable"—the antithesis "good" and "evil" originates elsewhere. The cowardly, the timid, the petty, and those who think only of narrow utility are despised; as are the mistrustful with their constricted glance, those who abase themselves, the dog-like man who lets himself be mistreated, the fawning flatterer, above all the liar—it is a fundamental belief of all aristocrats that the common people are liars. "We who are truthful"—thus did the nobility of ancient Greece designate themselves. . . . The noble type of man feels *himself* to be the determiner of values, he does not need to be approved of . . . such a morality is self-glorification. In the foreground stands the feeling of plenitude, of power which seeks to overflow, the happiness of high tension, the consciousness of a wealth which would like to give away and bestow—the noble human being also aids the unfortunate but not, or almost not, from pity, but more from an urge begotten by the superfluity of power. The noble human being honors in himself the man of power, also the man who has power over himself, who understands how to speak and how to keep silent, who enjoys practicing severity and harshness upon himself and feels reverence for all that is severe and harsh . . . belief in oneself, pride in oneself, a fundamental hostility and irony toward "selflessness" belong just as definitely to noble morality as does a mild contempt for and caution against sympathy and the "warm heart."—It is the powerful who *understand* how to honor, that is their art, their realm of invention. Deep reverence for age and the traditional . . . belief and prejudice in favor of ancestors and against descendants, is typical of the morality of the powerful; and when, conversely, men of "modern ideas" believe almost instinctively in "progress" and "the future" and show an increasing lack of respect for age, this reveals clearly enough the ignoble origin of these "ideas." (aphorism 260)

We, who have a different faith—we, to whom the democratic movement is not merely a form assumed by political organization in decay but also a form assumed by man in decay, that is to say in diminishment, in process of becoming mediocre and losing his value: whither must *we* direct our hopes?—Toward *new philosophers*, we have no other choice; toward spirits strong and original enough to make a start on antithetical evaluations and to revalue and reverse "eternal values" . . . so as to make an end to that gruesome dominion of chance and nonsense that has hitherto been called "history"—the nonsense of the "greatest number" is only its latest form—: for that a new kind of philosopher and commander will some time be needed, in the face of whom whatever has existed on earth of hidden, dreadful, and benevolent spirits may well look pale and dwarfed. It is the image of such leaders which hovers before *our* eyes. (Part 5: "On the Natural History of Morals," aphorism 203)

From *Human, All Too Human* (book I, aphorism 451, "Justice as a Party Lure," trans. Gary Handwerk, Stanford, 1995):

The *demand* for equality of rights made by socialists of the subjected caste never flows from a sense of justice, but instead from greed.—If someone holds bloody chunks of meat near an animal and then yanks them away until finally it roars: do you think that this roaring signifies justice?

Concerning Evola's disdain of "equal rights for all":

The inequality of rights is the precondition for the existence of any rights at all. . . . There is nothing wrong with unequal rights; only in the claim to equal rights . . .What is evil? . . . Everything arising in weakness, envy, and *revenge*. (*The Antichrist*, aphorism 57, trans. P. R. Stephensen, London, 1929)

Concerning his passionate arguments against Christianity:

> There is every reason for comparing the Christian and the anarchist because the impulse of both is toward destruction. . . . The Christian and anarchist are both decadents, both are only able to act for the purpose of disintegrating, poisoning, degrading, and *blood-sucking*. They both have the impulse of mortal hatred toward anything that stands up, and is great, and is lasting and shows promise for the future . . . Christianity was the vampire of the *Imperium Romanum* . . . (aphorism 58)

These few passages should give us enough insight. Of course, it must be emphasized that Evola, as much as he valued Nietzsche, always cautioned against his hubris of the "worldview" in the purely natural sense (see the introduction to *Revolt*, pp. 14–17). Nietzsche's influence was strong but should not be overrated, because he never even mentions the "transcendence" that was so important for Evola.

With that we turn to Oswald Spengler and his work that was so important for cultural history, *The Decline of the West*, which Evola later translated into Italian and for which he wrote a critical introduction. Concerning Evola's criticism of Spengler, especially his bondage to the natural and his lack of transcendent principles, see Evola's essay "Spengler e il Tramonto dell'Occidente" (Spengler and the Decline of the West, Fondazione Julius Evola, Rome, 1981, *Quaderni di Testi Evoliani*, no. 14). The fundamentally pessimistic outlook, which we have already encountered in Nietzsche and which figures in most of the "philosophers of crisis" up to Ortega y Gasset, found its most eloquent and pronounced expression in Spengler. After reading him, if not before, Evola was finally convinced that Western civilization was doomed to failure. Very important in this is Spengler's view that it is a sure sign of decadence when the economy wins the upper hand in a culture.

Evola's conviction that a new start was necessary—hence his conditional support of Fascism and, later, the transcendence of this world through "Tradition"—was indebted to this philosophy of decline.

But Nietzsche's ideas also appear in Spengler's work, as in the following passage, which defines the difference between the "deed" and "work," which is also decisive for Evola:

> And there is the same relation between the ethical passion of the great Baroque masters—Shakespeare, Bach, Kant, Goethe—the manly will to *inward* mastery of natural things that are felt to be far below oneself, and modern Europe's will

to *outwardly* clear them out of the way (in the form of state-provisions, humanitarian ideals, world peace, happiness of the majority) because one perceives oneself to be on the same level as they. This also is a manifestation of the will-to-
power as opposed to the Classical endurance of the inevitable; it also shows
passion and a longing for eternity, but there remains a fundamental difference
between the material and metaphysical scale of the achievements. The latter
lacks depth, it lacks what men formerly called God. The Faustian universal feeling of the *deed*, which . . . had been active in every great man, was reduced to a
philosophy of *work*. Whether such a philosophy attacks or defends work does
not affect its inward value. The cultural concept of the deed and the civilized
concept of work stand in similar relation as Aeschylus's Prometheus to Diogenes.
The one suffers and endures, the other is lazy. Galileo, Kepler, and Newton
performed deeds of science; the modern physicist *carries out scientific work*. And
in spite of all the great words from Schopenhauer to Shaw, it is the plebeian
morals of everyday life and "sound human reason" that are the basis for all
perceptions and discussions of life. (*The Decline of the West*, New York, 1934, p.
355, translation adapted)

Similarly, concerning the same theme: "What has occurred on the way from
Newton to Faraday—or from Berkeley to Mill—is the supplanting of the religious concept of the deed by the irreligious concept of work. In Bruno's, Newton's,
and Goethe's view of nature, something divine was active in deeds; in the worldview
of modern physics, nature *carries out work*" (German ed., p. 537).

A few words by Spengler that could also come verbatim from *Men among
the Ruins:* "The state is the inner form, the shape of a nation" (p. 179). "But
that is exactly what turned Faustian man into the slave of his creation. His
number and the layout of his standard of living are forced by the machine onto
a course of no rest and no return" (vol. II, p. 631).

"But the onslaught of money against this spiritual power has taken the same
titanic proportions. Even industry is bound to its place and to its sources of
elements, bound to the soil like the peasantry. Only high finance is *completely*
free, completely unsusceptible to attack. Since 1789, the banks and thus the
stock exchanges have come into their own as a power, feeding off the credit
needs of an industry growing into monstrous proportions. Now they, and money,
want to be the *sole* power in *all civilizations*" (p. 633). Like Evola, Spengler
considers that "Caesarism arises out of democracy" (p. 583). In his other work,
The Hour of Decision (original title *Jahre der Entscheidung*, Munich, 1933; English
edition: New York, 1934), for which Evola again authored an introduction to

its Italian edition, Spengler speaks of the "utilitarian morality of slave-souls" (p. 95), and further of a "Prussian style" to which Evola gives high marks in *Men among the Ruins* and which consists of an "aristocratic ordering of life according to the rank of achievement" and of the "preeminence of high politics over the economy and the latter's *disciplining* by a strong state" (p. 138).

This brings us to Gustave Le Bon (1841–1931) and his work *The Crowd* (London, 1896, seventh ed., 1910), which was valued not only by Pareto, Freud, Mussolini, and de Gaulle, but even by Horkheimer and Adorno. Evola's mistrust of democracy looked for and surely found its final confirmation in Le Bon's work. Properly, a faith in democracy has to be matched by a radical optimism, a belief in the good in man. Politically, Evola was a pessimist—and not just since reading Spengler—and thus was hard to win over to democratic ideas. He is convinced that the masses are incapable of following higher ideals, because they always follow the leader who is temporarily the strongest, no matter what ideas he preaches. He merely has to be able to fascinate. Evola fears what Le Bon likewise called the "feminine character" of the masses. The rejection of Christianity also shows itself in Le Bon, because at least at the time of its inception it was identifiable with the spirit of the masses.

Once again, some quotes to clarify Le Bon's influence:

Crowds exhibit a docile respect for force, and are but slightly impressed by kindness, which for them is scarcely more than a form of weakness. Their sympathies have never been bestowed on easy-going masters, but on tyrants who vigorously oppress them. It is to these latter that they always erect the greatest statues. It is true that they willingly trample on the despot whom they have stripped of his power, but this is because, having lost his strength, he has resumed his place among the weak, who are to be despised and not feared. The type of hero dear to crowds will always have the semblance of a Caesar. His insignia attracts them, his authority overawes them, and his sword instills them with fear. . . . Should the strength of an authority be intermittent, the crowd, always obedient to its extreme sentiments, passes alternately from anarchy to servitude, and from servitude to anarchy. (*The Crowd*, book I, ch. 2, section 4)

Ideas being only accessible to crowds after having assumed a very simple shape must often undergo the most thoroughgoing transformations to become popular. It is especially when we are dealing with somewhat lofty philosophic or scientific ideas that we see how far-reaching are the modifications they require in order to lower them to the level of the intelligence of crowds. (book I, ch. 3, section 1)

Still, though the wishes of crowds are frenzied they are not durable. Crowds are as incapable of willing as of thinking for any length of time. . . . Crowds are everywhere distinguished by feminine characteristics, but Latin crowds are the most feminine of all. (book I, ch. 2, section 1)

Le Bon states "On this point, however, as on many others, democratic ideas are in profound disagreement with the results of psychology and experience." Le Bon then goes on to explain that man cannot be taught by education (book II, ch. 1, section 5). And as a final quote: "In the case of human crowds, the chief . . . plays a considerable part. His will is the nucleus around which the opinions of the crowd are grouped and attain to identity. . . . A crowd is a servile flock that is incapable of ever doing without a master" (book II, ch. 3, section 1).

Another name should be mentioned briefly, even though his influence probably took effect later: that of Johann Jakob Bachofen, who has recently gained renewed respect. He certainly counts as the one who popularized in the scientific world the concept of "gynecocracy," the rule of women. Precisely through Bachofen's identification of the age of female rule with the age of earthbound, "chthonic" deities, a model was created that must imply as its opposite pole the solar, the Olympian, and the manly, with which Evola naturally identified. Thus Bachofen can be credited with the creation of that idea of "Olympian manliness" which is one of the foundations of *Revolt Against the Modern World*. Evola later translated a selection of Bachofen's work into Italian, adding an introduction and notes. (Julius Evola, *Le Madri e la virilita olimpica* [The Mothers and Olympian Manliness], Milan, 1949. Apparently, this translation did not have the same precision as Evola's translations of Spengler and Weininger.)

With that we have dealt with the most important "profane" philosophers to whom Evola is unmistakably indebted. But there is an essential element that is lacking in all these authors: the Transcendent. Everything that these people said might be apposite, but it amounts to nothing in an Evolian and traditionalist worldview if it is not elevated by and grounded in transcendence. These opinions become valid only when they are seen against the backdrop of a higher, timeless realm.

Papini had already introduced Evola to Meister Eckhart, who was probably the first to reveal this deeper knowledge to Evola. Meister Eckhart and Jan van Ruysbroeck are mentioned as early as Evola's *Arte astratta* (Abstract Art, Rome, 1920, p. 14). Concurrently, he was most likely starting to study Buddhism,

Taoism, and Hinduism. As already mentioned, it was a passage from the Buddhist Pali Canon that stopped Evola from committing suicide.

We should therefore investigate the extent to which religious and mystical writings complement the thinkers mentioned thus far, or better, place them in a timeless framework so that many passages that smack of the "worldview" will be spiritualized and given a different background as to their meaning.

First, let us deal with Meister Eckhart. Early on, Evola had mastered several foreign languages: Latin, ancient Greek, and above all French (his poetry, which will be mentioned later, was written in this language) and German. Thus he read Meister Eckhart in German. From his notes we even know that he first used the edition by E. Büttner, *Schriften und Predigten* (Works and Sermons). The important influence of this work cannot be underestimated: he quoted Eckhart with the greatest respect all his life, which is unusual given Evola's critical mind. Evola's concept of freedom, his "act, without looking toward success or failure" and his aforementioned aversion to sentimentality can be largely traced to this theologian and mystic. For example, Evola quotes Meister Eckhart in German in his early work *Saggi sull'Idealismo Magico* (1925, p. 48) as follows: "From this deepest foundation of being [where life exists for its own sake (Evola's note)], you should do all your works, *without asking why*. I decisively assert: as long as you do your works for the sake of heaven, God, or your salvation, and hence from the outside, you are really not in the right. If one asks a truthful man, one who acts from his own being: 'Why do you do your works?' and he answers honestly, he would also say: 'I do for the sake of doing!'"

The closeness of this thought to Taoism and Zen is self-evident. But more about this later.

Meister Eckhart's thought also already shows the traits that Evola's critics, in their thorough misunderstanding, have seen as selfish excess, total overestimation and obsession with the *Übermensch:* the fact that Evola holds the Self (of course, not the everyday self or "worldly self" in Graf Dürckheim's expression) to be absolute. Let us quote Eckhart: "Being is God . . . God and existence are identical. Should I be able to recognize God in an immediate way, then *I* must become *he* and *he* must become *I*, pure and simple . . . so completely at one, that this *he* and this *I* are one and will become and be one, and exist and act eternally in this way and form of being" (Meister Eckhart, *Deutsche Predigten und Traktate* [German Sermons and Treatises], ed. Josef Quint, Munich, 1978, p. 354). With this and his maxim of "action without questioning why" Eckhart also anticipates Evola's boundless conception of freedom. For as long as one is acting out of an inner urge, as a reaction to a shortcoming, or because an idea seems attractive, whether it is "material" or "spiritual," one continues to be bound in "slavery." The concept of "power" that is so important to Evola also derives from this precept. An absolute Self wields absolute power, even when it does not utilize it. Naturally, the concept of power leads through cross-references to Tantra, which Evola had already encountered very early on (see below as well as his work *L'uomo come potenza* [Man as Power], Rome, 1926). His main sources for this were the translations by Sir John Woodroffe (Arthur Avalon). Evola also knew Woodroffe personally, and thus certain translations of the latter's work first appeared in Italian before they were even published in English (one such example is contained in Julius Evola and the UR Group, *Introduction to Magic*, Rochester, Vt., 2001, p. 64 ff.).

The "arrogance" in spiritual matters that Evola has been accused of again and again also applies to Meister Eckhart—for example, when he writes: "Coarse-natured people must simply *believe* this, but the enlightened must *know* it" (Eckhart, p. 267).

Still another quote concerning action without looking for success, approval, or rejection by others: "He is just, who gives everybody what is due to him" (p. 182). And then: ". . . but in a different sense, those are just who take all things from God to be equal, whatever it may be, great or small, dear or not, completely the same, without less or more, the one like the other" (ibid.). Such an outlook presumes a separation from the world and especially from oneself ("All love in this world is built on self-love. If you would only leave that, you would have the whole world left"; p. 185) and must necessarily bring with it a separation from the concept of time and a turning toward the supra-temporal or, in other words, the "eternal." Eternity in this sense is not limitless time, but instead the atemporal, the realm beyond time, where before and after fuse into an absolute present. This timelessness is also the realm in which Tradition, in the Evolian sense, operates. It is the "most intrinsic of all being, the most real of all reality, the most certain of all certainty," which even though we cannot understand it intellectually is an area we can be open to.

A poem by Henry Vaughan (quoted by D. T. Suzuki in *Mysticism: Christian and Buddhist*, New York, 1957, p. 93f.) may open the way on an emotional level:

> *I saw Eternity the other night,*
> *Like a great ring of pure and endless light,*

All calm, as it was bright,
And round beneath it, Time, in hours, days, years
Driven by the spheres,
Like a vast shadow moved, in which the world
And all her train were hurled.

Meister Eckhart writes the following concerning this concept: "For the Now in which God created the first human being, and the Now in which the last human being will perish, and the Now in which I speak, are all identical in God and are nothing but a Now" (Eckhart, p. 162).

Evola's urge toward transcendence and the higher reaches, which was certainly already preconditioned (see the introduction to *Revolt Against the Modern World*, which deals with this quest in more detail), found its deeply-felt confirmation in Meister Eckhart. Other sources, especially Taoism, whose main work (Lao Tse, *Tao te Ching*) he translated into Italian in two different versions in 1923 and 1959, also strengthened and confirmed his notions. A few excerpts from this work will testify to the extent these esoteric truths additionally influenced and strengthened Evola's thought, including his political ideas. (All translations based on Lao Tse, *Tao Teh King*, ed. by K. O. Schmidt, Pfullingen, 1961.)

Tao te Ching (I, ch. 7; Evola mentions this explicitly in *Saggi sull'Idealismo Magico*, p. 100, as a maxim for right action):

Thus the awakened one,
Because he puts himself behind, he steps in front,
Because he gives away, he gains,
Because he cares not for himself, he is maintained.
That is it:
Because he is selfless,
He achieves self-fullfillment.

Here we have the famous *wei wu wei*, (subtle) action without acting in the normal sense, which is so prevalent in Taoism. Another quote from I, ch. 10:

To feed and to preserve, yet not to cling,
To act, yet not to hold back and not to hold forever,
To lead, yet not to lord over,
This is the virtue of a calm spirit.

From I, ch. 13:

> *Honors and disgraces are equally full of suffering*
> . . . .
> *Attain glory, and you will fear losing it.*
> *Lose glory, and the shame will terrify you.*
> *Both are accompanied by fear,*
> *Both are sources of suffering.*

From I, ch. 26:

> *Thus the sage is anchored in inner security and safeguards his weight.*
> *He remains calm, also when glory and riches tempt.*
> *For the one who gives up inner security and who sticks to something,*
> *Becomes weightless and insecure.*
> *Weightless he becomes thoughtless and restless,*
> *Insecure he remains defeated and powerless.*

From I, ch. 29 (this passage is especially important politically, in order to understand the attitude of the traditional monarch. Evola has admonished Fascism and National Socialism repeatedly for not comprehending this attitude):

> *To win the empire through action and to master it,*
> *That is the way that leads to failure.*
> *For the empire is a divine vessel,*
> *Which cannot be seized and acted upon.*
> *One who desires to grasp it, does not understand it.*
> *One who desires to take it, loses it.*
> *He believes he is getting ahead, but falls behind.*
> *He believes he is increasing, but he dwindles away.*
> *He thinks himself strong, and reveals his weakness.*
> *He thinks himself superior, and is defeated.*

From I, ch. 33 (central to his concept of power):

> *One who knows others is clever;*
> *One who knows himself is enlightened.*
> *One who conquers others is strong;*
> *One who conquers himself is power.*

From II, ch. 56, about the nobility of the wise:

> *Since he is all-one, he is touched by neither life nor hate, gain nor loss,*
> *exaltation nor humiliation. That is his nobility.*

This inner attitude of the enlightened one as goal is found in all of Evola's creative periods, from the philosophical to the magical, from the political to the cultural-historical. It must be emphasized again and again that Evola's political writings cannot be understood at all without this reference point and that anybody who reads them with the usual values in mind is doomed to misinterpret them.

Finally, we arrive at Hinduism and one of its main writings, namely the *Bhagavad Gita*, whose pronouncements strengthened Evola's existing warrior (Sanskrit: *kshatriya*) tendencies and provided them with the necessary metaphysical background. Again, we provide selected quotes (the edition we have utilized is *The Bhagavad Gita*, trans. Winthrop Sargeant, Albany, 1984):

> *He whose delight is only in the self,*
> *And whose satisfaction is in the self,*
> *And who is content only in the self;*
> *For him the need to act does not exist.*
> *He has no purpose at all in action,*
> *Nor any whatever in non-action,*
> *And he has no need of any purpose whatever*
> *in regard to any being.*
> (III, 17–18)

> *In a sense in relation to an object of that sense,*
> *Passion and hatred are seated.*
> *One should not come under the power of these two;*
> *They are indeed one's two antagonists.*
> (III, 34)

> *To whom honor and dishonor are equal;*
> *Dispassionate toward the side of friend or foe,*
> *Renouncing all undertakings,*
> *He is said to transcend the gunas* [attributes].
> (XIV, 25)

That action which is controlled and
free from attachment,
Performed without desire or hate,
With no wish to obtain fruit,
Is said to be sattvic [filled with being].
But that action which is performed
with a wish to obtain desires,
With selfishness, or, again,
With much effort,
Is declared to be rajasic [filled with passion].
(XVIII, 23–24)

Fixed in Yoga, perform actions,
Having abandoned attachment, Conqueror of Wealth [Arjuna].
Having become indifferent to success or failure.
It is said that indifference is Yoga [realization].
Action is inferior by far
To the Yoga of intuition, Conqueror of Wealth.
Seek refuge in intuitive determination!
Despicable are those whose motives
are based on the fruit of action.
He whose intuitive determination is disciplined
Casts off, here in the world, both good and evil actions . . .
(II, 48–50)

By relinquishing egotism, force, arrogance,
Desire, anger and possession of property;
Unselfish, tranquil,
One is fit for oneness with Brahman [the divine].
(XVIII, 53)

And it is hard to escape the greatness and tragedy of the *Bhagavad Gita* while reading about the warrior Arjuna's horror, when he stands on the battlefield and realizes that the opposing ranks include friends and relatives whom he has to kill.

My limbs sink down
And my mouth dries up

And my body trembles
And my hair stands on end.
Gandiva (Arjuna's bow) falls from (my) hand,
And my skin burns,
And I am unable to remain as I am,
And my mind seems to ramble . . .
(I, 29–30)

And he begs Lord Krishna to absolve him from his warrior duties, because he does not want to fight this battle. But what does Krishna answer him?

Thou hast mourned the not-to-be-mourned
And yet thou speakest as if with wisdom;
For the dead and for the not dead
The pandits [wise ones] *do not mourn.*
(II, 11)

These bodies inhabited by the eternal,
The indestructible, the immeasurable embodied one [i.e., the Brahman],
Are said to come to an end.
Therefore fight heroically, Descendant of Bharata [Arjuna]!
(II, 18)

He whose state of mind is not egoistic,
Whose intelligence is not befouled,
Even though he slays these people,
Does not slay, and is not bound [by his actions].
(XVIII, 17)

And, perceiving just thine own caste duty,
Thou shouldst not tremble.
Indeed, anything superior to righteous battle,
For the kshatriya [man of the warrior caste], *does not exist.*
And if by good fortune they gain
The open gate of heaven
Happy are the kshatriyas, Sons of Pritha,
When they encounter such a fight.
(II, 31–32)

Given Evola's predisposition, these words fell on fertile ground—even more so when he realized that the outward battle on the field is used by all wisdom teachings as a symbol for the inner struggle against one's own negative attributes, and can only be justifiably fought in this way; and that such a struggle through self-mastery can even lead to "liberation." Corresponding passages in the Koran and even the Bible must have strengthened his notion (see *Revolt Against the Modern World*, "The Greater and the Lesser Holy War," p. 116).

Of course, such excerpts raise the question of which code of ethics and morals one should follow. That the thoughts quoted above can be incorporated only with much difficulty into today's prevalent worldview is self-evident. It is even harder to see them as "religious" commandments. Only a vision directed exclusively at the eternal, to which our human world is irrelevant, makes their affirmation even possible. The unshakable conviction that this world is in reality *Maya*, a mere illusion, is the prerequisite. In reference to morals and ethics, we include another Taoist saying that Evola often quoted and which we will deal with in more detail further on: "When the Way [the immediate connection to the spiritual] has been lost, virtue [in the sense of manliness and honor] remains. When virtue is lost, ethics remain; when ethics are lost, moralism remains. Moralism is the exteriorization of ethics and defines the principle of decline."

When speaking of Evola's spiritual foundation, the drug experiences of his youth (circa 1917–18) cannot be left unmentioned, because to them he owes his *practical* approach to esotericism, his first personal experience of transcendence. They surely also contributed to the absolute and uncompromising nature of his idea of freedom. Evola never repeated his drug experiences because he had already taken from them all that he could. In describing them, he speaks of a "peremptory, absolute, resounding certainty" (see Iagla, "Experiences: The Law of Beings" in *Introduction to Magic*, p. 167ff.). Evola defines the expansion of consciousness caused by drugs as follows: "When I compare it to my previous and habitual consciousness, only one image comes to my mind: the most lucid, conscious state of wakefulness in comparison to the deepest, most hypnotic and torpid state of sleep."

Extensive experiences with mountain climbing also have their place in the formation of Evola's distinct spiritual worldview, because he preferred to visit the high alpine mountains, the glaciers and impassable regions, where he sensed the force of creation in their solitude and could measure his spirit against this force. It was neither sport nor romanticism for him; he saw mountaineering as a path to his Self. Following ancient traditions, Evola speaks of the mountain as the holy mountain, the seat of the gods, the mediator between heaven and earth (Olympus, Meru, Kailash, etc.). Mountain climbing for him is the symbol for the spiritual ascent toward the divine, the ever purer, clearer, and more crystalline realm. Evola speaks of the "transformation of the experience of the mountain into a way of being." And further: "This then is the strength of those who may be said to never return from the peaks to the plains. This is the strength of those for whom there is no longer going out or coming back because the mountain is in their spirit, because the symbol has become reality . . . " And: "The mountain is connected to something that has no beginning and no end and that, having become an inalienable spiritual conquest, has become part of one's nature, something one carries everywhere that bestows a new meaning to every action, every experience, and every struggle in everyday life" (*Meditations on the Peaks*, Rochester, Vt., 1998, p. 22). Or: "The mountain teaches silence. . . . It promotes simplification and the turning of one's attention inward" (p. 33).

Evola completed some difficult climbs—for example, the north wall of the Eastern Lyskam in 1927. He also requested in his will that after his death the urn containing his ashes be deposited in a glacial crevasse on Monte Rosa (see Renato del Ponte's report in Michel Angebert et al., *Julius Evola: le visionnaire foudroyé* [Julius Evola: The Devastating Visionary], Paris, 1977, p. 211f.). In Domenico Rudatis—who ranks among the best mountain climbers of this century and who, among other achievements, edited a book (with Reinhold Messner and V. Varale) about the sixth degree of difficulty in mountain climbing—Evola found a fellow traveler to write about the mountains for his later magazines.

The Artistic Experiences

Alongside the philosophical influences (of which the essential ones, such as Seneca, Spinoza, Vico, and the French Personalists, especially Hamelin and Lagneau, cannot be treated here), the artistic influences must be briefly mentioned: briefly, because their influence on Evola's political views—on which we concentrate here—was only a secondary one, noticeable only through their radical nature. On the other hand, their influence is of particular importance because it took effect in his early youth.

Besides Novalis, from whom he borrowed the name for his philosophical orientation, "Magical Idealism," Mereschkowski, Mallarmé, and Rimbaud must be mentioned: Rimbaud especially, because he fought against all convention and advocated an uncompromising brand of freedom. We have already discussed Futurism and the reasons for Evola's departure from its circles. Even more radical, and for Evola more consequential, was Dadaism ("True Dadaism is against Dadaism . . . "), whose cofounder Tristan Tzara he knew personally. Dadaism embodied a worldview in which the desire for total freedom tore down all logical, ethical, and aesthetic categories. The Dadaists spoke of a "strict necessity, without discipline or morals" and of the "identity of order and disorder, of Self and non-Self, of affirmation and negation." They said that the pure individuality could be revealed only after a condition of insanity, and that they looked for the "focused energy; pure, naked, single force; and the void." But on the other hand Tzara said himself: "Dada is not serious. . . ." Everywhere, he strove to introduce "idiocy." Evola was one of the first in Italy to try to write down these theories in his *Arte astratta* (Abstract Art, Rome, 1920). "Art is egoism and freedom," he asserts (p. 8, quoted from the new edition published by the Fondazione Julius Evola) and adds: "I view art as a disinterested creation that originates in the higher consciousness of the individual, and is therefore able to transcend and be independent of the passions and the crystallizations based on common experience."

We can already discern here Evola's quest for transcendence, for an inner "superiority," a breakthrough of levels, and release from the world. Because Dadaism ultimately could not provide him these things, Evola terminated this phase abruptly and radically, despite his recognition by others. He was able to exhibit his paintings, which were perceived as having strong parallels to Giorgio de Chirico's respected "metaphysical painting," and his poems were published by the leading modern art magazines such as *Dada* and *Bleu*, alongside the writings of André Breton, Aragon, and Cocteau. After 1922, his twenty-fourth year, Evola never again wrote a poem, and painted no more pictures for more than forty years. In this, he wanted to follow Rimbaud's example (*Cammino*, p. 23).

At this point we conclude our discussion of the artists and thinkers important to Evola. It becomes immediately apparent that Evola's spiritual and philosophical line of inheritance takes a very different course from that of most intellectuals today, whose path leads from Descartes to Hegel, Marx, Sartre, and the Frankfurt School. Evola's course, on the other hand, would be: Plato, Seneca, Spinoza, Vico, German Idealism, de Bonald, de Maistre (who, like Montesquieu, believed that the feudal regime was the most perfect system of rule that had ever existed on earth, and who through his writings convinced not only Evola of this, but Guénon as well), Donoso Cortès, Nietzsche, Weininger, Spengler, and Michelstaedter.

Naturally we are focusing here only on the development of Evola's political thought; as a result such important thinkers (if not the most important of all in Evola's life) as Arturo Reghini and René Guénon have hardly been mentioned. The nucleus of Evola's political views has now been established: the basic attitude toward the leader and the led, toward aristocracy and democracy, toward a spiritually based rule on the one hand and a government geared to general well-being on the other. Out of this, Evola wanted to construct a unified, interrelated, and therefore rigorous worldview that would incorporate all these elements and lead to wholeness. On the grounds of this inner coherence it is hardly possible to remove one element and replace it with a more "agreeable" one. One thing leads logically to the next, forcing one either to accept or to reject this worldview as a whole. It is indivisible.

The Philosophical Period

Evola's "academic" philosophy traces back in general to German Idealism, and thus further back to Plato. Even if originating from the same root, it goes against the Italian court philosophers of the time, Giovanni Gentile and Benedetto Croce. Despite this, the latter valued Evola's thought and even published him through his main imprint, Laterza. The strong voluntaristic streak in Evola, which decisively differentiates him from Croce and Gentile, can be traced back on the one hand to Nietzsche and on the other to French Personalism, whose main proponents Secrétan, Lachelier, Hamelin, and Lagneau he studied closely. Also originating from Lagneau is Evola's motto for his *Saggi sull'Idealismo Magico*, a work that gives a very good overview of Evola's thought development around 1923–1925, and already contains a nucleus of all his later views. The motto already indicates that purely academic philosophy would not suffice for him. What concerns him in this, as in his earlier artistic and his later political activity, is the "breakthrough of levels" to a "totally different" plane. The motto is as follows: "Philosophy is the train of thought that finally sees into its own inadequacy and realizes the need for an *absolute* action that originates from within."

Exoterically, this view is also comparable to the solipsism of the Stirnerian type—and Evola does not deny how strongly Stirner's anarchism had moved him—but he wants to overcome it by referring to the "totally different" plane, namely the transcendental. Unbridled freedom and the will-to-rule as essence of the individual are also Evola's code words; only he tries to proceed from the "transcendent" Self (in the sense of idealistic philosophy) to a true super-personality, an impersonality. The Self for him is the "center of *universal* responsibility" (*Teoria del Individuo Assoluto* [Theory of the Absolute Individual], new edition, Rome, 1975, p. 32; first published 1927). For this Self he desires a complete realization that is freedom and power at the same time, and which includes not only body, soul, and spirit, but also the whole cosmos. He wants to overcome any abstract speculation and actuate the knowledge completely within himself. An irresistible urge for self-transcendence and therefore self-salvation becomes apparent here. The identification of *Deus* = *Homo* and *Homo* = *Deus* (God is man and man is God) is to become reality for him. It seems only logical that the philosophical period is followed immediately by the magical one (see *Introduction to Magic*, vol. I of which is available in English; vols. II and III remain untranslated).

Evola's question is one of the primal questions of philosophy, and is also Descartes's question: Where is this point of certainty, which is completely fixed and on which I can build my construct of thought and life? At least at that point in time, for Evola this could only be the Self, but of course not the everyday self but the transcendent, primal foundation of one's own personality. In the philosophical magazine *Logos* (20/1931, p. 404, written at the beginning of the 1920s but first published in German in 1931), he writes: "One can only ascribe reality to those things whose principle and the cause of whose being . . . are found in the Self as the governing function. . . . Beyond the eternal problem of that which, according to Plato, 'simultaneously is and is not,' there lies only one certainty: the SELF. Only here does the individual find . . . an absolute and self-evident reality. The rest—the infinite ocean of forms of the inner and outer world—affords no such certainty."

Just a few words regarding Evola's conception of power, which is the source of so much misunderstanding, especially when used in the political realm: this concept, which Evola derived from esotericism, especially from Tantra and Taoism, must be strictly differentiated from "force." On the contrary: "power" loses its essential nature when it has to resort to material means—i.e., "force"— and is not acknowledged as self-evident. Power must function as its own "unmoved mover." To Evola, it is a meta-concept intended to overcome both rationalism and irrationalism, since on the one hand it makes use of reason, while on the other an elevation occurs through power to freedom, realization, and primordial being. In *Saggi* (p. 123), Evola writes: "Here one understands why Lao-Tse ascribes the characteristics of 'emptiness' and 'non-being' to the perfect man, and how he can say, from the depths of the consciousness of perfection, that every being has its primordial basis in non-being . . . and one also understands why the much abused concept of *maya* in Tantra means illusion, but also at the same time stands for creative *power;* and finally, one understands the meaning of the highest body of the Buddha, *Dharmakaya*, which is defined as the principle of nonexistence, which is the foundation of all reality." Or as he writes in *Imperialismo pagano* (Padua, 1996): "Superiority does not rest on power, but power rests on superiority. To *need* power is impotence; the one who truly comprehends this will perhaps understand in what sense the path of renunciation (a manly sacrifice that rests on 'not needing,' on 'having enough') can be a condition for the way to the highest power; and he will also grasp the hidden logic according to which (based on traditions that most people hold to be myths, but I certainly do not) ascetics, holy men, and initiates suddenly and naturally manifest suggestive and supernatural powers that are stronger than any powers of men and things. . . .

"A true ruler, imperial by nature, is he who has access to this higher quantity of *being,* which automatically also means a different quality of being by which others are inflamed, attracted, overpowered—without his even wanting them to be. It is he who imposes himself, so to speak, through his mere *presence:* like an embracing and threatening gaze that others are unable to resist; akin to that calm and relaxed greatness that magically stops even the armed man and the attacking beast; that immediately commands respect and the desire to obey, to sacrifice oneself, to search for the meaning of one's own truer life within this vaster life. . . . And so it is he who can say at the zenith: '*I* am the way, the truth and the life,' and thus give a unity, *meaning,* and *justification* to countless individuals, to that whole system of life's inferior determinisms, that they did not have before. For the inferior person never lives his *own* life as perfectly as when he is certain that this existence has a center and a goal in something superior" (pp. 49–50; emphasis original).

Concerning this we offer an excerpt from Georg Mehlis, *Italienische Philosophie der Gegenwart* (Philosophische Berichte, no. 12; chapter: "Der magische Idealismus"): "Man as power is in possession of total self-rule: he is content with the absolute possession of his self. He has no longer any 'deficiency' to compensate for. In his full possession of power, man reaches absolute indifference, so that it makes no sense for him to act any more. The magical man stands beyond good and evil, beyond pain or joy, beyond emotion or passion. Nietzsche's *Übermensch* is actualized within him, who rejects the paltry moral concepts of the bourgeois order, mainly built on utility and advantage, and who celebrates the singular great personality. However, Evola rises even above the *Übermensch*."

It is self-evident that these excerpts merely deal with the partial aspect of Evola's philosophy that is relevant to this inquiry. But they provide a glimpse that is already helpful for the comprehension of his political ideas. Those who are further interested in the philosophical phase of Evola's work may refer to Roberto Melchionda, *Il volto di Dionisio—filosofia e arte in Julius Evola* (The Face of Dionysus—Philosophy and Art in Julius Evola, Rome, 1984), which remains the deepest analysis so far of Evola's anything-but-simple philosophy.

The transition from the philosophical to the political world of ideas occurs wholly without constraint in that, according to Evola, on the political plane one replaces the Self in its freedom and power with the State, which rules the people as the Self rules its body.

The First Steps Toward Politics

This chapter is mainly based on the meticulous and excellent articles by the professor Marco Rossi: "L'Interventismo politico-culturale delle riviste tradizionaliste negli anni venti: 'Atanor' (1924) e 'Ignis' (1925)" in the respected journal *Storia Contemporanea* XVIII, no. 3, June 1987, and "'Lo Stato Democratico' e l'antifascismo antidemocratico di Julius Evola" in *Storia Contemporanea* XX, no. 1, February 1989. A further important source is Mario Bozzi Sentieri, "La via evoliana allo stato," in *Diorama Letterario*, no. 72, Florence, June 1984.

If Evola had already chosen an antidemocratic and voluntaristic direction after his previous issues, it was Arturo Reghini (1878–1946) who was responsible for the decisive step that finally fixed this position and gave it a spiritual framework. Reghini was a mathematician, linguist, thirty-third-degree Mason (Scottish Rite), and above all a follower of an esoteric "Italic Tradition." This tradition tried to revitalize Pythagoreanism for the modern age and was emphatically anti-Christian. Reghini had introduced the writings of René Guénon to Evola, and thus introduced him to the central idea of "Tradition." Guénon does *not* understand this to be the taking over of certain rules of behavior and traditions of the past, but instead holds it to be a *metaphysical* reality standing above time: a totality of principles and transcendental and therefore eternal, unchanging values that are completely anchored in Being—i.e., transcendence— and which appear in the historical world in a more or less materialized form. This tradition forms an organic whole that is hierarchically structured and which strives to overcome the nature-bound element to form a higher metaphysical principle (concerning this, see *Revolt Against the Modern World*, the entire first part of which is dedicated to explaining this traditional world).

For Reghini and, in his wake, Evola, the classical Roman and Greek religion and imperial conception of the state approached this ideal very closely. A constant decline, owing mainly to Christianity, which contributed to the dissolution of the Roman Empire, had then led the world to its modern state of dismemberment. A last grandiose gesture was the medieval empire of the Hohenstaufen, with its ideals of asceticism, knighthood, and the strict feudal division of society (see Dante, *De Monarchia*).

Reghini and others now hoped that the ancient *Imperium Romanum* could be revived in their lifetime. In his magazine *Atanor*, Reghini writes in 1924 that he has already foreseen and wished for the rise of an Italian regime in the ancient sense. This regime would primarily have the task of rejuvenating spiritual values, by which he meant anti-Christian and antidemocratic ones. It was precisely in this spirit that *Atanor* (for which Evola also wrote, although on other topics) already welcomed Fascism in its first issue (January/February 1924). The Traditionalists believed, as did the "Conservative Revolution" in the case of National Socialism, that Fascism merely had to be "corrected" in order to be steered onto the right path. They tried to initiate this "correction" repeatedly. This was also the reason for Reghini's, and later Evola's, campaign against the effort of the Fascist regime to come to an agreement with the Catholic Church. This was, of course, a hopeless struggle, which ended in 1929 with the ratification of the Lateran Accords between Italy and the Vatican and the defeat of the Traditionalists.

Within the framework of his campaign for a "pagan imperialism" modeled on antiquity, Reghini had sharply attacked Mussolini, who was acting prime minister, in his otherwise purely philosophical and esoteric magazine *Atanor*, which even drew a detailed and surprisingly knowledgeable response in the form of an article by Mussolini himself (writing under a pseudonym). Of course, in the interests of maintaining power, Mussolini could never pursue an anti-Christian line, but it is still interesting that he even responded to such a marginal opinion. Concerning this, there is some background that has not been completely elucidated and which points to Mussolini's connections to certain esoteric tendencies. Professor Renato del Ponte revealed some of this in his work *Il movimento tradizionalista romano nel novecento* (Scandiano, 1987; see also his preface to Julius Evola and the UR Group, *Introduction to Magic*).

A mysterious character named "Ekatlos" writes in the third volume of Julius Evola and the UR Group's *Introduzione alla Magia quale scienza dell'Io* (Rome, 1971, p. 381ff.) that as early as 1913, mysterious rites were being conducted night after night that were intended to hasten the return of the ancient Roman Empire. Thereafter, ancient sacred objects were discovered that harbored the corresponding spiritual power. Finally, when the first *fascio di combattimento* (combat unit) was founded on March 23, 1919, out of which the Fascist party developed in 1921, someone was present who was part of this magical-sacral group and had conducted the rites. This person said to Mussolini then and there: "You will become the Consul of Italy." On May 23, 1923, the very same person gave a fasces to Mussolini, who had been head of the government since 1922. The fasces (Italian *fascio littorio*, hence Fascism) was a symbol of the chief magistrates in ancient Rome. For this fasces that Mussolini received, an ancient Etruscan battle-ax was used, one of the sacred objects mentioned earlier. Also in 1923, the Palatine (one of the sacred hills of Rome in the ancient tradition) witnessed a performance of part of the tragedy *Ruman: Romae sacrae origines* (Ruman: Rome's Sacred Origins), with Mussolini present and cheering approvingly. In a letter dated March 7, 1923, he had written: "*Ruman* must happen under all circumstances. The government supports the initiative most passionately." However, this tragedy was not theater in the usual sense, but rather a real ritual and an act of consecration that showed a deep knowledge of Rome's ancient tradition.

Likewise, rites were conducted within the UR Group (which, as we know, was under Evola's leadership) with the purpose of ensouling Fascism with the spirit of ancient Rome. However, the Christian integralist Silvano Pannunzio writes in his magazine *Metapolitica* (XIII, 3–4, December 1988) that Mussolini was apparently taken aback when he heard that Reghini and Evola—supposedly in an Etruscan coffin—had conducted rites with this purpose. In the same breath he adds that Evola had no influence on Fascism at all, or certainly much less than had been assumed previously. At least the Catholic Church must have seen these rites and the parallel publishing activities as some kind of danger, for it reacted most vehemently. For example, the later Pope Paul VI indicted the magicians assembled around Julius Evola and their "fanatical re-evocations" in the periodical *Studium* (XXIV, 6, June 1928). In any case, the esoteric attempt to ensoul Fascism with ancient sacrality had failed. The later intellectual efforts of Evola as a writer that ran in the same direction likewise brought negative results.

This episode definitely shows one thing: at least in the beginning stages of Fascism, the most manifold political and even esoteric-political movements had a chance to articulate themselves, even though Mussolini soon closed down all Masonic lodges on behalf of the Church, despite the fact that the Masonic element was not only strongly represented at the founding of the Party, but was the majority as well, as Gianni Vannoni writes (*Massoneria, Fascismo e Chiesa Cattolica*, Rome, 1979). Mussolini was continually torn between Modernism (for example, his acceptance of Futurism as the "official" artistic tendency of Fascism) and Traditionalism.

Evola wrote his first real political essay at the behest of his friend Count Giovanni Colonna di Cesarò, who was a deeply committed democrat and led his own political paper named *Lo Stato Democratico*, which ran counter to the rule of Fascism in its espousal of democratic ideas. Colonna di Cesarò had approached Evola about a contribution for his magazine. Evola immediately let him know that he could only give a devastating indictment of democracy, which was really surprising (excepting his aforementioned studies) as at that time he still moved in Theosophical and Anthroposophical circles (for example, Colonna di Cesarò's mother was the Italian publisher of Rudolf Steiner's works) that were known for their democratic convictions. To this Colonna di Cesarò answered that free expression was the hallmark of democracy and that Evola could naturally write what he wanted. The latter agreed, and so the essay "Stato, Potenza e Libertà" came about (State, Power and Freedom, in *Lo Stato Democratico*, 1/7, May 1925), which consisted of an almost complete transposition of his solipsistic philosophical ideas to the state: "The State as Power," to paraphrase his work *Man as Power*. The foundation of justice and the legitimization of the state can lie only in its power, whereby the concept of power is to be understood in its spiritual meaning as discussed above. In this context, Evola portrayed Fascism as a "mere caricature" and a "grotesque parody, if one looks at the type of ruler and the state that ought to embody the principle of freedom." (In 1925, it was already the leading party.) He further elaborated that the Fascist movement "in no way possesses a cultural and spiritual root." Only after "purely material strength" had brought success did Fascism turn to the task of creating this root, "just as a newly rich man later tries to buy himself an education and a noble title."

These were not exactly amicable words. The "patriotic mythos" is reprimanded as a simplistic "sentimental complex" that reveals an "inner idealistic weakness" and which might be an "early sign of dangerous compromise." "The so-called Fascist revolution" is merely "an ironic revolution," because it has "formally accepted the existing constitutional, parliamentary, and legal order." Evola then goes even further and asserts that this is not so surprising, for "one can hardly trust" these "pseudo-revolutionaries to have the power to execute a real coup d'état."

Evola wrote all this despite the fact that he naturally had his hopes for Fascism. He simply wanted to "correct" it and steer it into aristocratic channels, as we will see him doing during the entire Fascist era. Evola always insisted (perhaps with the exception of his last years) on absolute standpoints and despised compromises because they stemmed from the consideration of advantage and utility. This is also one of the reasons he rejected democracy. This unbending search for a perfect inner coherence is both Evola's highest virtue and his greatest fault.

In this first political essay his special conception of power is also discussed repeatedly. Among other things, Evola criticizes those leaders of the Fascist party who ceaselessly emphasized that they held all the power and therefore possessed the ability to prevail, and opines: "To feel the need to refer to one's own power at every opportunity is already a sign of fear, inner weakness, and insecurity, which leads them in their desperation to resort to brutal violence, since they possess no inner point of real stability and power."

In the same article Evola also strongly condemns violent acts against politically different thinking people, as in the case of the parliamentary deputy Matteotti who was murdered by the Fascists because he wanted to annul the elections of 1924 due to terrorist influence.

This was Evola's not exactly timid entrance into the political debate. *Lo Stato Democratico*, no. 15, of the same year already included his next essay "Note critiche sulla dottrina democratica" (Critical Notes Concerning the Democratic Doctrine). Colonna di Cesarò found it necessary to introduce Evola as a "strict antidemocrat but definitely not a Fascist." Evola himself notes in this article: "Good heavens! To be undemocratic and to be a Fascist: those are surely two totally different things." Evola then expounds the theorem, based on Plato and Taoism, that only a truly spiritual group should hold the reins of power. Then all political and economic problems will be solved. He actually thinks it possible to find such a group in Italy. His later efforts with the UR Group surely followed this direction. Furthermore, he denies in this article that the political arena as such has any value in itself. That is why he has no interest in mere politics. Only the world of ideas has such real value, and therefore has to order the political realm beneath it. He then continues to present "communism, anarchism, and democracy" as different shades of the same thing, a view that he would steadily repeat from then on.

But he did not stop at the political essays for *Lo Stato Democratico*. In 1926 Evola was already published in the important magazine *Critica Fascista*, which was founded and headed by Giuseppe Bottai, later minister of education and governor of Rome. Evola knew Bottai from their time in World War I when they had served in the same artillery regiment. Both had agreed to "stir up the waters" a bit, which Evola accomplished immediately, as *Critica Fascista* was also read by high-ranking officials of the Fascist party.

The tenor was always the same: the fight against the Catholic Church, against the bourgeois element in Fascism, against the administration and its back-scratching toadyism, as well as the accusation that a real cultural revolution based on spirituality had not been achieved. Practical questions of statecraft did not interest Evola, nor did eventual difficulties with the conversion of his theories into reality. Thus he writes in "Idee su uno stato come potenza" (Thoughts about a State as Power; *Critica Fascista*, September 1, 1926): "We have constructed the present concept of the state entirely *a priori*, independently of any historical reality. But *a priori* does not mean abstraction. The idea must sit in judgment over reality, and not the other way round. The task of speculation is to ascertain which values *must* be valid in this insecure human world, not which ones exist. And if this does not correspond to everyday reality, one must nevertheless not call it abstract. Rather, it is the will and strength of those human beings who do not live up to the idea that must be called abstract and sluggish."

With words like these, it could be foreseen that he would not gain any support within the ruling regime, and even less with functionaries concerned for their careers and families. Finally, even his friend Bottai withdrew his support when the attacks on Evola (and by extension on himself, as the publisher responsible) grew in intensity, the immediate cause being the essay "Il fascismo quale volontà di impero e il Cristianesimo" (Fascism as the Will to Empire and Christianity), which appeared in *Critica Fascista* in 1927 and resulted in such vehement reactions that Bottai did not dare defend Evola any more, even suppressing his replies. The hardest attacks came from the Catholic Church.

These attacks reached a climax with the publication of Evola's highly polemical first political book, *Imperialismo pagano*. A storm of outrage broke loose against Evola in magazines and newspapers, even the *Osservatore Romano*, making the author famous overnight.

In this book, which Evola later characterized as too impetuous and of which he forbade new editions, he attacked not only the Catholic Church, but also Protestantism, lashed out equally against the Soviet Union and America, and above all indicted the faults of the Fascist regime, by then already all-powerful.

One example will illustrate this: "On the other hand, the so-called hierarchies of Fascism almost always consist of mere party leaders, who have often come up from lower strata, without a title or a true spiritual tradition, and who have more the suggestive ability of popular tribunes or *condottieri* in a secular Renaissance sense than any real aristocratic traits. Caught up in the struggles and worries of concrete politics, Fascism does not seem to be interested in creating a hierarchy in the higher sense, based on purely spiritual values and knowing only disdain for all pollutions due to 'culture' and modern intellectualism, so that the center might again shift to a position that lies beyond secular and religious boundaries alike. The Fascist conjuration of Roman symbols is far from being accompanied by a conjuration of the pagan Roman idea of the *Imperium* that is sacral, not just militaristic, and that would clearly expose the whole compromising and purely opportunistic side of the union of integral Fascism with any form of the Judeo-Christian religion" (p. 98 in the German edition).

It probably did not help that he immediately followed this by noting that the Fascist regime was "better than nothing."

The following quote elucidates what moved Evola and what he believed in: "In the same way that a living body stays alive only when a *soul* is present to govern it, so every social organization not rooted in a spiritual reality is outward and transitory, unable to remain healthy and retain its identity in the struggle of the various forces; it is not really an *organism*, but more aptly something *thrown together*, an aggregate. The true cause for the decline of the political idea in the West today is to be found in the fact that the spiritual values that once permeated the social order have been lost, without any successful efforts to put something better in their place. The problem has been lowered to the plane of economic, industrial, military, governmental, or even more sentimental factors, without considering that all this is nothing more than matter: necessary if you like, but never enough by itself, and unable to create a healthy and reasonable social order, any more than the mere interplay of mechanical forces can bring forth a living being" (ibid., p. 14). Therefore one thing was essential above all: "The principle and foundation of the new state must be the organic idea" (ibid., p. 26).

What else did Evola want? A resurrection of Rome's ancient greatness. Thus he writes: "Rome was simultaneously a material and a spiritual power: it arose 'to rule the earth's peoples with authority and discipline, to order peace, to be mild toward the vanquished, and to crush the defiant' [Virgil, *Aeneid*, VI, 852–854], and at the same time was something sacral . . . , in which there existed no expression of life, be it in public or private, in war or peace, that was not strictly accompanied by a ritual or symbol—a cultural formation of mysterious origin that had its demigods, its divine kings . . . " (p. 43f.). The resurgence of Rome should coincide with the formation of a true sacral monarchy. We quote: "Of course, this ideal implies the affirmation not only of the concept and right of the nobility, but *also of the monarchy*. . . . It must be renewed, strengthened, and dynamized as an *organic*, central, absolute function that embodies the might of power and the light of the spirit in a single being; then the monarchy is truly the *act* of a whole race, and at the same time the point that leads beyond all that is bound by blood and soil. Only then is one justified to speak of an *Imperium*. When it is awakened into a glorious, holy, metaphysical reality, the pinnacle of a martially ordered political hierarchy, *then the monarchy once again occupies the place and fulfils the function that it once had, before being usurped by the priestly caste*" (p. 24f., emphasis original).

Evola believed he would be able to rechannel Fascism with this battle cry and maybe prevent the concordat with the Church at the last moment. But no positive echo within Fascism was forthcoming. The practicalities of daily government and careerism were too far removed from such ideas. However, we know that Antonio Gramsci, a cofounder of the Italian Communist party and still its leading theoretician (and respected by both left and right), definitely took note of the work.

Even though the book found no positive echo in Italy, it was noticed in Germany, where it was published in 1933 by the Armanen Verlag in an expanded version. It was due to this book that Evola was able to make his first lecture tours in Germany and also make contacts within the "Conservative Revolution." The commentary of SS Brigadeführer Karl Maria Weisthor (real name Wiligut), which will be discussed later, is also interesting. In a report dated August 7, 1938 (R.A. III 2309/6/392) to the *Reichsführer*-SS Heinrich Himmler, after reporting on Evola's *Heidnischer Imperialismus* at the latter's behest, he writes as follows: "It is astounding that a man in today's strongly nationalistic Italy dares to publicly commit such thoughts to writing."

In 1929, Evola's famous essay "Americanismo e Bolscevismo" (Americanism and Bolshevism) appeared in the magazine *Nuova Antologia*. Following the ideas in *Imperialismo pagano*, this piece reveals the danger of a division of the world between America and the Soviet Union, by which Europe would only lose. Both powers strive to enslave man, although with different methods and toward different goals. In either case, the spiritual element is abandoned.

The year 1929 also saw the end of the magical workings of the UR Group, which from 1928 was called KRUR. As he did not have any more true inner or esoteric experiences to add to what he had already published, as he says in the last *Krur* journal, Evola now felt it his mission to become active in the exoteric realm. And because few publications were willing to accept his contributions, he founded his own magazine with a few friends, which he called *La Torre* (The Tower, new edition: Milan, 1977, published by Marco Tarchi), even though the times were extremely difficult, as he writes at the conclusion of *Krur* (new edition: Rome, 1981, p. 385). But he takes the words of the Indian sage Shankara to heart: "Just as the clouds move back and forth across the sky, so too do the experiences of the individual change. And just as all the dark clouds together cannot cloud its emerald calm, so the pains and passions of the world cannot disturb the detached state of an enlightened soul." It was called "The Tower" not as a "place of refuge, but as a place of resistance, of the struggle of a higher realism for the few, the lonely, the free, and the unbending."

With *La Torre*, Evola finally tested the extent of his influence on the cultural and political currents of his time. Among his contributors he counted the poet Girolamo Comi, the later famous psychoanalyst Emilio Servadio, the well-known mountain climber Domenico Rudatis, the Roman mystic Guido de Giorgio, and René Guénon. Contributions by Julien Benda, Krishnamurti, and even Paul Tillich, and excerpts from Nietzsche and Bachofen also appeared. (How many of these were authorized cannot be determined.)

In the editorial to the first issue of *La Torre*, Evola already writes: "Without weakening and compromise we oppose the lowering of the spiritual level, as it has been elevated into a system by contemporary man. . . . We are reacting against the loss of all higher meaning in life; against the materialization, socialization, and standardization to which everything is subjected. . . . We want to be a danger, a challenge, and an indictment . . . of all that is weak and directed toward compromising solutions, and which stands enslaved by prevailing opinion and small-minded adaptations to the moment. . . . [With this magazine we express] the unmoving protest against the tyranny of the economic and the social that insolently permeates everything, and against the decline of any higher viewpoint into the most pitiable humanism" (p. 21).

An "identity card" written by Evola for the magazine also appeared in the first issue (p. 43). Herein it says: "Our magazine was not created to 'whisper' and 'insinuate' something to Fascism or to Deputy Mussolini, because neither Fascism nor Deputy Mussolini would know what to do with that. Our magazine was created rather to defend *principles* that for us are always and absolutely the same, independently of whether we are under a communist, anarchist, or republican regime." Evola mentions his thoughts, as we have heard them, on hierarchy, the anchoring in the transcendental, and the imperial idea. Then he continues: "*Up to the point that Fascism follows and defends these principles, up to that point we can consider ourselves Fascists.* And that is all."

And further: "We are in open opposition to a certain mythos: the one that wants to turn spirituality and culture into a realm that is dependent on politics. We, on the other hand, claim that it is politics that must be dependent on spirituality and culture." It is thereby unmistakable what Evola's goals were in regard to Fascism, what his convictions were, and what his efforts were aiming for.

Already one month after the launch of the magazine (the publication appeared biweekly), an issue was confiscated because Evola had taken an energetic stance against Mussolini's plan to increase the population ("The fatherland needs people").

By the time of issue number five (April 1, 1930), he seems to have found it necessary to write a preamble under the following title: "Things Put in Their

Proper Place, and Some Plain Words." Among other things one can read there: "We are neither 'Fascists' nor 'anti-Fascists.' 'Antifascism' is nothing. But for us as integral advocates of the *Imperium*, for us as aristocratically inclined, for us as unbending enemies of plebeian politics, of any 'nationalistic' ideology, of any and all party ranks and all forms of party 'spirit,' as well as of any more or less disguised form of socialism or democracy, *Fascism is not enough*. We would have wanted a more radical, more fearless, a more absolute Fascism that would exist in pure strength and unbending spirit against any compromise, inflamed by a real fire for imperial power. We can never be viewed as 'anti-Fascists,' except to the extent that 'super-Fascism' can be equated with 'antifascism.' And we have no inhibitions that keep us from plainly speaking our minds. On the contrary, it is to our advantage that the censors know from the start: *even if in a humble form, with the experiment of* La Torre *we want to signal to the foreign world the point up to which strict imperial and traditional thought has a chance of survival in Fascist Italy, especially when it remains free of any political indenture and only obeys the pure will to defend an idea."*

Evola went even further: when he was reminded that Mussolini thought differently from him (one has to remember the totalitarian character of Fascism at that time), he answered in his paper: "So much the worse for Mussolini!" Especially in the column "L'Arco e la Clava" (The Bow and the Club—the title is an ironic expression of how distant opponents would be dealt with by the bow and closer ones with the club), Evola let his polemical and satirical side have free rein. His opponents were almost always functionaries who had climbed to their positions through long service and who had often been from the ranks of the street fighters. Education and culture were not their strong points, and hence Evola had an easy game. Expressions like "cabbage heads" and sentences like "these people should learn how to read before they talk about me" (p. 130) earned him many enemies. Soon the political department of the police warned him and recommended that he be more moderate, because the highest ranks of the Fascist party were already moving against him. He suffered daily attacks and could not move around in Rome without a bodyguard of friends. Consistently with his martial character, Evola did not worry about this, and so orders came down from the highest places to all potential printers of La Torre to refuse any orders placed by Evola. Thus this initiative was choked off after little more than six months. La Torre could no longer appear.

It is interesting to note that a non-Fascist, even anti-Fascist periodical like

Croce's *La Critica* could appear throughout the whole Fascist period, whereas a "super-Fascist" publication like *La Torre* was a victim of censorship. One can see from this who served the regime and its functionaries more, or at least damaged them less.

In his autobiography, Evola wrote about the epoch up to 1930 (*Cammino*, p. 102) that back then he was acting "with idealistic innocence and little practical and tactical sense." After these experiences it became clear to him that he needed "some kind of base within the castle" if he wanted to continue to be active. This base he soon reached with the help of Giovanni Preziosi, who had become aware of *La Torre* because he himself edited a very combative publication called *La Vita Italiana*. In addition, he was acquainted with Arturo Reghini. Preziosi, who came from a strict Catholic family, had won Mussolini's trust with his uprightness, in spite of some resistance; hence, he enjoyed a kind of immunity, as Evola writes, that gave him a large amount of freedom within his magazine. Thus, Evola was able to continue expressing his opinions in Preziosi's organ, and even had the opportunity to travel abroad—for instance, to Germany and Romania—at the magazine's expense. But Preziosi did even more for Evola when he introduced him to Roberto Farinacci. Like Preziosi, Farinacci had been on Mussolini's bad side for a time, because he had uncovered the dirty dealings of Mussolini's brother, but on account of his loyalty, honesty, and strength of character he had a direct connection to Mussolini and so was in a nearly unassailable position. Farinacci managed the publication *Il Regime Fascista*, which was then part of the official state media.

Now, Farinacci offered Evola the possibility to fill a special page every two weeks with the very ideas that he had always stood for, in complete freedom. And thus the absurd situation developed in which although *La Torre* could not appear any more, the same ideas continued to be published in a paper of the regime. And as he notes, Evola had found a "patron saint" in Farinacci who defended him to the utmost degree. It did not matter to Farinacci that Evola was not a party member and had no intention of becoming one. Evola had indeed found a "base within the castle itself." Farinacci was conscious of his own lack of learning, but saw this as a deficiency, and at least through this support wanted to bring "culture" into Fascism.

Thus, it was decided to create a philosophical podium to address a spiritual elite. It was called *Diorama Filosofico* (Philosophical Diorama) and subtitled "Problems of the Spirit in Fascist Ethics." (The reprint of a first volume of the

Diorama with the essays from 1934 to 1935 appeared in 1974 in Rome. It was prefaced with a knowledgeable introduction by Marco Tarchi, "Evola e il fenomeno storico del fascismo" [Evola and the Historical Phenomenon of Fascism].) This special page, which appeared almost uninterruptedly for ten years (until 1943), was a veritable anthology of rightist thinkers in which the unorthodox and nonpartisan dominated. In fact, Evola wanted to assemble a European nonconformist Right that would work as a corrective, in Evola's sense, in the Fascist-type regimes that then predominated everywhere. To this end, he visited numerous countries, all the while soliciting contributions for his *Diorama Filosofico*. This plan is articulated, for example, in the *Diorama* introduction (of February 2, 1934), where he mentions the need for an elite that will function as the "living soul in the center of the hierarchical totality."

The variety of authors whom Evola was able to win over was surprisingly colorful. This kind of freedom was possible in the first place only because *Diorama* appeared in one of the organs most loyal to the party, and thus little prone to attack. Among the authors we must mention Franz Altheim, Othmar Spann, Walter Heinrich, Gonzague de Reynold; and famous poets like Gottfried Benn, Karl Wolfskehl (who came from the circle surrounding Stefan George), and Paul Valéry. In addition, there were outstanding monarchists, like Prince Karl Anton Rohan, Edmund Dodsworth, Sir Charles Petrie, and the monarchist delegate A. E. Günter (not to be confused with H. F. K. Günther); and no less than Wilhelm Stapel, publisher of *Deutsches Volkstum*. Former collaborators of *La Torre*, like Guido de Giorgio and René Guénon, wrote for it as well. Even a Georgian, Grigol Robakadise, was among the contributors. G. Preziosi and G. A. Fanelli must perhaps be counted among the more official proponents. A submission by Heinrich Himmler also appeared, although only in the form of a summary because, as can be seen in the documents of the German Federal Archives in Koblenz, Himmler—or at least his staff—was not very happy about this (more details about the National Socialist episode below).

In addition, poetry by Proust, Joyce, and Thomas Mann was reviewed in the *Diorama*, and there were critiques of Freudian and Jungian psychoanalysis, Nietzsche, Bachofen, and Bergson. Beside these contributions, which must have been incomprehensible for many readers, there were discussions of themes connected to the current experiences of Fascism. Among these themes we can include the problems of the corporations, the question of a unique Fascist art and architecture, and ethical questions.

In the meantime, Evola's totally unpolitical but excellent study of alchemy had appeared in 1931 under the title *La tradizione ermetica* (The Hermetic Tradition, English edition: Rochester, Vt., 1995). The book betrays an unbelievable familiarity with hundreds of alchemical texts, and has been laudably mentioned by C. G. Jung and Mircea Eliade. Académie Française member Marguerite Yourcenar, at the end of her own *L'Oeuvre au noir*, calls it one of the best studies on alchemy that has ever been published.

In 1934 Evola released his "unofficial masterpiece," *Rivolta contro il mondo moderno*, in which he consolidated his thought on a traditional worldview. The work (which was also released in 1935 by the German Verlags-Anstalt, Stuttgart, under the title *Erhebung wider die moderne Welt*) was revised three times and published in its final form in Rome, 1969. The latter was the foundation for the English translation of 1995 with the title *Revolt Against the Modern World*. Because this book is still available, despite its importance it will be discussed only very briefly here. It is not a political book in the strict sense; rather it could be called metapolitical. Supported by a mass of quotes from ancient philosophical and religious writings, it presents the spiritual foundation on which all politics whatsoever, according to Evola, should be built. Without exaggerating, one can say that none of Evola's other writings, including the political ones, can be understood without prior knowledge of *Revolt*. The only exceptions are the works written before 1925, although even these are already infused with some isolated aspects of the traditional worldview.

The book is a merciless reckoning with everything we call modern, and especially with the concept of progress as such. According to Evola (and also according to the ancient world and the religious beliefs of India), the world is not in a state of improvement, but rather in an ongoing decline. The reason for this lies in an increasing desacralization of life and of history. The sacred, which penetrated and uplifted every aspect of life in the traditional world, from the family to the state, has been completely lost, replaced by a purely economic attitude entailing ever stronger mechanization and standardization. This is especially noticeable in the leadership of the state, which should be the domain of a priest-king acting as mediator between Heaven and Earth. And for all this, the traditional world for Evola (and he follows Guénon in this regard) is no nostalgic conjuration of the past, but instead the historical expression of a supratemporal reality.

In his review of the work in *Die Literatur* (vol. XXXVII, 1934/1935,

pp. 283–287), the famous expressionist poet Gottfried Benn called it: "A work
. . . whose extraordinary importance . . . will be clearly evident. An 'epochal'
book. He who has read it will be changed." And Mircea Eliade, ostensibly the
most well-known contemporary scholar of comparative religion, writes in
Vremea (March 31, 1935, p. 6): "Evola is one of the most interesting spirits of
the war generation. He wields a truly astounding amount of knowledge. . . .
We recommend this book to those who want to consider, if not answers to all
questions, then at least a fascinatingly broad explanation of the world and of
history" (quoted after *Les Deux Etendards*, I/1, Luisant, 1988).

Evola's Relations to Fascism in the Years 1935–1945

We have already become acquainted with Evola's strongly critical yet hopeful
attitude toward Fascism. In spite of this, and partly due to his very refusal to
compromise, he had friends and protectors in the ranks of ardent Fascists who
wanted to help build a better world and who, like Evola, saw their ideals van-
ishing before their eyes. Thus he enjoyed support, and was always able to pub-
licize, make contacts, and travel. There was only one thing he was never able to
do, interestingly enough: to reach the Russian front as a fighter. Evola had long
dedicated himself to this venture, as he wanted to do his part in beating back
Communism. But his application was delayed again and again, chiefly because as
an officer who was not a member of the Fascist party he was regarded as unde-
pendable. Even when he declared his willingness to seek party membership to
reach his goal, he received a negative reply to his request. He simply had too
many enemies in the bureaucracy.

Official Fascism did not think highly of him. In spite of this, he was able to
partake in one initiative, if only as a supplier of ideas. This was the Scuola
Mistica del Fascismo (The Mystical School of Fascism), which had been founded
in 1930 under the auspices of Arnaldo Mussolini. In this school Evola saw the
realization of one of his favorite plans, which would later surface again and
again (for example, in his evaluation of the SS or in *Men among the Ruins*). Its
purpose was to form a core with a strongly spiritual worldview, or, as Evola
would have rather called it, an Order that would take on the spiritual leadership of Fascism. It was a matter of the much desired "new Fascist type of man,"
who would correspond to the knightly and ascetic goal of sacrifice for a higher
ideal. But it soon became clear that the day-to-day problems of the regime and
finally the course of the war would leave no room for "Fascist mysticism."

What, then, were Evola's relations with Mussolini (the head of the government), and how can some authors—for example, Werner Gerson (a.k.a. Pierre Mariel) and, even worse, Elisabeth Antebi—describe Evola as Mussolini's *"éminence grise"*?

Already in 1935 Mussolini had noticed Evola's essay "Razza e Cultura" (Race and Culture) in the magazine *Rassegna Italiana*, which he was in agreement with, whereupon he had let the editors know that he supported such theses. It is unknown whether Mussolini knew of Evola before this, although it is very possible that he had studied *Imperialismo pagano*, just as he had read Reghini's political essays. However, the first personal meeting between Evola and Mussolini came about only in 1942, when the latter arranged a meeting after reading Evola's *Sintesi di dottrina della Razza* (Synthesis of a Doctrine of Race; Evola's racial ideas will be explored in a later chapter). Mussolini praised the book warmly (his personal copy has been preserved, complete with his notes in the margins)—really more so than the work deserved, as Evola himself writes (*Cammino*, p. 155). Mussolini even said it was exactly these ideas that he wanted to comprise the official Italian doctrine on race. In the same breath he proposed that Evola should call these teachings a "Fascist" (as opposed to "National Socialist") doctrine, as was then done in the title of the German edition, *Grundrisse der faschistischen Rassenlehre* (Berlin, 1942). With this, Mussolini had reached his aim: a racial doctrine of his own, different from Germany's. Il Duce also advised all the important papers and magazines to publish positive reviews of the work.

The next known meeting between Evola and Mussolini followed in September 1943, immediately after Mussolini's liberation by Skorzeny, at Hitler's headquarters in Rastenburg, near the East Prussian border. It came about in the following manner: Evola had excellent relations with Germany (more about this in the next section) and was, if only through his mastery of the German language, an ideal mediator between that country and Italy. Even though both countries were still allied militarily, Mussolini had already been deposed by the Badoglio government, and Germany feared that despite promises to the contrary, Italy would abandon the military front. Because Evola was well known, if not as a Fascist, at least as a friend of the Germans in Italy, he was invited to seek safety in Germany, which he declined. However, at the end of August 1943 he went to Berlin after all, to at least lead some discussions about the situation in Italy.

When he was ready to travel back, the Office of Foreign Affairs told him that his friend Giovanni Preziosi, who had become a minister, was staying incognito in Bad Reichenhall near Munich and wished to see him. Evola immediately went there. At the moment of departure, he and Preziosi received the news of the separate cease-fire that Badoglio had negotiated with the Allies, which, of course, had to be interpreted as treason by the Germans. Preziosi, and with him Evola, who acted as his interpreter, was asked to come to Rastenburg, where Hitler had his headquarters at that point, to discuss the new situation. Indeed, they were immediately received by Ribbentrop, who expressed Hitler's wish that the forces loyal to Mussolini form a counter-government as soon as possible. Naturally, this was barely possible since the fate of Mussolini, now imprisoned at Gran Sasso, was unknown. Then the news of Mussolini's liberation by Skorzeny arrived, and soon after Mussolini himself arrived in Rastenburg. According to Evola's descriptions, in the discussions that followed Mussolini revealed himself to be full of illusions, as he did not know (or did not want to know) what had transpired in Italy. And so the Salò Republic, with the more official title Repubblica Sociale Italiana (RSI), was proclaimed under German protectorate.

Evola supported this undertaking even though (or maybe because) it was obvious that one was fighting a losing battle—at this point there could be no doubt about the outcome of the war. This is all the more astounding since Evola, a monarchist, aristocrat, and "reactionary," was participating in a form of government that according to its name alone was "socialist" and "republican"—both tendencies that Evola had always rejected. This republic, for example, lacked the monarchical superstructure that Mussolini had upheld throughout the whole Fascist period until June 25, 1943. The socialist tendencies of early Fascism also played a larger role, probably as a reaction to the fact that it was King Vittorio Emmanuele who had had Mussolini arrested. But Evola did not want to desert something for which he had held such great hopes. His "legionnaire's spirit," the resolve to fight to the bitter end, also left him no choice, although there were great discussions with Mussolini about the monarchy that was so dear to him, and about Vittorio Emmanuele. As he writes in his autobiography: "I did not want to follow the 'Salò Fascism' in the ideological arena at all, but had to show my respect for the martial side that was bound to the legionary spirit: the decision of hundreds of thousands of Italians to stay loyal to their ally and to continue the war—as the king and Badoglio had falsely promised right after July 25—although these hundreds of thousands knew they were manning a lost position, so that at least their honor would be upheld. This was unique in the post-Roman history of Italy."

Because the Salò Republic did not meet his expectations, after his return to Rome Evola started to prepare the nucleus of a spiritually based rightist movement for the postwar period, which later might possibly develop into a party. This group, in which an old friend of Evola's, the constitutionalist Carlo Costamagna, also participated, bore the name Movimento per la Rinascita d'Italia (Movement for the Rebirth of Italy). But soon the Allies had taken Rome and, as Evola himself puts it, "men from their secret service were so kind as to promptly pay me a visit." While his mother kept the men at bay, Evola was able to get away, and to reach Vienna by way of Verona (the source of this report is J. Evola, *Diario 1943–1944*, Centro Studi Evoliani, Genoa, 1975). Evola's relations with Mussolini had hereby ended, even though another essay of his was circulated widely in magazine form at Mussolini's request: "Considerazioni sui fatti d'Italia" (Thoughts About the Events in Italy; *Politica Nuova*, September 28, 1943).

According to rumor, Mussolini was afraid of Evola's magical powers and formed the well-known gesture against the Evil Eye whenever he was mentioned. It seems that Evola even lost journalistic assignments because of this. It is also certain that Mussolini was superstitious, and that Evola had the reputation of bringing bad luck in the circles then current. This reputation remained intact even in the postwar era. It is supposedly the real reason that Evola could not publish in the very successful magazine *Il Borghese* in the 1960s. However, in 1990 Renzo de Felice published in Bologna the *Taccuini mussoliniani* (Mussolinian Diaries) by Yvon de Begnac. De Begnac had had very close contact with Mussolini and had kept continuous notes about this. Mussolini had mentioned Evola fairly frequently, and always in a positive sense. So at least at that time their relationship does not seem to have been characterized by fear.

Independently of Evola's sharp criticism of Fascism, as we have already discussed, the few direct contacts (not more than three or four times) that Evola had with Il Duce hardly make up the important role that an *"éminence grise"* plays.

An interesting story should be mentioned in this context, although it unfortunately cannot be proved. In the *Zeitschrift für Ganzheitsforschung* (Journal for

Holistic Research, vol. 34, no. I, Vienna, 1990), Dr. Theodor Veiter reports that Evola, through his work as coeditor at the official magazine *Affari Esteri* (Foreign Affairs), came to have strong differences of opinion with Mussolini and had to go underground forthwith. At the beginning of the war he had supposedly moved to Vienna, where he lived, as he told Dr. Veiter personally, as a "U-boat" out of fear of Mussolini's henchmen, who had orders even to "murder" him. Back then, he also had close contact with Professor Walter Heinrich, who beside his academic activities also had esoteric interests (see Walter Heinrich, *Der Sonnenweg* [The Solar Path], Ansata, Interlaken, 1985) and further with Rafael Spann, a son of Othmar Spann. They supposedly founded a sort of think tank called the Kronidenbund, so called in reference to *chronos* (the Greek word for "time") and the god of the same name (Saturnus in Latin) who ruled the Golden Age before Zeus ushered in decadence. At that time, Dr. Veiter had known Evola in person. He also knew Mussolini personally.

Domenico Rudatis has also told us that in Vienna Evola lived under a false name and with a forged passport, as there were efforts to keep him under surveillance. However, he could not ascertain when this had occurred, whether at the beginning of the 1940s or only following the aforementioned escape, after the Allies had captured Rome. Evola's own version of this episode of the forged passport (*Cammino*, p. 163) definitely seems to point to the time after the flight from Rome, even though his account mentions neither an exact time frame nor a motive. Maybe the reason for this is the fact that Evola had at that time been commissioned by certain circles within the SS to write the *Storia segreta delle società segrete* (Secret History of Secret Societies). As part of this effort, he had access to the archives of the SS, which had confiscated the documents of various esoteric societies, especially many Masonic lodges. Evola never desired to make more details of this known, but perhaps a false identity was an advantage in this work.

Summary of Evola's Relations to Fascism

Taken as a whole, one can look at Evola's attitude toward the historical phenomenon of Fascism in the following time sequence: first a great hope; then an immediate sobering that is nevertheless supported by the hope of being able to make corrections of a traditional kind; and finally the recognition that everything is lost, which in Evola's case, however, leads him to endure, out of "loyalty" and the "legionnaire's spirit," to the end and beyond. Finally comes *apoliteia*, the apolitical stance that betrays a total disillusion. We have discussed several times Evola's main point of contention regarding Fascism: its lack of spiritual roots. All his other criticisms are merely consequences of this. In countless essays he mentioned the totalitarian state, the bureaucracy, the populist elements ("Proletarian and Fascist Italy," as one slogan had it) that brought with them demagoguery and a primitive emphasis on outward things, the pedagogic urge of the state, the campaign for population increase, the "virtuous" attitude toward sexual morals, the absurd continuing existence of the party (which, after all, means "part," and thus stands in logical opposition to an autocratic assertion), with its pathetic election spectacles, the politicizing of leisure time, the Fascist corporative concept, the Catholic influence, and so on.

These "degenerations," as Evola termed them, were of course exactly the components that made up the political success of Fascism and National Socialism alike. The emphasis on bourgeois thought-patterns and the subsequent repression of the aristocratic element aroused his decisive opposition. By Evola's definition of aristocracy, it "has nothing in common with Machiavellian or demagogic forms of rule by violent and terrorizing types. . . . The foundation of every aristocratic type is above all spiritual, 'Olympian,' and refers to an order that is already metaphysical" (*Lo Stato*, April 1941). We are already familiar with his distaste of everything middle class, as well as its roots in Nietzsche, Plato, Le Bon, and so on. Evola's attitude becomes very apparent in the article "Unsere antibürgerliche Front" (Our Antibourgeois Front), which he published in issue no. 27 of the German conservative magazine *Der Ring*. We quote: "The bourgeoisie is identical to the Third Estate, the class of merchants and craftsmen who settled in the medieval cities. Now it is obvious that the 'progress' of history since the Middle Ages can be summarized as the abnormal development of the middle-class element and its unique occupations and interests, while the other, higher elements of the medieval hierarchy were shut out—a development that has the character of a cancerous growth. It is the *Bürger* [bourgeois citizen] who unloads the full curse of ridicule on the ideals of the previous knightly era. It is the *Bürger*, like the 'new men' whom Dante so despised, who is the first to give the signal to the antitraditional outrage by assuming the right to bear arms, by fortifying the centers of corrupt economic power, and so helping his standard to prevail; it is the *Bürger* who makes an anarchical claim of autonomy against imperial authority in the urban communities. It is the *Bürger* who has slowly brought things to the point that today a claim that would have been deemed an absurd heresy in other, normal times can appear to be the most natural thing in the world: that is, that the economy is our fate and destiny, that profit is our purpose in life, that bargaining and trading is a 'deed,' and that the conversion of every value into the notions of profitability, prosperity, and comfort, into units of speculation and of supply and demand, makes up the essence of our civilization . . . thus, modern civilization and bourgeois civilization have come to be almost identical expressions. It is to the *Bürger's* rise to power, who first through the Revolution and then through the democratic constitutions has been freed from the medieval 'residues,' that the Western world owes its illusory greatness, but at the same also its terrible spiritual destruction, whose witnesses we are today."

Evola made Edgardo Sulis's words his own: "The bourgeoisie: enemy number one of the Fascist revolution." For Evola, the bourgeoisie is identical with the destruction of true spiritual values in order to increase one's own profits, as well as the failure to recognize quality and the subsequent introduction of quantity as the sole criterion. Herein lie further roots of Evola's enmity toward democracy: it is not the majority—that is, quantity—that should decide, but the quality of realization that can be found only in the few. To the same category as the article quoted above belongs the essay "Bureaucracy and the Leading Strata" (in *Lo Stato*, IV, as well as a German version in *Der Vierjahresplan*, 1940), where Evola writes: "After the communist and bolshevist danger had receded, one rightfully saw Fascism's most dangerous opponents in the form of bourgeois culture and the bourgeois spirit. Fascism must be especially prepared for this danger, because it appears in a more refined and cunning form and finds a fertile ground in the natural inclinations of the majority of men, wherever the heroic tension . . . begins to weaken. . . . However, it is curious that one of the most typical forms [of the bourgeois spirit] has hardly received any attention, a form that is all the more dangerous because it flourishes in the center of the state: I mean the phenomenon of bureaucracy. Bureaucracy is the typical agent of the 'political bourgeoisie' and embodies the worst misdeeds of the middle-class spirit in its widest sense. In spite of eighteen years of Fascist rule, it must be honestly admitted that Italy is far removed from being able to show a really effective and not just nominal de-bureaucratization. . . . In this way, a very real kind of bureaucratic feudalism is being formed. . . ."

In his enmity toward the middle-class spirit, Evola could refer to Mussolini himself, who had stressed repeatedly that bourgeois and Fascist spirit, bourgeois and heroic ethic, are incompatible opposites. The expression "Fascism disdains the comfortable life" also originates from Mussolini.

Thomas Sheehan, in his interesting although strongly anti-Evolian essay "Myth and Violence: The Fascism of Julius Evola and Alain de Benoist" (in *Social Research*, vol. 48, pp. 45–73), in which he sees an absolute "demythologizing" and a veritable ban on the "mythic" as the only means against violence and extremism, quotes Mussolini as exhorting the Italian citizen to "attain that purely spiritual existence in which his value as a man consists." In a 1930 speech about Fascism, Mussolini also says: "This political process is flanked by a philosophical process; if it be true that matter was on the altars for a century, today it is the spirit which takes its place. . . . By saying that God is returning, we mean that spiritual values are returning" (p. 52).

Utterances of this sort must have surely given Evola new hope time and again; but a deep chasm opened between such words and the reality designed by administrators. It is hard to ascertain whether Evola made a fundamental error with regard to Fascism, by mistakenly identifying his private conceptions of it with the historical phenomenon. But we can hardly believe this, because the divergences were simply too great. Was it not Fascism that, as Philippe Baillet writes ("Les rapports de Julius Evola avec le Fascisme et le National-Socialisme" [The Relationships of Julius Evola with Fascism and National Socialism] in *Politica Hermetica*, p. 61f.), brought the people the modernism despised by Evola with its "invasion of radios, that mania of compulsory exercise for everyone, the political song, the cult of film stars, the invasiveness of bureaucracy, and the excessive industrialization"? And the mass marches where a "Caesar" was applauded? We also support the thesis of Baillet (one of the best Evola experts) and assume that Evola simply saw Fascism as the last chance of the West. From his standpoint, the visible alternatives were much worse; there was only liberalism paired with capitalism ("anything goes") and Communism, both of which worshiped a world of machines and limitless materialism. Because Fascism strengthened the state and the hierarchical concept, and, for all its demagoguery, praised honor, bravery, and loyalty, Evola saw in it at least a temporary bastion against the equalizing flood that seemed certain to succeed in liberalism and Communism.

In the same way, Evola's approach to the "much more consequential" National Socialism can be understood as a reaction to his disappointment with Fascism. The disappointment with National Socialism in addition led him to the even "more consequential" philosophy of the SS. But this is material for another chapter. The last "consequence" was *apoliteia*, the retreat into metaphysics.

Aside from this, Evola possibly believed in the "magical" effectiveness of the traditional ideas in the present. Through their continuous "invocation," the supra-mundane ideas were supposed to act like magnets on this earth, around which the best simply had to gather. But exactly here lies the crux of any concept of the state that is founded in transcendence: How does one translate the metaphysical values into mundane reality? And this poses a second question: Must not man assimilate himself to the supra-mundane world before he can recognize and then realize its values? Is not an inner transformation needed before the outer?

Another aspect that brought Evola into conflict with the ruling Fascism was his disapproval of the nation concept as a creation of the French Revolution, which had led to an impermissible rise of the ethnic concept. For him, nation and folk were concepts rooted in nature, and thus subversive and anti-traditional. Rooted in nature means rooted in life, and thus geared toward one's own survival, which excludes any form of sacrifice for a higher ideal. The whole philosophy of self-interest derives from being rooted in life. By definition, true spirituality stands above life and therefore cannot be concerned with it. That is why overcoming the fear of death is a prerequisite of free spirituality.

In the essay "Processo alla Borghesia" (Indictment of the Bourgeoisie) from March 1940 (reprinted in the anthology *Gli articoli de la Vita Italiana durante il periodo bellico* [The Articles from *Vita Italiana* during the War Period], Treviso, 1988), he says: "For us the word 'people' comes from the jargon of demagogues and agitators, because in reality it is either a passive substance and belongs to him who understands how to possess it, or else it is the end phase of a process of dissolution and of a societal equalization." To Fascism, and even more so to National Socialism, such words amounted to sacrilege—as they would in the contemporary world as well.

In his summarizing critique of Fascism, *Il fascismo visto dalla Destra con in appendice: "Note sul Terzo Reich"* (Fascism Viewed from the Right with an Appendix: 'Notes on the Third Reich,' Rome, 1970), which, however, was written after the war—which is why we have focused on the works of the Fascist period—Evola even writes the following: "We are not afraid to invert the thesis of a certain antifascism, and assert that it was not Fascism that had negative effects on the Italian people, but rather the other way round: it was this people, this 'race,' that negatively affected Fascism, i.e., the Fascist experiment, because it showed that it did not have enough men on the necessary plane of certain higher qualifications and symbols . . . capable of further developing the positive possibilities that could have been contained in this system."

This is not necessarily as malicious as it seems, even though it is of course provocative (provocation being, after all, one of the special inclinations of our author), for the concept of the state that Evola represents presupposes the overcoming of the purely human. That is why Evola strives to form the "new man," only not in the mass but instead in the form of an elite, an Order, which takes up the reins of the state as Plato's wise men did. In this he is different from the leftist utopians, who also want to create a new man, but who want to see him in the people as a whole, and thus mercilessly want to reeducate everyone. As their head there should be a monarch because, as Evola writes in *Fascismo* (p. 45): "A true Right without a monarchy would be lacking its natural gravitational and crystallizing point" (see also the collection of essays published by Renato del Ponte with Evola's relevant articles: *Monarchia, Aristocrazia, Tradizione*, San Remo, 1986, and "Significato e funzione della Monarchia" [Significance and Function of the Monarchy] in the appendix to his translation of Karl Löwenstein, *La Monarchia nello stato moderno*, Rome, 1969).

With this emphasis on a spiritual monarchy ("by the grace of God") and the consequent imperial idea, Evola stood in sharp contrast to the principle of Fascism's and National Socialism's leaders, who both derived their legitimacy from the people: thus the monarchs came from above, the leaders from below. This leadership principle corresponds exactly to the picture of Caesarism that Spengler unfolds in his *Decline of the West*, and which is a sign of a declining civilization. Mussolini seems to have had a clear understanding of these contexts, and tried to cut off the spread of Spenglerian ideas as much as possible. It is interesting that the communist theoretician Antonio Gramsci accused Fascism of "bourgeoisation" and Caesarism (see Marcello Veneziani, *La Revoluzione Conservatrice in Italia*, Milan, 1987, p. 51).

On the other hand, Evola did not intend his traditional concepts to remain mere idle plays of thought. In order to at least put something into action, he also had to compromise and, for instance, accept the nominal status of the monarchy in the Fascist epoch. Of course, this led to other unavoidable contradictions. A real solution to these inconsistencies was to come only with Evola's *apoliteia*.

Evola led a special struggle against the "bolshevist" tendencies in Fascism—that is, the opinion of some that communism had to undergo only a few positive developments in order to turn into Fascism. The communist idea, with its collectivism, was for Evola the most radical negation of his ideal of the personality, which, bound to transcendence, rose above the purely human element. This "antibolshevism," as he often called it, was also the reason for his decisive opposition to all similar tendencies in National Socialism, which also approached communism, in that among other things it wanted to abolish private property and dreamed of the introduction of the Russian *mir*. That is why he opposed National Bolshevism more and more, even though he also wrote for Ernst Niekisch's journal *Widerstand*.

Evola attacked; however, he was also himself attacked, not only because of his strict theoretical convictions and his often personal attacks on some representatives of Fascism and its culture, but also because he was seen as a "narcissistic magician" who studied Tantrism, Buddhism, Hinduism, alchemy, and so on. One of the accusations from Catholics and Fascists asserted that these occult activities in themselves already proved his "antifascism," because a real Fascist would have totally different ideals. Accusations of this kind must have been frequent, because Evola at least once felt compelled to answer the charges in an essay (see "Oriente non e antifascismo" [Orient Does Not Equal Antifascism"], in *Critica Fascista*, October 10, 1927).

Official Fascism was equally unhappy about Evola's public agreement with the thesis of the "philosophers of crisis"—Spengler, Benda, Massis, Guénon, Keyserling, and Ortega y Gasset—that the world was in the midst of a decline. This amounted to a denunciation of the modern age, whereas to be modern and progressive was the declared goal of Fascism. Especially hard hit by this rejection by the Fascist regime was Oswald Spengler, who was spurned even by such well-known philosophers as Croce and Cantimori.

For the evaluation of Evola's attitude toward Fascism, the following seems to us expressive and telling. In the middle of the war, when the very survival of Fascism was at stake, Evola authored an extensive work on Buddhism, which, truly free of any hint of the desperate times, speaks in an erudite fashion about ascetics, nirvana, karma, and rebirth, unlocking these concepts in true Evolian fashion in a new way, while directly referring to the ancient Buddhist texts, contradicting the then current pseudo-Oriental prejudices: a work that was translated and published by Luzac, one of the most respected English publishers in this field. Even declared enemies of Evola agree about its merits.

After these fairly numerous references, which should allow the reader a differentiated picture of Evola's activities in relation to Fascism, it is surely interesting to read a few opinions and judgments about him.

Renzo de Felice, no doubt the most important expert on Fascism and the well-known Mussolini biographer, writes in *Der Faschismus: Ein Interview* (Stuttgart, 1977, p. 97ff.): "Who is Evola? Throughout the whole Fascist period he was an outsider, and not by accident; he never held any office within the Fascist party . . . and at least many of the Fascists criticized him and viewed him with mistrust. Evola represents a form of Traditionalism that consists of cosmic history on the one hand and prophecies of doom on the other. These are convictions that one finds only in very small fringe groups in Fascism, if at all."

Ernst Nolte opined in his *Der Faschismus in seiner Epoche* (Fascism in Its Epoch, Munich, 1979, p. 589): "Giulio Evola played no political role. Still, he was no 'unpolitical archaicist,' because he worked diligently with the racial campaign." (A following chapter examines Evola's racism in detail.)

Mircea Eliade (as a historian of religion no "expert" on the subject, and then still young) declared in his article in *Vremea:* "Evola is not subject to influences. This is exactly why we sympathize with him."

Gottfried Benn had the following to say in his review of *Revolt:* "Because they put their racial-religious axiom into action, Evola sees in the movements of Fascism and National Socialism the possibilities of a relinking of peoples to the world of Tradition, promises for the production of real history, and a new legitimate relationship of spirit and power. Indeed, with Evola's teachings as a background, one can see the epochal depth of these movements very clearly."

Surely, Evola was no Fascist in the historical meaning of the term, but was even less of an "anti-Fascist." One could label him as a critical sympathizer with Fascism, who because of his martial and spiritual archaisms remained without political influence.

A pointed word from Dino Cofrancesco (in Paolo Corsini and Laura Novati, *L'eversione nera*, Milan, 1985, p. 105) concludes this chapter: "To paraphrase the saying of De Felice, Fascism was an illegitimate child of 1789. For Evola, in contrast, Fascism is a degenerate child of Tradition." As is well known, for De Felice, Italian Fascism is part of a revolutionary line of a "leftist" Enlightenment that demands a "new man" in a "new society."

Evola and National Socialism

Early on, Evola had already striven to maintain good relations with Germany. He admired German culture, and we have already noted how strongly his worldview was influenced by German philosophers and thinkers. He had

especially tried to connect with proponents of the so-called Conservative Revolution (to use a term coined by Armin Mohler), such as Edgar Julius Jung (murdered by the National Socialists in 1934), Christoph Steding, Wilhelm Stapel,
A. E. Günter, and Ernst Niekisch. He also contributed writings to their magazines *(Der Ring, Europäische Revue, Deutsches Volkstum, Widerstand)* and popularized their philosophies in Italy (with regard to this, see Marcello Veneziani,
La Rivoluzione Conservatrice in Italia, Milan, 1987). From the beginning, he also
had relations with the Viennese Kulturbund as well as with the group around
Othmar Spann (persecuted by the National Socialists) and Prince Karl Anton
Rohan, with whom he had especially close contact.

In 1934 Evola embarked on his first series of lectures in Germany and spoke
at Berlin University and at the aristocratic, conservative Berliner Herrenklub
(Berlin Gentlemen's Club) under Baron Heinrich von Gleichen. Evola can
probably be equated with the proponents of the Conservative Revolution—
that is, as their Italian counterpart, as his ideological opponent Professor Franco
Ferraresi confirms in *La destra radicale* (Milan, 1984, p. 26). Though these circles
tried at least initially to collaborate with the National Socialists, they distanced
themselves from the "populist, plebeian, and fanatical" aspects of the Hitler
regime. They believed they could influence National Socialism, which, of
course, turned out to be an illusion in the face of Hitler's great political and
also economic success. As a general rule, the more radical element will always
triumph over the moderate when their forces are fairly equal.

Evola had developed a sympathy for Germany during World War I that set
him at odds with his Futurist friends. Later he developed the idea of the unification of "the two eagles"—the German and the Italian—based on the
Ghibelline notion of Empire during the Hohenstaufen period. He pointed out
that the two peoples complement each other, and would reap benefits only by
moving closer together. With this idea, he invited enmity on both the German
and the Italian side, given the ultranationalist climate of the time. Concerning
this question, an interesting National Socialist document has been preserved
in the Political Archive of the Ministry of Foreign Affairs in Bonn (file AA
Referat DIII, e.o. 9685) that was marked for the internal use of the Foreign
Office (Auswärtiges Amt). It reports on an article entitled "The Contribution
of Rome to the New Germany," which Evola published in *Regime Fascista* on
November 16, 1941. After discussing the main thesis, the author of the document continues: "This impudent article, which . . . is in no way suited to ad-

vance German-Italian collaboration, cannot remain uncontested. . . ." In this article, Evola, among other things, "spoke of the formidable confusion and spiritual aberrations that can be detected in some circles of the German Reich, and have to be prevented." These circles' view of what really constitutes the Nordic ideal rests on "one-sided and arbitrary interpretations" and "confused and often dilettante authors" who sought the essence of Nordicism in a "naturalistic mysticism" and a "foggy, Nibelungen-like romanticism." Evola further characterized Richard Wagner (for whom Hitler's admiration is notorious) as a "forger and usurper of the old mythology."

We have already mentioned that, aside from his Germanophilia, the main reason for Evola's rapprochement with National Socialism lies in his disillusionment with Fascism. In National Socialism, he saw a much greater inner coherence, a stronger emphasis on the warrior element and the culture of the conservative Right (although the latter was disdained by the actual NS). He was similarly impressed by the motto of the "struggle for the worldview" and welcomed the absence of the marching in line and vying for position that were so common in Italy. As Maria Zucchinali adds (*A destra in Italia oggi*, Milan, 1986), Evola was also closer to National Socialism because its socialist origins were less noticeable; in their place, the link with the First and Second Empires was emphasized. Tradition seemed more essential there than progress (also because of the prevalence of the Prussian element). National Socialism likewise strove to breathe new life into ancient Germanic man and to restore the original brilliance of the North (Hermann the Cherusker, for example). Added to this were the notion of the *"Ordensstaat"* (Order-based state) with its accompanying ascetic attitude and readiness for sacrifice, loyalty, honor, discipline, and selflessness. Even the obsession with ancient symbols must have impressed Evola, even though it was clear to him that they were often misused. He knew this manipulation well; as early as 1931, René Guénon had indicted the misuse of the swastika in his *Symbolisme de la Croix* (see Evola's essay in *Hochschule und Ausland* 12, 1934, "Das Hakenkreuz als polares Symbol" [The Swastika as a Polar Symbol]), in which he attributes this symbol not to the Indo-Germanic cultures but instead to a Hyperborean primordial race.

In spite of all this, Evola early on had expressed reservations about National Socialism, as in an article in *Vita Nova* with the title "Problemi attuali" (Current Problems), in which he uses an article in the *Europäische Revue* about the Third Reich as a pretext to present his arguments. Beneath the already challenging subtitle "Counterrevolution or Reaction?" he writes: "The inferiority of National Socialism is obvious from the standpoint of 'doctrine,' compared to the traditional values defended by groups like those around Hugenberg and Düsterberg. Instead of a tradition with clear outlines that is still ensouled by the ethos and spirit of order, hierarchy, aristocracy, and a heritage that stands in a direct line from the greatest imperial cultures of ancient Europe, we see vague demands, compromises, and national concessions even to Marxism and to positions whose content is dictated mainly by the necessities of the moment and who owe their effectiveness solely to that fact."

Even earlier he had polemicized against Alfred Rosenberg, the "Ideologue of National Socialism," whom he also met in person. Here the November 1930 essay "Il 'Mito' del nuovo nazionalismo tedesco" (The "Mythos" of the New German Nationalism) in *Vita Nova* must be mentioned. Evola's dislike was based mostly on the fact that Rosenberg valued modernity so much. Another article against Rosenberg was "Paradossi dei tempi: paganesimo razzista = Illuminismo liberale" (A Current Paradox: Racist Paganism = Liberal Enlightenment) in *Lo Stato*, VI, 7 (July 1935), pp. 530–532. Evola also polemicized against Walther Darré, who was already NSDAP Reichsleiter at this time, in *Lo Stato* ("Il Nazismo sulla via di Mosca" [Nazism on the Same Path as Moscow], March 1935, pp. 186–195). Later in *Cammino* (p. 147), Evola stated about Rosenberg that "he lacked any understanding for the transcendental dimensions of the sacral."

The absence of any transcendent background was, of course, one of Evola's main objections against National Socialism. "One can organize a state in the name of the spirit or in the name of matter," he wrote in 1937 ("Sulle premesse di un'antibolscevismo positivo" [On the Prerequisites for a Positive Antibolshevism], in *Lo Stato*. This and a few other quotes we have culled from Alessandro Campis's interesting contribution "Organicismo, Idea Imperiale e Dottrina della Razza" in *Trasgressioni*, I/1, Florence, 1986). This lack of reference to transcendence also leads to the other points criticized by Evola, such as National Socialism's great attachment to nature (the *Volk* as guiding principle); the Führer principle that answers only to the people and has no legitimation from above, and the resulting demagoguery; as well as populism and purely biological racism.

Evola also spoke out against the *Anschluss* of Austria into Germany, because he wanted to see the Austrian monarchy revived (see "Il problema monarchio in Austria" [The Monarchist Question in Austria], in *Lo Stato*, IV, February 2, 1935, and "Orizzonte Austriaco" [Austrian Horizon], also in *Lo Stato*, 1935, pp. 22–29). In "Orizzonte Austriaco" we even read: "National Socialism has forsworn the ancient, aristocratic tradition of the Empire. Being nothing but a semi-collectivist nationalism and equalizing in its centralism, it has not hesitated to destroy Germany's time-honored division into duchies, counties, and cities that all enjoyed a measure of independence."

Evola did not hesitate to go further. In an essay of November 1940 (that is, after the start of the war, when Evola was repeatedly visiting Berlin and Vienna) he attacked one of the main slogans of National Socialism and declared: "One of the catchphrases that is especially dear to National Socialism and is expressed in the words: '*Ein Volk, ein Reich, ein Führer*' [One people, one empire, one leader] is already outdated." ("Il problema dei futuri 'spazi imperiali' e il contributo romano-germanico" [The Problem of the Future "Imperial Regions" and the Romano-Germanic Contribution] in *Vita Italiana*). As late as 1942 there appeared a German version of this article under the heading "Reich und Imperium als Elemente der neuen europäischen Ordnung" (Empire and *Imperium* as Elements of the New European Order, in *Europäische Revue*, no. 18) in which Evola expressed the same sentiment in somewhat milder form.

Two excerpts from Evola's postwar work about Fascism (*Fascismo*, p. 171) should also illustrate his feelings in that period: "For Hitler, the people were *the* principle of legitimacy. No higher principle existed or was tolerated by him (his polemics against the Hapsburgs were often marked by an unparalleled vulgarity)."

And "When one took a look at the masses of 'Aryan' folkish comrades of the KdF and the arrogance of the 'de-proletarianized' modern Berlin worker, one could only shudder with revulsion at the thought of a future Germany that would develop in this direction."

But in spite of all these negative aspects, there was something in National Socialism that attracted Evola: the concept of a state ruled by an Order, which he felt was embodied by the SS. "We are inclined to the opinion that we can see the nucleus of an Order in the higher sense of tradition in the 'Black Corps,'" he wrote in *Vita Italiana* (August 15, 1938). Again in *Vita Italiana* (August 1941, "Per una profonda alleanza italo-germanica" [For a Deep Italian-Germanic Alliance]) he writes: "Beyond the confines of the party and of any political-administrative structure, an elite in the form of a new 'Order'—that is, a kind of ascetic-military organization that is held together by the principles of 'loyalty' and 'honor,' must form the basis of the new state." As mentioned, Evola held the SS, which Himmler strove to design according to the model of the Teutonic Order, to be this elite. The castles of the SS Order, with their "initiations," the emphasis on transcending the purely human element, the prerequisite of physical valor, as well as the ethical requirements (loyalty, discipline, defiance of death, willingness to sacrifice, unselfishness), strengthened Evola in his conviction. He also was of the opinion that the ethics of the SS were borrowed from the Jesuits.

Conversely, the SS was interested in Evola and began to maintain a file on him. All his lectures after 1937 were attended, summarized, and archived. Through the meritorious work of Hans Werner Neulen, a real expert in the area of recent historical relations between Italy and Germany, these files have been found in the Political Archive of the Ministry of Foreign Affairs in Bonn (most of them were translated into Italian and published by Nicola Cospito and Hans Werner Neulen as *Julius Evola nei documenti segreti del Terzo Reich* [Julius Evola in the Secret Documents of the Third Reich], Rome, 1986). Nicholas Cospito authored another essay regarding this theme in *Intervento* (no. 80/ 81, Rome, 1987: "Julius Evola e il Nazionalsocialismo"). The first facsimiles of this material were publicized in Rudolf Mund's work illuminating Himmler's occult side, *Der Rasputin Himmlers* (Vienna, 1982). This book deals with the aforementioned Karl Maria Wiligut (alias Weisthor), who wanted to instill Himmler with a Germanic esoteric foundation.

Especially important to this study is the final report on Evola's June 1938 lectures, kept in the handwritten files of the personal staff of the *Reichsführer-SS* (file AR/126). After a short summary of his life, it says there: "Today Evola—and really only in northern Italy—is regarded as a fanatic and dreamer, mostly misunderstood and merely tolerated by official Fascism." Then the content of the three lectures is summarized and on page 12 comes the conclusion, which must be quoted in full:

> The ultimate and secret motivation for Evola's theories and plans must be sought in a *revolt of the old aristocracy* against today's world, which is totally alienated from the upper class. This confirms the initial German impression: that we are dealing with a 'reactionary Roman.' The whole impression is one of an old-fashioned aristocratic feudalism. Thus even his scholarship displays a trait of dilettantism and literary affectation.

In conclusion, there exist no grounds for National Socialism to place itself at the disposal of Baron Evola. His political plans for a Romano-Germanic *Imperium* are of a utopian character and moreover very apt to cause ideological confusions. Since Evola is also only tolerated and barely supported by Fascism, it is tactically not necessary to accommodate his tendencies from our side. It is therefore recommended to:

1. Not support Evola's current efforts for the establishment of a secret supranational order and the founding of a magazine directed toward this goal.

2. Curb his public activities in Germany after this lecture series, without taking any special measures.

3. Prevent his further penetration into leading offices of the party and the state.

4. Observe his propaganda activity in neighboring countries.

In a short letter (AR/83) dated August 8, 1938, it then says laconically: "The *Reichsführer*-SS has acknowledged the report regarding the lectures of Baron Evola and is in full agreement with the thoughts and recommendations stated in the last paragraph thereof."

According to this, the SS as a whole was not favorably inclined toward him, even though he was apparently unaware of it. His ideas were just too different from official National Socialist thought. The scope of this difference is displayed by a written report from one of Evola's lecture evenings (October 12, 1937 at the Studienkreis, Berlin), which bore the title "Abendländischer Aufbau aus urarischem Geist" (Western Rebirth Out of the Primordial Aryan Spirit) and is archived in the same file. Because this lecture documents very well Evola's attitude toward National Socialism, some especially telling excerpts will be quoted at length. First, Evola lists some areas in which he thinks National Socialism (which he refers to as "the new views") has made a positive development (the formation of a front against liberalism, rationalism, Bolshevism, "the myth of the economy," for instance). But then he goes on to declare that much work remains to be done. For example, National Socialism should be replaced by a supranationalism in order to fight against the internationalist forces, and an "Olympian elite, so to speak" must take up the task of superseding with spiritual aims, and thus eliminate all modern streams of thought, such as rationalism, materialism, and collectivism. Then he goes into detail about the points that should be improved, and explains:

> In this respect, I want to be totally straightforward with you, since you shouldn't view me as someone whose ideas are conditioned by his ethnicity and who speaks to you as a foreigner, or who follows any other interest but the pure truth. The only important fact is that we have some knowledge concerning these matters and want to contribute to the common cause, on the basis of unconditional loyalty, lack of prejudice, and selflessness.

> This said, we note the first principal fault in the new views [i.e., National Socialism], which is that these are composed more of myths than of real ideas. To a great extent, these seem to be unclearly received truths that essentially have turned to crystallization points for irrational and passionate forces of belief, that have their effect not because of their spiritual truthfulness but because of their power of suggestion. Because of this impure makeup, these new myths are prone to all manner of infiltration; they are not equipped to prevent dangerous mixtures and are even in danger of becoming the instruments of an unconscious demagoguery, differing from the myths of our opponents only by their distinguishing symbol. I don't want to be misunderstood; therefore I happily admit that it would be utopian to want to influence the masses without resorting to the realm of myth, the irrational, and the passional. But that which constitutes myth and irrationality for them should be pure knowledge, truth, and reality for the others—for a strongly organized and cohesive elite. Due to a regrettable incompetence and pressure from immediate interests, Nordic thought, paganism, primordial symbols, and so on, today all too often see new life in the distorted form of personal affectations and slogans. . . .

> As they are frequently understood today, Nordic thought, Aryanism, the imperial idea, and the concept of a super-race are burdened with an interpretation entirely foreign to the great free breath of the corresponding primordial traditions. According to the Aryan primordial conception, the *Reich* is a metaphysical solar reality. The Nordic heritage is not semi-naturalistic, only conceivable on a blood-and-soil basis, but rather constitutes a cultural category, an original transcendent form of the spirit, of which the Nordic type, the Aryan race, and the general Indo-Germanic moral being are only outward manifestations. The concept of race itself, according to its higher traditional significance, cannot have anything in common with the rational idols of modern biology and profane science. Above all, race is a basic attitude, a spiritual power, something primal and creative, whose outer, tangible forms are only a last echo. . . .

The truly original Nordic essence melts with the Hyperborean; and here we see a primordial culture that is solar and sacral, that possesses the power and irresistibility of the universal, and that encompasses paganism and spirit, Olympian sovereign superiority and will-conditioned originality, in a grand synthesis of the mundane and the supra-mundane. Once one has reached this realization, then one can truly say that Tradition in its higher sense is synonymous with the Hyperborean, or primordial Nordic, tradition, and that the Nordic element has been present wherever a people has had a tradition, and vice versa. That is not all. In this way we can even approach the mystery of prehistory and sense a fateful correspondence between physical circumstances and higher, metaphysical meanings. If the tradition in question indeed had the polar region as its original seat, it must therefore have been geographically polar and so has always embodied the spiritual significance of a pole as an unshakable axis for any ordered movement, as a center point for any normal hierarchy and every true tradition-based *Reich*. . . .

Now, can one present such streams of thought in certain circles without being accused of an alien universalism, of Roman notions that are anti-Germanic, or even of having Jewish ideas? And yet all this belongs to the highest Aryan inheritance; this is the true level to which the motifs and symbols that the new Germany has called forth must be elevated if it really wants to stand at the forefront of the resistance and attack against the dark powers of world revolution. We must really return to the origins, and the Nordic essence must be freed from any interpretations that are infected by modern, profane intellectual prejudices and by the superstitious religion of life, becoming, and being bound to nature. We must once again find out how to imbue the Nordic-Aryan symbols and their logical consequence, the *Reich*, with a spiritual power and a universal gravity, something truly Olympian and transcendental. And this is indeed possible. This must be our task. The new Germany has talented and qualified powers for this and it remains only to give them the right points of orientation, true principles instead of myths and slogans. . . .

We repeat: race is secondary, spirit and tradition the primary factor, because, in a metaphysical sense, race dwells in the spirit before being expressed in the blood. If it is true that without racial purity, spirit and tradition are deprived of their most precious means of expression, then it also true that pure race deprived of spirit is condemned to be a biological mechanism and, in the end, doomed to extinction. The proof of this lies in spiritual decay, the ethical stupefaction, and the slow death of many tribes that did not commit any of the sins against the blood that have been discovered by materialistic racial science. . . . It

follows that without the rejuvenation of the higher spiritual power latent in the
Nordic symbol, all measures for the biological protection of the race will have a
limited and relative effectiveness, as opposed to our superior task of a Western
reconstruction of the Nordic-Aryan spirit. . . .

Leader and followers, organic structure, overcoming of individualism and collectivism through a virile spiritual concept of community—these foundations
for an inner rebuilding of the Folk should now be valid above and beyond the
individual nations, and should lead the way to an organic conception, to which
independence contributes as well as unified higher leadership, ethnic diversity,
as well as spiritual, supranational community. That is what Western rebirth fu-
eled by the Aryan spirit means. . . .

It follows that our front should also take account of all the surviving conservative and traditionalist forces in Europe and even strive toward a new active conservatism on a Nordic foundation, which will have this dual purpose: to rid the
world in revolutionary fashion of a culture of decadence and the new materialist
and collectivist barbarism and to call forth to new life the primal creative power
of the ancient Aryans, in close connection with the values of personality, hierarchy, spiritual virility, and the *Reich* as both worldly and metaphysical reality.
The first condition for this is the desecularization of the world and of man, of
realization and of action. If this prerequisite is not fulfilled, then all roads toward the understanding of primordial Nordicism remain blocked. The first assumption is that there is a higher world beyond this one. Therefore, we have to
abandon any mysticism of this world, any adoration of nature and of life, any
pantheism. At the same time we must strongly oppose the curious interpretation of Aryanism invented by the dilettante Chamberlain that relates to a purely
rational praise and glorification of profane science and technology for the sur-
mounting of a supposedly un-Aryan supersensible worldview. It is indeed high
time that we were done with such foolery. . . .

1. The supra-mundane realm should mean Doric clarity, cosmos, light in its
   supra-rational sense, and thus has no concern for feelings, longing, mere
   faith, or the unconscious. This is the fundamental condition of understanding the true meaning and content and the true awakening power of the primordial symbols of our tradition, and of using them to rediscover the paths
   to a metaphysical, supra-rational and supra-individual knowledge.

2. Two main attitudes toward the supra-mundane reality are possible. One is
   solar, virile, affirming; the other is lunar, feminine, religious, passive, corresponding to the priestly ideal. The second attitude is mostly that of the

southern Semitic cultures, whereas the lordly Nordic and Indo-Germanic man has always been solar; the subjugation of the creature and the pathos of its absolute distance from the Almighty were totally unknown to him. He felt the gods to be his equals; he felt himself to be descended from heaven and to be of the same blood as the gods. From this there arises a conception of the heroic that does not end with the physical, soldierly, or tragically choreographed aspects, and a conception of the *Übermensch* that has nothing in common with the Nietzschean-Darwinist caricature of the beautiful blond beast, because this Nordic *Übermensch* also exhibits ascetic, sacral, and supra-natural traits, and culminates in the type of the Olympian ruler, the Aryan *Chakravartin* as wielder of the two powers and King of Kings. . . .

These excerpts not only are useful in determining Evola's exact attitude toward National Socialism, but also explain what the concepts of "race," "Nordic," and so on, meant to him. All these interpretations must be kept in mind if one wants to do justice to his work, especially that which dates from this period. By using these emotive words, very positively received at the time, he wanted to slowly bend their meaning in his own direction and thereby influence the decisive circles. This was of course a hopeless undertaking for one man who could count on scarcely any support.

How was it possible for Evola to speak his mind so freely and critically in a public lecture? It seems that the Germans initially thought Evola to be the man who would propagate their racial ideas in Italy, since he was introduced by "racists" as a "racist" into the German Foreign Office. When it was realized (especially by the Ahnenerbe) that Evola wanted to spread totally different ideas and that his racism was far removed from the NS version, both interest and support for him waned. In spite of this, as he notes in his autobiography, Evola was long able to say things for which a German would have landed in prison.

Another document from Himmler's personal staff should be mentioned here (archived in the aforementioned file under no. II 2113), because it shows that Himmler personally received and collected information about Evola. It reports that Himmler again ordered a thorough examination of Evola's *Heidnischer Imperialismus*, in which the German translation should even be compared to the original Italian text in order to eliminate errors in translation. At the same time, the opinion of the chief of the Sicherheitshauptamt (main security office) is given:

> Evola possesses no understanding of the German folkish *(völkisch)* past, whereby it must be noted that he is a foreigner and probably does not know Germany's

historical conditions enough to really grasp the origins of our folkish history. His results remain a spiritual and speculative impossibility. . . .

His [Evola's] words about the "superstition of the Fatherland" clearly display that these traditionalist values of his are only theoretical and are not rooted in profound historical views and realizations. The following passage of Evola's shows his basic lack of understanding of National Socialism and Germanic values (p. 98): "If it is true that the swastika, the Aryan pagan symbol of the sun and of the flame burning by its own volition, certainly belongs to those symbols that more than any others might lead the way to a real Germanic rebirth, it nevertheless must be realized that the name of the political party that has taken it as its emblem and that is today revolutionizing Germany in the spirit of Fascism is anything but a fitting choice. Indeed, aside from the association with the working class, both 'Nationalism' and 'Socialism' are elements that have a hard time fitting in with the noble Teutonic tradition, and it should be clear that what Germany urgently needs is a counterrevolution against democratic socialism. The resurrected Harzburg front already showed the right path: an anti-Marxist and anti-democratic movement of revolt that called upon the front of conservative and traditionalist elements as such. One will have to be careful that the 'socialist' element, even if it is a 'National Socialism,' does not get the upper hand *and let everything become a mass phenomenon grouped around the momentary prestige of a Führer.'"* [emphasis original]

During the war, Evola had three main goals:

1. To usher in a spiritual unity between Germany and Italy.

2. To propagate his ideas concerning racism.

3. To provide early on for a new order in Europe after the war.

His ambitions for this "new Europe" are also expounded in *Men among the Ruins*. Essentially, it incorporates a federal ruling system based on the old concept of the Empire. It therefore stands opposed to a rigid centralism, has organic foundations, and rests on a spiritual basis. Churchill and Roosevelt supposedly also discussed the possibility of such a European Empire for the postwar era. A sort of "super-monarchy" was supposed to form a strong dam against Communism. The names of Otto von Hapsburg and Lord Mountbatten were mentioned in this regard. That it was the destruction of the Hapsburg Empire that first made possible the expansion of Communism in all of Eastern Europe is today recognized by many experts, even by liberal historians like Golo Mann.

This should suffice to establish Evola's fundamental attitude within and toward National Socialism. For a complete evaluation of his political beliefs, it remains only to examine his attitude toward racism and the Jews.

Evola and Racism

Evola dealt with the question of race in much detail and in countless newspaper and magazine articles. He also at least touches upon this theme in most of his books, and four are devoted to it exclusively. This wealth can certainly be ascribed partly to the fact that there was no other field in which he received so much attention, both positive and negative. Mussolini's reaction and his proposal to make Evola's racial theories the official "Fascist" doctrine has already been mentioned. If one could ever credit Evola with an "official" character and the resulting influence, it would be here. However, this was the case only after 1938, when under German pressure Italy passed its own racial laws and Mussolini was looking for his own way that would be different from the National Socialist racial views.

But recognition alone was not the motivation. Evola was genuinely interested in the question itself, and had long studied it. He always regretted that people saw him only as the "racist" and did not realize that his position regarding race was a consequence of his entire worldview. He always saw racial themes as one area among many, which had its importance but was hierarchically below the all-important primal principles. In later Fascism and in National Socialism this question dominated everything and, in addition, had been approached from the wrong angle, as Evola saw it. In *Grundrisse der faschistischen Rassenlehre* (p. 8), he writes as follows: "Up until now, mainly the propagandistic and polemical aspect of race has been emphasized, in respect to the anti-Jewish struggle and other practical and preventive tasks aimed against the mixing of white Italians with races of other colors. But Italy has lacked any preparations concerning the positive, truly educative, and finally the spiritual side of racial thought."

Since we already know that Evola views any and all questions in their relation to transcendence (which he calls "spirit" in man, as opposed to "soul"), it comes as no surprise to learn that when it comes to race, he places the emphasis on the spiritual factor.

The following quote gives us a first access to his concept of "race" (*Rassenlehre*, p. 18): "To 'have race' in its perfect and higher meaning is a characteristic that towers above both intellectual values and so-called 'natural' talents. In normal linguistic usage, the expression 'a man of race' has been around for a long time. In general, this was an aristocratic concept. Out of the mass of common and mediocre beings rise men 'of race' in the sense of higher, 'noble' beings. Of course, this nobility did not necessarily have a heraldic sense to it: characters from the countryside or originating in a true and healthy people could evoke this impression of 'race' to the same extent as the honorable representatives of a true aristocracy."

Here Evola is already introducing a nonquantifiable concept of "quality" that is tied to spiritual values and which is absent in the anthropological view of race. Man can thereby differentiate himself and rise above the shapeless masses. According to Evola's view, this lends to the racial concept "the sense of defending quality against quantity, cosmos against chaos . . . and form against the formless" (ibid., p. 15).

As late as in his postwar work *Fascismo* (p. 106), Evola dares to say the following: "Race alone is and contains an elite, whereas the folk merely remains the folk and the masses."

Of course, Evola does not intend to totally cut off the idea of "race" from its biological background, the fact of belonging to a folk. But he goes somewhat further and assigns to each nation a nonbiological but "spiritual" and "soul" race. Sometimes he uses the word in this fashion; speaking for example of an "Italian race."

Concerning this, he writes in the *Rassenlehre* (p. 15f.): "The racial concept . . . refuses to look at the 'individual in itself' as an atom that somehow has to create everything out of nothing, and which hence acquires value. On the contrary, every man is . . . regarded spatially as a link in a community, and temporally as a being that in its past and future is indivisibly bound to the continuity of a family, a clan, to blood and tradition."

With this he emphasizes the rootedness of man in contrast to the "individualistic" rootlessness, as he calls it, in which all individuals are interchangeable, lacking their own face and "personality." He thereby elevates the racial idea above the strictly naturalistic concept of the folk and the nation. He writes (ibid., p. 37):

> In this context, the "race"—as a higher race—certainly has a greater importance than "folk and nation": it is the leading and creative element of a nation and its dominant culture, which is in full agreement with Fascist thought. Indeed, Fascism refuses to think of nation and folk as being outside the state.

According to Fascist doctrine, it is the state that gives form and consciousness to the nation. The state, on the other hand, is no abstract and impersonal object in Fascism; it is rather the tool of a political elite, the most valuable part of a "nation." Fascist racial doctrine even goes one step further: *This elite is predestined to reassume the heritage of the higher race and tradition that is present in the national makeup.* And when Mussolini said in 1923: "As it will be tomorrow and through the millennia, Rome has been the powerful heart of our race: it is the eternal symbol of our higher existence," he clearly set the direction for an irrevocable decision: *The super-race of the Italian nation is the "Race of Rome," that which we will call the "Aryan-Roman" race.*

Thus the purely biological element is not enough for Evola. This is especially clear in the following quotation (ibid., p. 41): "In a cat or a thoroughbred horse the biological is the deciding element, and thus the racial observation can be restricted to this criterion. This, however, is no longer the case when dealing with humans, or at least with beings that are worthy of that name. Man is indeed a biological being, but also connected to forces and laws of a different kind, that are as real and effective as the biological realm and whose influence on the latter cannot be overlooked. Fascist racial doctrine therefore holds a purely biological view of race to be inadequate."

On p. 43 of the same book he slowly arrives at the central thought that occupies him:

Our racial doctrine is determined by tradition. Thus the traditional view of the human being is our foundation, according to which this being has a tripartite nature; that is, *it consists of three principles: spirit, soul, and body.* . . .

This stated, the Fascist racial doctrine rises above both the attitude of those who see the purely biological race as the deciding element, as well as the attitude of those who profit from the standpoint of a racial science only concerned with anthropological, genetic, and biological problems, and who hold that, while race is a reality, it has nothing to do with the values, problems, and the strictly spiritual and cultural activity of man. Fascist racial doctrine, on the other hand, maintains that race exists in the body but also in the spirit and the soul. Race is a deeply embedded force that reveals itself in the biological and morphological realm (as race of the body), the psychical (as race of the soul), as well as in the spiritual (as race of the spirit).

Then (ibid., p. 47) follows the hierarchy that is to be expected of Evola: it is the spirit that builds its body. He writes: "Fascist racial doctrine understands the correlations between race and spirit on the basis of the principle already mentioned: *the exterior is a function of the interior, the physical form is symbol, tool, and means of expression of a spiritual form.*"

These thoughts were not newly developed at the beginning of the 1940s, when the *Rassenlehre* was published; they had existed much earlier. Already in *Heidnischer Imperialismus*, from the year 1928, we can read (p. 55):

> Thus, according to our view, the teachings of Count Gobineau contain a glimmer of truth, but not much more. The decline of the qualities and factors that make up the greatness of a race is not—as he states—the outcome of the mixing of this race with others, the outcome of its ethnic, biological, and demographic deterioration: the truth is rather that a race deteriorates *when its spirit deteriorates*, when the inner tension relaxes, to which it owes its original form and its spiritual type. *Then* a race degenerates or changes, because its most secret root has been severed! Then it loses that invisible and unconquerable transforming virtue, which, far from infecting them, moves other races even to adopt the form of its culture and to be swept away by it as by a wider stream.
>
> That is why for us the return to the race cannot be merely the return to the blood—especially in these twilight times in which almost irreversible mixtures have taken place. It must mean a return to the spirit of the race, not in a totemistic sense but in an aristocratic sense, relating to the primordial seed of our "form" and our culture.

And in July of 1931, Evola writes in *Vita Nova:* "The error of some extreme 'racists' who believe that the return of a race to its ethnic purity *ipso facto* equals its rebirth as a people consists of exactly this: they treat the human being as if he were a purebred cat, horse, or dog. To an animal, the conservation or restoration of its racial unity (in its narrow definition) can be everything. But it is not so with the human. . . . It would be too convenient if the simple fact that one belongs to a pure race were to bestow, without further ado, a 'quality' in the higher sense."

Or in 1934, in *Rassegna Italiana* (XVII, pp. 11–16, "Razza e Cultura" [Race and Culture]): "This (aristocratic) style is precisely the feature that in a higher sense, i.e., concerning man as man and not as animal . . . can be called 'race.'"

As early as 1933, Evola started to criticize the racial attitudes of the National Socialists ("Osservazioni critiche sul 'razzismo' nazional-socialista," [Critical Observations on the Subject of National Socialist "Racism"] in *Vita Italiana*, XXI, 248, pp. 544–549): "The racial doctrine is of value as far as it represents the primacy of quality over quantity, the differentiated over the formless, and the organically grown over the mechanical. Above all, when it has as its starting point the ideal of a deep and living unity of spirit and life, of thought and race, of culture and instinct."

In the already mentioned article against Rosenberg ("A Paradox of Our Time . . .") it further states: "Is it the spirit that gives shape to the race (especially to the nation), or is it the race that gives shape to the spirit? Or even more to the point: Does determination come from above or from below?"

Then in the *Grundrisse* (p. 7), he writes: "In its higher form the racial doctrine has the importance of a culturally and spiritually revolutionary idea. It can even assume the value of a 'mythos' (in Sorel's sense, i.e., that of a power idea), of a crystallizing center for the creative energies and developments of an epoch."

As can be seen upon investigation, Evola's racial teachings reveal that he understands "race" differently from what is generally the case. Primarily, he introduces a tripartite structure and differentiates between the race of the body (which covers the usual concept of race), the race of the soul (the type of character, lifestyle, and the emotional attitude toward environment and society), and the race of the spirit (the kind of religious experience and position regarding the "traditional" values). Thus, as Mussolini expressed it on the occasion of that first meeting with Evola, Evola's categories would correspond to Plato's division of the populace into three groups: the general masses, the warriors, and the wise ones.

Since it is the "race of the spirit" that is the most difficult to grasp, and since Evola himself does not always define it in the same way, another quotation follows ("L'equivoco del razzismo scientifico" [The Mistake of Scientific Racism], in *Vita Italiana*, September 1942. The review in *Diorama Letterario*, no. 138, July 1990, of *Gli Articoli de la Vita Italiana*, to which we owe much inspiration, gives a good overview of Evola's articles in that journal): "We wish to clarify that for us spirit does not signify philosophical games, 'Theosophy,' or mystical-devotional escapism from the world, but simply that which in better times was called *race* by well-born persons: that is, straightforwardness, inner unity, character, dignity, manliness, immediate sensitivity for all values that are at the core of all human greatness and which, since they are situated far above fortuitous reality, govern this same reality. That race which, on the other hand, is a construct of science and a little figurine from the anthropological museum, we leave to that pseudo-intellectual bourgeoisie that still clings to the nineteenth-century idols of positivism."

The same article later contains one of Evola's strongest attacks against so-called "scientific" racism, which hurt him very much in official circles. One cannot forget that in 1942, because of the war, the racial campaign was seen as very important. He says: "Those who are striving for a 'purely scientific racism' today want to ingratiate themselves with 'the people.' Instead of contributing to the elimination of a leftover myth that is present in the lesser educated strata of society, they believe they can use it as a sure basis, to 'make an impression,' to give authority to half-baked ideas and a dilettante racism, which wants to be as untouchable in its surface assumptions as it is incoherent and contradictory upon closer inspection."

As the above shows, Evola fought vehemently against a purely physical racism because of its superficiality, and he ranted several times against skull measuring and similar practices. Because of his emphasis on the spiritual, his rejection of what Trotsky called "zoological materialism" was only natural. In addition, Evola traced the origin of "racial thought" in his sense back to aristocratic custom, in which the physical counted for nothing: the deciding factor was membership in the same stratum. Thus, the royal dynasties only in the rarest cases originated in the people that they ruled over. And the fact that ruling dynasties always marry across their frontiers (for example, the Hapsburgs even had Mongolian ancestors) also testifies to this same attitude. (Concerning this, see "Sull'essenza e la funzione attuale dello spirito aristocratico" [On the Essence and the Present Function of the Aristocratic Spirit], in *Lo Stato*, XII, 10). This "spiritual racism" is also evident in Evola's saying (which was vehemently opposed by nationalist circles) that the "common ideas are the fatherland" and not the region in which one was born, because "all peoples of today are racial mixtures, and in general elements other than the racial count as the foundation of their unity."

Just as Evola's definition of race veers from the customary delineations, so also does his use of the term "Aryan." Of course, Evola is strongly influenced by the Zeitgeist, so that the word "Aryan" automatically has a positive meaning for him. (We already know from his speech of December 1937, which we quoted above, the essential aspects of what Evola means by "Aryan" and "Nordic.") In spite of this, one cannot forget his studies of the Buddhist scriptures that continuously mention the *arya*, which generally means the "noble." (One also cannot overlook that Evola's Buddhist and racial studies stem from the same time period.) In his book about Buddhism (*La dottrina del risveglio*, 1942, p. 23ff. [English edition: *The Doctrine of Awakening*, Rochester, Vt., 1995]), he deals with this term in detail. In so doing, he mentions that *arya* is very hard to translate, because several meanings are hidden in the word. Thus even prominent Orientalists like Rhys Davids and Woodward have left this word untranslated in their translations and writings. *Arya* does indeed mean aristocratic, noble, but with a fourfold meaning:

1. In the spiritual sense, in which *arya* is often equated with the "awakened" in the Buddhist canon.

2. In the aristocratic sense, in order to denote the actual membership in a higher caste.

3. Also in a clearly racial sense, in order to differentiate between the Aryan peoples that had immigrated from the North and the conquered indigenous strata of the population (*varma*, Sanskrit for "caste," originally meant "color," as the Nordic conquerors were of much lighter skin color).

4. In the sense of a special "style" that finds its expression in crystalline clarity, lack of emotion, and an ascetic attitude. Here Evola does not hesitate to compare this "style" with Meister Eckhart's concept of "detachment."

This also sheds a different light on Evola's ideal of the "Aryan-Roman" race. His brand of "Roman character" should be seen in this same sacral, aristocratic sense. And even if Evola himself did not always keep these interpretations clear and constant (especially in his numerous newspaper articles), they certainly resonated in his imagination. One must therefore be careful when reading about the "Aryan-Roman" style or similar subjects in his works. If today, after the excesses of the National Socialist era, one uses such words as "Aryan" and even the neutral "race" with some discomfort, one must consider that this problem did not exist at that time. However, as Giovanni Monastra emphasizes ("Anthropologie aristocratique et racisme: l'itinéraire de Julius Evola en terre maudite" in *Politica Hermetica*, II, Paris, 1988), Evola must also have considered that most peoples class themselves as "noble" and look down upon other ethnic groups, in the era of ancient Buddhism just as today.

Later, in 1952, when Evola was standing trial, he stated in his famous *Self-Defense*: "It must be realized that in modern racial studies, 'Aryan' and even 'Nordic' do not in fact mean 'German'; the term is synonymous with 'Indo-European,' and is correctly applied to a primordial, prehistoric race, from which were derived the first creators of the Indian, Persian, Greek, and Roman civilizations, and of which the Germans are only the final adventitious branches."

As one can see from all these citations, Evola's racial views were not taken from Vacher Lapouge, Gobineau, Chamberlain, Rosenberg, and so on; instead, his forefathers were Montaigne, Herder and his *Völkergeist* (spirit of the people), Fichte, Le Bon, and L. F. Clauss, who probably influenced him the most in this direction. It was Clauss, through his *Rassenseelenkunde* (racial soul doctrine) who most likely inspired Evola directly to develop his doctrine of the racial spirit *(Rassengeisteskunde)*. Clauss, who was never a member of the NSDAP, also revolted against the purely biological tendencies of German racism. He tried to distinguish between different peoples on the basis of their varying psychological qualities (today this would be called ethnic psychology). But when it was discovered that his most important assistant, a woman who also lived with him, was Jewish, trouble came his way, and in 1942 he lost his teaching position at Berlin University. Evola was in personal contact with Clauss and greatly respected him (see Robert de Herte, "Profil bio-bibliographique de L. F. Clauss" in *Etudes et Recherches*, no. 2, 1983, p. 25). Clauss himself seems to have had a precursor in Gustave Le Bon, who developed the thesis that the forms of community in different peoples were expressions of their "race soul." This "race soul" remained in effect even when the physical racial characteristics had changed due to mixing with other races (Gustave Le Bon, *Lois psychologiques du developpement des peuples*, Paris, 1894).

In general, Evola tried to construct a racial theory that combines the history of the spirit with racial history, fusing them together: a view that according to Othmar Spann goes back to Schelling's second phase.

It goes without saying that Evola's racial views did not avoid criticism—if only because of competition, as Mussolini had had such a positive impression of them. Through his polemics he also managed to increase the number of his enemies. For example, after the passage of the Italian race laws in 1938 ("Manifesto della Razza") when he accused the many people who all of a sudden "discover a deep racial calling in themselves that is dictated by the despicable toadying spirit," this could hardly have made him any friends.

Evola's theses were very hotly debated because in the last analysis (due to the difficulty of applying them) they pulled the rug out from under the notion of a factual and "exploitable" racism. In the end, outward physical characteristics did not count exclusively anymore. The important thing was the inner attitude; and who could test that? Even worse, was anyone good enough for this "higher" conception of race?

In order to show how vehemently his opponents fought against Evola, probably in part to demote him from his "privileged" standing with Mussolini, a selection of his critics follows.

We begin with the Jesuit publication *Civiltà Cattolica* (XCII, vol. III, September 1941), which indicted Evola's racism as an "abstruse and unscientific construct." (For this reference, we are indebted to Mario Bernardi Guardi's essay "Julius Evola: Scandalo e Ter" in *Avallon*, X, April 1986, in which Evola is referred to a "cave-explorer of the spirit," among other things.) Today it might seem strange that such a prominent religious organ would deal with these questions. But this merely illustrates that the entire intellectual world of that time was concerned with the racial problem. It was especially the Church publications that later brought Evola's magazine project *Sangue e Spirito* (Blood and Spirit) to an early end. The other quotations are from the *Bolletino del Centro Studi Evoliani*, no. 18, Genoa, 1977, and were compiled by Professor Giovanni Conti.

Giorgio Almirante, later longtime leader of the MSI (Italy's "neofascist" party), says in his article "Che la diritta via era smarrita . . ." (Since the Straight Path Was Lost . . .; subtitle: "Against the 'Lost' Sheep of Anti-Biological Pseudo-Racism," in *La Difesa della Razza*, V, no. 13, April 5, 1942): "Our racism must be that of the blood that I feel within me and that I can compare to the blood of others. Our racism must be a racism of flesh and muscle . . . otherwise we will ultimately play into the hands of the bastards and Jews. . . . Therefore the 'absolute spiritualists' should convince themselves that this is not the moment to, as they say, 'deepen' our racism."

Ugoberto Alfassio Grimaldi (at the time one of the exemplary personalities in the racial and Fascist areas; after the war, he became a deputy of the Communist party) wrote in his review of Evola's *Grundrisse der Faschistischen Rassenlehre* (*Civiltà Fascista*, IX, no. 4, February 1942, pp. 252–261): "After many efforts, Julius Evola's racism finally ends up in a special form of anti-racism. . . . As Fascists we must refuse the validity of an 'autonomous' racial teaching, especially when the concept of race conceals a metaphysical view that did not originate in our cultural sphere. . . . That is why the reader of Evola feels some discomfort that Fascism is dealt with only as something very distant—I might almost say finite and mortal—which is used as an *'instrumentum regni'* for the empowerment of other principles having merely a coincidental connection to politics. Here, Fascism is not the goal, but only the means to an end."

Also in *Civiltà Fascista* (IX, no. 10, August 1942, pp. 647–652), the same Grimaldi writes the following in his article "Ali margini di una polemica sulla validità di un esoterismo razzista" (On the Margins of a Polemic about the Validity of a Racial Esotericism): "The reasons that Fascism is fighting against a certain brand of modern culture that includes the Hebrew element are only in small part identical with the reasons that esotericists like Evola are fighting a culture that does not correspond to the one fought by Fascism, not even in the purely racial area. . . . One can have no doubt that Evola is aware of Fascism's weakness (as he represents it) in comparison to his esoteric world, after re-reading what Evola himself has declared in the biweekly *La Torre* (no. 5, April 1, 1930): 'We are neither "Fascists" nor "anti-Fascists" '."

Even Guido Landra, the extremely important director of the Racial Studies Department in the Ministry for National Culture, coeditor of the official periodical *La Difesa della Razza* (The Defense of the Race), and coauthor of the official 1938 *Manifesto Razzista*, attacks Evola vehemently. In his article "Razzismo biologico e scientismo" (Biological Racism and Scientism), in *La Difesa della Razza*, VI, no. 1, November 1942, pp. 9–11, aptly subtitled "For Science and Against the Melancholic Apostles of a Nebulous Spiritualism," we read: "Those poor racists of the first hour who are guilty merely of having initiated the race campaign in Italy and of having remained loyal to the original as well as the official line, are now being accused of nothing less than Jacobinism and Bolshevism. The accusation—and this is painful to report— originates from a publication that can really be proud of a noble anti-Jewish tradition; and the accuser is the author Evola, who, while claiming to expatiate upon Professor Canella, attacks all those who remain loyal to the notion of biological racism. . . . If the expressions 'biological' and 'scientific' have a negative connotation for the spiritualists, we answer that for us it is a great honor to be called biological and scientific racists."

In *Vita Italiana* (XXXI, no. 359, February 1943, p. 151ff.) Landra adds: "And this is the weakest point in Evola's teachings: that an Aryan can possess the soul of a Jew and vice versa. And that a Jew could therefore be discriminated against even though he possesses the soul of an Aryan is for us theoretically untenable. In practice, the assumption of such a principle would have terrifying consequences for racism, and ones that would exclusively benefit the Jews."

Landra, probably the highest official racial theoretician, makes his sharpest attack in his own publication *La Difesa della Razza* (VI, 1, November 5, 1942, p. 20), singling out the following for criticism: "The essays about the problem of race, 'Due razze' [Two Races] by Giulio Evola and 'I nostri nemici' [Our Foes] by Guido Cavalluci, that have appeared in a well-known monthly *Diorama* [Evola's aforementioned *Diorama Filosofico*] and in which every realistic foundation of racism is doubted, even going so far as labeling anti-Semitism as a mere polemical view . . . [and] that article 'The Misunderstanding of Scientific Racism' by Evola, which is the most exemplary document and monument of the present campaign that has been unleashed against racism in Italy . . .'"

Attacks of this sort and the resulting sanctions from high places were also responsible for the demise of a project that surely was very dear to Evola. He was to have been the editor of a bilingual German-Italian periodical on race. The project had been worked out together with Mussolini, who moreover had already pledged his full support. Even the title of the magazine had been determined: *Sangue e Spirito—Blut und Geist* (Blood and Spirit). The intention was to unify the approaches to the race problem in Germany and Italy, whereby both sides hoped to present their own views to each other. The steady efforts by the Church and orthodox Fascists to influence Mussolini finally succeeded in swaying him toward the "biological" racist position, which also corresponded to the NS ideology. In the end, Mussolini withdrew his approval of the magazine. Since the German Foreign Affairs Office had also noticed that Evola did not intend to champion the racism dear to the Germans, it also withdrew its support. In addition, the dramatically increasing wartime confusion made this and other similar plans seem less important. Thus the project was doomed to certain failure.

Now we turn to another question that logically follows from Evola's racial thought: his anti-Semitism.

Evola's Attitude Toward the Jews

In the above-mentioned polemic, Grimaldi characterized Evola as a "Jew lover." It goes without saying that this misses the mark by a long shot and merely reflects the anger of the attacker. There are so many comments against the Jews in Evola's work, ranging from simple criticisms to truly painful ones, that there can be no doubt about his basic attitude. Evola himself would have been the last to deny that. But here a distinction has to be made. His writings never spoke out against orthodox, religious Judaism. On the contrary; as an example, he writes in his *Tre aspetti del problema Ebraico* (Three Aspects of the Jewish Problem), Rome, 1936, p. 23: "There are elements and symbols in the Old Testament that possess metaphysical and therefore universal value." Or in *Revolt Against the Modern World* (p. 281): "In contrast to orthodox Judaism, early Christianity can at most claim a mystical character on the same line as the prophets. . . . And whenever a true esotericism was subsequently created in the West, it was essentially found outside of Christianity with the help of non-Christian currents, like the Hebraic Kabbalah. . . ." Evola even names operative Kabbalah as one of the few paths that can still be followed successfully in the West today.

Evola's attacks are more often directed against the Jews as symbol of the rule of economic-materialistic individualism and the hegemony of money. In other words: in the Jews he is fighting materialism. The fact that in doing so he again brings up all the well-known prejudices and generalizations shows that he too was dependent on the preeminent Zeitgeist. Thus, he speaks of the groveling hypocrisy, the Mammonism of the Jews, and their desire to dissolve hierarchical societies, as well as of a "Jewish threat" in general. These are the same accusations that Martin Luther brought up, and which Karl Marx presented in his tract *Zur Judenfrage* (Concerning the Jewish Question), published 1844 in the *Deutsche-französische Jahrbücher* in Paris. The worst passages seem to be those to which Professor Franco Ferraresi of the University of Turin refers in his contribution "Julius Evola et la Droite radicale de l'après-guerre" ("Julius Evola and the Radical Right in the Postwar Era," in *Politica Hermetica*, I, p. 100) and which deal with the death of Corneliu Codreanu.

Codreanu, the charismatic leader of the simultaneously political and mystical Christian "Iron Guard" movement in Romania, which saw itself as a part of the army of the Archangel Michael, was definitely one of the very few indisputable "heroes" and models for Evola. Everything he wrote about him amounted to a panegyric and therefore the pain about Codreanu being "shot while escaping," which he attributed to the Jews, seems to have been genuine and to explain the decline of his high standards. (De Felice writes in his *Der Faschismus:*

Ein Interview, p. 98: "Strictly speaking, Codreanu is no Fascist. He fights against middle-class values and institutions. His movement is everything but petit-bourgeois; it is rather a movement of students of the lower classes, a popular peasant movement. Anything but a middle-class movement.")

It general, it is obvious that Evola chose a much more incisive and polemical tone in his newspaper articles than in his books. But we do not believe that Evola aimed at a "gripping journalistic style" (as still practiced today), used for effect; rather, it seems likely that he wrote these articles under the pressure of a deadline, and therefore in a tone that was much too immediate and emotional. In any case, the fact remains as such.

A lot certainly has to be attributed to the Zeitgeist, which apparently included certain patterns of thought that were never questioned. It is indeed astonishing that even recognized critical minds like Karl Kraus (a Jew himself) continually spouted the usual anti-Jewish prejudices (regarding this, see the interesting research of Jacques le Rider, *Der Fall Otto Weininger* [The Case of Otto Weininger], Vienna, 1985, and *Das Ende der Illusion* [The End of Illusion], Vienna, 1990). If one adds the amount of slander that was spread about the Jews in the Fascist era by newspapers that are still important to the present day, such as *La Stampa* and *Corriere della Sera*, then the situation becomes a little easier to understand (regarding this, see excerpts in Renzo de Felice's *Storia degli Ebrei Italiani sotto il Fascismo* [The History of the Italian Jews under Fascism], Turin, 1972, p. 260).

In light of all of Evola's well-known anti-Jewish remarks, how could he ever have been called a "Jew lover"? We have already shown a few reasons. Since Evola set supreme importance on the spiritual attitude, a Jew could of course also espouse "Aryan" thought (see "Scienza, razza e scientismo" [Science, Race, and Scientism], in *Vita Italiana*, XXX, no. 357, December 1942, pp. 556–563; there, he writes verbatim: "For example, can an 'Aryan' have a Jewish soul or inner race and vice versa? Yes, it is possible. . . ."). And Evola had surely noticed that especially in Germany some Jews felt more "Aryan" than many Germans, and this was not only in intellectual circles. In exactly this sense one must assume that Evola did not at all regard the Jews Weininger and Michelstaedter, to whom he owed so much, as "Jews," independently of their heritage. That an opinion like this was a danger to mass propaganda could not go unnoticed by the political observers of the day. Basically, Evola did not indict the Jewish people (although naturally there were exceptions), for

he did not even acknowledge them as a "biological" race, due to the miscege-
nation that they themselves admitted; it was Jewry as an idea and "spiritual
race" that had been forged together by a common, strictly preserved body of
thought (Old Testament, Torah, Talmud, for example). If one rereads (see above)
what Otto Weininger said about Jewry as "spiritual direction," "psychic constitution," and "Platonic idea," one will understand what Evola really meant.
Contemporary quotes from his own hand will underscore this view.

Thus he writes in the aforementioned *Tre aspetti del problema Ebraico* (p. 42):

> Are "rationalism" and "calculation" purely Jewish phenomena? If one wanted
> to answer "yes," one would also be forced to believe that the first antitradi-
> tional, critical, antireligious, and "scientific" upheavals of ancient Greece had
> also been introduced and supported by Jews; that therefore Socrates was a Jew,
> and that not only the medieval nominalists, but also Descartes, Galileo, Bacon,
> etc., were Jews. . . . Even if the passion for the lifeless number and abstract
> reason is an outstanding characteristic of the Semites . . . , it nevertheless seems
> clear that one can speak of a Jewish spirit in this regard only if it destroys every-
> thing through rationalism and calculation, if it leads to a world that consists only
> of machines, objects, and money instead of persons, traditions, and fatherlands,
> and if one uses the expression "Jewish" in a symbolic sense, without necessarily
> referring to the race. . . . In the concrete development of modern civilization,
> the Jew can be seen as a force that worked together with others for the prolif-
> eration of the "civilized," rationalized, scientific, mechanistic, modern deca-
> dence. But he certainly cannot be singled out as the single, far-seeing cause. It
> would be nonsense to believe anything of the kind. The actual truth is that one
> would rather fight against personalized forces than against abstract principles
> and general phenomena, because the former can also be attacked in a practical
> manner. And so people have turned against the Jew to the degree that he seems
> to embody a type that is also present in other areas, and even in nations that
> have been virtually unaffected by Jewish immigration.

Even in his introduction to the notorious *Protocols of the Elders of Zion*, which
we will deal with later, he writes on page xix: "We want to mention right away
that we personally cannot follow a certain fanatical anti-Semitism that sees the
Jews everywhere as *deus ex machina* and finally ends in a kind of ambush itself.
Guénon himself has referred to the fact that one of the means used by the masked
forces to defend themselves consists of directing the entire attention of their
enemies in a tendentious way toward those who are only partially the real cause

of certain upheavals. Once they have created a scapegoat in this manner, which suffers the full brunt of reaction, they themselves are free to continue with their intrigues. In a certain way, this is also true of the Jewish question. . . ."

In "Inquadramento del problemo ebraico" (Categorization of the Jewish Question; in *Bibliografia Fascista*, XIV, no. 8/9, 1939, pp. 717–728), he writes concerning the same question: "A serious formulation of the Jewish problem cannot overlook that which concerns the 'Aryan' peoples themselves: the Jew must be prevented from becoming a kind of scapegoat for everything that in reality the non-Jews also have to answer for."

In 1942, Evola writes in his above-mentioned essay "The Misunderstanding of Scientific Racism": "Because it is useless to try to hide it from oneself, people today are often wondering if the Jew isn't ultimately a kind of scapegoat. The cases are so frequent in which the characteristics that our doctrine attributes to the Jews are fully and brazenly exhibited by 'Aryan' speculators, profiteers, upstarts, and—why not—even by journalists, who do not hesitate to use the most twisted and disloyal means for polemical ends."

Even in a publication such as *La Difesa della Razza*, which was remarkable for its viciousness concerning the Jewish question and sometimes included despicable articles of the *Stürmer* variety, Evola expounded his views (for example, in the article "Razza, eredità, personalità" [Race, Heredity, Personality], April 5, 1942).

Evola also confirms his values in his book *Il Fascismo* (p. 180), although this was not written until 1970: "One must realize that with Hitler anti-Semitism had the role of a veritable obsession, whereby it is not possible to fully explain the causes of this anti-Semitism in its almost paranoid aspect, which had such tragic consequences." Then Evola adds: "Hitler's anti-Semitism had a forced, fanatical character and points to a lack of inner control. This has led to a stain of infamy on the Third Reich that will be very hard to wash away."

We have already discussed the difficulties that Evola had to deal with during the Fascist era on account to his opinions, which may well stand as evidence for the integrity of his attitude. Despite her understandable condemnation of Evola's views, even Adriana Goldstaub admits that Evola did not deem all Jews, nor the Jews exclusively, responsible for the decline of the modern world (see her contribution to the debate at the symposium at Cuneo in 1982: "Fascismo Oggi: Nuova destra e Cultura reazionaria negli anni ottanta," Istituto storico della Resistenza in Cuneo, p. 175).

The oft-quoted and knowledgeable expert Renzo de Felice confirms in his
History of the Italian Jews under Fascism (p. 465):

> . . . we are forced to admit that among the creative and cultured ones—as among
> the politicians—seen from a certain standpoint, the most respectable ones were
> the convinced racists. With this we do not mean a Landra or a Cogni, those pale
> and submissive "vestal virgins" of Nazi racism, but an Evola and an Acerbo,
> who both created their own path that they followed to the end with dignity and
> seriousness. And this in contrast to many who chose the way of the lie, of slan-
> der, and the total obscuration of every cultural and moral value. . . . Evola him-
> self also very decidedly discounted any theory of pure biological racism, going
> so far that he attracted the attacks and sarcasm of the Landras upon himself. I
> do not mean by this that the "spiritual" theory of races is acceptable, but it at
> least had the advantage of not completely discounting certain values. It also
> renounced the German and German-derived confusions and tried . . . to con-
> fine racism to the plane of a cultural problem worthy of the name.

The attitude of Evola toward the Jews that we have sketched here—that is, to
see "Jewishness" as a certain "spiritual attitude," an idea derived from Weininger—
was anything but singular or rare. As Jacques le Rider shows in his book *The End
of Illusion*, this attitude characterized a whole epoch: the era of fin-de-siècle Vienna,
which Weininger was a part of. And perhaps we should not underestimate the
influence of Michelstaedter, who studied in Vienna at this time and was surely
much affected by the intellectual life that flourished there. Because not only
"anti-Jewishness" characterizes the Viennese modern era (even though the Jews
were the essential proponents of that modernism); it was marked also by "anti-
democratism," "antifeminism," and "anti-intellectualism," which are all found
in Evola's work in modified form. Even the passion for Meister Eckhart was
especially pronounced during this time and, for example, influenced the philosopher Fritz Mauthner, who was also interested in Buddhism.

In his study, Jacques le Rider introduces many examples and an interesting
analysis of this negative attitude toward the Jews. We have mentioned Karl
Kraus and his famous publication *Fackel* (Torch). Even the intellectual poet
Hermann Bahr, copublisher of *Die Zeit*, who is above suspicion, speaks of the
"judaicized Viennese" whereby he obviously means the intellectual attitude
and not the biological heredity. According to him, the Viennese were already
judaicized "even before the first Jew arrived" (quoted after Jacques le Rider,
Das Ende der Illusion, p. 239). Le Rider shows further that Sigmund Freud him-

self exhibited some rudiments of a similar theory. As with Weininger, his anti-Semitism is the hatred for the Jewish part of his self. To quote le Rider verbatim: "Why not continue with Weininger's thoughts and see a similar subjective conflict between the inner Jew and non-Jew in anti-Semitism, just as antifeminism might be a protest of the masculine against his own femininity? . . . An image that characterizes many anti-Semitic phobias is the fear of having to discover a Jewishness in oneself. Likewise the woman-hater shudders at being unmasked as effeminate."

With Evola, there was probably a component too of this "spiritual" anti-Semitism that concerned "actual" Jewry, although immediate proof is missing. His friendship with Giovanni Preziosi was again influential in this regard. Preziosi, who was certainly a thoroughly honest Fascist, belonged to a strict Catholic tradition and had taken on the anti-Semitism present in those circles as well as a deeply felt aversion to Freemasonry. Generally this culminated in a theory of a "global conspiracy" by Jewish and Freemasonic circles, with the intention of toppling Christianity and traditional state institutions. Preziosi himself collected numerous facts to prove this theory. Evola was undoubtedly attracted to this, even though he considered the conspiratorial circles in question not so much as the movers but more likely the instruments of other forces, not necessarily human. After all, René Guénon had voiced the same suspicions—also in regard to the Jews—and thus surely contributed to Evola's position. This explains but does not excuse his preface and appendix to the *Protocols of the Elders of Zion* published by Preziosi, which would become a lasting hindrance in Evola's later life. It reduced to a minimum his contacts with "official" and well-known personalities who nonetheless respected him (for example, Mircea Eliade, with whom he exchanged letters for a long period, and the famous Tibetologist Giuseppe Tucci, for whose academic publication *East and West* he wrote numerous contributions).

Such conspiracy theories might astound many, but in the first half of this century they were very popular and nothing unusual (and are still current today, in slightly altered form, among both "Nationalist" and "Green" circles). Even Winston Churchill, early on when he was still attacking Bolshevism frequently and vehemently in his speeches, often quoted at length from Nesta Webster, probably the most famous "conspiracy theorist" of that time and still published today.

As an appendix to the actual *Protocols*, Evola published an essay ("L'autenticità dei protocolli provata dalla tradizione ebraica" [The Authenticity of the Protocols as Proved by the Jewish Tradition]) in which he included a mass of quotations allegedly from the Talmud and other Jewish religious writings. However, these quotes were taken not from the original writings but from second- or thirdhand sources, such as Rohling's *Talmudjuden* and Theodor Fritsch's *Handbuch der Judenfrage*, whose dubious scholarship and zealous bias should have been obvious to Evola. In making such a serious accusation it would have been his duty either to look up the primary sources himself or to consult knowledgeable and unbiased experts. Evola certainly did this in other areas: his studies of the ancient scriptures of Buddhism and Tantrism, Zen and alchemy were marked by an all-encompassing meticulousness. As Professor di Vona of the University of Naples confirms (*Hermeneutica*, 6, p. 84), Evola's esoteric studies were far more important and their research methods more strict than his comparable political works, which were characterized by an emotionality rooted in the times.

Carlo Mattogno, who is probably more partial toward Evola, in a series of articles for *Orion* examined the aforementioned quotes allegedly stemming from old Hebrew sources, and proved that they were either falsified (though long before Evola), taken out of context, or in some cases freely invented. Barely a single quote was reproduced correctly! (See Carlo Mattogno's articles in *Orion*, no. 22, July 1986, p. 169; vol. IV, no. 12, December 1987, p. 94; vol. VI, no. 3, March 1989, p. 232.)

Even if some things announced in the *Protocols*, although already easy to recognize at the time of their publication, such as Liberalism and Rationalism and the dissolution of family ties, have come to pass, there are scores of contradictions and absurdities in them that destroy their "authenticity." In his preface, Evola himself described certain parts of the *Protocols*, especially toward the end, as "fantasy." A list of these contradictions is presented in Pierre Charles's *Les Protocoles des sages de Sion* (Paris-Tournai, 1938). A condensed Italian version of this book also appeared in *Orion* (no. 46, July 1988, a National-Bolshevist magazine that even partially subscribes to these conspiracy theories, and therefore can hardly be classified as pro-Jewish). Further details regarding the *Protocols* can be found in the works listed in the bibliography[see page 104]. The thirteenth chapter of *Men among the Ruins* contains Evola's detailed views regarding this subject.

In spite of these factual and intellectual derailments, we do not wish to ascribe any malice, dishonesty, or egotism to Evola in this matter—just sheer carelessness, a lack of serious research, and the reckless assimilation of prejudices that happened to coincide with his own views. But here it also applies that it is easier to recognize the prejudices of others in the past than our own current ones. Without wanting to belittle them, because these questions can rightly unleash incredible emotional currents (and, of course, quite apart from the much greater personal suffering of those who were affected) there seems to be a certain psychological analogy between the past persecution of the "Jew" and today's hunt for the "multinational." In this century, mechanization, technological advance, dehumanization, and the dire dependence of large parts of the world have grown to such an extent that one simply longs for clear, simple, monocausal explanations for the misery. And "proof" for the "guilt" of the Jews yesterday and the "multinationals" today can be found or constructed again and again, which does not necessarily imply malice, but can be an expression of mere overzealousness. As is so often, here too the road to Hell can be paved with good intentions. After all, the real direction of both attacks is essentially the same. One is aiming for "free capital" that according to our economic laws is always invested where the highest returns are expected, without caring much for the resulting human consequences. But the much despised "capitalists," or rather the "managers" who actually wield the power today, are, in the present as in the past, the expression of a materialist worldview to which we all contribute our support. Only a different order of values, in which the material values are important but do not occupy the highest position, can change this situation. The mere search for scapegoats certainly will not solve anything, for he who seeks will always find. And those somewhat familiar with the shadow problem of psychology will know that the "scapegoat" thus discovered is nothing but a rejected, suppressed part of our personality that is forcibly projected to the outside.

To conclude this chapter on Evola's racism, we want to mention Robert Melchionda's thesis that views Evola as "antiracist" par excellence (*Il volto di Dionisio*, p. 208). The reasoning behind this thesis, which seems strange after all the foregoing arguments, is as follows: since someone's race, in the usual sense of the word, is connected to the corresponding physical characteristics that cannot be changed at will, the word "race" really expresses the "unchangeable," the "immutable." In contrast, to Evola it is the spirit and not the body that contains the primary racial characteristics. But according to Evola, the spirit above all represents "absolute freedom" and rules the physical body. However, this "absolute freedom" also makes a change in the "spiritual race" possible and thus race has ceased to be the deciding, unchangeable factor. The reality is a "freedom of race" of a scope not even postulated by the "antiracists."

In summarizing, we will let Giovanni Monastra have the final word *(Anthropologie aristocratique et Racisme)*: "Evola's ambition was to apply the traditional worldview as he understood it to a specific aspect of reality: the differences that can be found in humans, both collectively and individually."

Evola and Neofascism

As we have already reported, at least in the later war years Evola lived in Vienna while probably going through the archives of various secret societies. His exact intentions are not known, since he never wanted to talk about them. During this time Vienna was bombarded heavily, but Evola had adopted the habit of working instead of fleeing into the bunker. He did this "because I did not want to evade danger; I sought it out, in the spirit of a silent questioning of fate" *(Cammino,* p. 177). Then it happened, a few days before the Russians marched into Vienna: Evola was seriously wounded during an air strike. His spinal cord was damaged, and in spite of numerous operations he remained paralyzed from the waist down for the rest of his life. (Erik von Kuehnelt-Leddihn informed us that this bomb attack occurred on March 12, 1945, the anniversary of the *Anschluss* of Austria to the Third Reich.) For a year and a half, he lay in a hospital in Bad Ischl in upper Austria, until the Red Cross brought him first to Varese and then to a Bologna hospital. A cure was no longer possible and so Evola returned to Rome in 1948, where he lived the rest of his life (except for the time he was imprisoned on remand) in his apartment in the Via Vittorio Emmanuele II.

By 1949 he was already writing in new rightist publications and had soon assembled a small band of mostly young followers (regarding this, see Fausto Gianfreschi, "L'influenza di Evola sulla generazione che non ha fatto in tempo a perdere la guerra" [Evola's Influence on the Generation That Did Not Make It in Time to Lose the War"], in AA. VV, *Testimonianze su Evola* [Testimonies about Evola], Rome, 1985, p. 130). They urged him to write an "orientation" for them, a compendium that would set down the most important core values of a traditional rightist group. The result was Evola's pamphlet *Orientamenti* (Orientations), which was published in 1950 in the periodical *Imperium* and which has since seen countless authorized and unauthorized editions in Italian and other languages.

In turn, this pamphlet led to the writing of Evola's main political work, *Men among the Ruins*. During his hospital stay in Bad Ischl, Evola had already written to the poet Girolamo Comi: "However, in contrast to your opinion, I see nothing but a world of ruins, where a kind of front line is possible only in the catacombs" (letter of April 20, 1948; quoted in *Lettere di Julius Evola a Girolamo Comi 1934–1962*, Rome, 1987). *Men among the Ruins* was written in the hope of being able to change something about the postwar order. Even though it probably was and has remained the only "practical" handbook for a truly traditional right wing, no reaction was forthcoming from the circles in question. Evola was visibly disillusioned by this, and so this work has remained his only book with an actual "political" doctrine. A few parts of the book may have become outdated because of the ongoing events of history, but since nothing comparable has ever been written, it has been reprinted again and again, the last edition being issued 1990 in Rome by Gianfranco de Turris. Therefore, it was Evola's only book that was somewhat of a commercial success (in total, it probably sold about 10,000 copies). There were also two editions in France (1972 and 1984), even though the work was originally intended only for Italy. But the underlying principles are so universal that the references to the Italian situation do not detract from them. This was also the reason for the German edition [and for the present English edition—*Editor's note*].

Almost concurrently with *Men among the Ruins*, Evola authored a complementary work, even though this appeared only in 1961 in Milan. This work is *Cavalcare la tigre* (Riding the Tiger). These books belong together and cannot really be judged apart from each other. *Men among the Ruins* shows the universal standpoint of ideal politics; *Riding the Tiger* deals with the practical "existential" perspective for the individual who wants to preserve his "*hegomonikon,*" his inner sovereignty. In *Riding the Tiger*, Evola advocated, as already reported, the teaching of "*apoliteia*" as the only proper attitude for the traditional person. One must have the freedom to go along with the follies of the world on the outside while, on the inside, being detached and able to let go whenever one wants to. Because of its inherent inner contradictions and ever-increasing tensions, modern civilization (the tiger) will drive itself to death. One just has to remain on the tiger's back and not fall off in order to evade its claws and fangs. If one just waits long enough, its ceaseless running will make it weaker and tired until it finally collapses from exhaustion. Then one can strangle it with one's bare hands. Concerning this, Evola says: "Today there is no idea, no object, and no goal that is worth sacrificing one's own true interest for" (*Cavalcare la tigre*, p. 174) and: " '*Apoliteia*' must be the principle of the differentiated [i.e., traditional] man [*Uomo differenziato*] (*Cavalcare la tigre*, p. 202). With this he admitted that his book *Men among the Ruins* was really a failure.

Interesting in this regard is the opinion of Evola's declared enemy Furio Jesi (*Cultura di Destra*, Milan, 1979, p. 89), according to whom the later Evola considered that all worldly action was senseless and meaningless, but that those who did not dare to take the step over to "*apoliteia*" (i.e., the "noninitiates" that have not reached the "other shore") should still be encouraged to action by the truly "wise ones," because this was the only way they could learn their lesson. If Evola was indeed of this opinion, then it must have originated in his own life experience.

After *The Metaphysics of Sex* (1958) and *L'"Operaio" nel pensiero di Ernst Jünger* (The "Worker" in the Thought of Ernst Jünger; Rome, 1960), his already cited analysis of Fascism was issued in 1964. In 1970, an enlarged edition was published with the addition of the appendix *Note sul Terzo Reich* (Notes on the Third Reich). The themes contained therein have already been discussed. Evola's last complete book was his spiritual autobiography, *Il cammino del cinabro*, which appeared in 1972.

In his final years Evola suffered from constant and severe pain and was probably quite embittered. Erik von Kuehnelt-Leddihn has also confirmed this during a conversation with the author. At this point, Evola wrote only for a few magazines from the rightist spectrum and gave a few interviews, notably for the sex magazine *Playmen* ("Gespräch ohne Komplexe," no. 2, 1970). His two wishes—to put out a new magazine with the provocative title *The Reactionary* and to write a book about Stoicism, for which he had already collected the material—were not fulfilled, for he died on June 11, 1974, in the early afternoon. He had asked to be led from his desk to the window from which one could see the Janiculum (the holy hill sacred to Janus, the two-faced god who gazes into this and the other world). There he tried to die "upright," as far as was possible with his paralysis—upright because, according to mythical tradition, many heroes died in this manner (Roland, for example, who passed away leaning against a tree after being mortally wounded).

In his testament, Evola had decreed that his corpse be cremated and that there be no funeral procession or Catholic funeral rite. He also forbade an obituary. As chance would have it, the crematorium both in Rome and in Naples was out of order, while the next one, in Pisa, was out of business. After some time, Evola's body was finally cremated in Spoleto. The urn with his ashes was then, as reported elsewhere, lowered into a glacial crevasse on Monte Rosa in accordance with his last wishes.

After this short historical overview, we now turn to Evola's influence on the Italian postwar neofascist scene. It is not very easy to determine this influence, for the only ostensibly right-wing party known to its enemies as "neofascists," and officially as the MSI (Movimento Sociale Italiano), always left Evola out of the picture, despite the fact that a number of its leading members (for example, Pino Rauti) had been influenced in their youth by Evola's thought. The name Evola is not even mentioned in the official history of the MSI (Gianni Roberti, *Opposizione di Destra in Italia, 1946–1979*, Naples, 1988). Only the long-standing party chairman Giorgio Almirante once, maybe ironically, called Evola "the Marcuse of the Right, only better" but otherwise he was smilingly referred to as the *"magico barone"* (magic Baron). Nevertheless, one cannot understand the history of Italy's right wing without Evola. Especially the young, and among them the more "radical" elements (derived from the Latin *radix*— "root, origin"), have repeatedly made use of Evola's thought in their ideologies, even though he himself had lost his faith in "practical" politics at least since the mid-1950s.

So it came to Evola's arrest in April 1951, which led to six months of detention. The charge was the "glorification of Fascism." He was also accused of being the "intellectual instigator" of secret combat groups. The police really believed in a far-reaching conspiracy of rightist elements, but the trial ended with Evola being proved innocent and his acquittal. Apart from a few quotes from publicly accessible writings, there had been no evidence against him. All his life Evola had never owned anything (he constantly gave away even his books and pictures). The prominent attorney Francesco Carnelutti defended him free of charge, not because of his political beliefs, for, as Carnelutti emphasized, he understood nothing of those, but because he wanted to rid the world of an injustice. [For more details on the accusations that were leveled against him, and Evola's own response, see his *Autodifesa* (self-defense testimony) which is included as an appendix to this book—*Editor's note.*]

How then is Evola's attitude toward the postwar rightist groups in Italy to be classified? And where, if at all, is his influence to be found? One thing is certain: Evola certainly was no *"nostalgico,"* who looked back with longing to the historical Fascist era. On the contrary, he rather despised such people. This could be one explanation for his lack of popularity within the MSI. He also had little good to say about the right National-Bolshevists and the right-wing Maoists (yes, they also have these in Italy), since they combined traditional ideas with "leftist" efforts aimed at the masses. He gave his most avid support to "rightist anarchism," as this was closest to his *apoliteia* and reminded him of his youthful dadaist ambitions (see Julius Evola, *L'arco e la clava*, p. 208, where he discusses this type). His positive attitude toward the Beatnik movement and people such as Jack Kerouac and Henry Miller must be viewed in the same light. So he says: ". . . we are of the same opinion as some Beatniks . . . , that in today's culture and society, especially in America, the healthy person can be generally recognized in the rebel and the asocial type that does not fit in" (ibid., p. 210). But Evola warned the Beatniks that their attitude can only be sustained if one possesses a strong inner center. Here, perhaps to the surprise of many, the proximity to Herbert Marcuse becomes obvious. But in contrast to Marcuse, he says: "One must know *in whose name* one says no to a whole civilization." Here Evola is referring to the necessary transcendental foundations that are totally missing in Marcuse. Giorgio Galli even writes (*La crisi italiana e la Destra internazionale*, Milan, 1974, p. 20): "The analogies between Evola and the Frankfurt School (Marcuse, Horkheimer, Adorno) doubtless exist, especially concerning the critique of mass society and its manipulated democracy. Evola can even claim the fame of being the first." In spite of Evola's approval of the 1968 Revolution (when excerpts from *Riding the Tiger* were read publicly at Roman universities), he felt that the revolt of '68 had only superficially attacked the terror of consumerism, and that the revolution in the 1930s (the "Fascist revolution") had gone much deeper, because it had aimed at reforming the whole person and the corresponding institutions, even if that had failed.

Italo Mancini and Massimo Cacciari, one a university professor and the other a delegate of the Italian Communist Party, have also confirmed the parallels between Evola and Marcuse. Their radical critique of rationalism, the unmasking of modern middle-class society and the revolt against the same, the lack of faith in progress, and the recognition of the alienated direction of man are certainly present in both, and probably go back to a common root in Nietzsche.

But if one wants to speak of Evola's actual political influence, one must keep this in mind: Evola's traditionalism cannot be used by modern political movements. Even Evola himself saw this: his teachings are too aristocratic, too demanding, and too much directed against progress and modernity. It is unimaginable how these thought patterns could be successful in the industrialized democracies of the West. Evola's ideas did not even have any hope of being realized during the time of Fascism, which certainly was fertile ground. His antimodernism is simply too radical. Italy's New Right under Marco Tarchi (which received major impetus from the French New Right under Alain de Benoist) even regards the Evolian philosophy as a *"mito incapacitante,"* an incapacitating myth. Indeed, reading Evola has kept many young people from pursuing political activities, because he speaks of a past that is too remote and of which nothing is left, as well as of ideals that are too lofty. He leaves no hope for contemporary man (thus the adoption of *apoliteia* as the last consequence). But a "tragic" attitude toward life is not enough for political activism. And since according to Evola we cannot change the cosmic, metaphysical course of history, any political engagement becomes meaningless. Thus the myth of the eternally vanquished hero is born. But, interestingly enough, there are other inconsistencies. Evola writes in *Orientamenti* (p. 15): "It is senseless to harbor illusions: we are at the end of a cycle." And (p. 28): "History, that mysterious entity beginning with a capital letter, does not exist. It is humans, as far as they are *truly* human, that make history or tear it down." (Concerning this, see "Julius Evola: Tra mito e attualita," in *Diorama Letterario*, no. 72, June 1984.)

Marcello Veneziani also writes that Evola's teachings lead "to a traditionalism without tradition, since it lacks real continuity" and to a frustrating immobility (ibid., p. 212; Veneziani was himself one of the "affected"). The only allowable engagement is one that is totally detached from all that is political and historical today, as Veneziani continues. In Evola's *Revolt Against the Modern World*, we read the following (pp. xxix–xxx): "The only thing that matters today is the activity of those who can 'ride the wave' and remain firm in their principles, unmoved by any concessions and indifferent to the fevers, the convulsions, the superstitions, and the prostitutions that characterize modern generations. The only thing that matters is the silent endurance of the few, whose impassible presence as 'stone guests' helps to create new relationships, new distances, new values, and helps to construct a pole that, although it will certainly not prevent this world inhabited by the distracted and restless from being what it is, will still help to transmit to someone the sensation of truth—a sensation that could become for them the principle of a liberating crisis."

The abyss between the world of facts and the world of Tradition is too great. The construction of a bridge no longer seems possible. Traditionalists must hold onto ideas and principles, not institutions (*Men among the Ruins*), or in other words: "The idea and only the idea can be the true fatherland for them. Not the fact that they are of the same nationality, that they speak the same language, and that they are of the same blood, but the fact that they belong to the same idea, should be the deciding factor that unites or divides them" (*Revolt*, first chapter).

In his interesting essay "Evola e la generazione che non ha fatto in tempo a perdere il Sessantotto" (Evola and the Generation That Did Not Make It in Time to Lose '68), in *Testimonianze su Evola*, Rome, 1985, p. 324, the same Veneziani says, perhaps hitting the mark: "Evola's doctrine remains a teaching about the roots and not about the fruits. An unpolitical thought, then. Daring, noble, but desperately nonpolitical." Further: "The mistakes that have been made by those who have tried to transfer Evola onto the earthquake-fraught terrain of politics must be blamed on those who committed them, and not on Evola himself."

Other rightists accused Evola of "sterility" and "retrograde utopias." In spite of this, Evola was doubtlessly a model, even if only for very small groups that did not intend to break into competitive politics. But why? Antonio Lombardo, one of the young people who looked to Evola for "orientation" right after the war, writes in "La funzione delle minoranze e l'opera di Evola" (The Function of the Minorities and Evola's Work), in *Ordine Nuovo*, vol. X, no. 5/6, 1964, p. 30: "Evola offered a system of principles and correspondences that was organic and closed within itself, an interpretation of history and a systematic analysis of the ruling ideologies in the modern world." In this way, Evola offered the more intellectual elements a "meaning" for life and history that could be used to combat the all-powerful Frankfurt School. And Marco Tarchi (also one of those immediately "affected") wrote in "La Rivolta contro l'uomo qualunque" (Revolt Against Anybody), in *Civiltà*, vol. II, 8/9, 1974, p. 41: "He gave the consciousness of being *different* in a world that tends to be shapeless and colorless: the consciousness of realizing something on the inside that the others, in their superficiality, could not even approach, the certainty of having foundations on which one can build while everything is collapsing around oneself." Obviously, Evola was compensating for the difficult role in the outside world that rightists had to play after the war.

Is it completely impossible that Evola's thought will ever be transformed into political action? Evola would probably have answered that his ideas (i.e., traditional ones) should serve as centers, like poles or bridge piers, around which something slowly builds itself up that will then make the transition from the spiritual into the material realm. Not Voluntarism (as in Ernst Jünger, for instance) but the "magical effect" of fascination could usher in change. Not causality, but analogy. In *Orientamenti* (p. 21), Evola formulates it thus: "a silent revolution that reaches the depths, so that first inside and in the individual the prerequisites to that order are met that will dominate on the outside at the right moment, by replacing in a flash the form and forces of a ruined and corrupt world."

Of course, one could call Evola the "spiritual father" of a group of radical "neofascists" (in the broadest sense of the word), just as Nietzsche has been called the father of National Socialism, Stirner the father of terrorist anarchism, and Hegel the father of Stalinism. But it is questionable that this leads to better understanding. Even though he himself would have strictly denied this characterization (see his "Superamento del Romanticismo" [Overcoming Romanticism] in *Il Progresso Religioso*, Rome, 1928, no. 3, p. 97), one could instead see him, in spite of his "Olympian clarity," as a "romantic" latecomer.

Some Concluding Thoughts

A few of the more controversial aspects of Evola's thought must be raised before proceeding with this characterization.

Especially since his "doctrine" runs counter to our usual conceptions, misjudgments can be avoided only by a certain thoroughness. But despite the wealth of facts offered here, many other important questions have had to be bracketed out. Above all, those concern Evola's esoteric side, the supra-rational and spiritual, with which the majority of his books deal. At this point it must be stressed that *supra-rational* does not in any way equal *irrational*. On the contrary: irrational means under or before the *ratio* (reason); supra-rational, on the other hand, goes beyond the rational but still includes reason itself. The triumph of reason alone first began with Nominalism. Before that, there was hardly a doubt that the spiritual (in a pure, elevated sense; the *nous* in the ancient meaning in which Plato and Plotinus used it) ranks above mere reason, just as "intellectual intuition" (the "vision" connected to the supra-rational, the so-called "intel-lectual contemplation," of Dante and Thomas Aquinas) lies above discursive knowledge and thus rules over it. Apart from Guénon and Evola, this view is also found in incomparably more famous philosophers, from Spinoza, Fichte, and Schelling up to Schopenhauer and Heidegger (albeit in a different form).

It should be stressed again that Evola's experiences with the supra-rational are the foundation of his political doctrine. We have tried to prove this point repeatedly throughout this introduction, because it seems that this presents the greatest difficulty in the political analysis of Evola. For "modern" man, the foundations are now totally different. That is why we have so many difficulties in understanding the fundamentalist currents of Islam and Christianity that are primarily connected to transcendence. However, in these cases there are many other aspects at work as well, so that they often result in a narrowing and restriction of the spiritual standpoint, instead of in the expansion and univer-sality demanded by Tradition.

The fundamental question Evola asks is the same fundamental question of all philosophy: Where can I find the point of absolute certainty on which I can build my cosmic system? At first Evola found this point in the "Self," which in its "might" and "freedom" merged with the absolute "I am who I am." Various traditional esoteric teachings pointed the way to this conclusion, teachings whose prerequisite was always a stepping out of the purely human condition. And this overcoming of the "human" that leads to the a-human (lying beyond the con-ception of the human; not to be confused with inhuman) is what is so hard for today's Western mind to comprehend. In the Tradition, "turning toward God" also means turning away from purely human concerns, not in the sense of de-spising them but because God is more "important." Even Jesus Christ demanded of his apostles that they leave behind their parents and brethren, if they wanted to follow him.

Two excerpts from *Imperialismo pagano* (p. 80 in the German edition) eluci-date this attitude: "This 'human' feeling for life that is so typical of the West merely betrays its very plebeian and inferior aspect. That which is an object of shame to some—the 'human'—is praised by others. Antiquity elevated the in-dividual to godhood, strove to free him from the passions in order to raise him to the transcendental sphere, that liberating air of the peaks, be it in contem-plation or in deed; they knew of traditions of nonhuman heroes and men of divine blood." And: "The 'human' is to be overcome absolutely, without remorse. But to achieve this it is necessary for the individual to attain the feeling of *inner liberation*. One must know that this feeling cannot be the object of thirst, of the hungry search of the captive whose path to this state is blocked. Either it is a simple matter, which is neither proclaimed nor discussed—something that does not need a second glance, like a natural, elemental, unmanifested presence of the elect—or it is nothing at all. The more it is seen and desired, the more distant it becomes, because desire is fatal to it."

Such an attitude totally contradicts our contemporary view of life. Today, whether in philosophy or in politics and science, moral and ethical views predominate that are directed only toward the human or social spheres. That is why there is constant talk of "human rights," and surprise when these values are not followed in other cultures (as in the fundamentalist ones, for example), where "divine" commandments remain at the center. Jean-Paul Sartre was certainly one of those who contributed the most to our increasing emphasis on purely moral values; but he was also an Atheist.

One could also formulate it in this admittedly provocative way: the more "humane" man becomes, the less he contemplates the "divine"—unless he considers "man" and "God" to be equal, which a mystic, a Mahayana Buddhist, or a Sufi would accept, at least in the spiritual sense. But in today's practice, this usually results in a "denial of God," which again leaves only the "human." The purely linguistic problems in defining what is "human" and "divine" to each individual must, of course, be omitted here. These thoughts should also by no means prevent anyone from treating his fellow men humanely, without which no ordered coexistence is possible; they are intended only to provoke thought.

The following excerpt from an already cited magazine article may help to clear up Evola's attitude toward the "moral" question ("Our Antibourgeois Front"):

> In the text of a document that was written two thousand years before Nietzsche we read: "When the path (i.e., the immediate connection to the pure spiritual state) is lost, virtue remains; when virtue is lost, ethics remain; when ethics are lost, moralism remains. Moralism is only an exteriorization of ethics and denotes the principle of decline." This saying clearly differentiates the stages of the decline that has led down to the bourgeois idol: moralism. Such an idol remained wholly unknown to the great traditional cultures: they had never known a system of egalitarianism and training built on convention, compromise, hypocrisy, and cowardice, a system founded on an inferior, societized utilitarianism—

that is, a system of taboos for the protection of undisturbed gluttony, pleasure, and commercial dealings. Moralism has developed in parallel with the parasitic degeneration of Western bourgeois civilization, so its attitude is not hard to connect with the characteristic statements of the most important ideological exponents of this civilization.

Incidentally, it must be mentioned that when before the rise of the bourgeois spirit ethics are mentioned instead of morals, these ethics are really nothing more than a secular spirituality and a laicized religion. That which today has the value of a conventional morality and yesterday had the value of an inner ethos possessed a "sacral" justification in the Tradition. This can already be seen in symbolic guise from the fact that in ancient times every system of law was "supernaturally" revealed or of divine origin, or else decreed by lawgivers of not quite human origin: Manes, Minos, Manu, Numa, and so on. This fact follows from the real essence of every traditional culture, which is always striving to connect man with an energy from above, an energy of such intensity that it is able to tear away, subjugate, and tame everything lowly (i.e., the purely human element) and thus create possibilities for superhuman ascent, instead of damming up and canalizing every rise, every manifestation of power and audacity, in order to reach the goal of creating petty beings and petty lives running on identical tracks. Even when this energy from above is no longer present, its traces remained for a time in ethics, in the classical sense: an ethos as inner character and tradition-bound lifestyle, imbued with a spontaneous love for self-control, discipline, daring, loyalty, or for authority. When even this ethos had run dry, it was replaced by morals and the constant worry about propriety—that is, moralism. The center of gravity shifted to the Philistine in his various disguises, from the fanatical Puritan to Candide and Babbitt.

Especially because morals present something purely human, they differ from culture to culture. Transpositions of moral positions into other cultural circles are therefore not permissible if one is not to become guilty of a new form of colonialism. Concerning this, Oswald Spengler, one of the fathers of Evolian thought, writes in *The Decline of the West* (German ed., vol. I, p. 434)

Western mankind, without exception, is under the influence here of an immense optical illusion. Everyone *demands* something of the rest. We say "thou shalt" in the conviction that so-and-so in fact will, can, and must be changed, fashioned, and arranged conformably to the order, with unshakable belief both in the efficacy of such orders and in our right to issue them. That is what we call morality. In the ethics of the West everything is direction, claim to power, will to action at a distance. Here Luther is completely at one with Nietzsche, the popes with the Darwinians, the Socialists with the Jesuits; for one and all, the beginning of morality is a claim to general and permanent validity. This is one of the necessities of the Faustian soul. He who thinks or teaches otherwise is sinful, a backslider, an enemy, and he is fought without mercy. "Thou shalt," the State shall, society shall—this form of morality is self-evident; it represents the only real meaning that we can attach to the word. But it was not so either in the Classical world, in India, or in China. Buddha, for instance, gave an example to take or to leave; Epicurus offered good advice. These are also forms of high morality, and neither contains the will element.

But if Evola falls back on an a-human viewpoint, this should not be taken to mean that he was against humane and "social" programs, as his support of the social laws as part of the RSI proves. He merely fought vehemently against the demagoguery that is usually connected with such initiatives.

This supra-moral attitude kept many thinkers away from Evola who might otherwise have stood closer to him, as, for example, Count Hermann Keyserling. Hermann Hesse also seems to have gone in this direction, when he says of Evola in a letter to Peter Suhrkamp dated April 27, 1935: "This dazzling and interesting, but very dangerous author . . ." Hesse then goes on to accuse Evola of dilettantism in esoteric matters, which seems unjustified considering the many competent and distinguished positive voices, such as C. G. Jung, Mircea Eliade, Giuseppe Tucci, and Marguerite Yourcenar. His works about Tantrism and Buddhism were even published in India, which is very rare for Western authors.

Amusingly enough, Hesse adds the following remark: "In Italy, almost no one will fall for him, but it will be different in Germany."

As with René Guénon, it is difficult to classify Julius Evola within the intellectual history of the twentieth century: the innermost conviction of both that modernity equals decadence led them to break with this world. Guénon went to Cairo, after he had already converted to Islam, and joined a traditional Sufi group. Evola completely withdrew in Rome, did not leave his apartment, and received only a few visitors. Only his combative nature (in contrast to Guénon's Brahmanic nature) encouraged him to publish an article here and there.

Evola may be studied at various Italian universities (Turin, Genoa, Florence, Rome, Naples, and Pisa) and be the subject of an increasing number of dissertations, but his radically antimodern, antidemocratic (though not at all antiliberty!), reactionary, aristocratic, even theocratic statements will always remain a stumbling block. Incidentally, Evola was also a "practicing" antidemocrat. He never voted in elections, and party politics were always thoroughly alien to him.

With Evola's traditional worldview and the modern one, we actually have two possible solutions to a fundamental problem of man: the problem of his weakness in the face of the immense universe, or in other words the problem of his "being thrown" into this world (as Sartre says). Should we in answer to this inferiority complex try to *soar up* to the universe, or must we, when we sense a discrepancy with something "higher" and more "spiritual" (that is, we feel inside that we cannot meet its standards), *bring it down* to our human plane? Should we—and here we again connect with the moral question—transcend ourselves and turn man into a "divine" man, or must we strip the "divine" of its attributes and feel merely human? Should we acknowledge an aristocratic, hierarchical order whose ranks are impulses to higher realms, or do we unite according to our most common denominator "down here," and are all equally high or low? Should we strive to fulfill "eternal" values, or do even temporal ones exceed our abilities and possibilities? Basically, is the direction "up" or "down"? (the "inner" being very much feels the difference). Here we have two opposing value systems: which one do we follow? Does the purely pragmatic answer apply here: right is that which leads to the happiness and satisfaction of the majority of people? So do we try, in Popperian manner, to "falsify" these two value systems? Or are there perhaps some archetypes that tower above the individual, fascinating primal images in the collective unconscious, that downright force us to strive for "higher" things? Or is the human substance somehow conditioned from the beginning so that "liberation" from the earthly burden is possible only through physical well-being? Questions upon questions, which we each have to answer according to our inclinations.

This is what makes Evola's thought so interesting, because he leaps ahead of us in his radicality and paints a powerful total picture of his version of an upwardly-directed traditional guidance. In this we are able to search for our likeness and see whether we can find ourselves there.

Evola's critique of today's world is among the most embittered and fundamental that have ever been heard. Thomas Sheehan writes in his aforementioned essay "Myth and Violence" (p. 61): "In no other contemporary European thinker that I know of is the rejection of history—and, *a fortiori*, of the modern world—so absolute and so violent." Incidentally, Sheehan characterizes Evola, whom he holds *intellectually* responsible for some terrorist acts, as "perhaps the most original and creative—and, intellectually, the most noncon-formist—of the Italian Fascist philosophers" (p. 50).

But even this can be understood as originating from Evola. His principles are "eternal" and thus one cannot negotiate about them. They are not a compromise between the individual efforts of various people in order to arrive at a *contrat social* (social contract). For Evola, they are truths carried over from transcen-dence, and there is no room for compromise in truth.

Therefore, the motto throughout his life remained: "Act, without heeding the fruits, without letting the prospects of success or failure, victory or loss influence you, nor even joy or pain, or the approval and rejection of others." Or expressed in other words: "Be whole, even in fragments; be upright even when bent." In a time when the marketing techniques devised by business are used in every arena, especially in politics, these sentences will most likely not be understood. Only shortly before his death he is supposed to have uttered: "One must rescue that which can be rescued, choose the lesser evil, and ally oneself with the moderate in order to fight the subversion." A step in the right direction or a sign of weakness?

Today one hears such radical sentiments mainly among the fundamentalist Greens. While their critique of progress, technology, and the hegemony of sci-ence is outwardly identical, when measured against Evola it remains superficial. The fact that quality, the immeasurable, is always coming up short against quan-tity, the measurable, is, however, a thorn in the sides of both.

Evola "engaged" himself and for almost sixty years fought for the same principles, albeit in various interpretations. Part of these was what he always called a cardinal attribute of traditional man: the "legionary spirit" (in refer-ence to Codreanu?). In *Orientamenti* (p. 20), Evola defines this term: "The attitude of him who can choose the hardest life, who is able to continue fight-ing even when he knows that the battle is materially lost, who holds to the ancient precept that 'loyalty is mightier than fire,' and who carries the tradi-tional idea of honor and dishonor within. This attitude creates a substantial, even existential difference between men, almost as though between one race and another. . . ."

Compare to this (and to other ideas of Evola's that we know) the ideas of Toni Negri, the Italian theoretician of radical neo-Marxism living in French exile, when he speaks of the conviction that true Marxists are a "different race," descended from a "virgin mother," and are engaged in a "struggle between truth and falsehood," all the while being led by the party that is compared to a "martial religious order" (Antonio Negri, *Il dominio e il sabotaggio: Sul metodo marxista della trasformazione sociale* [Rule and Sabotage: On the Marxist Method of Societal Change], Milan, 1978).

"The 'style' that must assert itself is the style of one who remains strong in his position of loyalty to himself and to an idea, a strength marked by concentrated intensity, resistance to any compromise, as well as a total engagement that shows in every phase of existence." And further, as an explanation: "Tradition as we understand it is that which is most revolutionary in the face of today's prevailing values" (interview with Evola in *Pianeta*, no. 44, January 1972, quoted from R. del Ponte's introduction to Evola's *Saggi sull'Idealismo Magico*, Genoa, 1981).

In any case, a certain desire of Evola's to shock with his pronouncements cannot be denied. Again and again he uses terms with a meaning totally different from the publicly accepted one, and in so doing almost deliberately invites misunderstanding.

Related to this is his perfect ability to continually "fall between two stools," even where he could have enjoyed sympathies. Domenico Rudatis once said in a personal conversation about Evola: "His greatest obstacle was his intellectual brilliance." He was certainly no easy character, as is confirmed by some episodes from his youth, and was easily insulted and hurt. Such natures (combative because of their very fragility) with the corresponding verbal excesses seem to have been more common in the first half of the twentieth century than today. Would National Socialism and Fascism have been as successful with their methods otherwise?

But it is also obvious to Evola that he is not really fighting against Bolshevism, Americanism, and consumer culture, but rather against contemporary man. All these currents would have had no chance if we were not already "inner" "Bolshevists," "Americans," or "consumers." A term like "Americanism" is only a symbol for something that is found deep inside us. The "outer enemy" has chances of winning only because an "inner enemy" inside of ourselves collaborates with him. This also explains Evola's esoteric efforts, intended to counteract this, because he who can control the inner can also control the outer domain. The outward fight, as we have said, is regarded as an "existential moment" or "inner experience" (E. Jünger), as metaphor for a spiritual or intellectual conflict. Apart from Jünger, this insight can be also be found in Gottfried

Benn, Knut Hamsun, Ezra Pound, and Ferdinand Céline, all of whom, interestingly enough, sympathized for a longer or shorter time with Fascism or National Socialism. Even Luigi Pirandello, one of the most important dramatists of the twentieth century and, like Hamsun and Pound, a recipient of the Nobel Prize for Literature, said as he signed a manifesto of Fascist intellectuals: "I have always struggled against words" (quoted by Sheehan, p. 53).

In Evola, this martial, warrior element (his "Kshatriya" essence) led to a special conflict. How can one be simultaneously active in this world and detached from it? And how can one feel oneself to be part of Tradition and yet act in the "factual" world? The necessary "active indifference" is a problem already encountered in Plato's philosopher. In reality, his goal is spiritual self-realization, and yet he has the task of ruling a state. Evola finally saw *"apoliteia"* as a way out and thus ended the dilemma.

To see Evola as a thinker (in the philosophical, esoteric, and metapolitical sense of Gramsci), as we have done in this study, is one approach. Pierre-André Taguieff uncovers another possibility. He views Evola above all as an artist for whom the "aesthetic" side of his ideas lies closest to his heart. Taguieff even calls Evola's metaphysics those of an artist. If one agrees with this assessment, then many doors might open for Evola, because an artist has more freedom in our society than is allotted to a philosopher or even a political thinker. Above all, the artist can claim freedom from the usual moral norms: *he* is allowed to stand *beyond*, while also changing society on this side.

Henry de Montherlant sees the Evola phenomenon in yet another light: "I have read Julius Evola and I continue to read him. . . . He is what he is. *But, he sees*" (quoted in Pierre Pascal, "Lux evoliana," in *Julius Evola, Le philosophe foudroyé*). The same article quotes René Guénon, who despite his differences was one of the closest fellow travelers of Evola. He says of Evola: "Fire in ice and ice in fire . . . the eagle's cry . . . the demon of action."

And Gerd-Klaus Kaltenbrunner opines about this "pilgrim of the absolute": "For many, reading Evola might be an offense, in the exact biblical sense. . . . But this at least one cannot take away from the author: his consistency, a universal education, and the courage to make a daring, sovereign formulation" ("Das letzte Licht kam vom Gral. Anmerkungen zu Julius Evolas Traktat: *Revolte gegen die Moderne Welt*" [The Last Light Emanated from the Grail: Notes on Julius Evola's *Revolt Against the Modern World*], in *Die Welt*, December 28, 1982).

Jay Kinney, publisher of *Gnosis* magazine, writes the following in issue 14

("Who's Afraid of the Bogeyman? The Phantasm of Esoteric Terrorism," San Francisco, 1990): "It remains to be seen whether his Hermetic virtues can be disentangled from his political sins. Meanwhile, he serves as a persuasive argument for the separation of esoteric 'Church and State.' "

To conclude this study, we will mention a characterization that Joseph Roth gave of the Austrian poet Franz Grillparzer that seems to me both amusing and appropriate, for it suits Evola just as well: Roth called Grillparzer an "anarchist individualist reactionary."

Bibliography to the Introduction
(works not already mentioned in the text)

Billig, Michael. *Die Rassistische Internationale*, Frankfurt, 1981.

Cohn, Norman. *Warrant for Genocide: The Myth of the Jewish World Conspiracy and the Protocols of the Elders of Zion*, New York, 1969.

Ferracuti, Giovanni. *Julius Evola*, Rimini, 1984.

Forschbach, Edmund. *Edgar Julius Jung*, Pfullingen, 1984, pp. 85–118.

Garin, Nacci, et al. *Tendenze della Filosofia nell'eta del fascismo*, Livorno, 1985.

Heilbutt, Iwan. *Die öffentlichen Verleumder: Die "Protokolle der Weisen von Zion" und ihre Anwendung in der heutigen Weltpolitik*, Zurich, 1937.

Kaltenbrunner, Gerd-Klaus. *Europa: Seine geistigen Quellen in Portraits aus zwei Jahrtausenden*, vol. II, Heroldsberg, 1983, p. 405 ff.

Poliakov, Leon. *The Aryan Myth*, New York, 1974.

Raes, R. "Julius Evola en het fascisme," in *Dietsland-Europa*, 1985, no. 6/7, pp. 15–25.

de Turris, Gianfranco. "Il Gruppo di UR, tra magia e Superfascismo," in *Abstracta* 6/1987, p. 12ff.

Vasallo, Piero. *Modernità e tradizione nell'opera evoliana*, Palermo, 1978.

Weissmann, Karl-Heinz. "Bibliographie der Werke Julius Evolas" in Julius Evola, *Menschen inmitten von Ruinen*, Tübingen, 1991.

PREFACE TO THE
THIRD ITALIAN EDITION (1972)*

When the present book was written, it was with reference to a definite situation in Italy. In 1953, when the first edition appeared (from Edizioni dell'Ascia), it seemed that conditions were present there for the initial formation of a realignment of the Right—a Right not in the political sense, but above all in the ideal and spiritual sense. Hence, it did not seem in vain to formulate the principles, values, and main lines of a doctrine of the State that might serve for this eventual realignment, not with the idea of their possibly being adopted and realized, but essentially to point out a direction for them to take. Moreover, the preface written for the book by Junio Valerio Borghese was intended to have a particular symbolic value, due both to the name of Borghese and to what he represented as a combatant.

Unfortunately, the possibilities that seemed to be dawning have developed no further, and the process of Italy's political and moral fragmentation has continued. Nonetheless, I have thought it timely to reprint the book, which had become unobtainable. In point of fact—and it is depressing to have to say so—it represents the one and only exposition of a "reactionary" thinking that is anti-democratic, anti-Marxist, and free from dilutions and concessions that has been published since World War II, not only in Italy but in all of the rest of Europe as well. Thus it may still have value in terms of its testimony, its presence, and its point of reference, whatever the current situation, as it takes its place among the anti-conformist publications courageously issued by Giovanni Volpe. In this new edition, the text has been revised and completed in various respects, but without changing the essentials.

In my work *Il fascismo—Saggio di una analisi critica dal punto di vista della Destra* [Fascism—An Essay of Critical Analysis from the Point of View of the

---

*Translated by Joscelyn Godwin.

Right], which has appeared in the interim also from Volpe, I inevitably referred to some of the ideas already expounded in the present book. I do not think that any annoyance will be caused by the consequent repetitions, because one cannot insist too strongly on principles and truths that are being systematically denied, forgotten, or avoided by the vast majority today, for want of intellectual and even physical courage, and by the general subjection to the myths and slogans of the dominant order.

The first edition of the present book found a particular resonance among the young. If the same happens with this new edition, that can only be considered a positive sign with regard to a new generation.

—J. E.

INTRODUCTION TO
THE ITALIAN EDITION*

Prince J. Valerio Borghese

In the face of the growing crisis in higher moral and political values that the world is currently undergoing, with this book Julius Evola raises a cry of protest of exceptional frankness and courage, seeking at the same time to indicate the bases for the radical reconstruction of a civic reality that has been shattered by a precise, destructive will and by the corrosive action of materialism of every type and color.

Even if certain historical judgments cannot be wholly shared, even if certain points of view can be justified only from very particular perspectives, the spirit that animates this courageous statement, and which addresses primarily *men*—in their virility, in their personal and civic dignity, in a word, in the higher aspect of their being—will find a broad consensus among all of those who, like ourselves, believe that man lives not by bread alone; that the development and affirmation of the human personality is possible only through a heroic vision of life; that the economic factor is important but not supreme and much less the exclusive factor in true history; and that the value of a State and a people rests not on their standard of living and level of economic production, but instead on their civic and political greatness.

One should see on this topic the insightful pages that the author dedicates to the "demonic nature of the economy," where a trenchant criticism lays bare the common myth that keeps today's world in slavery, according to which the sole purpose of life is comfort: a fetish to which must be sacrificed serenity, the inner life, a truly free way of life, and every fertile, noble, and serious aspiration, so that men are trapped as slaves of the mechanism of production, which would fall into crisis if the illusion of this myth were dispelled.

---

*Translated by Joscelyn Godwin.

In a certain sense, the author stands outside the disputes and divergences of commonplace politics—between fascism and antifascism, liberalism and communism, capitalism and socialism—because he refuses to let the discussion unfold on the essentially materialistic plane chosen by our adversaries. By the latter are understood those who put self-interest above duty, duplicity above loyalty; who consider wealth to be the basis of civilization and resignation, cowardice, and egoism to be virtues, but heroism, ardor, and courage to be shortcomings; who substitute permissiveness for order, and give more weight to undifferentiated democratic numbers than to the aristocracy of values; all who support quantity against quality, matter against spirit.

Avoiding certain extreme or partial positions, *Men among the Ruins* defends the organic character of the State, which is also transcendent and "anagogical." It is a sense that is lost today, caught as we are in a dilemma: on the one hand, the overvaluation of the individual as such and the corrupt parliamentary systems; on the other hand, the formless pressure of a bureaucratic and totalitarian machine of the Soviet type. He reclaims the value of *auctoritas* and of hierarchy, the primary conditions of any true justice and, note well, of any true liberty, against the democratic idol of equality that is unrealistic and unjust at the same time; the value of Tradition, understood as the supreme civic patrimony of eternally valid principles, as against the historicist myth that holds that not only the particular institutions but also their very raison d'être must perish, and hence that revolution infallibly furthers progress. He asserts, at the basis of the rise and dividing of peoples and nations, the value of the political idea, of the vision of the world, of a center of authority, of the religious sentiment of social life, above and beyond their own ethnic characters. The author does not fear to be called a reactionary—that is, a man of the Right—when he warns that revolution makes sense only when it is reconstructive, being the violent removal of an unjust condition and perturbation of the civic and political order, whereas revolution is purely negative when it destroys for the sake of destruction and negates the higher moral validity of Tradition. This view suggests to him, among other things, some original thoughts about what has been called the "fascist parenthesis."

Notwithstanding its philosophical tone, sometimes animated by an energetic polemical spirit, the book speaks also of our passion for our country, and one feels the scarcely repressed emotion when it mentions "liberated Italy—'liberated' from the difficult task of forming itself on the inspiration of its highest traditions."

But the central ideas of this work, which perhaps could be developed differently in many aspects, but only with difficulty on any other basis, are the superiority of the *imperium* and of the State to individual interests and the exaltation of aristocratic heroism. The first idea affirms with great clarity a solar reality, albeit denied and violated today on every side, namely that "the State, incarnation of an idea and a power, is a higher reality with respect to the world of the economy" and that "political necessity always takes precedence over economic necessity," the economic order being an order of means of existence that ought never to become ends in themselves.

The second idea encourages our higher hopes, for it is not a matter of morals or civilization, where the heroic and hence aristocratic sense of life is wanting. The author does well to warn us that when he speaks of aristocracy, he is referring to a certain vision of the world: an aristocracy of character, not economic nor even intellectual, for intellectuality "exists in a sphere separated from the living wholeness of the individual, and above all from everything that is character, spiritual courage, and inner decision."

It is precisely this aristocracy of character that the best Italians desire and must constitute, beyond the ruins that surround us.

Perhaps there is a pattern of it laid up in heaven for him who wishes to contemplate it, and, in so doing, make himself its citizen. It makes no difference whether it exists now or ever will exist: the politics of this city alone will be his, and none other.

—**Plato,** *The Republic* [1]

MEN AMONG THE RUINS

One

REVOLUTION
COUNTERREVOLUTION
TRADITION

Recently, various forces have attempted to set up a defense and a resistance in the sociopolitical domain against the extreme forms in which the disorder of our age manifests itself. It is necessary to realize that this is a useless effort, even for the sake of merely demonstrative purposes, unless the disease is dealt with at its very roots. These roots, as far as the historical dimension is concerned, *are to be found in the subversion introduced in Europe by the revolutions of 1789 and 1848.* The disease must be recognized in all of its forms and degrees; thus, the main task is to establish if there are still men willing to reject all the ideologies, political movements, and parties that, directly or indirectly, derive from those revolutionary ideas (i.e., everything ranging from liberalism and democracy to Marxism and communism). As a positive counterpart, these men should be given an orientation and a solid foundation consisting of a broad view of life and a stern doctrine of the State.

Strictly speaking, the watchword could then be *counterrevolution;* however, the revolutionary origins are by now remote and almost forgotten. The subversion has long since taken root, so much so as to appear obvious and natural in the majority of existing institutions. Thus, for all practical purposes, the formula of "counterrevolution" would make sense only if people were able to see clearly the last stages that the world subversion is trying to cover up through revolutionary communism. Otherwise, another watchword is to be preferred, namely *reaction*. To adopt it and call oneself "reactionary" is a true test of courage. For quite some time, left-wing movements have made the term "reaction" synonymous with all kinds of iniquity and shame; they never miss an

112

opportunity to thereby stigmatize all those who are not helpful to their cause and who do not go with the flow, or do not follow what, according to them, is the "course of History." While it is very natural for the Left to employ this tactic, I find unnatural the sense of anguish that the term often induces in people, due to their lack of political, intellectual, and even physical courage; this lack of courage plagues even the representatives of the so-called Right or "national conservatives," who, as soon as they are labeled "reactionaries," protest, exculpate themselves, and try to show that they do not deserve that label.

What is the Right expected to do? While activists of the Left are "acting" and carrying forward the process of world subversion, is a conservative supposed to refrain from reacting and rather to look on, cheer them on, and even help them along the way? Historically speaking, it is deplorable that a "reaction" has been absent, inadequate, or only half-hearted, lacking people, means, and adequate doctrines, right at the time when the disease was still at an embryonic stage and thus susceptible to be eliminated by immediate cauterization of its infectious hotbeds; had that been the case, the European nations would have been spared untold calamities.

What is needed, therefore, is a new radical front, with clear boundaries drawn between friends and foes. If the "game" is not over yet, the future does not belong to those who share in the hybrid and crumbling ideas predominant even in groups that do not belong to the Left, but rather to those who have the courage to espouse radicalism—namely, the radicalism of the "absolute negations" or of "majestic affirmations," to use expressions dear to Donoso Cortès.

Naturally, the term "reaction" intrinsically possesses a slightly negative connotation: those who react do not have the initiative of action; one reacts, in a polemical or defensive way, when confronted by something that has already been affirmed or done. Thus, it is necessary to specify that reaction does not consist in parrying the moves of the opponent without having anything positive to oppose him with. This misperception could be eliminated by associating the formula of "reaction" with that of "conservative revolution," a formula in which a dynamic element is evident. In this context "revolution" no longer signifies a violent overthrow of a legitimate established order, but rather an action aimed at eliminating a newly emerged disorder and at reestablishing a state of normalcy. Joseph De Maistre remarked that what is needed, more than a "counterrevolution" in a polemical and strict sense, is the "opposite to a revolution," namely a positive action inspired by the origins. It is curious how words evolve: after all, *revolution*, according to its original Latin meaning (*re-volvere*), referred to a motion that led again to the starting point, to the origins. There-fore, the "revolutionary" force of renewal that needs to be employed against the existing situation should be derived from the origins.

However, if one wants to embrace the idea of "conservatism" (i.e., a "con-servative revolution"), it is necessary to proceed with caution. Considering the interpretation imposed by the Left, the term "conservative" is as intimidating as the term "reactionary." Obviously, it is necessary to first establish as exactly as possible what needs to be "preserved"; today there is very little that deserves to be preserved, especially as far as social structures and political institutions are concerned. In the case of Italy, this is true almost without exception; to a lesser degree it was valid for England and France, and even less for the nations of central Europe, in which vestiges of higher traditions continued to exist even on the plane of everyday life. In fact, the formula "conservative revolu-tion" was chosen by German intellectuals immediately after World War I, even with very recent historical references.[2] As far as everything else is concerned, we must acknowledge the reality of a situation that is an easy target for the polemics of the Left, according to which conservatives are not the champions of ideas, but rather of the interests of a particular economic class (i.e., the capi-talist one), which organized itself politically in order to perpetuate, for its own advantage, what is alleged to be merely a regime of privileges and social injus-tices. Thus, it has become all too easy to lump together conservatives, "reac-tionaries," capitalists, and bourgeoisie; in this way, a "*faux* target," to use a military term employed in artillery barrages, was successfully chosen. More-over, the same tactic was employed at a time when the avant-garde of world subversion did not yet wave the flag of Marxism and communism, but instead were represented by liberalism and by constitutionalism. The efficacy of this tactic was due to the fact that yesterday's conservatives (not unlike the contem-porary ones, even though the former were of an undeniably higher caliber) limited themselves to defending their sociopolitical positions and the material interests of a given class, of a given caste, instead of committing themselves to a stout defense of a higher right, dignity, and impersonal legacy of values, ideas, and principles. This was indeed their fundamental and most deplorable weakness.

Today we have sunk to an even lower level; therefore, the "conservative" idea to be defended must not only have no connection with the class that has replaced the fallen aristocracy and exclusively has the character of a mere eco-nomic class (i.e., the capitalist bourgeoisie)—but it must also be resolutely op-posed to it. What needs to be "preserved" and defended in a "revolutionary fashion" is the general view of life and of the State that, being based on higher values and interests, definitely transcends the economic plane, and thus everything that can be defined in terms of economic classes. In regard to these values, what refers to concrete orientations, positive institutions, and historical situations is just a consequence; it is not the primary but rather the secondary element. If things were set up in this way, by absolutely refusing to set foot in the field where the Left trains its aim on the "*faux* target," its polemics would be rendered totally ineffective.

Moreover, what is needed is not to artificially and coercively perpetuate particular forms tied to the past, despite having exhausted their vital possibilities and being out of touch with the times. For the authentic revolutionary conservative, what really counts is to be faithful not to past forms and institutions, but rather to *principles* of which such forms and institutions have been particular expressions, adequate for a specific period of time and in a specific geographical area. And just as these particular expressions ought to be regarded as changeable and ephemeral in themselves, since they are connected to historical circumstances that are often unrepeatable, likewise the corresponding principles animating them have a value that is unaffected by such contingencies, as they enjoy a perennial actuality. New forms, corresponding in essence to the old ones, are liable to emerge from them as if from a seed; thus, even as they eventually replace the old forms (even in a "revolutionary" manner), what remains is a certain continuity amid the changing historical, social, economic, and cultural factors.

In order to ensure this continuity, while holding fast to the underlying principles, it is necessary to eventually throw away everything that needs to be discarded, instead of stiffening, panicking, or confusedly seeking new ideas when crises occur and times change: this is indeed the essence of the true conservative spirit. Therefore, conservative spirit and traditional spirit are one and the same thing. According to its true, living meaning, Tradition is neither servile conformity to what has been, nor a sluggish perpetuation of the past into the present. Tradition, in its essence, is something simultaneously meta-historical and dynamic: it is an overall ordering force, in the service of principles that have the chrism of a superior legitimacy (we may even call them "principles from above"). This force acts through the generations, in continuity of spirit and inspiration, through institutions, laws, and social orders that may even display a remarkable variety and diversity. An analogous mistake to the one I have just condemned consists of identifying or in confusing the various formulations of a more or less distant past with the tradition itself.

Methodologically, in the quest for reference points, a given historical form must be considered exclusively as the exemplification and more or less faithful application of certain principles: this is a perfectly legitimate procedure, comparable to what in mathematics is called the shift from the differential to the integral. In such a case there is no anachronism or regression; nothing has been turned into an idol, or made absolute, that was not already so, since this is the nature of principles. Otherwise it would be like accusing of anachronism those who defend certain peculiar virtues of the soul merely because the latter are inspired by some person in the past, in whom those virtues were exhibited to a high degree. As Hegel himself said, "It is a matter of recognizing in the apparitions of temporal and transitory things, both the substance, which is *immanent*, and the eternal, which is *actual*."

With this is mind, we can see the ultimate premises of two opposing attitudes. The axiom of the revolutionary-conservative or revolutionary-reactionary mentality is that the supreme values and the foundational principles of every healthy and normal institution are not liable to change and to becoming: among these values we may find, for instance, the true State, the *imperium*, the *auctoritas* [authority], hierarchy, justice, functional classes, and the primacy of the political element over the social and economic elements. In the domain of these values there is no "history," and to think about them in historical terms is absurd. Such values and principles have an essentially *normative* character. In the public and political order they have the same dignity as, in private life, is typical of values and principles of absolute morality: they are imperative principles requiring a direct, intrinsic acknowledgment (it is the capacity for such an acknowledgment that differentiates existentially a certain category of beings from another). These principles are not compromised by the fact that in various instances an individual, out of weakness or due to other reasons, was unable to actualize them or to even implement them partially at one point in his life rather than another: as long as such an individual does not give up inwardly, he will be acknowledged even in abjection and in desperation. The ideas to which I am referring have the same nature: Vico called them "the natural laws of an eternal republic that varies in time and in different places." Even where these principles are objectified in a historical reality, they are not at all conditioned by it; they always point to a higher, meta-historical plane, which is their natural domain and where there is no change. The ideas that I call "traditional" must be thought of along the same lines.

The fundamental premise always revealed, more or less distinctly, in the revolutionary mentality is the total opposite. The truths it professes are historicism and empiricism. According to the revolutionary mentality, "Becoming" rules in the spiritual realm as well: everything is believed to be conditioned and shaped by the age and by the times. According to the revolutionary mentality, there are no principles, systems, and norms with values independent from the period in which they have assumed a historical form, on the basis of contingent and very human aspects such as physical, social, economic, and irrational factors. According to the most extreme and up-to-date trajectory of this deviant mind-set, the truly determining factor of every structure, and of what resembles an autonomous value, is the contingency proper to the various forms and development of the means of production, according to its consequences and social repercussions.

In chapter 7 I will discuss at greater length the historicist thesis I have merely outlined here, in order to clarify the fundamental and unbridgeable gap between the two premises. It is therefore useless to engage in a discussion when this gap is not acknowledged as given, *a priori*. The two views are as irreconcilable as the patterns of thought behind them. The former is the truth upheld by the revolutionary conservative, and by any group that, in the political realm, can be properly characterized as part of an authentic "Right"; the latter is the myth upheld by world subversion, the common background of all its forms, no matter how extreme, moderate, or watered down they may be. The previous considerations concerning the method and the meaning of some historical references also have a practical value. As a matter of fact, in a nation there is not always a sufficient living traditional continuity, whereas referring to existing or relatively young institutions may serve directly as a reference to the corresponding ideas. Conversely, it may happen that, when the continuity is broken, the previous procedure is adopted: then one must look to other eras, but only in order to derive from them ideas that are valid per se. This is especially the case for Italy. In previous books of mine I have often wondered what could actually be "preserved" in this country. In Italy we find no basis of political forms that have been preserved sufficiently intact from a traditional past; this is due mainly to the fact that such a past is lacking and that, unlike in major European states, in Italy there was no secular and continuous unitary formation

connected to a symbol and to a central, dynastic political power. More specifically, in Italy there is no trace of a strong ideological legacy (not even as the
legacy of a few) that would enable people to feel everything connected with the
ideologies that arose with the French Revolution as extraneous, unnatural, and
destructive. In fact, it was precisely these ideologies, in various forms, that
propitiated the unification of Italy, continued to prevail in the unified Italy, and
multiplied in the most virulent forms after the Fascist era. Thus, there is a
hiatus and a *vacuum*—and, in the case of Italy, the reference to traditional principles will necessarily have an ideal rather than a historical character. And even
if we refer to historical forms, we should only acknowledge them to be the
mere basis for an integration that will immediately leave them behind, having
in mind ideas instead; the historical distance being (as in the case of the ancient
Roman world, or certain aspects of medieval civilization) too great for that
reference to serve any other purpose.

Such a circumstance does not represent a disadvantage from all points of
view—for instance, if the ideas to which I allude were implemented by a new
movement, they would appear in an almost pure state, with only a minimum of
historical dross.

Unfortunately, Italian representatives of these principles will not be able to
benefit from what some states, especially the central European ones, displayed
as a residual historical positive basis or as a predisposition for a conservative
revolution; the positive counterpart of this disadvantage is that if the formation I
have in mind will come into existence, it will be endowed with an absolute and
uncompromising character. Precisely because there is no material support still
alive emanating from a traditional past and made concrete in historical forms
that are still valid, the conservative revolution in Italy must emerge as a pre-
dominantly spiritual phenomenon, based on a pure idea. However, since the
present world looks more and more like a world of ruins, sooner or later the
same line of action will assert itself everywhere: in other words, people will
realize that it is useless to lean on what still has vestiges of more normal institutions, but which is compromised by several negative historical factors, and
that it is imperative to go back to the origins and to start anew from them, as if
they towered over history, moving ahead with pure forces along the path of an
avenging and reconstructive reaction.

It may be useful to make another brief consideration of the term "revolution"
applied in a particular context, namely in relation to the fact that in various

national right-wing movements opposed to the present system we find a yearning to be "revolutionary." This tendency, after all, was present in the movements of the most recent past, considering the choice of designations such as "Fascist revolution," "revolution of the Brown Shirts," and "revolution of order" (e.g., Salazar's movement in Portugal). Naturally one should ask: revolution against what? Revolution in the name of what? In any event, every word has its "soul" and one should be careful not to be unconsciously influenced by it. I have made it clear, from my perspective, that one could speak of "revolution" only in a relative sense—as Hegel used to say, a "negation of the negation"—in reference either to an attack against something that has a negative character or to a number of changes, whether violent or not, aimed at reinstating normalcy, just as a person who has fallen down gets up again, or an organism is freed from degenerative growths by halting the spread of cancerous cells. Thus, it is necessary to prevent the hidden "soul" of the term "revolution" from influencing even those who are not Leftists, leading them away from the right course when they claim to be revolutionaries, in a sense that diverges from the one I have just indicated, in virtue of being somehow positive.

The danger may consist in appropriating, more or less implicitly, foundational premises that are not different from those of one's opponents, espousing the idea that "history marches on" and that it is necessary to be open to the future by creating new things and formulating new principles: in that case the "revolution" becomes an aspect of a forward direction, a course that would then imply breaking points and upheavals. There are some who believe that in this fashion the "revolutionary spirit" acquires a greater dignity and as a myth exercises a greater power of suggestion. I believe this amounts to a capitulation; it is then difficult, even without being aware of it consciously, not to espouse the progressive ideology according to which every new thing represents something more and better than what preceded it.

We already know what the true foundation of progressivism is: the mirage of technological civilization, the lure exercised by some undeniable material and industrial progress that, however, is appreciated without paying much attention to its negative drawbacks, which often affect other, more important and valuable domains of human life. Those who are not subject to the predominant materialism of our times, upon recognizing the only context in which it is legitimate to speak of progress, will be on guard against any orientation in which the modern "myth of progress" is reflected. In ancient times the matter was very clear. In Latin, the word denoting subversion was not *revolutio* (which had a different meaning, as I have explained before) but rather *seditio*, or *eversio*, or *civilis perturbatio*, or *rerum publicarum commutatio*. Thus, the term "revolutionary," in its modern meaning, was rendered with circumlocutions such as *rerum novarum studiosus*, or *fautor*, namely one who aims at and promotes new things. According to the traditional Roman mentality, "new things" were automatically regarded as negative and subversive.

Thus, in regard to "revolutionary" ambitions it is necessary to clear the misunderstanding and to choose between the two aforementioned opposing positions, which determine two likewise opposing styles. Again, on the one hand there are those who acknowledge the existence of immutable principles for every true order and who abide by them, not allowing themselves to be swept along by events. Such people do not believe in "history" and in "progress" as mysterious super-ordained entities, but instead attempt to dominate the forces of the environment and lead them back to higher, stable forms: according to them, this is what embracing reality amounts to. On the other hand there are those who, having been "born yesterday," have nothing in the past, who believe only in the future and are committed to a groundless, empirical, and improvised action, deluding themselves that they are able to direct events without knowing or acknowledging anything that rises above the plane of matter and contingency; such people devise many systems, the end result of which will never be an authentic order, but instead a more or less manageable disorder. The "revolutionary" vocation belongs to this second line of thought, even when it does not directly serve the interests of unadulterated subversion. In this context, the lack of principles is supplied with the myth of the future, through which some dare to justify and sanctify recent destructions that have occurred, since in their view they were necessary in order to move ahead and to achieve new and better horizons (any trace of which, I am afraid, it is difficult to point out).

Once things are clearly seen in these terms, it is necessary to thoroughly examine one's "revolutionary" ambitions, all the while aware that if these ambitions are kept within their legitimate limits, one would then be a part of history's demolition squad. Those who are still standing upright in this world of ruins are at a higher level; their watchword is *Tradition*, according to the dynamic aspect I have just made evident. When circumstances change, when crises occur, when new factors come into play, where the previous dams begin to crack, these people know how to retain their sangfroid and are capable of letting go of what needs to be abandoned *in order that what is truly essential may not be compromised.* These people know how to move on, upholding in an impassive way the forms that are proper to the new circumstances, knowing how to assert themselves through them; their goal is to reestablish and maintain an immaterial continuity and avoid a groundless and adventurous course of action. This is the method of the true dominators of history, which is very different from and more virile than that of the merely "revolutionary."

I will end this series of considerations with a particular application for them. Since, as I have said, Italy lacks an authentic "traditional" past, there are some who, in their attempt to organize themselves against the avant-garde of world subversion, and in order to claim some concrete and historical basis, have found a reference point in the principles and institutions of the Fascist era. I wish to uphold the following fundamental principle: if the "Fascist ideas" still deserve to be defended, they should not be defended simply insofar as they are "Fascist," but rather insofar as they have represented a particular form of the apparition and affirmation of ideas that were older and more elevated than Fascism, ideas that have the character of "constants," so that they may found again as integral parts of a great European political tradition. To cherish these ideas not according to this spirit, but solely because they are "revolutionary," original, and proper only to Fascism, would amount to belittling them, adopting a limiting perspective, and making difficult a much needed task of clarification. To those for whom everything begins and ends with Fascism, including those whose political horizons are confined by the mere polemics between Fascism and antifascism and who have no other reference point beside these two poles— these people would hardly be able to distinguish the best potential of the Italian world of the past from some of its aspects that were affected by the same evils that it is necessary to fight against today.[3]

Thus, when I will later discuss ideas for which the Italy and Germany of yesterday fought, I will always do so within revolutionary-traditional parameters; I will take the utmost care to limit as much as possible any contingent reference to the past and to emphasize the principles' pure ideal and normative character, which is not connected to a particular period or movement.

Two

SOVEREIGNTY
AUTHORITY
IMPERIUM

⟡⟶◉⟵⟡

The foundation of every true State is the transcendence of its own principle, namely the principle of sovereignty, authority, and legitimacy. This essential truth has been variously expressed in the course of history; if this truth was not recognized, the meaning of everything that belongs to political reality would be misunderstood, or at least distorted. Through the multifaceted variety of these forms we always find as a "constant" the notion of the State as the intrusion and the manifestation of a higher order, which is then actualized in a *power*. Therefore, every true political unity appears as the embodiment of an *idea* and a *power*, thus distinguishing itself from every form of naturalistic association or "natural right," and also from every societal aggregation determined by mere social, economic, biological, utilitarian, or eudemonistic factors.

In previous eras it was possible to speak of the *sacred* character of the principle of sovereignty and power, namely of the State. For instance, the ancient Roman notion of *imperium* essentially belonged to the domain of the sacred. This notion, in its specific meaning, even before expressing a system of territorial, supernational hegemony, designated the pure power of command, the almost mystical power and *auctoritas* inherent in the one who had the function and quality of Leader: a leader in the religious and warrior order as well as in the order of the patrician family, the *gens*, and, eminently, of the State, the *res publica*. In the Roman world, which was intensely realistic (or, I should say, precisely because it was intensely realistic), the notion of this power, which is simultaneously *auctoritas*, always retained its intrinsic character of bright force from above and of sacred power, beyond the various and often spurious techniques that conditioned its access in different periods.[4]

It is possible to deny the principle of sovereignty; but if we acknowledge it, it is also necessary to recognize its attribute of *absoluteness*. A power that is also *auctoritas* (*aeterna auctoritas* [eternal authority], as the Romans would say) must necessarily have in itself the decreeing power of something that represents the ultimate application. A power and authority that are not absolute, are not real authority or real power, as De Maistre made very clear. Just as in the order of natural causes, likewise in the political domain it is not possible to regress indefinitely from condition to condition; the series must have its limit in one point, which is characterized by the unconditioned and by an absoluteness in the act of deciding. This will also be the point of *stability* and of consistency, the natural center of the entire organism; if it lacks this, a political association would be merely an aggregate, an unstable formation. Conversely, the above-mentioned power refers to a transcendent order that alone can ground and legitimize it in terms of a sovereign, autonomous, and underived principle that is the basis of every right without being subject to another right. These two aspects and two necessities mutually condition each other in reality; in doing so they express the nature of the pure political principle of the *imperium* and also the figure of the one who, as true Leader, must embody and represent it.

The juridical view of sovereignty (the so-called "State of right," cf. Kelsen), no matter what form it embodies, refers only to a *caput mortuum*, namely the condition proper to a dead political organism, which lives in a mechanical fashion and is characterized by a latency or an absence of its center and original generating force. If *order*, the form that triumphs over chaos and disorder (thus the law and the right), is the very substance of the State, all this has its sufficient reason and ultimate justification only in the above-mentioned transcendence. Thus it was rightly said: *"princeps a legibus solutus"*—namely, the law does not apply to the one who acts as Leader, just as Aristotle stated concerning those who, being themselves the law, have no law. In particular, the positive essence of the principle of sovereignty has rightfully been recognized in the power of making absolute decisions, in exceptional or emergency situations, beyond any duties and discussions, whenever the existing right and laws are suspended or their suspension is required.[5] In such instances and circumstances, one can witness the new arising and manifestation of the absolute power from above, which, though it remained invisible and silent in every other period and at other times, nevertheless should not cease to be present wherever the State remains steady in its generating principle, or wherever the State is a living organism and not a mechanical thing or a mere routine.[6] The "exceptional powers" and a "dictatorship" are devices of necessity, or the "life belt" that is required in such circumstances when the awaited awakening of the central principle of the State does not occur. In the same way, a dictatorship is not a "revolutionary" phenomenon; it represents legitimacy but it does not constitute a new political principle and a new right. In the best period of the Roman civilization, the dictatorship was conceived and allowed as a temporary remedy; far from replacing the existing order, it was its reintegration. In every other regard, dictatorship equals usurpation.

The State is not the expression of "society." The basis of sociological positivism, namely the "social" or "communal" view of the State, is the index of a regression and naturalistic involution. It contradicts the essence of the true State, inverting every proper relationship; it divests the political dimension of its proper character, original quality, and dignity. The "anagogical" end (namely, of a power drawing upward) of the State is thus completely denied.

The political domain is defined through hierarchical, heroic, ideal, antihedonistic, and, to a degree, even anti-eudemonistic values that set it apart from the order of naturalistic and vegetative life. Authentic political ends are mostly autonomous ones (i.e., not derived from something else): they are connected to ideas and interests different from those of peaceful living, pure economics, and physical well-being, pointing to a higher dimension of life and a separate order of dignity. This opposition between the political and the social domains is fundamental. It has the value of a "category"; the more it is emphasized, the more the State is animated by a metaphysical tension, displaying solid structures and representing the faithful image of a superior type of organism. In fact, the superior functions in such an organism are not the expression of its biological and vegetative part; aside from cases of obvious degradation, these functions are not even at the service of this part. Rather, these superior functions carry on an activity that may eventually assert itself over the physical life in order to direct it toward ends, actions, or disciplines that the mere physical life cannot explain or justify. All this has an analogical application concerning the relationships that, in a condition of normalcy, must exist between political order and "society."

The differentiation between the political and the physical domains was well articulated in the origins (i.e., the traditional past). It was also found in various primitive societies, in which some primordial meanings appeared in a purity that would be vainly sought in the shallow and crumbling sociologies of our times.

According to an old view, the State derives from the family: the same

principle responsible for shaping the family and the *gens*, having been integrated and extended, allegedly gave rise to the State. Whether or not this is the
case, it is possible, from a logical point of view, to trace the origins of the State
to a naturalistic plane only by committing an initial mistake: to assume that in
ancient civilized areas, and especially those populated by Indo-European civilizations, the family was a unity of a purely physical type, and that the sacred,
together with a well-articulated hierarchical social system, did not play a decisive role in it. Even if we were to rely on the findings of modern investigations,
thanks to the evidence marshaled by Fustel de Coulanges, there should be no
doubts about this matter. But if the family is thought of in naturalistic terms, or
in the terms in which it presents itself today, the generating principle of the
properly political communities must be traced to a context that is very different from the one typical of the family: it must be traced to the plane of the so-
called *Männerbünde*.[7]

Among several primitive societies, the individual, up to a certain age, being
regarded as a merely natural being, was entrusted to the family and to maternal
tutelage, since everything related to the maternal, physical aspect of existence
fell under the maternal-feminine aegis. However, at a certain point what happened, or better, what could happen, was a change of nature and status. Special
rites, known as "rites of passage," which were often preceded by a period of
detachment and isolation, and which were accompanied by harsh trials, generated a new being according to a scheme of "death and rebirth" who alone could
be regarded as a "man." In fact, prior to this initiation, the member of the group,
no matter what his age, was believed to belong to the same category that included women, children, and animals. Once the transformation occurred, the
individual was incorporated into the *Männerbund*. It was this *Männerbund*, in
which the qualification of "man" had simultaneously an initiatory (i.e., sacred)
and a warrior meaning, that wielded the power in the social group or clan. This
Männerbund was characterized by special tasks and responsibilities; it was different from all other societies to which other members of the tribe belonged.[8]

In this primordial scheme we find the fundamental "categories" differentiating the political order from the "social" order. First among these is a special
chrism—namely, that proper to "man" in the higher sense of the word (*vir* was
the term employed in Roman times) and not merely of a generic *homo:* this
condition is marked by a spiritual breakthrough and by detachment from the
naturalistic and vegetative plane. Its integration is *power*, the principle of command belonging to the *Männerbund*. We could rightfully see in this one of the

"constants" (i.e., basic ideas) that in very different applications, formulations, and derivations are uniformly found in the theory or, better, in the metaphysics of the State that was professed even by the greatest civilizations of the past. Following the processes of secularization, rationalization, and materialization, which have become increasingly accentuated in recent times, those original meanings became obscured and attenuated; and yet, wherever they are entirely obliterated, even though they exist in a transposed form, without an initiatory or sacred background, there no longer is a State or a political class in the specific, traditional sense. In reference to this, someone was able to say that the "formation of a ruling class is a divine mystery"; in some cases, though, it could be a "demonic mystery" (e.g., the tribunes of the people; demagogy; communism), but never something that could be defined in mere social or, worse yet, economic factors.

The State is under the masculine aegis, while "society" and, by extension, the people, or demos, *are under the feminine aegis.* Once again, this is a primordial truth. The maternal domination, from which the political-virile principle subtracts itself, was also understood as the domination of Mother Earth and the Mothers of life and fertility, under whose power and tutelage existence was believed to unfold in its physical, biological, and collective-material aspects. The common mythological background is that of the duality of the luminous and heavenly deities, who are the gods of the political and heroic world on the one hand, and of the feminine and maternal deities of naturalistic existence, who were loved by the plebeian strata of society on the other hand. Thus, even in the ancient Roman world, the idea of State and of *imperium* (i.e., of the sacred authority) was strictly connected to the symbolic cult of the virile deities of heaven, of light and of the super-world in opposition to the dark region of the Mothers and the chthonic deities. The same ideal line runs through the themes found in primitive societies (i.e., *Männerbünde*), up to the central, bright motif of the Olympian-state tradition of the Classical world and several superior Indo-European civilizations.

Later on in history this line leads, if not to the *imperium*, to the divine right of Kings; where there were no groups created by the power of a rite, there were Orders, aristocracies, political classes defined by disciplines and dignities that cannot be reduced to social values and economic factors. Then the line was broken, and the decadence of the State idea—parallel to the degeneration and the obfuscation of the pure principle of sovereignty and authority—ended with the inversion through which the world of the *demos* and the materialized masses emerged on the political horizon, engaging in the struggle for power. Such is the primary meaning of any democracy in the original sense of the term, and of every kind of "socialism": in their essence they are both anti-State, and represent the degradation and contamination of the political principle. Both democracy and socialism ratify the shift from the masculine to the feminine and from the spiritual to the material and the promiscuous. This is an involution, the basis or counterpart of which is an involution occurring within the individual himself, expressed by the inner triumph of faculties and interests connected to the naturalistic, obtuse, and merely vitalistic part of the human being. According to the correspondences already acknowledged by Plato and Aristotle, injustice—namely, the distortion and the external collective subversion—always reflects the internal subversion: that which is present in a given human type that has prevailed in a given civilization.

Today there are political forms in which such a fall of level and inversion are very clear and unmistakable; they are expressed in unequivocal terms in the political and ideological platforms of political parties. In other cases this is a less noticeable phenomenon; in regard to them, it will be helpful to make the following clarification.

The previously mentioned gap between the political idea of State and the physical idea of "society" is found again in the *opposition that exists between State and nation*. The notions of nation, fatherland, and people, despite their romantic and idealistic halo, essentially belong to the naturalistic and biological plane and not the political one; they lead back to the "maternal" and physical dimension of a given collectivity. Wherever these concepts were emphasized and bestowed with the dignity of a primary element, this has always happened in a revolutionary or even polemical function toward the concept of the State and the pure principle of sovereignty. With the passage from the expression "by grace of God" (as approximate and stereotypical as it was, it still designated the true right "from above") to that of "by will of the nation," what really occurs is the above-mentioned inversion, which is not a shift just from an institutional structure to another, but also from one world to another world, separated by an unbridgeable hiatus.

A brief historical overview will clarify this regressive meaning of the myth of the nation. The origin of this myth should be traced to the deviation proper of those European States that, while acknowledging the political principle of the pure, higher sovereignty, assumed the form of "national States." This phenomenon had an essentially antiaristocratic (i.e., anti-feudal), schismatic, and anti-hierarchical function, vis-à-vis the European *ecumene*, in that it refused to acknowledge the superior authority of the Holy Roman Empire and conferred an absolute anarchical character to the particular political units over which the individual princes ruled. These princes, after they ceased to receive support "from above," sought their support "from below" and pursued a policy of centralization destined to occasion their downfall, since a more or less formless and inarticulate human conglomerate increasingly gained preeminence. Thus they shaped the structures that eventually ended in the hands of the "nation" first understood as the Third Estate, and later on in the hands of the nation understood as the "people" and the masses. This shift, as it is well known, was brought about by the French Revolution. In the French Revolution the "nation" emerged in an exclusively demagogical function; since then, nationalism allied itself with revolution, constitutionalism, liberalism, and democracy, becoming the symbol of the revolutionary movements that from 1789 to 1848, all the way to 1918, were responsible for subverting whatever remained of traditional Europe's preceding order. These "patriotic" ideologies were responsible for the upheaval in virtue of which a given naturalistic factor (such as that of belonging to a particular stock and historical society) is transformed into something mystical and assumes a supreme value; in this context the individual matters only as *citoyen* and as *l'enfant de la patrie*. The cumulative unity of citizens eventually detracts from authority, undermines or subordinates every higher principle to itself (i.e., to the "will of the people"), beginning with the principle of sovereignty.

We know what high consideration the social matriarchate held in Marxist historiography; it was regarded as the primordial social constitution and the original state of justice, which were ended by the institution of private property and by the political forms associated with it. However, the regression from the masculine to the feminine is equally visible in the previously mentioned revolutionary ideologies. The image of the fatherland as Mother, as Land of which we are all children and before which we are all equals and brothers, clearly recalls that physical, feminine-maternal order from which "men" separate themselves in order to create the virile and luminous order of the State, while the physical order, per se, has a pre-political character. Moreover, it is a very significant fact that country and nation have prevalently been allegorized through feminine figures, even among peoples whose land had a neuter or masculine, rather than a feminine, name.[9] The sacred character and inviolability of "nation" and of "people" are merely the transposition of features attributed to the Great Mother in ancient plebeian gynecocracies and in societies that ignored the virile and political principle of the *imperium*. Thus, it has rightfully been suggested by Bachofen and by Steding that "men" uphold the idea of State, while feminine natures, which are spiritually matriarchical, side instead with "fatherland," "nation," and "people." This casts a sinister light on the nature of the influences that have been predominant in the political history of the West, beginning with the French Revolution.

An additional insight could be gained by considering this problem from yet a different perspective. An idea also embraced by Fascism was that the nation exists and has an awareness, a will, and a superior reality only in service of the State. This idea has a specific historical confirmation, especially in reference to what Vico called "the right of heroic peoples" and the origin of the main European nations. Even though "fatherland" certainly means "land of the fathers," the term could have acquired this meaning only a very long time ago, since the historical fatherlands and nations known to us, almost without exception, have been established in lands that were not the primordial ones, and, in any event, in areas wider than the original ones. Their establishment occurred through conquests and aggregative and formative processes that presuppose the continuity of a power, of a principle of sovereignty and of authority, as well as the bond of a group of men sharing the same *idea* and loyalty, pursuing the same goal, and obeying the same inner law reflected in a specific political and social ideal. Such is the generating principle and the basis of every great nation. Understood in naturalistic terms, the political nucleus therefore relates to the nation in the same manner as the soul (as "entelechy") is related to the body: it shapes it, unifies it, and makes it partake of a higher life. In reference to this, we could say that a nation exists and overcomes geographical and even ethical boundaries wherever we find the reproduction of the same "inner form," namely the consecration or the imprint bestowed by the higher political force and its representatives. Thus it would be absurd, for instance, to call ancient Rome a "nation" in the modern sense of the word: one could refer to it as a "spiritual nation" or as a unity defined by the "Roman man." The same applies to the creations of the Franks and the Germans, as well as the Arabs who spread Islam, just to cite a few examples. Maybe the most significant case is the Prussian State, which originated from a knightly Order (a classic example of a

Männerbund), namely the Order of Teutonic Knights, which later on became the structure and the "form" of the German Reich.

Only when the tension decreases do differences become attenuated and the group of men gathered around the supra-ordained symbol of sovereignty and authority weakens and crumbles; only then may that which is a by-product and an artificial creation (i.e., the "nation") become autonomous and separate itself, thus acquiring the appearance of a living entity in its own right. Then what emerges is the "nation" as people, collectivity, and mass—namely, that which such a concept has increasingly signified since the French Revolution. When a sovereignty is no longer allowed other than one that is the expression and the reflection of the "will of the nation," it is almost as if a creature overtook its creator. From the political class understood as an Order and a *Männerbund* a shift occurs to demagogues and to the so-called "servants of the nation," to the democratic ruling classes who presume to "represent" the people and who acquire for themselves various offices or positions of power by flattering and manipulating the masses. The natural and fatal consequence of the above-mentioned regression is the inconsistency and, most of all, the *cowardice* of those who, in our time, constitute the "political class." It has rightly been said that in previous times there has never been a sovereign so absolute that he could silence an eventual opposition of the nobility and clergy;[10] yet today nobody dares to blame the "people" and they refuse to believe in the "nation," or at least are openly defiant toward it. However, this does not mean preventing the ruling classes from playing with, deceiving, and exploiting the people as their Athenian demagogic counterparts did and as, in more recent times, courtesans used to do with degenerate and vain sovereigns; this happens because the *demos*, which is feminine by nature, will never have its own, clear will. The real difference between then and now lies in the cowardice and servile attitude of those who today no longer have the moral stature of *men* or of representatives of a higher legitimacy and authority from above. At most, we find what Carlyle referred to when he spoke of a "world of domestics that yearns to be ruled by a pseudo-hero" and not by a real master; I will return to this idea in chapter 4, when discussing the phenomenon of Bonapartism.

Action through "myths," namely through formulas lacking any objective truth and that appeal to the sub-intellectual dimension and passions of individuals and the masses, is the inseparable counterpart of the aforementioned political climate. In the most characteristic modern trends, the notions of "country" and "nation" display to an eminent degree the quality of myths, susceptible to receiving the most varied contents depending on which way the wind blows and on the political parties, with the only common denominator being the denial of the political principle of pure sovereignty.

We may add that the system that was established in Europe through the advent of democracies (i.e., the majority system based on universal suffrage) is characterized from the start by the degradation of the ruling class. In fact, the majority, being free from every restriction and qualitative clause, is necessarily on the side of the lower social strata; in order to win the favors of these strata and be elected to office by their votes, it will always be necessary to speak the only language they understand and to give priority to their predominant interests (which are naturally the most coarse, material, and illusory), always promising but never demanding.[11] Thus, every democracy is also a school of immorality, an offence to the dignity and inner code of conduct that ought to be the trademark of a true political class.

I wish now to continue to discuss the genesis of the great European nations in service of the political principle, in order to derive some orientations. The substance of every true and stable political organism is something resembling an Order, a *Männerbund* in charge of the principle of the *imperium*, comprising men who see loyalty as the basis of their honor (as the saying of the Saxon Code goes).[12] But in time of crisis and of an overall moral, political, and social disintegration (as is the case in our day and age), a generic reference to the "nation" does not suffice for reconstructive work unless such an idea assumes a revolutionary overtone, including elements of a properly political order, weakened to various degrees. The "nation" will always be a promiscuous entity; in the above-mentioned situation what needs to be done is to emphasize the fundamental duality of the origins: on the one side stand the masses, in which, besides changing feelings, the same elementary instincts and interests connected to a physical and hedonistic plane will always have free play; and on the other side stand men who differentiate themselves from the masses as bearers of a complete legitimacy and authority, bestowed by the Idea and by their rigorous, impersonal adherence to it. The Idea, only the Idea, must be the true fatherland for these men: what unites them and sets them apart should consist in adherence to the same idea, rather than to the same land, language, or blood. The true task and the necessary premise for the rebirth of the "nation" and for its renewed form and conscience consists of untying and separating that which only apparently, promiscuously, or collectively appears to be one entity, and in reestablishing a virile substance in the form of a political elite around which a new crystallization will occur.

I call this the *realism of the idea:* realism because what are needed for this work are strength and clarity, rather than "idealism" and sentimentality. This realism, however, is opposed both to the coarse, cynical, and degenerate realism of politicians and to the style of those who abhor "ideological prejudices"; the latter, in fact, are capable only of reawakening a vague feeling of "national solidarity" (a herdlike spirit) by means that do not really differ from the general techniques employed to arouse the excitement of the masses.

All this falls below the level of what politics is, in the virile, traditional sense; moreover, it is inadequate for the times. It is inadequate because a realization of the idea is already present on the opposite front. In fact, today we can witness the gradual formation of blocs that have the supernational character proper to units essentially based on political ideas, as barbaric as they may be. This is the case of communism, in which the aggregating and uniting factor beyond "nation" and "country" consists of being proletarian communists belonging to the Third International. This is also the case of democracy when it pretends to summon "crusades." The so-called Nuremberg ideology established certain principles—not at all the only conceivable ones—even though they are supposed to be categorically upheld, without regard to country or nation, according to the official formulation: "with precedence over the duty of obedience of the individuals toward the State to which they belong."

In this way, too, we can see the insufficiency of the simple notion of "nation" as a guiding principle, and the need for its *political* integration, in terms of a higher idea that alone must be the standard, uniting and dividing factor. The essential task ahead requires formulating an adequate doctrine, upholding principles that have been thoroughly studied, and, beginning from these, giving birth to an Order. This elite, differentiating itself on a plane that is defined in terms of spiritual virility, decisiveness, and impersonality, and where every naturalistic bond loses its power and value, will be the bearer of a new principle of a higher authority and sovereignty; it will be able to denounce subversion and demagogy in whatever form they appear and reverse the downward spiral of the top-level cadres and the irresistible rise to power of the masses. From this elite, as if from a seed, a political organism and an integrated nation will emerge, enjoying the same dignity as the nations created by the great European political tradition. Anything short of this amounts only to a quagmire, dilletantism, irrealism, and obliquity.

Three

PERSONALITY
FREEDOM
HIERARCHY

The beginning of the disintegration of the traditional sociopolitical structures, or at least whatever was left of them in Europe, occurred through *liberalism*. Following the stormy and demonic period of the French Revolution, the principles espoused by the Revolution first began to act under the guise of liberalism; thus, liberalism is the origin of the various interconnected forms of global subversion.

It is therefore necessary to expose the errors on which this ideology is based and especially those of the "immortal principles" by which it is inspired. This is necessary not only from a doctrinal point of view, but also from a practical one. Nowadays the intellectual confusion has reached such an extent that liberalism, which according to ancient regimes and the Church was synonymous with antitradition and revolution, is portrayed by some as a "right-wing" movement, bent on protecting human dignity, rights, and freedom against Marxism and totalitarianism. The following considerations are aimed at exposing this misconception.

The essence of liberalism is *individualism*. The basis of its error is to mistake the notion of the *person* with that of the *individual* and to claim for the latter, unconditionally and according to egalitarian premises, some values that should rather be attributed solely to the former, and then only conditionally. Because of this transposition, these values are transformed into errors, or into something absurd and harmful.

Let us begin with the egalitarian premise. It is necessary to state from the outset that the "immortal principle" of equality is sheer nonsense. There is no need to comment on the inequality of human beings from a naturalistic point of view. And yet the champions of egalitarianism make equality a matter of principle, claiming that while human beings are not equal *de facto*, they are so *de jure*: they are unequal, and yet they should not be. Inequality is unfair; the merit and the superiority of the liberal idea allegedly consists of not taking it into account, overcoming it, and acknowledging the same dignity in every man. Democracy, too, shares the belief in the "fundamental equality of anything that appears to be human."

I believe these are mere empty words. This is not a "noble ideal" but something that, if taken absolutely, represents a logical absurdity; wherever this view becomes an established trend, it may usher in only regression and decadence.

Concerning the first point, the notion of "many" (i.e., a multiplicity of individual beings) logically contradicts the notion of "many equals." First of all, ontologically speaking, this is due to the so-called "principle of undiscernibles," which is expressed in these terms: "A being that is absolutely identical to another, under every regard, would be one and the same with it." Thus, in the concept of "many" is implicit the concept of their fundamental difference: "many" beings that are equal, completely equal, would not be *many*, but *one*. To uphold the equality of the many is a contradiction in terms, unless we refer to a body of soulless mass-produced objects.

Second, the contradiction lies in the "principle of sufficient reason," which is expressed in these terms: "For every thing there must be some reason why it is one thing and not another." Now, a being that is totally equal to another would lack "sufficient reason": it would be just a meaningless duplicate.

From both perspectives, it is rationally well established that the "many" not only *cannot* be equal, but they also *must not* be equal: inequality is true *de facto* only because it is true *de jure* and it is real only because it is necessary. That which the egalitarian ideology wished to portray as a state of "justice" is in reality a state of *injustice*, according to a perspective that is higher and beyond the humanitarian and democratic rhetorics. In the past, Cicero and Aristotle argued along these lines.

Conversely, to posit inequality means to transcend quantity and admit quality. It is here that the two notions of the *individual* and the *person* are differentiated. The individual may be conceived only as an atomic unit, or as a mere number in the reign of quantity; in absolute terms, it is a mere fiction and an abstraction. And yet it is possible to *lean* toward this solution, namely to minimize the differences characterizing the individual being, emphasizing mixed and uniform qualities (what ensues from this, through massification and standardization, is a uniformity of paths, rights, and freedoms) and conceiving this as an ideal and desirable condition. However, this means to degrade and to alter the course of nature.

For all practical purposes, the pure individual belongs to the inorganic rather than to the organic dimension. In reality, the law of progressive differentiation rules supreme. In virtue of this law, the lower degrees of reality are differentiated from the higher ones because in the lower degrees a whole can be broken down into many parts, all of which retain the same quality (as in the case of the parts of a noncrystallized mineral, or those parts of some plants and animals that reproduce themselves by parthenogenesis); in the higher degrees of reality this is no longer possible, as there is a higher *organic* unity in them that does not allow itself to be split without being compromised and without its parts entirely losing the quality, meaning, and function they had in it. Therefore the atomic, unrestricted *(solutus)*, "free" individual is under the aegis of inorganic matter, and belongs, analogically, to the lowest degrees of reality.[13]

An equality may exist on the plane of a mere social aggregate or of a primordial, almost animal-like promiscuity; moreover, it may be recognized wherever we consider not the individual but the overall dimension; not the person but the species; not the "form" but "matter" (in the Aristotelian sense of these two terms). I will not deny that there are in human beings some aspects under which they are approximately equal, and yet these aspects, in every normal and traditional view, represent not the "plus" but the "minus"; in other words, they correspond to the lowest degree of reality, and to that which is least interesting in every being. Again, these aspects fall into an order that is not yet that of "form," or of personality, in the proper sense. To value these aspects and to emphasize them as those that truly matter is the same as regarding as paramount the bronze found in many statues, rather than seeing each one as the expression of distinct ideas, to which bronze (in our case, the generic human quality) has supplied the working matter.

These references clarify what is truly a person and personal value, as opposed to the mere individual and the mere element belonging to a mass or to a social agglomerate. The person is an individual who is differentiated through his qualities, endowed with his own face, his *proper nature*, and a series of attributes that make him who he is and distinguish him from all others—in other words, attributes that make him fundamentally *unequal*. The person is a man in whom the general characteristics (beginning with that very general characteristic of being human, to that of belonging to a given race, nation, gender, and social group) assume a differentiated form of expression by articulating and variously individuating themselves.

Any vital, individual, social, or moral process that goes in this direction and leads to the fulfillment of the person according to his own nature is truly ascending. Conversely, to give emphasis and priority to that which in every being is equal signifies regression. The will to equality is one and the same with the will to what is formless. Every egalitarian ideology is the barometric index of a certain climate of degeneration, or the "trademark" of forces leading to a process of degeneration. Overall, this is how we should think about the "noble ideal" and the "immortal principle" of equality.

After establishing this first point, it is easy to recognize the errors and misunderstandings associated with other liberal and revolutionary principles.

To begin with, I find it odd that the title "natural right" has been given to that which appears to be the most unnatural thing conceivable, or to that which is proper to primitive societies. The principle according to which all human beings are free and enjoy equal rights "by nature" is truly absurd, due to the very fact that "by nature" they are not the same. Also, when we go to an order that is not merely naturalistic, being a "person" is neither a uniform quality or a quality uniformly distributed, nor a dignity equal in everybody, being automatically derived from the mere membership of the single individual in the biological species called "mankind." The "dignity of the human person," with everything that this expression entails, and around which the supporters of the doctrine of natural law and liberals rally, should be acknowledged where it truly exists, and not in everybody. And even where this dignity truly exists, it should not be regarded as equal in every instance. This dignity admits different degrees; thus, *justice* means to attribute to each and every one of these degrees a different right and a different freedom. The differentiation of right, and the hierarchical idea in general, derives from the very notion of a person, since this notion, as we have seen, is inconceivable without referring to the difference, to the form, and to the differentiating individuation. Without these presuppositions, the respect for the human person in general is only a superstition, or rather one of the many superstitions of our time. In the domain of the person there is nothing on which the idea of a universal right could be based, or of a right that, as the doctrine of natural law claims, is to be enjoyed by everyone without discrimination.[14] Anybody who has the conscience and the dignity of a "person" cannot help but feel offended when that which is supposed to be one's own law becomes a law binding everybody else (as is the case in Kant's categorical imperative). Conversely, ancient wisdom believed in the principle *suum cuique tribuere*, to each his own. According to Plato's view, too, the highest responsibility of the Guardians is to ensure that justice (understood in this sense) prevails.

Hence, the conundrum facing those who uphold the principle of "equality": equality can exist only among equals, namely among those who are objectively at the same level and who embody an analogous degree of "personhood," and whose freedom, right, and also responsibility are not the same as those characterizing other degrees, whether higher or lower. "Brotherhood," too, which was included among the so-called "immortal principles" as a sentimental complement to the other two abstract principles (freedom and equality), is subject to the same restrictions: it is insolent to impose it as a norm and universal duty in indiscriminate terms. In the past, precisely thanks to the acknowledgment of the hierarchical idea, "peers" and "equals" were often aristocratic concepts: in Sparta, the title *homoioi* ("equals") belonged exclusively to the elite in power (the title was revoked in cases of misconduct). We find an analogous idea in ancient Rome, among the Nordic peoples, and during the Carolingian and the Holy Roman Empire periods. Moreover, in the days of old, the title "peers" was attributed to English lords.

The same applies to freedom, the first term of the revolutionary triad. Freedom must be understood and defended in the same qualitative and differentiated manner as the notion of "person": everybody enjoys the freedom he deserves, which is measured by the stature and dignity of his person or by his function, and not by the abstract and elementary fact of merely being a "human being" or a "citizen" (as in the much acclaimed *droits de l'homme et du citoyen*). Thus, according to the Classical saying *libertas summis infimisque aequanda*, freedom ought to be equally distributed above and below. It has been rightly remarked that "there is not one freedom, but many freedoms. There is no general, abstract freedom, but there are articulated freedoms conformed to one's own nature. Man must not generate within himself the idea of a homogenous liberty, but rather that of the whole of such differentiated and qualified liberties."[15] The other freedom, which is upheld by libertarianism and by natural law, is a fiction just like the idea of "equality." Practically speaking, it is only a revolutionary weapon: freedom and equality are the catchwords certain social strata or groups employed in order to undermine other classes and to gain preeminence; having achieved this task, they were quickly set aside.

Again, in regard to freedom, it is important to distinguish between the freedom *to do* something and the freedom *for doing* something. In the political domain, the former is a negative freedom that corresponds to the absence of bonds while remaining itself formless. It generally culminates in arbitrariness and in anomie, and where it is granted to everybody, in an egalitarian and democratic fashion, it becomes an impossibility. Where there is equality there cannot be freedom: what exists is not pure freedom, but rather the many individual, domesticated, and mechanized freedoms, in a state of reciprocal limitation. Paradoxically, that kind of freedom could approximately be realized in the system that is most opposite to liberal preferences: namely, in the system in which the social question is resolved in such a way as to guarantee certain privileges for a small group, at the cost of the total subjugation of everybody else. If carried to its extreme consequences, the figure of a tyrant would then be the most perfect concretization of this concept or ideal of formless freedom.

The freedom for doing something that is connected to each one's own nature and specific function is quite another thing. This freedom mainly signifies the power to actualize one's potential and to achieve one's particular perfection within a given political or social context; it has a functional and organic character, and is inseparable from an immanent and unmistakable end. It is characterized by the Classical saying *"Be yourself,"* and thus by quality and by difference; this is the only true freedom, according to justice and to right. In the Classical view, as it was expressed by Aristotle, Plato, and Plotinus, the only institution conformed to justice is the one in which everybody has, does, and realizes what is proper to himself. Catholicism itself, during the golden age of Scholasticism (an age that is reviled today by progressive and liberal Catholics as "feudal" and "obscurantist"), upheld the same truth and ethics. The foundations of medieval Catholicism's social doctrine were the idea of "proper nature," which varies with every being; the freedom in terms of such nature as "willed by God"; and the adherence to one's condition within a socially organic and differentiated system. Luther, too, upheld this doctrine. More recently, Benedetto Croce has written about the modern "religion of freedom," though what he is referring to should rather be called the "fetishism of freedom."

In the same order of ideas, we should consider the vexed question whether man comes before society or vice versa, and which of the two is the ultimate goal. From the traditional point of view, this question is definitely resolved by upholding man's rather than society's primacy. Every "social" thesis is a deviation connected to the same leveling and regressive tendency that I have criticized before—so much so, that individualism and anarchism have undoubtedly their good reasons and a much less degrading character when seen as reactions against such regressive tendency. Everything that is social, in the best of hypotheses, falls in the order of means and not in the order of ends. Society as an entity in itself is but a fetish and a personified abstraction; in reality, the plane proper to society is entirely material, physical, and subordinated. "Society" and "collectivity" are synonyms; if we exclude the individualistic interpretation of society as a sum of atoms coming together on the basis of a hypothetical contract, we are left with the idea that society is just a background before which the person is the positive, primary, and real thing.

Moreover, there are cases in which I am willing to acknowledge the priority of the person even before the State. The statolatry of the modern age has nothing to do with the traditional political view; the impersonal State, when regarded as a heavy juridical and bureaucratic entity (e.g., Nietzsche's "cold monster"), is also an aberration. Every society and State is made of people; individual human beings are their primary element. What kind of human beings? Not people as they are conceived by individualism, as atoms or a mass of atoms, but people as persons, as differentiated beings, each one endowed with a different rank, a different freedom, a different right within the social hierarchy based on the values of creating, constructing, obeying, and commanding. With people such as these it is possible to establish the true State, namely an antiliberal, antidemocratic, and organic State. The idea behind such a State is the priority of the person over any abstract social, political, or juridical entity, and not of the person as a neuter, leveled reality, a mere number in the world of quantity and universal suffrage.

The perfection of the human being is the end to which every healthy social institution must be subordinated, and it must be promoted as much as possible. This perfection must be conceived on the basis of a process of individuation and of progressive differentiation. In this regard we must consider the view expressed by Paul de Lagarde, which can be expressed approximately in these terms: everything that is under the aegis of humanitarianism, the doctrine of natural law, and collectivity corresponds to the inferior dimension. Merely being a "man" is a *minus* compared to being a man belonging to a given nation and society; this, in turn, is still a *minus* compared to being a "person," a quality that implies the shift to a plane that is higher than the merely naturalistic and "social" one. In turn, being a person is something that needs to be further differentiated into degrees, functions, and dignities with which, beyond the social and horizontal plane, the properly political world is defined vertically in its bodies, functional classes, corporations, or particular unities, according to a pyramid-like structure, at the top of which one would expect to find people who more or less embody the *absolute person*. What is meant by "absolute person" is the supremely realized person who represents the end, and the natural center of gravity, of the whole system. The "absolute person" is obviously the opposite of the individual. The atomic, unqualified, socialized, or standardized unity to which the individual corresponds is opposed in the absolute person by the actual synthesis of the fundamental possibilities and by the full control of the powers inherent in the idea of man (in the limiting case), or of a man of a given race (in a more relative, specialized, and historical domain): that is, by an extreme individuation that corresponds to a de-individualization and to a certain universalization of the types corresponding to it. Thus, this is the disposition required to embody pure authority, to assume the symbol and the power of sovereignty, or the form from above, namely the *imperium*.

Going from humanity, through "society" or a collectivity based on natural law and the nation, and then proceeding in the political world all the way to a personality variously integrated, and finally to a dominating super-personality, means to ascend from lower degrees to degrees that are increasingly filled with "being" and value, each one the natural end of the previous one: this is how we should understand the principle according to which man is the end or the primary end of society, and not vice versa.

By way of example we may refer to the hierarchical place proper to the "nation" when it has a positive and constructive, rather than a revolutionary, meaning. "Nation" is a *plus* in regard to "humanity." Thus, it is a positive and legitimate thing to uphold the right of the nation in order to assert an elementary and natural principle of difference of a given human group over and against all the forms of individualistic disintegration, international mixture and proletarization, and especially against the mere world of the masses and pure economy. Having set this demarcation as a protective fence, it is necessary to actualize inside it further degrees of differentiation that need to be implemented in a system of bodies, of disciplines and hierarchies, in virtue of which the *State* is created out of the substance of the *nation*.

It should be noted that the above-mentioned hierarchical notion is based on, among other things, freedom understood in a further special and ethical sense. The freedom upheld by the antitraditional ideologies has an undifferentiated, nonfunctional and subversive character, as well as an external and almost "physical" one. These ideologies usually ignore the emancipation of the single individual, which consists of being not so much free in relation to an external situation, whether real or imaginary, and in relation to others, as in being free *toward oneself*, namely toward the naturalistic part of one's self. Usually every dignity within qualitative hierarchies should be legitimated with this kind of freedom, without love for which one could not call oneself a person. With this kind of assumption, the political domain interferes with the ethical one ("ethical" in the spiritual, rather than moralistic, sense of the term). In this context what will be paramount is the virile quality of him who, in the case of conflict between opposite needs, knows how to assert the right of given principles and a given law over that which belongs to the naturalistic and material realm, whether in his case or that of others. Thus, family bonds or special affections will not limit such a person, nor will he be guided by the mere notions of utility and well-being, even if these notions were defined in social and collective terms. The personality is realized and consolidated along the path of the special "asceticism" required by freedom understood in this way—namely, by inner freedom and control over oneself as a physical individual; likewise, the foundations of the hierarchical connections proper to that which can be rightly called "the natural right of heroic peoples" are not to be sought elsewhere.

The first of these foundations is that the measure of what one can demand from others is dictated by the measure of what one can demand from oneself; he who does not have the capability to dominate himself and to give himself a code to abide by would not know how to dominate others according to justice or how to give them a law to follow. The second foundation is the idea, previously upheld by Plato, that those who cannot be their own masters should find a master outside of themselves, since practicing the discipline of obeying should teach these people how to master their own selves; thus, through loyalty to those who present themselves as the representatives of an idea and as the living approximations to a higher human type, they will remain as faithful as possible to their best nature. This has always been recognized in a spontaneous, natural way, and has created in traditional civilizations a special fluid, the vital substance of the organic and hierarchical structures, long before people fell under the spell of the suggestions or shallow rationalism espoused by subversive ideologies. In normal conditions all this goes without saying; thus, it is absurd to say that the only way in which the highest degrees in the social hierarchy were able to retain control was to apply physical force, violence, and terror and that people obeyed only out of fear or servility, or for their self-serving purposes. To think so is to denigrate human nature even in its most humble representatives, and to suppose that the atrophy of every higher sensibility that characterizes most people in this final age has always and everywhere ruled supreme.

Superiority and power need to go hand in hand, as long as we remember that power is based on superiority and not vice versa, and that superiority is connected with qualities that have always been thought by most people to constitute the true foundation of what others attempt to explain in terms of brutal "natural selection." Ancient primitive man essentially obeyed not the strongest members of society, but those in whom he perceived a saturation of *mana* (i.e., a sacred energy and life force) and who, for this reason, seemed to him best qualified to perform activities usually precluded to others. An analogous situation occurs where certain men have been followed, obeyed, and venerated for displaying a high degree of endurance, responsibility, lucidity, and a dangerous, open, and heroic life that others could not; it was decisive here to be able to recognize a special right and a special dignity in a free way. To depend on such leaders constituted not the subjugation, but rather the elevation of the person; this, however, makes no sense to the defenders of the "immortal principles" and to the supporters of "human dignity" because of their obtuseness. It is only the presence of superior individuals that bestows on a multitude of beings and on a system of disciplines of material life a meaning and a justification they previously lacked. *It is the inferior who needs the superior, and not the other way around.*[16] The inferior never lives a fuller life than when he feels his existence is subsumed in a greater order endowed with a center; then he feels like a man standing before leaders of men, and experiences the pride of serving as a free man in his proper station. The noblest things that human nature has to offer are found in similar situations, and not in the anodyne and shallow climate proper to democratic and social ideologies.

We should note in passing the irrationalism of the so-called utilitarian sociology, which could have been valued only in a society of merchants: in this doctrine, the "useful" is regarded as the positive foundation of every sociopolitical institution. However, there is hardly anything more relative than the concept of "useful." "Useful" for what? In view of what? For if utility is restricted to its coarsest, most materialistic, calculating, and petty form, we must say that, whether for better or for worse, human beings rarely think and act by following the "useful," understood in this narrow sense. Everything that has an emotional or irrational motivation has and will play a larger role in human conduct than that played by petty utility; if we did not acknowledge this fact, a great part of human history would be unintelligible. Among this order of non-utilitarian motivations (all of which lead man beyond himself), there is certainly a class that reflects higher possibilities, a certain generosity and a certain elementary heroic disposition; the above-mentioned forms of natural acknowledgment animating and sustaining every true hierarchical structure are derived from them. In these structures, authority as power may also play a part or, more specifically, it must have one. Thus, we can agree with Machiavelli's saying that where one is not loved one should at least be feared (feared, not *hated*). It is a distortion to begin from a mutilated and degraded image of man in general and believe that in all the historical hierarchies, other than strength, the principle of superiority and the direct and proud acknowledgment of the superior by the inferior did not play a relevant part.[17] Burke's saying that every political system that presupposes the existence of heroic virtues and of higher dispositions leads to vice and corruption is not so much an index of cynicism, but instead of short-sightedness about knowledge of the human species.

The higher and more genuine legitimization of a true *political* order, and thus of the State itself, lies in its *anagogical* function: namely, in arousing and nourishing the individual's disposition to act and to think, to live, to struggle, and eventually to sacrifice himself for something that goes beyond his mere individuality. This disposition is so real that it is possible not only to implement it, but also to abuse it; thus, alongside currents in which the single individual is led beyond himself by something that is spiritual and metaphysical (as was the case in all the major traditional forms), we can see other currents in which a demonic element is responsible for promoting an individual's ecstasies (i.e., the experience of being "outside one's self"). What is at work here is not an anagogic power, but rather a catagogic power—namely, the power that acts in the revolutionary phenomenon and is concretized in every collectivist ideology. In both cases, a sociology adopting utilitarian and individualistic perspectives is refuted; it proves to be merely a sophisticated and intellectual construction, especially when we consider human nature in its reality and concreteness.

The progress of one form of human organization over another is not measured by the fact that in it things are materially and socially fine and that the materialistic need of utility is satisfied to a higher degree; rather, progress is measured by the degree to which certain interests and criteria of evaluation have become differentiated and predominant in it. These criteria should rise above the mediocre concept of "utility," which happens to be the only perspective adopted by positivist sociology.

Coming back to liberalism, I wish to say that it represents the antithesis of every organic doctrine. Since according to liberalism the primary element is the human being regarded not as person, but rather as an individual living in a formless freedom, this philosophy is able to conceive society merely as a mechanical interplay of forces and entities acting and reacting to each other, according to the space they succeed in gaining for themselves, without the overall system reflecting any higher law of order or meaning. The only law, and thus the only State, that liberalism can conceive has therefore an extrinsic character in regard to its subjects. Power is entrusted to the State by sovereign individuals, so that it may safeguard the freedoms of the individuals and intervene only when these freedoms clash and prove dangerous to one another. Thus, order appears as a limitation and a regulation of freedoms, rather than as a form that freedom itself expresses from within, as freedom to do something, or as freedom connected to a quality and a specific function. Order, namely the legal order, eventually amounts to an act of violence because, practically speaking, in a liberal and democratic regime a government is defined in terms of a majority; thus, the minority, though composed of "free individuals," must bow and obey.

The specter that most terrifies liberalism today is totalitarianism. It can be said that totalitarianism may arise as a borderline case out of the presuppositions of liberalism, rather than out of those of an organic State. As we shall see, in totalitarianism we have the accentuation of the concept of order uniformly imposed from the outside onto a mass of mere individuals who, lacking their own form and law, must receive one from the outside, be introduced in a mechanical, all-inclusive system, and avoid the disorder typical of a disorganized and selfish expression of partisan forces and special-interest groups.

Events have recently led toward a similar solution, after the more or less idyllic view proper to the euphoric phase of liberalism and of laissez-faire economy has turned out to be simply a fancy. I am referring here to the view according to which a satisfactory social and economic equilibrium allegedly arises out of the conflict of particular interests: almost as if a preestablished harmony à la Leibniz would take care of ordering everything for the better, even when the single individual cares only for himself and is freed from every bond.

Thus, not only ideally, but historically too, liberalism and individualism are at the beginning and at the origin of the various interconnected forms of modern subversion. The person who becomes an individual, by ceasing to have an organic meaning and by refusing to acknowledge any principle of authority, is nothing more than a number, a unit in the pack; his usurpation evokes a fatal collectivist limitation against himself. Therefore, we go from liberalism to democracy: and then from democracy to socialist forms that are increasingly inclined toward collectivism. For a long time Marxist historiography has clearly recognized this pattern: it has recognized that the liberal revolution, or the revolution of the Third Estate, opened a breach and contributed to erode the previous traditional sociopolitical world and to pave the way to the socialist and communist revolution; in turn, the representatives of this revolution will leave the rhetorics of the "immortal principles" and the "noble and generous ideas" to naive and deluded people. Since every fall is characterized by an accelerated motion, it is not possible to stop halfway. Within the system of the predominant ideologies in the West, liberalism, having absolved its preliminary task of disintegration and disorganization, has quickly been set aside—thus, the claim of some of its contemporary epigones to be able to contain Marxism, which represents the last link in the chain of causes, rings hollow indeed and is indicative of lack of wisdom. There is a saying from Tacitus that summarizes in lapidary style what has happened since the "liberal revolution": *Ut imperium evertant, libertatem praeferunt; si perventerint, liberatem ipsam adgredientur* [18]—that is, "in order to overthrow the State (in its authority and sovereignty: i.e., *imperium*) they uphold freedom; once they succeed, they will turn against it too." Plato said: "Probably, then, tyranny develops out of no other constitution than democracy—from the height of liberty, I take it, the fiercest extreme of servitude." [19] Liberalism and individualism played merely the role of instruments in the overall plan of world subversion, to which they opened the dams.

Thus, it is of paramount importance to recognize the continuity of the current that has generated the various political, antitraditional forms that are today at work in the chaos of political parties: liberalism, constitutionalism, parliamentary democracy, socialism, radicalism, and finally communism and Sovietism have emerged in history as degrees or as interconnected stages of the same disease. Without the French Revolution and liberalism, constitutionalism and democracy would not have existed; without democracy and the corresponding bourgeois and capitalist civilization of the Third Estate, socialism and demagogic nationalism would not have arisen; without the groundwork laid by socialism, we would not have witnessed the advent of radicalism and of communism in both its national and proletarian-international versions. The fact that today these forms often appear either to coexist or to be in competition with each other should not prevent a keen eye from noting that they sustain, link, and mutually condition each other, being only the expression of different degrees of the same subversion of every normal and legitimate institution. It necessarily follows that, when these forms clash, the one that will prevail will be the most extreme, or the one located on the lowest step. The beginning of the process is to be traced to the time when Western man broke the ties to Tradition, claiming for himself as an individual a vain and illusory freedom: when he became an atom in society, rejecting every higher symbol of authority and sovereignty in a system of hierarchies. The "totalitarian" forms that are emerging are a demonic and materialistic counterfeit of the previous unitary political ideal, and they represent "the greatest and most savage slavery," which, according to Plato, arose out of formless "freedom."

Economic liberalism, which engendered various forms of capitalist exploitation and of cynical, antisocial plutocracy, is one of the final consequences of the intellectual emancipation that made the individual *solutus*—that is, lacking the inner, self-imposed bond, function, and limit that are found instead in every organic system's general climate and natural hierarchy of values. Moreover, we know that in more recent times, political liberalism has become little more than a system at the service of laissez-faire—namely, economic liberalism—in the context of a capitalist-plutocratic civilization; from this situation new reactions arose, pushing everything lower and lower, to the level of Marxism.

The above-mentioned connections are also visible in the special sector of property and wealth, especially when we consider the meaning of the change that occurred within it, following the institutions created by the French Revolution. By denouncing everything in the economic world that was still inspired by the feudal ideal as a cruel regime based on privileges, the organic connection (displayed mainly in various feudal systems) between personality and property, social function and wealth, and between a given qualification or moral nobility and the rightful and legitimate possession of goods, was broken. It was the Napoleonic Code that made "property" neutral and "private" in the inferior and individualistic sense of the word; with this code, property ceased to have a political function and bond. Moreover, property was no longer subject to an "eminent right," nor tied to a specific responsibility and social rank and subject to a "higher right." In this context, rank signified the objective and normal consecration in a hierarchical system that the superior one, as well as the personality formed and differentiated by a supra-individual tradition and idea, receives. Property, and wealth in general, no longer had any duties before the State other than in fiscal terms. The subject of property was the pure and simple "citizen," whose dominant concern was to exploit the property without any scruples and without too much regard for those traditions of blood, family, and folk that had previously been a relevant counterpart of property and wealth.[20]

It was only natural that in the end the right to private property came to be disputed; whenever there is no higher legitimization of ownership, it is always possible to wonder why some people have property and others do not, or why some people have earned for themselves privileges and social preeminence (often greater than those in feudal systems), while lacking something that would make them stand out and above everybody else in an effective and sensible manner. Thus the so-called "social question," together with the worn-out slogan "social justice," arose in those conditions where no differentiation is any longer visible other than in terms of mere "economic classes" (wealth and property having become "neutral" and apolitical; every value of difference and rank, of personality and authority having been rejected or undermined by processes of degeneration and materialization; the political sphere having been deprived of its original dignity). Thus, subversive ideologies have successfully and easily unmasked all the political myths that capitalism and the bourgeoisie have employed, in the absence of any superior principle, in order to defend their privileged status against the push and final violation by the forces from below.

Again, we can see that the various aspects of the contemporary social and political chaos are interrelated and there is no real way to effectively oppose them other than by returning to the origins. To go back to the origins means, plainly and simply, to reject everything that in any domain (whether social, political, or economic) is connected to the "immortal principles" of 1789, as a libertarian, individualistic, and egalitarian thought, and to oppose it with the hierarchical view, in the context of which alone the notion, value, and freedom of man as *person* are not reduced to mere words or excuses for a work of destruction and subversion.

Four

ORGANIC STATE
TOTALITARIANISM

One of the catchphrases that have become a rallying cry in the intellectual confusion of our contemporaries is *antitotalitarianism*. This catchphrase is employed mostly by democracies; the reference point that is upheld is basically the confused and formless view of the individual's freedom that I have criticized in the previous chapter. In this formula many different things are lumped together, as is shown by the distinction, expressed in very primitive terms, between a "right-wing" and a "left-wing" totalitarianism. But in the above-mentioned currents, it is clear that quite often "totalitarianism" is only a pretext. Just as communists and socialists find it useful and agreeable to brand anybody and anything that does not agree with their ideology with the label of "fascism," likewise the confusion about totalitarianism is employed in a tactical fashion by various parties in democratic regimes, and is exploited in order to try to discredit and to portray the traditional view of the true State in a heinous way.

In order to put an end to this misunderstanding, it will be helpful to introduce a fundamental distinction between the *totalitarian State* and the *organic State*. In regard to the terminology I have adopted, I want my readers to know that it is not in order to make concessions to my opponents that I have refrained from categorizing the traditional political view that I uphold as "totalitarian." In this regard, I am already vindicated by the fact that *totalitarianism* is a recent and rather modern term, and as such it is inseparably connected to the situation of a world that in no way, shape, or form should be employed as a reference point. Therefore, it is better to let the word *totalitarianism* designate what the representatives of democracy mean by it, applying instead to the idea of "organic State" whatever positive meaning may be found, despite everything, in totalitarianism (understood in a general fashion). In this way both concepts will be defined and contrasted with each other in a sufficiently clear manner.

The idea of the organic State was not born yesterday. This needs to be recalled both for those who have forgotten it and for those whose intellectual horizons are restricted to the polemics between "fascism" and "antifascism," as if nothing else ever existed previously in history. The idea of the organic State is a traditional one, and thus we can say that every true State has always had a certain organic character. A State is organic when it has a center, and this center is an idea that shapes the various domains of life in an efficacious way; it is organic when it ignores the division and the autonomization of the particular and when, by virtue of a system of hierarchical participation, every part within its relative autonomy performs its own function and enjoys an intimate connection with the whole. In an organic State we can speak of a "whole"—namely, something integral and spiritually unitary that articulates and unfolds itself— rather than a sum of elements within an aggregate, characterized by a disorderly clash of interests. The States that developed in the geographical areas of the great civilizations (whether they were empires, monarchies, aristocratic republics, or city-states) at their peak were almost without exception of this type. A central idea, a symbol of sovereignty with a corresponding, positive principle of authority was their foundation and animating force. Almost as if thanks to a spontaneous gravitation, men and social bodies found themselves working in synergy; though they retained their autonomy, they undertook activities that converged toward the same fundamental direction. Even contrasts and antitheses had their part in the economy of the whole; as they did not have the character of disorderly parts, they did not question the super-ordained unity of the organism, but rather acted as a dynamic and vivifying factor. Even the "opposition" of the early British parliamentary system was able to reflect a similar meaning (it was called "His Majesty's most loyal opposition"), though it disappeared in the later party-ruled parliamentary regime.

Reading G. B. Vico and Fustel de Coulanges helps us to realize the power that the organic ideal had in antiquity. The main thing that emerges in ancient forms is that unity in them did not possess a merely political character, but rather a spiritual and quite often religious one, the political domain apparently being shaped and upheld by an idea or a general view that was also articulated in thought, law, art, customs, cult, and the form of the economy. A unitary spirit was manifested in a choral variety of forms, corresponding to the various possibilities of human existence; in this context, *organic* and *traditional* are more or less synonymous terms. The *spirituality* of the whole was that which occasioned the *integration* of the particular, rather than its compression and coercion. A relative pluralism and decentralization are essential features in every organic system. The criterion for this decentralization is that it can be accentuated in proportion to the degree to which the center enjoys a spiritual and even transcendent character, a sovereign equilibrating power, and a natural prestige.

An objective observer cannot help but find it odd that all these things have been entirely forgotten, despite the fact that not long ago, before the advent in Europe of liberalism, individualism, and revolutions, there were political systems that reflected in a sensible way some aspects of the organic idea, and these systems appeared entirely normal and legitimate in the eyes of most people. But this is also the reason for the aforementioned confusion about totalitarianism, and for the fact that, displaying a bovine obtuseness and playing into the hands of the communists, the Italian people these days repeatedly view and denounce as "fascism" any system different from those glorified by the apostles of democracy and the "immortal principles."

However, totalitarianism merely represents the counterfeited image of the organic ideal. It is a system in which unity is imposed from the outside, not on the basis of the intrinsic force of a common idea and an authority that is naturally acknowledged, but rather through direct forms of intervention and control, exercised by a power that is exclusively and materially political, imposing itself as the ultimate reason for the system. Moreover, in totalitarianism we usually find a tendency toward uniformity and intolerance for any partial form of autonomy and any degree of freedom, for any intermediate body between the center and the periphery, between the peak and the bottom of the social pyramid. More specifically, totalitarianism engenders a kind of sclerosis, or a monstrous hypertrophy of the entire bureaucratic-administrative structure. These structures become all-pervasive, replacing and suppressing every particular activity, without any restraints, due to an insolent intrusion of the public sphere into the private domain, organizing everything into rigid schemes; these schemes eventually turn out to be meaningless because, starting from a formless center of power, what eventually arises is a sort of intrinsic and gloomy enjoyment of this relentless leveling process. Concerning the most materialistic aspect—namely, that of the economy (which has gained preeminence in this "era of economics")—super-organization, centralization, and rationalization play an essential part in this rigid and mechanical type of unity.

Though this type of unity has become predominant in the contemporary era, it was foreshadowed in various places and in other ages, although always in the terminal and twilight phases of a given cycle of civilization. Among the most notable examples we may recall the forms of bureaucratic-governmental centralization that developed during the decline of the Roman, Byzantine, and Persian Empires; what ensued was eventually a definitive dissolution.

Examples of this sort indicate the proper locus and meaning of "totalitarian" centralizations: they follow the crisis and the dissolution of previous unities of an organic nature, and the dissolution and turning loose of forces that were previously united by an idea in a differentiated civilization and in a living tradition. These forces are now mastered and brought together in a violent and extrinsic manner within an order, without any characteristic of true, recognized authority, and without anything connecting the single individuals from within.

In the previous chapter I have suggested that totalitarian or semi-totalitarian systems often arise as an unavoidable reaction against the libertarian-individualistic disintegration. In other times, all this was reduced to the final, short-lived reactions of an already doomed and senescent political organism. In the modern world, due to the predominance of materialistic, economic, and technological factors, this phenomenon may enjoy a certain stability (e.g., communism in the USSR), though the meaning remains the same.

In fact, the best image to illustrate these processes is the analogy with living organisms: after enjoying life and movement, a stiffening sets in when they die that is typical of a body turning into a corpse. This state, in turn, is followed by the terminal phase of disintegration. Thus, in these totalitarian systems we may note two processes that, though they appear to run toward opposite directions, eventually converge into one and the same effect, and up to a point even permeate each other. Totalitarianism, though it reacts against individualism and social atomism, brings a final end to the devastation of what may still survive in a society from the previous "organic" phase: quality, articulated forms, castes and classes, the values of personality, true freedom, daring and responsible initiative, and heroic feats. An organism of a superior type includes multiple functions retaining their specific character and a relative autonomy, all the while mutually coordinating and integrating each other, converging into a superior unity that never ceases to be ideally presupposed. Thus, in an organic State we find both unity and multiplicity, gradation and hierarchy; we do not find the dualism of center and formless mass typical of a totalitarian regime. Totalitarianism, in order to assert itself, imposes uniformity. In the final analysis, totalitarianism rests and relies on the inorganic world of quantity to which individualistic disintegration has led, and not on the world of quality and of personality. In such a system, the authoritarianism we encounter is such as we may expect from a drill instructor or a pedagogue wielding a whip, if I may use an image dear to Toynbee. The attitudes that totalitarianism requires are: obedience, even though such obedience does not amount to acknowledgment and adhesion; conformism; and irrational forms of aggregation, among which it is possible to detect a fanatical, sinister, and blind capability of sacrifice. The whole system has an undefined character because it lacks a true authority; moreover, there is a lack of true commitment among people living in a totalitarian society; a lack of the sense of responsibility; and a lack of the dignity of free beings who acknowledge this authority and arrange themselves in one efficient formation. In this perspective, totalitarianism is a school of servility and a pejorative extension of collectivism: it acts not as an influence from above, capable of leading and unifying people, but rather as a formless power that has become crystallized in a center, in order to absorb, bend, mechanize, control, and impose uniformity on the rest of society.

In these terms, two perspectives stand most visibly in irreducible antithesis: an antithesis that first of all must be understood as that of the *spirits* animating the two systems.

This must be taken into account in regard to those special situations of an economic order that require a strengthened coordinating intervention, regulating the central powers, as happened recently. Even in these circumstances (in which, due to a congestion of forces and to a complexity of factors that are likewise difficult to control, the "managerial" mania must be assigned a relevant role) it is possible to retain the organic ideal as the shaping principle, in opposition to every totalitarianism; this will be shown later when I discuss the idea of corporatism.

I wish to make one more comment in regard to the terminology used. *Statolatry* and *statism* are two expressions that have been recently used with polemical intent, as in the case of the term *totalitarianism*. Polemical remarks are pointless when aimed at criticizing the preeminence that legitimately belongs to the political principle of the State over "society," "people," "national community," and, in general, over the entire economic and physical dimension of any human organization. To refuse to acknowledge this preeminence amounts to denying that very principle in its proper reality and function, in contrast to what appears to be a constant element in traditional thought. Thus, there is no need to employ the neologism "statism" (which has a negative connotation) in order to describe the aforementioned preeminence.

As far as the term *statolatry* is concerned, it is necessary to examine the effective basis of the two fundamental principles of *imperium* and *auctoritas*. There is a profound and substantial difference between the deification and absolutization of what is profane and the case in which the political reality derives its legitimization from reference points that are also spiritual and somehow transcendent. There is usurpation and fetishism in the former instance but not in the latter; only in the former instance it is legitimate to talk about "State worship." State worship falls in the same context of totalitarianism; its limit is the theology or the mysticism of the omnipotent totalitarian State, having as its background the new earthly religion of materialism.

Conversely, the organic view presupposes something "transcendent" or "from above" as the basis of authority and command, without which there would automatically be no immaterial and substantial connections of the parts with the center; no inner order of single freedoms; no immanence of a general law that guides and sustains people without coercing them; and no supra-individual disposition of the particular, without which every decentralization and articulation would eventually pose a danger for the unity of the whole system.

I must admit that nowadays, considering the climate of general materialization and desacralization, it is not easy to indicate solutions conforming to the latter perspective. But the fact remains that even in the modern political reality there are still remarkable residues that would be entirely absurd without a similar frame of reference. This is the case, for instance, with an *oath*. An oath transcends the categories of the profane and secular world. And yet we see that even in the modern, democratic, republican, and secular States there is the requirement and even the obligation to take an oath: as in the situation, for example, of judges, cabinet ministers, and even members of the armed forces. This is indeed absurd or even sacrilegious when the State, in one way or another, does not embody a spiritual principle: an oath in such a case would be an instance of State worship. Where the meaning of what an oath is all about has been completely lost, how can one be willing or required to swear such an oath, if the State is nothing more than what modern "enlightened" ideologies claim it to be? A mere secular authority—*weltliche Obrigkeit*, to employ a Lutheran expression—as such has no right to require an oath, no matter what the circumstances. Conversely, we find oaths to be a normal and legitimate essential element in the political organization of an organic and traditional type; an example is found with the oath of loyalty, which was regarded as a true sacrament, the *sacramentum fidelitatis*, in the feudal world. In Christianity, this type of oath represented the most terrible of all oaths: in the words of a historian, "it made martyrs out of those who gave their lives in order to remain faithful to it, just as it damned those who violated it."

This is not without relation to a second point. In the communitarian and democratic views, we find the recurrent idea of sacrifice and of service; "altruism," the subordination and sacrifice of the single individual for the common good, all play a role in these views. Again, in this we have yet another instance of statolatry or at least of "sociolatry" or, in any event, of fetishism. We must ask what meaning these appeals have in the context of an organization, when its foundation is assumedly "positivist" and contractual. True, there are also forms of the capability to sacrifice oneself that are instinctive, heedless, irrational; sometimes we even find this capability among animals. A classic example of this instinctive and naturalistic type is the sacrifice of a mother for her children. However, these are dispositions that fall short of the sphere in which the concept of "person" is defined, and thus of the political sphere in its proper sense. Hofler has explained through an adequate comparison how things exist within this context: imagine a corporation, he writes, that truly represents a communion of interests on a purely contractual basis. In this type of organization (i.e., a corporation), to expect one of the stockholders to sacrifice himself to any degree for the common good and, worse yet, in favor of another stockholder would be regarded as absurd. This is because the foundation and the only sufficient reason of the system is the utilitarian interest of the single individual.

However, things are just the same in a society or in a State lacking any spiritual consecration or a transcendent dimension: when in such a State appeals are made to act according to a principle other than a pure individual selfish interest, or subjective, affective or emotional motifs, they can only be a manifestation of fetishism, statolatry, or sociolatry. It is useless to employ surrogates such as the "Ethical State" (Hegel), with their confused dialectical identifications of the individual with the universal; these are just speculative games, since the whole is perceived through "secular" and "humanistic" lenses. Those who gain no comfort in empty words find no serious foundation in concepts like "immanent ethics" and "ethics based on the universal"; rather, they see in them a rhetoric in support of the system. Such people are also aware that this rhetoric or mysticism, when it develops into a coherent totalitarian system, is not as efficient as a well-designed system based on terror: in that case, everybody knows what he is dealing with—the fact that the "idealist" mythology created around innerly desacralized political forms is done away with can even be regarded as a purifying and realistic measure.

Last but not least I wish to make a few comments about a formula that is often associated with totalitarianism in the polemics of a democracy: the *one-party system*. Fascism claimed that the State was the only party "governing the country in a totalitarian fashion." This is an unhappy or hybrid formula, to say the least, and it is a residue of the partisan-parliamentary view, though an instance of a higher order is also present within it.

Strictly speaking, *party* means faction. In that case, "one party" is either a contradictory or an aberrant notion, almost as if a faction wished to be the whole or dominate the entire system. Practically speaking, the notion of "party" belongs to parliamentary democracies, and it signifies an organization that defends a given ideology against other ideologies upheld by other groups, to which the system recognizes the same right and the same legitimacy. In these terms, the "one-party system" is that which, in one way or another, whether "democratically" or through the use of violence, succeeds in gaining control of the State and, once in a position of power, no longer tolerates other parties, using the State as a tool and imposing its particular ideology on the nation.

In these terms, the idea of "one party" is doubtless problematic. But even in this example our opponents make sweeping generalizations: they do not consider the case of developments through which such negative and contradictory aspects may be rectified and a shift adopted from one system to another. Their criticism loses its weight where, instead of "party" we speak simply of a minority: since the idea that a group of people should control the State, not as a party, but as a minority or political elite, is something perfectly legitimate, if not a necessity for every political regime. So we must say that a party that becomes the "one and only party" should cease to be a "party" *de facto*. Then its representatives, or at least its most qualified ones, should present themselves and rule as some sort of Order, or as a specifically political class, not creating a State within the State, but rather protecting and strengthening the State's key positions; not defending their particular ideology, but rather embodying in an impersonal manner the very pure idea of the State. The specific character of this type of upheaval should be expressed not with the formula of the "one party," but rather with that of the antipartisan and organic State. This would mark the return to a traditional type of State, following a period of interregnum and transitional political forms.

Five

BONAPARTISM
MACHIAVELLIANISM
ELITISM

R. Michels and J. Burnham are responsible for coining the term *Bonapartism*, designating a particular category of the modern political world. These authors suggest that the phenomenon of Bonapartism is a consequence that the democratic principle of popular representation (namely, the political criterion of majority and of the brute masses) may generate in given circumstances. In his *Political Parties: A Sociological Study of the Oligarchical Tendencies of Modern Democracy* (1915), Michels indicated both the technical and the psychological causes through which the iron law of oligarchies is reaffirmed even in the context of a system of democratic representation. It cannot be helped that, despite the formal institutions and the democratic doctrines, the effective power in democracies themselves ends up in the hands of a minority, or of a small group that will become more or less independent from the masses after gaining power. The only distinctive feature lies in the idea that this oligarchy, in such a case, allegedly represents the "people" and expresses its "will"; this is what the famous formula of "the government of the people" amounts to. However, this turns out to be pure fiction and a myth when developments lead to so-called Bonapartism.

The two above-mentioned sociologists suggest that once the principle of representation is legitimized, Bonapartism may be regarded as the extreme consequence, rather than the antithesis of democracy. Bonapartism represents a despotism based on a democratic view, which it denies *de facto* while fulfilling it in theory. Further on I will point out the ambiguity that derives from this in relation to the figure and the type of the leaders.

Burnham, in his *The Machiavellians*, has correctly identified Bonapartism as a general tendency of our modern age: in this trend new forms of government emerge in which a small number of rulers or a leader pretend to represent the people and to speak and to act on behalf of them. And since he personifies the will of the people, which is conceived as the political *ultima ratio*, the leader ends up claiming for himself an unlimited authority and regarding all the intermediate political bodies and all the branches of government as completely dependent on the central power, which alone is believed to legitimately represent the people. Regimes of this type are often legalized democratically through the technique of the plebiscite: once this happens, the formula of the people's self-government or similar formulas (e.g., "the will of the nation," "the dictatorship of the proletariat," and "the will of the Revolution") are employed to destroy or ultimately to restrict those individual rights and those particular freedoms that were originally associated with the idea of democracy. Thus, Burnham noted that, theoretically speaking, the Bonapartist leader may be considered the perfect embodiment of the democratic type; in his despotism, it is as if the omnipotent people led and disciplined themselves. Modern autocracies are created at the sound of the hymns to the "workers," to the "people," or to the "nation." Thus, according to Burnham, the "century of the people," the "People's State," the "classless society," and "National Socialism" are euphemisms or cover-ups, the only and real meaning of which is the "century of Bonapartism." It is rather evident that, when the trend gains momentum and the political structures are stabilized, totalitarianism is the direct and final result.

The historical antecedents of Bonapartism are well known: the popular tyrannies that arose in ancient Greece after the decline of previous aristocratic regimes; the tribunes of the people in ancient Rome; various princes and even *condottieri* (i.e., leaders of mercenary troops in the fourteenth through fifteenth centuries) who lived at the time of the Renaissance. In all of these cases we find an authority and a power lacking any higher consecration. This is more evident in the modern forms, in which the leaders pretend, more than in the previous forms, to speak and to act exclusively in the name of the people or of the collectivity, even when the practical result is an authentic despotism and a regime based on terror.

Otto Weininger described the figure of the great politician as one who is a despot and at the same time a worshiper of the people, or simultaneously a pimp and a whore, which is something people instinctively perceive. Though it is certainly wrong to apply such a view to every type of political leader, it nevertheless captures the essence of Bonapartism. What occurs here is an inversion of polarity: the leader has a value only by relating to the collective group, to the masses, establishing with them—namely, with the lower end of society—an essential relationship. This is why, despite all, or should I say, precisely because of it, we are still within the boundaries of "democracy." While the traditional view of sovereignty and authority is characterized by the *distance* from the people, and the feeling of distance induces in the inferiors a sense of veneration, a natural respect and disposition to obedience and loyalty toward the leaders, in the phenomenon I am describing the opposite is true: what we find instead is the abolition of, and even an intolerance for, any distance. The Bonapartist leader is and cares to be regarded as a "son of the people," even when the reality is different. He ignores the traditional principle according to which the wider the base is, the higher the pinnacle should be. He is enslaved to the complex of "popularity": thus, he attends all those rallies from which he may derive the feeling, illusory though it may be, that the people follow and approve him. In this case, it is the superior that needs the inferior, instead of the other way around. Of course, there is a counterpart to this: at least during the phase when he rises to power, the prestige of the Bonapartist leader depends on the fact that the masses perceive him to be close to them or as "one of us." In a similar situation the "anagogic" power (i.e., drawing upward), which is the essence and the reason for existence in every true hierarchical system, is excluded *a priori*. So what we are left with is what Weininger described with a crude expression: mutual prostitution.

To clarify this point we should recall that any power, in order to last, always needs the support of the foundation, which is constituted by a collective feeling; whether directly or indirectly, it needs to win certain social strata over to its side. But in the above-mentioned situation, things are otherwise. Various faculties of the human being react to political phenomena according to the nature of what we may call the corresponding "center of crystallization." In other words, here as elsewhere, what matters is the law of elective affinities, which may be formulated in this manner: "Like awakens like; like attracts like; like rejoins like." The nature of the principle on which the *auctoritas* is based is very important, and acts as the test of the elective affinities and as a determinant factor in the process of crystallization. The process has an anagogic character and causes the integration of the individual when the center of the system, or its fundamental symbol, is such that it appeals to the higher faculties and possibilities of the human being and awakens and moves these faculties, acting as a reference point for them, in the adhesion and in the acknowledgment of the collectivity. Thus, there is a substantial difference between the adhesion on which a political system of a warrior, heroic, or feudal type is based (the foundation of which is both sacred and spiritual) and the adhesion found in movements led by a tribune of the people, a dictator, or a "Bonapartist" leader. In the latter case, which I regard as negative, the leader appeals to the lowest and almost pre-personal levels of human beings, flatters them, manipulates them, and makes sure that any higher sensibility is stifled by them. This is also a reason that the leader presents himself in a democratic manner as a "son of the people," and not as the embodiment of a higher humanity and the bearer of a higher principle. Thus, this phenomenon has a regressive character, insofar as the values of the personality are concerned. The single individual in these collective movements or systems is restricted not so much in this or that exterior freedom (which is, after all, of little consequence) but rather in the inner freedom—the ability to free himself from his lowest instincts, which, as I have said, the general climate tends to foster, elevate, and flatter.

We should also note the relevant difference that exists whenever an acknowledgment is obtained and a certain prestige is acquired through promising or demanding. In the lowest, modern forms of democracy, we exclusively find the first: the prestige of the leaders is consolidated not so much on the basis of a high ideal tension (as was the case in the early forms of Bonapartism, which had a partially revolutionary and partially military character), but rather on the basis of "social" or "economic" promises, of factors and myths appealing to the purely physical aspect of the *demos*. This happens not only with the Marxist leaders in "left-wing totalitarianism"; various solutions of the "social question," materialistically considered, are one of the fundamental ingredients in the modern techniques employed by popular leaders in general, which is something that suffices to qualify the level and moral stature of such leaders.

The notion of *dictatorship* is usually associated with totalitarianism and Bonapartism. In this way we are led to consider the mistake incurred by some views that strive to be antidemocratic but nonetheless have only a very distorted understanding of aristocracy. According to traditional thought, it is necessary to distinguish clearly between the symbol, the function, and the principle, on the one hand, and man as an individual, on the other hand; starting from this premise, what matters is that a man be valued and recognized in terms of the idea and the principle he upholds, and not vice versa. In the situation of the dictator and the tribune of the people, we have the other alternative, that of a power leaning only on a person and on his action upon the irrational forms of the masses.

In the last century, under the influence of evolutionism, some views of aristocracy and the elites emerged that were based on "natural selection"; these views were plagued by a major misunderstanding of what was typical of ancient hierarchical societies, as even a purely historical investigation has shown. Later, what emerged was the romantic-bourgeois theory of "hero worship," compounded by the most problematic aspects of Nietzsche's theory of the *Übermensch*. With all this, we are still in the domain of forms of individualism and naturalism that are unable to formulate any doctrine of true, legitimate authority. And yet most people, even when they admit the notion of aristocracy in principle, ultimately settle for a very limited view of it: they admire an individual for being exceptional and brilliant, instead of for being one in whom a tradition and a special "spiritual race" shine forth, or instead of whose greatness is due not to his human virtues, but rather to the principle, the idea, and a certain regal impersonality that he embodies.

The Machiavellian model of the "prince" and its derivatives are confined to the plane of individualism. Machiavelli's "prince" does not lower himself as far as the leaders of modern demagogy and democracy: naturally, he does not believe in the "people" and does not care to become acquainted with the passions and elementary reactions of the masses in order to use them to his advantage and to exercise an adequate method of governing. However, his authority no longer comes "from above": its foundation is mere strength, which is the *virtus* of the prince. Power, as pure power of a man, is the ultimate end; everything else, spiritual and religious factors included, is only a means to be employed without any scruples. An intrinsic superiority does not come into play at all: Machiavellianism cares only for political *skills*, combined with individual gifts of shrewdness and strength (the well-known image Machiavelli employs is that of a breed between a fox and a lion). Here the leader does not consider the higher faculties that can be reawakened, in certain conditions, in his subjects; he harbors contempt and a fundamental pessimism toward people in general, on the basis of an alleged political "realism." This prevents the Machiavellian despot from prostituting himself: he is far from being a dupe of the means that he employs in order to gain power or to retain it. Deceit, lies, and acting skills contribute to keep the prince in power.[21] And yet this does not mean that in such a context there is no room for the concept of a true aristocracy and an effective authority. Once this view is developed, it leads to "dictatorial" forms, which are characterized by an individual preeminence and by a formless power, and to an era that has been called one of "absolute politics."

Machiavellianism may be regarded as an application of the method of modern physical sciences to the sociopolitical plane. The modern and profane sciences are committed in principle to abstract from everything that has characteristics of quality and individuality in nature, and concern themselves only with its purely material aspect; thus, they provide a body of knowledge that affords, through various techniques, a wide control over things. Machiavellianism does exactly the same in regard to social and political forces: once it operates an analogous abstraction from the qualitative and spiritual factor and a necessary reduction to that which is physical and material in the individual and in collectivity, it bases its domain on a mere *technique*.

This is the essence of Machiavellianism. Now, in the modern forms of Bonapartism—especially those connected to dictatorial totalitarianism—we may detect a mixture of the Machiavellian notion of the "prince" and the notion of the demagogue who is the son of democracy, insofar as an inverted mysticism conferring on the leader a "charismatic" character here has as its counterpart a perfected technique. This technique is unscrupulous and sometimes even demonic, considering the means it employs to establish power and to control the irrational forces of the masses: it amounts to "absolute politics," which ignores the potential value of man as free personality. The Machiavellian leaders themselves ignore that respect for oneself and for one's dignity that is the requirement for any aristocratic superiority.

Aside from Napoleon III, the term *Bonapartism* naturally recalls Napoleon Bonaparte, a figure who would be unfairly judged if we did not distinguish two aspects of his personality: the political and the military. When dealing with Bonapartism as a political category, I have considered only the first aspect, according to which Napoleon, rather than as a military leader, appears as the son of the French Revolution: the spirit of the revolution was essentially developed and actualized, rather than denied, in the "imperial" fulfillment. Concerning the military aspect, I have nothing to say against the prestige that a leader may acquire on the battlefield: on the contrary, such prestige has nothing to do with democracy or with demagogy, but instead is connected with heroic factors and, as it is with everything that pertains to the military dimension, it integrates the very notion of hierarchy, as long as this prestige does not go beyond its proper sphere. I wanted to make this point in order to distinguish the higher notion of authority and aristocracy from its problematic surrogates and by-products.

The ancient world offers a good example in this regard. In ancient Rome, as well as among Germanic people and other civilizations, a clear distinction was made between the *rex* on the one hand and the *dux* or *imperator* on the other hand; the latter was essentially conceived as a military leader who was qualified, through some purely individual gifts, to perform certain tasks. In similar terms, which differ only concerning the field of application, the same distinction existed between the leader and the one who was invested with exceptional, though temporary, powers in order to restore control over a difficult or emergency situation. Originally the "dictator" was defined in these terms, and a particular tradition or political idea was connected to him as well as to the *dux*. The nature, function, and prestige of both types were different. Some laws, like the ones that existed among ancient Germans, contemplated the choice of the *rex* not among those who distinguished themselves for certain human qualities (as was the case in the choice of a *dux* and a *heretigo*) but instead among those who descended from a "divine" line: such laws should not be attributed to a "mythological" and anachronistic mentality. This idea may be demythologized and even formulated in terms of a simple typological contrast. The essential is the leader's "upward" rather than "downward" reference: it is necessary that in him something superhuman and not-human shine forth, regardless of what form (usually dictated by the historical circumstances and milieu) this element of "immanent transcendence" may assume. This element is different from what is proper to the "hero" or to the military or dictatorial leader. To employ an Oriental expression, we may speak of two forms of authority, attributed to those who win or assert themselves without needing to struggle and to those who win or assert themselves after a struggle. In the former instance, what asserts itself in a natural way is essentially an Olympian element, or an "actionless activity," that is exercised not through material channels, but rather in a spiritual way. In the latter instance, we are still on a high plane if we are dealing with a *dux* or a military leader (especially if trained in a strict tradition, as was the case, in modern times, with Prussian officers) but we sink to a lower level when we deal with political interferences in the sense of dictatorial usurpations. Eventually the bottom is reached with the emergence of the Bonapartist leader, who is a mixture of a demagogical tribune in a democracy and a Machiavellian figure who is an expert in a degrading and cynical technique of power.

I hope I have introduced sufficient reference points to distinguish between the different types of leader and the varieties found in two spiritually antithetical systems.

"Aristocracy" is an indeterminate concept. Literally speaking, "the best ones" is a relative term. "Best" in terms of what, in view of what? There are indeed "best" gangsters, "best" technocrats, "best" demagogues, and so on: thus, it is obviously necessary to specify the basis of the values shaping a society or a civilization and giving it its specific character. In different cases, then, we are going to have very different "aristocracies" and elites.

This shows the limits of Pareto's sociology in regard to the law of circulation of the elites, as it was formulated by Pareto himself. The starting point is the acknowledgment of the fatal character of elitism and of the iron law of the oligarchies. But in Pareto everything remains on a formal plane, because in the changes that the constant phenomenon allows for, the qualitative, spiritual factor is not considered. The elite considered here has the character of an abstract category, and in the "circulation" or change of the guard that occurs there is no consideration for the specific meanings and changes of value, but rather consideration is given to processes of an almost mechanical and indifferent social dynamism. In essence, Pareto limited himself to studying the part variously played by those that he called the "residues of the persistence of aggregates" and the "residues of combinations"—in other words, the conservative forces and the innovative, progressive, and revolutionary forces—yet all the while, without specifying what is to be preserved and what is to be introduced. With the exhaustion of the vital possibilities of a given dominant class, a circulation of elements occurs (an ascent of some and a descent of others) beyond which the phenomenon of the elites is preserved. Here "elite" is understood in a general way, as an abstract category. This is related to the methodology proper to Pareto, which attributes to every principle, idea, value, or doctrine the mere character of "derivation," namely of secondary and dependent character, of something that does not have a determining force in itself, but instead variously expresses elementary, uniform, and irrational tendencies ("residues"), which alone are believed to be efficient.

As I see it, things are totally different because the primary and most important element is not represented by the existence of the abstract phenomenon of the "elites" in power, beyond the rotation or change-of-guard of the single elites, but vice versa, by the change of values and meanings that occurs when an elite is followed by another, and when it is one elite rather than another that occupies the center and shapes the whole system.

The considerations I have made so far concerning these transformations, and thus concerning the varieties of elitism, are meant as a clarification. From a historical perspective, the shift from one form of elite (or "aristocracy" in general) to another has obeyed a specific law, the law of *regression of the castes*, which I will not dwell upon here, having described it in detail in my principle work, *Revolt Against the Modern World*.[22] Here it will suffice to say that there are four stages: in the first stage, the elite has a purely spiritual character, embodying what may be generally called "divine right." This elite expresses an ideal of immaterial virility. In the second stage, the elite has the character of warrior nobility; at the third stage we find the advent of oligarchies of a plutocratic and capitalistic nature, such as they arise in democracies; the fourth and last elite is that of the collectivist and revolutionary leaders of the Fourth Estate.

Six

WORK
THE DEMONIC NATURE
OF THE ECONOMY

I have previously discussed the analogy that exists between the single individual and a collective entity, and the legitimacy that this analogy was accorded in the ancient past. I have also remarked that in modern times the dimension of sociopolitical organization has descended from a plane in which the vital, material part is subordinated to higher faculties, forces, and goals, to a plane in which this higher dimension is lacking or, worse yet, through an inversion, deprived of its own dimension and subordinated to inferior functions, which in the single individual correspond to the merely physical plane. The counterpart of this, in the State, is the *economy*. I will now consider the phenomenon in question from the perspective of this particular aspect.

Sombart's thesis that we are living in the *age of the economy* expresses in an accurate manner the above-mentioned anomaly. He is referring, first of all, to the general type of an entire civilization. All the exterior aspects of power and of technical-industrial progress of contemporary civilization do not detract from its involutive character—rather they depend on it, because all this apparent "progress" has been realized almost exclusively in terms of the economic interest, insofar as this interest has overshadowed all others. Nowadays it is possible to speak of a *demonic nature of the economy*, because in both individual and collective life the economic factor is the most important, real, and decisive one. Moreover, the tendency to converge every value and interest on the economic and productive plane is not perceived by Western man as an unprecedented aberration, but instead as something normal and natural, and not as an eventual necessity, but as something that must be accepted, willed, developed, and praised.

As I have said before, when the right and primacy of interests higher than those of the socioeconomic plane are not upheld, there is no hierarchy, and even if there is one, it is only a counterfeit; this is also true when a higher authority is not accorded to those men, groups, and bodies representing and defending these values and interests. In this case, an economic era is already by definition a fundamentally anarchical and antihierarchical era; it represents a subversion of the normal order. The materialization and the soullessness of all the domains of life that characterize it divest of any higher meaning all those problems and conflicts that are regarded as important within it.

This subversive character is found both in Marxism and in its apparent nemesis, modern capitalism. Thus, it is absurd and deplorable for those who pretend to represent the political "Right" to fail to leave the dark and small circle that is determined by the demonic power of the economy—a circle including capitalism, Marxism, and all the intermediate economic degrees.

This should be firmly upheld by those who today are taking a stand against the forces of the Left. Nothing is more evident than that *modern capitalism is just as subversive as Marxism.* The materialistic view of life on which both systems are based is identical; both of their ideals are qualitatively identical, including the premises connected to a world the center of which is constituted of technology, science, production, "productivity," and "consumption." And as long as we only talk about economic classes, profit, salaries, and production, and as long as we believe that real human progress is determined by a particular system of distribution of wealth and goods, and that, generally speaking, human progress is measured by the degree of wealth or indigence—then we are not even close to what is essential, even though new theories, beyond Marxism and capitalism, might be formulated.

The starting point should be, instead, a firm rejection of the principle formulated by Marxism, which summarizes the entire subversion at work today: *The economy is our destiny.* We must declare in an uncompromising way that in a normal civilization the economy and economic interests—understood as the satisfaction of material needs and their more or less artificial appendices—have always played, and always will play, a subordinated function. We must also uphold that beyond the economic sphere an order of higher political, spiritual, and heroic values has to emerge, an order that neither knows nor tolerates merely economic classes and does not know the division between "capitalists" and "proletarians"; an order solely in terms of which are to be defined the things worth living and dying for. We must also uphold the need for a true hierarchy and for different dignities, with a higher function of power installed at the top, namely the *imperium*. ✶

But where is the battle waged today in these terms? The "social question" and various "political problems" are increasingly losing any higher meaning, and are being defined on the basis of the most primitive conditions of physical existence, conditions that are then made absolute and removed from any higher concern. The notion of justice is reduced to this or that system of distribution of economic goods; the notion of civilization is measured mostly by that of production; and the focus of people's attention tends to be on topics such as production, work, productivity, economic classes, salaries, private or public property, exploitation of the workers, and special-interest groups. According to supporters of capitalism and to Marxists, nothing else exists or matters in this world. According to Marxists, everything that exists is regarded as a "superstructure" and as a derivative; supporters of free-market economy are not inclined to be as drastic, though their standard and main concern is always the economy.

All this is proof of the true pathology of our civilization. The economic factor exercises a hypnosis and a tyranny over modern man. And, as often occurs in hypnosis, what the mind focuses on eventually becomes real. Modern man is making possible what every normal and complete civilization has always regarded as an aberration or as a bad joke—namely, that the economy and the social problem in terms of the economy are his destiny.

Thus, in order to posit a new principle, what is needed is not to oppose one economic formula with another, but instead to radically change attitudes, to reject without compromise the materialistic premises from which the economic factor has been perceived as absolute.

What must be questioned is not the value of this or that economic system, but the value of the economy itself. Thus, despite the fact that the antithesis between capitalism and Marxism dominates the background of recent times, it must be regarded as a pseudo-antithesis. In free-market economies, as well as in Marxist societies, the myth of production and its corollaries (e.g., standardization, monopolies, cartels, technocracy) are subject to the "hegemony" of the economy, becoming the primary factor on which the material conditions of existence are based. Both systems regard as "backward" or as "underdeveloped" those civilizations that do not amount to "civilizations based on labor and production"—

namely, those civilizations that, luckily for themselves, have not yet been caught up in the feverish industrial exploitation of every natural resource, the social and productive enslavement of all human possibilities, and the exaltation of technical and industrial standards; in other words, those civilizations that still enjoy a certain *space* and a relative freedom. Thus, the true antithesis is not between capitalism and Marxism, but between a system in which the economy rules supreme (no matter in what form) and a system in which the economy is subordinated to extra-economic factors, within a wider and more complete order, such as to bestow a deep meaning upon human life and foster the development of its highest possibilities. This is the premise for a true restorative reaction, beyond "Left" and "Right," beyond capitalism's abuses and Marxist subversion. The necessary conditions are an inner detoxification, a becoming "normal" again ("normal" in the higher meaning of the term), and a renewed capability to differentiate between base and noble interests. No intervention from the outside can help; any external action at best might accompany this process.

In order to resolve the problem, it is necessary, first of all, to reject the "neutral" interpretation of the economic phenomenon proper to a deviated sociology. The very economic life has a body and soul of its own, and inner moral factors have always determined its meaning and spirit. Such spirit, as Sombart has clearly shown, should be distinguished from the various forms of production, distribution, and organization of economic goods; it may vary depending on individual instances and it bestows a very different scope and meaning on the economic factor. The pure *homo oeconomicus* is a fiction or the by-product of an evidently degenerated specialization. Thus, in every normal civilization a purely economic man—that is, the one who sees the economy not as an order of means but rather as an order of ends to which he dedicates his main activities—was always rightly regarded as a man of lower social extraction: lower in a spiritual sense, and furthermore in a social or political one. In essence, it is necessary to return to normalcy, to restore the natural dependency of the economic factor on inner, moral factors and to act upon them.

Once this is acknowledged, it will be easy to recognize the inner causes in the actual world (which have the economy as their common denominator) that preclude any solution that does not translate into a steeper fall to a lower level. I have previously suggested that the uprising of the masses has mainly been caused by the fact that every social difference has been reduced to those that exist between mere economic classes and by the fact that under the aegis of antitraditional liberalism, property and wealth, once free from any bond or higher value, have become the only criteria of social differences. However, beyond the strict limitations that were established within the overall hierarchical system prior to the ascent of the economy, the superiority and the right of a class as a merely economic class may rightly be contested in the name of elementary human values. And it was precisely here that the subversive ideology introduced itself, by making an anomalous and degenerative situation into an absolute one and acting as if nothing else had previously existed or could exist outside economic classes, or besides external and unfair social conditions that are determined by wealth alone. However, all this is false, since such conditions could develop only within a truncated society: only in such a society may the concepts of "capitalist" and "proletarian" be defined. These terms lack any foundation in a normal civilization, because *in such a civilization the counterpart constituted by extra-economic values portrays the corresponding human types as something radically different from what today is categorized as "capitalist" or "proletarian."* Even in the domain of the economy, a normal civilization provides specific justification for certain differences in condition, dignity, and function.[23]

Moreover, in the contemporary chaos it is also necessary to acknowledge what is caused by an ideological infection. It is not entirely correct to say that Marxism arose and took hold because there was a real social question that needed to be addressed (at best this may have been the case during the early stages of the industrial revolution); the opposite is true—to wit, that for the most part the social question gains precedence in today's world only as a result of the presence of Marxism. The social question artificially arises through the concerted effort of agitators, those who are engaged in "rekindling class consciousness." Lenin did not assign to the Communist Party only the task of supporting "workers' movements" where they arose spontaneously, but rather the task of creating and organizing them everywhere and by every means. Marxism gives rise to the proletarian and class mentality where it previously did not exist, stirring excitement and creating resentment and dissatisfaction in those societies where the individuals still lived in the station allotted to them by life. In those societies an individual contained his need and aspirations within natural limits; he did not yearn to become different from what he was, and thus he was innocent of that *Entfremdung* ("alienation") decried by Marxism. Incidentally, we should recall that Marxism proposes to overcome this alienation through something worse—namely, the "integration (or, we should say, disintegration) of the person into a collective entity (i.e., the 'people,' or 'the party')."

I am not espousing an "obscurantism" for the benefit of the "ruling classes"; as I have stated previously, I dispute the superiority and the rights of a merely economic class living in a materialistic fashion. Nevertheless, we need to side against the idea or myth of so-called social progress, which is another of the many pathological fixations of the economic era in general, and not the legacy of leftist movements alone. To this effect, the eschatological views of Marxism do not differ very much from the "Western" views of *prosperity:* both *Weltanschauungen* [worldviews] essentially coincide, as do their practical applications. In both Marxism and free-market economies we find the same materialistic, antipolitical, and social view detaching the social order and people from any higher order and higher goal, positing what it is "useful" as the only purpose (understood in a physical, vegetative, and earthly sense); by turning the "useful" into a criterion of progress, the values proper to every traditional structure are inverted. In fact, we should not forget that the law, meaning, and sufficient reason for these structures have always consisted in references for man to something beyond himself and beyond the economy, wealth, or material poverty, all these things having only a secondary importance. Thus, it can legitimately be claimed that the so-called improvement of social conditions should be regarded not as good but as evil, when its price consists of the enslavement of the single individual to the productive mechanism and to the social conglomerate; or in the degradation of the State to the "State based on work," and the degradation of society to "consumer society"; or in the elimination of every qualitative hierarchy; or in the atrophy of every spiritual sensibility and every "heroic" attitude. Hegel wrote, "Happiness is not to be found in the history of the world [in the sense of material comfort and social prosperity]; even the few happy periods found here and there are like white pages." But even at an individual level, the qualities that matter the most in a man and make him who he is often arise in harsh circumstances and even in conditions of indigence and injustice, since they represent a challenge to him, testing his spirit; what a sad contrast it is when the human animal is granted a maximum of comfort, an equal share in a mindless and "bovine" happiness, an easy and comfortable life filled with gadgets, radio and TV programs, planes, Hollywood, sports arenas, and popular culture at the level of *Reader's Digest.*

Again, spiritual values and the higher degrees of human perfection have nothing to do with either the presence or the absence of socioeconomic prosperity. The notion that indigence is always a source of abjection and vice— and that "advanced" social conditions represent its opposite—is the fairy tale told by materialistic ideologies, which contradict themselves when they uphold the other myth, according to which the "good guys" are on the side of the people and the oppressed workers and all the "bad guys" are to be found on the side of the wealthy classes, which are corrupt and exploitative. Both of these are fairy tales. In reality, true values bear no necessary relation to better or worse socioeconomic conditions; only when these values are put at the forefront is it possible to approximate an order of effective justice, even on the material plane. Among these values are: being oneself; the style of an active impersonality; love of discipline; and a generally heroic attitude toward life. Against all forms of resentment and social competition, every person should acknowledge and love that his station in life, which best corresponds to his own nature, thus acknowledging the limits within which he can develop his potential; and should give an organic sense to his life and achieve its perfection, since an artisan who perfectly fulfills his function is certainly superior to a king who does not live up to his dignity. Only when such considerations have weight will this or that reform carried out on the socioeconomic plane be conceived and implemented without any negative consequence, according to true justice, without mistaking the essential for the accessory. Unless an ideological detoxification and a rectification of attitudes is carried out, every reform will be only superficial and fail to tackle the deeper roots of the crisis of contemporary society, to the advantage of subversive forces.

It has been reported that in a non-European country, which could boast an ancient and rich past, an American company, upon realizing the scarce participation of local inhabitants who had been hired for a certain project, believed that the right way to motivate them consisted in doubling their pay. The result was that a majority of the workers cut their working hours in half. Believing the initial pay was enough to satisfy their natural and normal needs, those people thought it was absurd to spend more time than necessary to procure their pay. It has also been reported that Renan, after visiting an industrial exposition, left, saying: "There are so many things in life that I can do perfectly well without!"

Compare these two views with contemporary Stakanovism, economic "activism," "civilization of wealth," and "consumer society" and its applications. These two examples, better than any abstract consideration, supply us with the criteria to distinguish between two fundamental attitudes, the former healthy and normal, the latter deviant and pathological.

In the case of the first anecdote, some might adduce the usual prejudices about the alleged laziness or indolence of races that are not as "dynamic" and "goal-oriented" as the Western ones. Such comparisons are artificial and unilateral. In fact, it is enough to abstract from the notion of "modern civilization" (which is no longer exclusively "Western") to find even here, in Italy, the same view of life, inner attitude, and emphasis on profit and work. Prior to the advent in Europe of what textbooks call "mercantile economy" (the term is very appropriate, because it describes the tone given to the entire economy by the figures of the merchant and the moneylender), from which capitalism rapidly developed, the fundamental criteria of the economy were that the acquisition of external goods had to be restricted and that work and the quest for profit were justifiable only in order to acquire a level of wealth corresponding to one's status in life: this was the Thomist and, later, the Lutheran view.

The ancient corporative ethics shared this perspective: in this ethics the values of personality and quality were given priority, and the amount of work was always in relation to a specific level of natural needs and to a specific vocation. The fundamental idea was that work was meant not to bind man, but to free him and allow the pursuit of worthier interests, once the demands of existence were satisfied. No economic value was cherished enough to sacrifice one's independence to it, nor was the quest for the means of subsistence deemed worthy to consume one's entire life. Overall, the above-mentioned truth was acknowledged—that human progress must be defined not on an economic and social level, but rather on an inner plane; in other words, progress does not consist in leaving behind one's ranks "to become successful," or in increasing the amount of work in order to gain a position that one is not qualified for. At a higher level, the formula *substine et abstine* ["keep back, but stand firm"] was an axiom of wisdom that echoed through the Classical world; one of the possible interpretations of the Delphic saying "Nothing in excess" could also be applied to this order of considerations.

Therefore, all these were Western views too: they were the views of European man when he was still healthy, before he was *bitten by the tarantula,* so to speak, or not yet dominated by an insane restlessness that was destined to distort every criterion of value and to lead to the paroxysms of contemporary civilization. The "demonic nature of the economy" has developed from this distortion, following a chain of processes: thus, morally speaking, the responsibility falls squarely on the shoulder of the individual. The turning point was the advent of a view of life that, instead of keeping human needs within natural limits in view of what is truly worthy of pursuit, adopted as its highest ideal an artificial increase and multiplication of human needs and the necessary means to satisfy them, in total disregard for the growing slavery this would inexorably constitute for the individual and the collective whole. The limit of this deviation consists of the inner situation out of which the forms of industrial capitalism have developed: here the activity aimed at profit and at production has turned from a means to an end, ensnaring man's heart and soul, condemning him to a nonstop race and an unlimited growth of frantic activity and production. This race is imposed from the outside, because to stop, in the economic system, means to regress or even to be undermined and swept away. In this race, which is not "activism" but pure and senseless restlessness, the economy puts thousands of workers in "chains" just as it does the ambitious entrepreneur, the "producer of goods," and the "owner of the means of production," occasioning concordant actions and reactions that in turn generate increasingly wider spiritual destruction. The background of the "selfless" love of that American politician who put as the basis of his international political program the "economic improvement of the most underdeveloped countries of the world" can be seen in this light: its meaning consists of completing the new barbaric invasions (the only ones worthy of this name), and generating an obsession with economic concerns in some peoples whom so far have been spared the "tarantula's bite"—all this because the growing amount of capital seeks to be utilized and invested and the degenerated productive mechanism seeks wider and new markets for its overproduction. Lenin saw clearly through all this and how, in such upheavals, one of the traits of "dying capitalism" consists of digging its own grave, being forced by the mechanism it set in motion to unleash (through industrialization, proletarianization, and Europeanization) forces that eventually will react against it and against the white man's societies: the representatives of "progress" are not aware of it, and so the process snowballs. In the socialist systems that claim to be the rightful heirs of a capitalism doomed to perish because of its inner contradiction, the enslavement of the single individual is reaffirmed rather than alleviated; it is sanctioned no longer simply *de facto*, but *de jure* as well. In socialist regimes this enslavement obeys a collective imperative. If the great entrepreneur devotes his entire self to economic activity, turning it into some kind of drug that has a vital importance to him—the consequence of an unconscious self-defense mechanism, for he suspects that if he ceased the activity he would see the emptiness surrounding him and feel the utter horror of a life devoid of meaning[24]—in the ideologies of the opposing side an analogous situation is made to correspond to an ethical imperative. This imperative is also accompanied by anathemas and repressive measures against those who intend to raise their heads and reclaim their freedom from everything that is work, production, productivity, and social ties.

At this point it is necessary to denounce another pathological fixation of the economic age, or one of its fundamental slogans: I am referring to the *modern superstition of work* that has become common to both left-wing and right-wing movements. Just like the notion of "the people," "work" too has become one of those sacred cows and intangible entities that modern man dares only to praise and exalt. One of the characteristics of the economic era, considered in its most plebeian and shallow aspect, is this kind of self-inflicted sadism that consists of glorifying "work as an ethical value and as an essential duty," and in conceiving every form of activity as some kind of work. A future and perhaps more normal mankind will regard the notion in which the means becomes an end as a peculiar perversion. Thus, work ceases to signify something that is imposed only in view of the material needs of existence, and to which no more room should be given than is required according to the individual and the status of his rank; on the contrary, work is absolutized and seen as a value in itself, and is associated simultaneously with the myth of paroxysmal and productive activity. Moreover, we come to a real inversion. The term *work* has always designated the lowest forms of human activity, those that are more exclusively conditioned by the economic factor. It is illegitimate to label as "work" anything that is not reduced to these forms; rather, the word to be used is *action*: action, not work, is what is performed by the leader, the explorer, the ascetic, the pure scientist, the warrior, the artist, the diplomat, the theologian, the one who makes or breaks a law, the one who is motivated by an elementary passion or guided by a principle. But while every normal civilization, thanks to its upward orientation, intended to bestow a character of action, creation, and "art" even upon work (see, for instance, the corporations in the ancient world), exactly the opposite is happening in the present economic civilization: even action (or whatever is still worthy of the term) is increasingly attributed the character of "work" (i.e., an economic and proletarian character), almost out of a masochistic pleasure in degradation and contamination.

Thus, we have gone as far as formulating the "ideal" of a "State based on work" and fantasizing about a "humanism of work," even in milieus that profess to be anti-Marxist. Giovanni Gentile began to glorify the "humanism of culture" as a "glorious stage in the emancipation of man"—which must be seen as the liberal, individualistic-intellectual phase of world subversion. Gentile said that this stage is insufficient because "it was still necessary to recognize the worker's high dignity that man had previously discovered in intellectual activity." Thus, according to him, "there is no doubt that the social upheavals and the parallel socialist upheavals of the twentieth century have created a new humanism: the humanism of work, the establishment of which as an actual and concrete reality is the real task and responsibility of our century." The logical development of the liberal deviation, which I have previously documented, is here expressed in very clear terms. This "humanism of work" is one and the same with the "integral humanism" or "realist humanism" or "new humanism" proclaimed by communist intellectuals,[25] and the "ethical character" and "high dignity" attributed to work are only a meaningless fiction attempting to make man forget every higher interest and gleefully accept his obtuse and meaningless organization in barbaric structures: I say "barbaric" because they do not recognize anything besides work and hierarchies of production. The most peculiar thing is that this superstitious and insolent cult of work is proclaimed in an era in which the irreversible and relentless mechanization eliminates from the main varieties of work whatever in them still had a character of quality, art, and the spontaneous unfoldment of a vocation, turning it into something inanimate and devoid of even an immanent meaning.

Thus, those who rightfully invoke a "deproletarization" delude themselves if they see in this only a social problem. The task ahead, first of all, is *to deproletarize the view of life*; if this task is not accomplished, everything remains distorted and tied up. The proletarian spirit, the quality that is spiritually proletarian,[26] subsists when no higher human type than the "worker" is conceived; when one describes "the ethical character of work"; when one praises "society" or the "State based on work"; when one does not have the courage to take a resolute stand against all these new contaminating myths.

An ancient image, taken from a Buddhist text, is that of a man running breathlessly under the burning sun. At a certain point this man may ask himself:

"Why am I running? What if I were to slow down?" and then, walking more slowly, he asks: "Why am I walking in this heat? What if I paused under a tree?"—and in doing so he may come to see that his previous running was caused by a foolish and feverish state of mind. Such an image indicates the inner transformation, or *metanoia*, required to strike at the heart of the "hegemony" of work and to regain inner freedom: this, however, not in order to shift to a renunciatory, utopian, and miserable civilization, but in order to clear every domain of life of insane tensions and to restore a real hierarchy of values.

Here the fundamental point is to be able to recognize that there is no external economic improvement or social prosperity worthy enough (and the temptations of which should not be absolutely resisted) when its counterpart is an essential limitation of freedom and of the space necessary for everyone to realize his possibilities beyond the dimension conditioned by matter and by the needs of ordinary life.

Moreover, this does not apply only to the single individual, but to the collective whole and the State as well, especially when its material resources are limited and foreign economic forces are pressuring it. Here *autarchy* may be an ethical precept, because what weighs more on the scale of values must be the same for a single individual and for a State: it is better to renounce the allure of improving general social and economic conditions and to adopt a regime of *austerity* than to become enslaved to foreign interests or to become caught up in world processes of reckless economic hegemony and productivity that are destined to sweep away those who have set them in motion.

The overall contemporary situation is naturally such that my considerations mean nothing less than swimming against the current; while this does not affect their intrinsic value, it must nonetheless be acknowledged that the single individual cannot react and subtract himself from the overall mechanism of the economic era other than in a restricted and limited way, and also given certain more or less privileged conditions. A general change may occur only if a superordained power intervenes. After acknowledging the fundamental principle of the primacy and sovereignty of State over economy, the State can then produce an action of limiting and ordering the economic domain; this action will be able to facilitate what derives from the essential and unavoidable factor, that of the detoxification, the change of mentality, and the return to normalcy for people who have learned anew what is sensible activity, right effort, values to be upheld, and loyalty to oneself. Only on such a basis can one simultaneously be a "protester" in an integral and legitimate sense, and an "achiever" in a higher sense.

I will again discuss the relationship between State and economy. Here I want to recall Nietzsche's words as a parting shot regarding the social question: "The workers shall live one day as the bourgeois do now—but *above* them, distinguished by their freedom from wants, the *higher* caste: that is to say, poorer and simpler, but in possession of power."[27] A differentiation on this basis will act as the principle for the rectification of the inversion I have lamented, and as the principle for defense of the idea of the State and for the resurgence of a different type of dignity and superiority. Such dignity and superiority must be consolidated and validated beyond the world of the economy, through a continuous struggle, both *inner* and outer, through the confirmation of one's being and the conquest of each moment.

Seven

HISTORY
HISTORICISM

At the end of chapter 1, when discussing the premises proper to the revolutionary-conservative idea, I declared my intention to return to the topic of historicism. I will do so in this chapter, also in order to introduce the topics that I will analyze later (e.g., choice of traditions; the third dimension of history; domestic clarifications [concerning Italy]). What I will say may cause a few difficulties for those who have not renounced the historicist mind-set.

We should begin by noticing that the emphasis given to the notion of "history" is recent and alien to every normal civilization; much more so is the personification of history into some kind of mystical entity that is the object of a superstitious faith, as are many of the other personified abstractions that have become fashionable in an age that claims to be "positivist" and "scientific." Many people are accustomed to writing History with a capital H, just as in the past the first letter of a name of a deity was capitalized.

The first and more general meaning of historicism refers to the collapse or disastrous shift from a *civilization of being* (characterized by stability, form, and adherence to super-temporal principles) to a *civilization of becoming* (characterized by change, flux, and contingency).[28] This should be our starting point. In a second phase, values have been inverted, and this caving-in has come to be seen as a positive thing that not only should not be resisted, but also should be accepted, extolled, and willed. On this basis, the ideas of History, "progress," and "evolution" have been intimately associated with one another; thus, historicism has often appeared as an integral part of the progressive and enlightened nineteenth century, constituting the background of rationalist, scientific, and technological civilization.

Aside from this, historicism in a specific sense is the basic view of the philosophy, originally inspired by Hegel, that was represented in Italy by the

178

philosophers Benedetto Croce and Giovanni Gentile. I will now expound upon the spirit and the "morality" of the latter type of historicism.

As it is known, Hegel saw a coincidence between the spheres of reality and of rationality, hence his famous axiom: "Everything that is real is rational, and everything that is rational is real." I will not examine this problem from a metaphysical perspective, or *sub specie aeternitatis* [from the perspective of eternity]. However, it is certain that from a concrete and human point of view this axiom is dubious for two reasons. The first reason is that, in order for it to be useful, one would first have to know directly, *a priori*, and in a determinate way what must be called "rational" and used as the order or the law that History and every event are always supposed to reflect. The disagreement among historicists on this issue is significant: the truth is that each one of them is inspired by his own subjective speculations, on the level of college philosophy; what is truly lacking here is even the most modest bird's-eye view that is required to grasp not only what lies beyond the world of phenomena, but also what is hidden behind the most evident causes of historical upheavals. The second reason is that (even if we were to believe in what this or that philosopher postulates as "rational") in the course of ordinary experience it is not possible to detect the complete identity of the rational and the real; thus, we may wonder if one affirming this identity calls something "real" because it is rational, or vice versa, if he calls something "rational" only because it is merely real, or because it presents itself as factual reality.

Even without engaging in an appropriate philosophical critique—as I have done elsewhere, when I criticized so-called "transcendental idealism"[29]—this suffices to expose the ambiguous and ephemeral character of historicism. It is precisely because we live in the world of becoming, which is characterized by a rapid change of events, circumstances, and forces, that on the one hand historicism reduces itself to a "passive philosophy of the *fait accompli*" and a theory that bestows a "rationality" on everything that has successfully asserted itself;[30] on the other hand, historicism may equally promote "revolutionary" claims when one does not want to acknowledge the real as "rational." In this case, in the name of "reason" and "History," interpreted to one's advantage, a condemnation is passed on what is. A third solution is still possible, as a mixture of the previous two—namely, to label everything as "anti-History" that seeks to assert itself or that tends to realize or to restore an order other than the existing one, yet without succeeding except to justify it and to lend a "rationality" to it, in the case of its victory and assertion, since by then it has become "real."

Thus, depending on the situation, historicism may be equally on the side of a second-rate conservatism or that of revolutionary utopias, or, as probably occurs more often, on the side of those who know how to adapt to changing circumstances, shifting allegiance according to which way the wind blows. Thus, "History" and "anti-History" become slogans devoid of any concrete content that may be used in both senses, according to personal preferences, in the context of a dice game that representatives of this view call "dialectics" or "historical dialectics."

The typical example of this was the development that occurred in Germany, out of the premises of Hegelian historicism, of both a theory of authority and of the absolute State on the one hand (a worthless theory behind a system that, being rooted in traditional values, had no need whatsoever for a philosophical justification), and of the Marxist revolutionary and "dialectical" ideology on the other. A more recent example, in Italy, is the enmity between Gentile and Croce, both of whom were committed historicists. However, Gentile, by assuming as rational what asserted itself in the political arena, bestowed the character of "historicity" upon Fascism, putting his philosophy at its service. Conversely, Croce, due to his personal and ideological preferences, thought the "rational" corresponded to liberal anti-Fascism; thus, he stigmatized the Fascist order, although it was "real," as being "antihistorical." After the wind changed direction, many people who were yesterday's Fascists awoke a few years later as anti-Fascists; these turncoats may be regarded as the representatives of the third possibility—becoming up-to-date about what "History" and its "rationality" will desire from time to time.[31]

These brief references show what historicism amounts to. It is essentially a formless, useless, and vain philosophy, at times even cowardly and opportunistic; it is either unrealistic or coarsely realistic, depending on the circumstances. But aside from the lucubrations of historicism as a philosophy and the corresponding mental deformity of which a sector of Italian academic culture is guilty, *we must expose the myth of History with the capital H*, especially when this myth fosters the narcosis of those who are not aware of the forces they have surrendered to, and when it helps those who want the current to become more rapid, any opposition to cease, and the last dams to be broken; appealing to the "sense of history," these people stigmatize every attitude different from their own as "antihistorical" or "reactionary."

This type of historicism, when it is not a senseless hallucination of shipwrecked people, is obviously the smokescreen behind which the forces of world subversion operate. Surprisingly enough, even among those who yearn to restore the old order there are some who are not aware of this; they are unable to reject the historicist myth in all of its forms, failing to acknowledge that it is men who make or undo history, if given the opportunity. We must be opposed to any consecration and "rationalization" of the status quo and must deny any acknowledgment of the forces or currents that have assumed power. We should recall that the anathema of being "antihistorical" and "outside of history" is cast against those who still remember the way things were before and who call subversion by its name, instead of conforming to the processes that are precipitating the world's decline.

Having made this clear, man is restored to a fundamental freedom of movement; at the same time, the groundwork is laid for a possible investigation aimed at judging the effective influences that have promoted this or that upheaval in history. In regard to the first point, what I have said will constitute the introduction to the next topic, *the choice of traditions*. Having overcome all historicism, we are rid of both the idea that the past is something that mechanically determines the present and the concept of a teleological, evolutionary, and transcendental law that, for all practical purposes, leads us back to determinism. Then, every historical factor will appear to have a *conditioning* role, but never a *determining* role. The possibility of an active attitude toward the past will be safeguarded, especially the possibility to uphold everything that is inspired by super-temporal values.

After these general references, I wish to examine some historical problems concerning Italy.

Eight

CHOICE OF TRADITIONS

In the case of every historical nation it is not always possible to speak of "tradition" in the singular, if this term is understood according to the most current meaning, and not according to the higher meaning that I have previously discussed. In almost every instance, the processes that have unfolded within a nation in the course of centuries have a complex character, and are influenced by multiple factors and trends that sometimes have been harmonious and at other times have clashed and neutralized one another. What was a predominant force at a certain time may have shifted later into a latent form, and vice versa; only an obsolete "historicism" can be so presumptuous to reduce everything to a linear development. And just as historicism is characterized by the passive acceptance of the status quo, which it sanctions with the myth of an "ideal necessity of history" or with similar formulas, likewise it regards a nation as a temporal unit that does not allow revisions. On the contrary, a more open-minded outlook is able to recognize multiple and at times even contrasting possibilities in the history of a nation, possibilities that in some way reflect just as many "traditions." Such an outlook realizes the specific importance such an acknowledgment has from a practical point of view, as what is required is a *choice of traditions*, especially at turning points and in times of crisis (when it is necessary to react, command, and organize on the basis of a central idea the forces of a people who are wavering and falling apart). It is necessary to choose the ideas in one's past that are perceived as more congenial by the men who, at such times, are entrusted to begin a new cycle.

When these considerations are applied to Italy, we are confronted with a difficult problem, since multiple factors hinder the exercise of discrimination and choice. The greatest impediment lies in the existence of a "patriotic" historiography that, due to its partisan spirit, suggestions, and catchphrases, precludes the objective comprehension of many aspects of the past, and is often responsible for serious distortions. After all, the character of history that has generally been "fabricated" (and there is no other word for it) in the last century is not altogether different. Overall, such a history is nothing but the alibi that revolutionary liberalism, democracy, and the thinkers of Freemasonry and the Enlightenment have created for their own benefit; these movements were later followed by the interpretations proper to Marxist "historical materialism" and its "revolutionary progressivism."

Because of this situation, the choice of traditions in view of a true reconstruction is particularly difficult, since measures have already been taken to preclude the acknowledgment of certain values, to falsify the real meaning of some fundamental historical upheavals, and to ensure that only the direction chosen by the authors and popularizers of such historiography will prevail. This tactic is very apparent, especially in the case of Italy: to historically endow everything with a national character that in the past had a subversive and anti-traditional tendency so that, after establishing some taboos, people will scream "sacrilege" and mobilize a passionate "patriotic" reaction as soon as any other interpretation is put forth.

Thus, things are not easy. It is necessary to have the strength to slow down a well-established tendency: according to this tendency, being "one of us" or belonging to "our history" automatically and indiscriminately places certain upheavals, people, and facts beyond criticism. This is necessary because, unfortunately, after Italy's more ancient history (connected to Roman civilization and its extension in time), we can say there is a "tradition" of the Italian past that fostered the subversive ideas that have shaped the later political world, a tradition therefore of which there is truly no grounds to be proud, but rather just the opposite.

It is important to realize this by "deconstructing" the patriotic myth that was fabricated by the aforementioned historiography. In this context, I will limit myself to addressing briefly some specific points: the real meanings of the revolt of the Italian Communes, the Renaissance, the Risorgimento, and Italy's military intervention in 1915.

It is commonplace to glorify the Italian civilization of the Communes and to bestow the meaning of a national awakening upon their rebellion against the Empire. Another myth has usually been associated with the latter, namely the *anti-German myth*, according to which the Germans have always been the nemesis of the Italian people. According to this view, the insurrection of the Communes allegedly represented the dawn of the new Italian national consciousness, or the first attempt on the part of Italy to break the yoke of centuries, become united, and extricate itself from the tyranny of the hated foreigner, the "barbarian" beyond the Alps. All this is sheer nonsense.

The truth is that the national element played no role in the struggle, nor could it have. The conflict was not at all between two nations, but rather between two ideas and two supernational castes. Frederick I fought against the Communes not as a Teutonic prince but as "Roman" emperor, upholding the supernational and sacred principle of authority that was exclusively derived from his qualification and function. It was not in order to defend the interests of his lineage, which he rather neglected, but to prevent the lessening of the Empire's authority that Barbarossa took to the field, having been asked to do so by some Italian cities that were being oppressed and harassed by others: he did so, not really because it was his right, but because it was his unavoidable duty. Frederick understood his task to elevate the regal and imperial authority to its highest degree, vindicate the rights that were lost or had fallen into neglect, uphold the law, and reestablish order and peace. In the terms of the peace that he dictated, he referred to the principles of Roman law. If the Communes had remained loyal and retained the hierarchical position that belonged to them in the medieval ecumene, they would have enjoyed their space within the Empire, and would not have been opposed. What Frederick or any other representative of the Empire (whether Spanish, Italian, or French, instead of German) could not have tolerated was the Italian Communes' antihierarchical pretense of self-emancipation, becoming independent, taking up arms almost as if they were States within the State, and revoking their natural dependence on the higher caste—namely, that of the warrior and feudal nobility—all according to the spirit of a new civilization. This new civilization, tendentiously democratic and capitalist, was the same under which modern people have progressively denied every principle of legitimate authority (i.e., "from above"), thus becoming subjects of the various "kings" of a faceless and nationless finance and industry. In this sense Sombart has rightly called Florence "the New York of the Middle Ages."

These were the real terms of the conflict. The Communes were the forerunners of the revolution of the Third Estate, and thus the Communes' "tradition" found its natural development in the antitraditional world that arose with the French Revolution. Official historiography has placed great emphasis upon the battle of Legnano (A.D. 1176) not because it was a national event, and not even because it was a great military success (hardly so, if we read the terms of the peace that was signed), but precisely because it was raised to the value of a revolutionary symbol.[32]

Concerning what affects the national factor more closely, we must recall that Italians fought both on the side of the emperor and against him. On the side of the emperor we find almost the entire Italian nobility: the Ezzelino, Monferrato, and Savoia families; however, a prince of the same stock of Frederick, Henry the Lion of Bavaria, abandoned him at the decisive moment, thus becoming largely responsible for the upset at the battle of Legnano. As far as the Communes are concerned, I do not see why Lodi should be regarded as less Italian than its rival, Milan: Lodi preferred certain ruin rather than betraying the loyalty sworn to the emperor at a time when he certainly could not have come to the city's rescue. Thus, the war of the Communes was mainly a fratricidal war between Italians, between those Italians who remained loyal to the "Roman" symbol of the Empire (which Dante fully acknowledged, regarding it as a healthy principle for Italy itself) and the Italians who did not accept, or even denied, this symbol.[33]

Nor is it possible after the struggle against Barbarossa to see anything vaguely resembling Italy's awakening or its unification. Least of all is it possible to see what an unconditional adherence to the thesis of "our nation's history" would require: we do not see Italians capable of opposing the German prince *in the name of the same idea*, the same ideal, and the same "Roman" symbol of the emperor (Frederick himself was to describe with harsh words what the "Romans" of those days had been reduced to). We see nothing of the sort in all this. The League of Communes was not followed by a national unification, not even of the purely political, schismatic, and antiaristocratic type that was first exemplified in France by Philip the Fair. The Communes were followed by the Seignories, with their suspicious figures of petty, tyrannical princes and *condottieri*—while in Florence we could witness the unprecedented case of the elevation of a money-lending family to the status of a princely dynasty: thus, the Medici were entrusted with the political government of the city. Generally speaking, what ensues is political chaos, struggle, and turmoil—in the name not of the nation, but rather of the faction and the most extreme particularism.

And yet all this does not matter to patriotic historiography, which cared only to sanction a "choice of traditions" espousing the forms of revolutionary, secular, and democratic thought that had inspired it. The fact that there was a Ghibelline Italy, to which the idea of the empire was not at all foreign, is briefly mentioned, without giving to it any national relevance, even though it represented a traditional and healthier Italy.

I have devoted many pages in the past to the real meaning of the Italian Renaissance. In the present context I will limit myself to briefly highlighting whatever in it has more pertinence to the political sphere. Patriotic historiography perceives the Renaissance more accurately than the history of culture does, since the latter glorifies that period only from the humanistic and artistic points of view. Official historiography considers and extols these achievements as well, but it does so from a specific polemical orientation against the previous medieval civilization, which it depicts as "obscurantist," thereby failing to acknowledge its greatness and the high metaphysical tension that permeated it. Thus, according to such historiography, the same current runs from the Italian Renaissance to what later on became the Enlightenment, "free thought," and the "modern spirit" (that is, a rationalist and antitraditional spirit), just as a river flows into the ocean. Therefore, in the same sense in which Renaissance Italy becomes the mother of geniuses and artists, it also becomes the forerunner of subversion. And just as the Communes represent the first rebellion against an alleged political despotism, the civilization of the Renaissance likewise represents the "discovery of man" and of freedom of the spirit in the creative individual, as well as the principle of the intellectual emancipation that constitutes the "basis of human progress." These are views in which different elements are mixed together. However, we cannot deny that the "efficacious direction" of the civilization of the Renaissance is largely subject to a similar interpretation; thus, from a traditional point of view, specific reservations should be made about all that is said about the Renaissance in exclusively praiseworthy terms from the standpoint of the history of the arts and culture. After all, it is not arbitrary to see a parallel between the individualism that is expressed in the more or less visible and genial creations of the artistic Renaissance and the individualism that raged in Italy during the same period (in the political dimension) in the regime of factions, rival cities, and *condottieri*, namely in a body of phenomena that bear witness to the absence of a unitary political force and a national consciousness. The legacy bequeathed to us by the "tradition" of the Renaissance, besides what belongs to art galleries, museums, and civic monuments, presents rather clear and not very edifying traits. Here, too, the perspectives have been distorted by a unilateral view. Thus, what the official historiography attributes to Italy's glory—the Renaissance—is also a phenomenon of which those who abide by traditional, more austere values should often be suspicious.

When we come to the third example, the Risorgimento, we discover that the tendentious interpretations of a historiography of Masonic inspiration have been, and continue to be, applied with particular virulence: this Masonic historiography has tried to disguise its most cherished ideas with the alibi of a generic and rhetorical patriotism. It is necessary to distinguish within the Risorgimento the aspect of a national movement from the ideological aspect. We owe the unification of Italy to the Risorgimento. I am not here going to evaluate people and movements to which, thanks to a rather complex convergence of circumstances, Italy owed its unification and political independence. Things change, however, and very much so, when we consider the main ideas in the service of which all this was realized (eliminating, among other things, a federalist solution such as the one Bismarck utilized to build the German Reich), and which continued to predominate in Italian political life up to the Fascist era.

From this latter perspective, the Risorgimento was only accidentally a national movement; it fell within the trend of revolutionary movements that sprang up in a group of States following the importation of the ideas of the Jacobin revolution. The revolutions of 1848 and 1849 had the same features and followed the same watchwords in the Italian movements as those that arose in Prague, Hungary, Germany, and Hapsburg Vienna. Here we simply had many columns advancing in the service of a single international front, driven by liberal-democratic and Masonic ideology, a front whose leaders were often hidden from view. In a similar way, the contemporary communist insurrections taking place in various nations are many aspects of the action of the Third International and of the network of "cells" working for it. The representatives of what at the time was still traditional Europe regarded liberalism and Mazzinianism in the same way as today's liberal and democratic parties regard communism; the truth is that the subversive intentions of the former were not much different from the latter's, the main difference being that liberalism and Mazzinianism employed the national and patriotic myth at the early stages of the disintegrating action.

There are significant documents (which have conveniently been utilized only in part), such as those gathered by the papal state police, which show the way things really were to those who are willing to explore the third dimension of the Italian history of that period. To the forces that were acting backstage and at an international level, Italy's unification and independence were rather of secondary importance; in any event they represented not the end but the means. The true end, which the Italian patriots and idealists did not need to know about (one of these chilling documents says that if they were too curious, "let the knife answer their questions"), was to deal mortal blows to Austria (which represented the imperial idea) and to the Church, to Rome. To this effect, it is significant that in the Masonic degree of the Kadosh Knight, the neophyte, as a way of sealing his oath, ritually stabs the tiara and the crown with a knife, these being the symbols of the double traditional authority.[34] The relationships that existed between Masonry and the Carbonari, which played a major role in the Risorgimento, are well known. Things in Italy did not go as planned, due to a number of factors, but the roles were not inverted either—the ideologies borrowed to unify Italy were not dispensed with after they fulfilled their function. They continued to be predominant in Italy, which was unified through a policy that today may be characterized as "possibilism," though the new State lacked its own idea, supra-ordained symbol, and formative force, for the monarchy appeared as little more than a superstructure, characterized almost by "private" and merely representative features. The true test occurred in 1915, when Italy not only left the Triple Alliance, but also broke its neutrality by joining the Allies.

Thus, we can see what the "tradition" of the Risorgimento amounts to. Apart from the absurd thesis of its alleged continuity with the spirit that informed the League of Italian Communes during the Middle Ages, we do not see what its "Italian" character allegedly consists of; if anything, we can discern French influences that later characterized an international revolutionary front. One need only examine the writings of that time, especially those inspired more or less directly by secret societies, to see that while there are frequent mentions of Italy and of the struggle against the foreigner, more emphasis was given to the exaltation of Jacobin principles of freedom and equality (i.e., the cause of the French Revolution) and to a relentless war "against tyrants" (this is most explicit in the oath of Carbonari neophytes), it being of little consequence whether the alleged tyrant was Italian or a foreigner. For the same ideological reason, we have seen that in the case of the medieval League of Communes, the Italians who fought on the side of the emperor according to "patriotic historiography" were either almost nonexistent or regarded as non-Italians. During the Risorgimento too, a war was waged mostly against a principle and a sociopolitical idea, though the "nation" was invoked. The anti-German myth itself, which views Germany as an oppressive foreign power and is an integral part of the Risorgimento's idea, is specious; if anything, the "foreigner" was not Germany, but rather the House of Austria and a dynastic stock that meant to order different peoples (Bohemians, Hungarians, Croats, as well as Italians) in a common geographical area, granting them a government with partial autonomy.[35] After all, according to the "possibilism" of the realistic politics of the Risorgimento, the Franco-Prussian war represented a particularly important factor. Cavour himself said: "Alliance with Prussia is written in golden letters in the book of future history."[36]

Yet this was not the direction pursued by the forces that controlled the unified Italy at a deeper level. Even though they are seldom discussed, following the unification of Italy there were Italians who attempted to extricate the new State from French influences and from the currents inspired by Jacobinism. In this regard, the Triple Alliance could have played a decisive role if only the themes of realistic politics that had propitiated its inception had been integrated by a corresponding, resolute spiritual orientation. In effect, the Triple Alliance appeared for some time as the partial implementation of an incipient supernational coalition built on an ideological-traditional rather than merely a political foundation, in which the issues that shaped the Holy Alliance tried to assert themselves. In 1893, referring to the Triple Alliance, Wilhelm II suggested to the future Russian emperor Nicholas II the idea of a *league of the three emperors* (Germany, Austria, Russia), supported by Italy. This league was meant not only as a mutual safeguard for the territories and interests of the participating States, but especially as a united front against socialism, radicalism, and anarchism, or as the solidarity of the European authoritarian and monarchical States against the Marxist International and the revolutionary and liberal currents that had their center in France. Nicholas II, in 1906, returned to this idea, approving the report of Count Lamsdorf, his foreign minister, in which the latter outlined the bases for an alliance and a crusade against the revolutionary, Judeo-Masonic threat, and against all the anti-Christian and anti-monarchical forces. According to this plan, the support of Germany and of the Vatican had to be won as well.[37] This idea could be traced back to Bismarck, who, in a note sent to Wilhelm I in 1887 on the occasion of a visit from Alexander III of Russia, also wrote: "The struggle today is not so much between Russians, Germans, Italians, and French, but rather between revolution and monarchy. The Revolution has conquered France, affected England, and is strong in Italy and in Spain. There are only three Emperors who can oppose it. . . . An

eventual future war will have less the character of a war between governments, but more so that of a war of the red flag against the elements of order
and preservation."

These were prophetic words, just like the above-mentioned plans for defensive solidarity of those who, by upholding the principle of authority (which
was then concretized in the monarchical form), had promoted the Triple Alliance. This bestowed on Italy as well the direction for its natural development
as a strong, antirevolutionary State, following the clearing away of the dross and
miserable ideological baggage from the previous period. Unfortunately, Italy
took the Triple Alliance superficially, or as a mere diplomatic affair; this alliance did not act as the incentive for an *inner* creative development leading our
nation to the same level as its allies. This alliance was not "felt," but rather sabotaged from within; the decision became clear at the time of testing, in 1915.

Even with regard to Italy's intervention in World War I (1915) we need to
deconstruct the nationalistic alibi. We know that Italy, with opportune diplomatic negotiations, and even by remaining neutral, could have obtained what
her new democratic allies were to grant her reluctantly at the end of the war.
Likewise, it is clear that even in terms of mere "realistic" politics, in regard to
the control of the Mediterranean, Italy's national interests could not be recon-
ciled with those of France and England; thus, the Triple Alliance appeared as
the only reasonable, coherent, and efficient choice. We see, then, that it was
not national and realistic considerations that prevailed in 1914 and 1915, but
rather the ideological "tradition" of the Risorgimento. This tradition, besides
reviving anti-German feelings, portrayed the central empires as "fascist" *avant
la lettre*, oppressive, and "aggressive" States and established the congruence of
Italian "national interests" with the *true* Italian goals of World War I. These
goals were proclaimed at an international secret Masonic congress (Paris, 1918),
in these precise terms: the war was to be a crusade aimed at furthering the
cause of democracy, which inherited the principles of the French Revolution,
and eliminating the remnants of intolerable obscurantist regimes (those of Central Europe, as they still retained structures based on hierarchy, authority, and
tradition, despite the increasing power of high finance and capitalism).

Moreover, right at the time of Italy's intervention in the war on the side of the
Allies, Italian Masonry voted an order of the day in which satisfaction was expressed for this decision, because it corresponded to the ideas that Freemasonry
had always upheld. Only at the last minute the text was modified for the sake of

prudence, limiting itself to state that the Italian military intervention reflected the ideals for which the patriots and prophets of the Risorgimento, who were singled out as an example in the various lodges, had fought.

Given these precedents, we cannot ignore the meaning that Fascism had: a break with the past, a different and bold choice of traditions, and the will to undertake a new direction, solely upon which the reference to Rome as a political symbol could be legitimized ("We dream of a Roman Italy," Mussolini once said). This direction was followed only after a last threat was thwarted, as Scottish Rite Masonry had initially hoped to use Fascism to reach its goals and thus had financed it at the time of the March on Rome, counting on Fascism's republican and generally leftist tendencies, which were eventually neutralized by Mussolini's later policy. The establishment of the Axis and the war against the democratic powers (I am not going to discuss here the problem of the war's timeliness, its lack of preparation, and blatant mistakes) was exactly what was needed in 1914, if only Italy had not been dominated by the wretched ideological legacy of the Risorgimento and of the international influences connected to it. Some have seen a sort of historical nemesis and a secret relationship between concordant actions and reactions in the fact that Italy, having won a war that it should not have waged (1915–18), lost the war that it should have waged (1940–45). There may be some truth in that view.

In any event it is clear that Italy's defeat, or "liberation," marks a regression to the most problematic direction of its history—namely, to endeavors that are nothing to be proud of. Thus, it became possible to talk of a "Fascist parenthesis," almost as if the "constant" of the Italian tradition were to be interpreted in antitraditional terms and as if in Fascism there were no ideas to be found that were not internally conceived and that preexisted in various European nations as well. Such ideas, apart from the incidental designation of "Fascism" and what was added to it, will certainly continue to emerge in history, given a proper climate and an adequate inner attitude. Thus the so-called Resistance claimed for itself the glory of a "second Risorgimento"; the betrayed ally of 1943 (who was betrayed almost in the same terms as in 1915, even in a juridical context) was then labeled the "invading German," according to the trite anti-German myth.

Because of the actual situation, it is necessary to get rid of the above-mentioned suggestions in regard to "our nation's history," and, having regained an insightful and accurate perspective, to again pose the problem of the choice

of traditions. As I have said before, this implies a renunciation of the nationalistic infatuation. In fact, if the criterion to be employed is the quantitative and
historicist one—in other words, if we were to endorse that which in the Italian
past (following the Roman era and the Ghibelline phase) has in practice played
a dominant role—we would not be at an advantage. In that case the scales
would tip in favor of those who see no higher goal than introducing a democratic Italy (lacking any higher ideal of authority, hierarchy, and aristocracy)
into the bloc of democratic powers confronting the ultimate form of world
subversion: communism.

Nine

MILITARY STYLE
"MILITARISM"
WAR

As everybody knows, *militarism* is the *bête noire* of any democracy. The "fight against militarism" has been one of democracy's favorite rallying cries. This formula was associated with a hypocritical pacifism and with the attempt to legitimize the "just war," which was conceived merely in the terms of a necessary international police operation against an "aggressor." During the first half of this century, so-called Prussian militarism has been a thorn in the side of democracies, since they perceived it as the prototype of the phenomenon they deprecated. What we have here is a characteristic antithesis that does not refer to the relationships between groups of rival nations, but rather to two general views of life and of the State, and even to two distinct, irreconcilable forms of civilization and society. Historically speaking, such an antithesis is reflected in the opposition between the view of the Germanic-Prussian tradition and the view that first emerged in England and in America, and later in all democratic nations; the latter view is characterized by the predominance of economic and mercantile values and by their development in the context of capitalism. The origins of the former view can be traced to an ascetic warrior organization, the ancient Order of Teutonic Knights.

In essence, the antithesis that I will discuss refers to the different relationship between the military and the bourgeois elements, and to the different meaning and function that the former is supposed to play in society and in the State. The view of modern democracies that first emerged in England, under the aegis of mercantilism, is that in society the primary element is the bourgeois type and the bourgeois life during times of peace; such a life is dominated by the physical concern for safety, well-being, and material wealth, with the cultivation of letters and the arts serving as a decorative frame. Thus, according to this view, the "civilian" or "bourgeois" element is usually, and as a matter of principle, entrusted with running the State. It is this human type that engages in politics; when politics—that is, international politics—must be continued with other means, to use the famous expression of Clausewitz, the armed forces are then employed. In this view the military and warrior element has the subordinated meaning of a mere instrument: it should have no particular influence or exercise any interference whatsoever in daily social life. Even if it is acknowledged that the military element has its own code of ethics, it is not desirable that this code be applied to the normal, overall life of a nation. The view I am referring to is closely associated to the humanitarian-liberal beliefs that true civilization has nothing to do with that tragic necessity and useless carnage called "war"; that a true civilization's foundations are not the warrior, but the "civic" and "social" virtues inspired by the "immortal principles"; and that "culture" and "spirituality" are expressed in the world of "thought," the sciences, and the arts, while everything that is related to war and military matters amounts to brute strength, to something materialistic and soulless.

However, it seems that in this context one should speak of a "soldierly" rather than of a military or warrior element. In fact, the term "soldier" originally referred to a man who engaged in the armed profession for pay. It is a term that referred to the mercenary troops a town hired and supported in order to defend itself or to attack its enemies, since citizens did not engage in war, preferring instead to take care of their private business.[38] Opposite to the "soldier" was the type of the warrior and the member of the feudal aristocracy; the caste to which this type belonged was the central nucleus in a corresponding social organization. This caste was not at the service of the bourgeois class but rather ruled over it, since the class that was protected depended on those who had the right to bear arms.

Despite the mandatory draft and the establishment of standing armies, the role played by the military man in modern democracies is that of a mere "soldier." As I have said, modern democracies distinguish between military and civic virtues and emphasize the latter, upholding them as the most important ones in life. According to the most recent formulation of the corresponding ideology, armies should be used only as an international police force to maintain the "peace"; in most cases, this amounts to allowing wealthy nations to live undisturbed. Otherwise, aside from any pretense, what is repeated is the example of the East India Company and similar enterprises: the armed forces are used by modern democracies to impose or retain an economic hegemony; to gain new markets and to acquire raw materials; and to create new space for capital seeking investment and profit. No mention is made of mercenaries, and many nice and noble words are uttered, appealing to the ideas of country, civilization, and progress. And yet, all things considered, things do not change much: we still have the "soldier" working for the "bourgeois" or for the "merchant"; the "merchant," in the wider sense of the word, is the social type or caste that is at the forefront in this capitalist civilization.

More specifically, the democratic view does not admit that the political class should have military traits and structure; this would be the worst-case scenario and amount to a real "militarism." In modern democracies, the members of the bourgeoisie must govern the affairs of the state as politicians and as representatives of a numerical majority. But, as is well known, in modern democracies the ruling class is often at the service of economic, financial, labor, or industrial interests and groups.

This order of ideas is opposed by the truth professed by those who uphold the *higher right of a warrior view of life*, which has its own spirituality, values, and ethics. Such a view finds a specific expression in everything that has particular pertinence to war and the military profession, yet it is not reduced to or exhausted by it; it is susceptible to manifestation in other forms and domains as well, and to imparting an overall tone to a given, unmistakable type of sociopolitical organization. In this context the "military" values approximate the specifically "warrior" ones, and it is regarded as desirable that they join political and ethical values and supply the State with a firm foundation. The antipolitical bourgeois view of what is "spirit" is rejected here, as are the humanistic-bourgeois ideals of so-called "culture" and "progress"; a limit to the bourgeoisie and the bourgeois spirit is established in the State's articulations and overall order. This does not mean that the military must manage the affairs of the state (with the exception of emergency cases, as recently happened in Spain, Turkey, and Greece, in order to contain the spread of subversion), but rather that virtues, disciplines, and feelings of a military type acquire preeminence and a superior dignity over everything that is of a bourgeois type. We may add that this view does not uphold the "barracks as an ideal," nor does it seek a strict regimentation of daily life (one of the traits of totalitarianism), which is synonymous with a stiffening and with a mechanical and obtuse discipline. Love for hierarchy; relationships of obedience and command; courage; feelings of honor and loyalty; specific forms of active impersonality capable of producing anonymous sacrifice; frank and open relationships from man to man, from one comrade to another, from leader to follower—all these are the characteristic, living values that are predominant in the aforementioned view. These are the values found in what I have called the *Männerbund*. Everything that has exclusive pertinence to the army and warfare is only a detail in a wider order of things.

However, this does not exclude that, when needed, heroic values are given a precise acknowledgment and that the phenomenon of war in this context has a different meaning from the merely negative one attributed to it by democracies and humanitarianism, as well as by a hypocritical "anti-imperialist" and pacifist communism; nor does it exclude that certain spiritual and even metaphysical dimensions are felt as real possibilities in this phenomenon. There is no antithesis, but rather identity between spirit and superior civilization on the one hand and the world of war and of warriors on the other, according to the general sense I have pointed out.

We may note that, in a sense, the above-mentioned contrast of views on the meaning and role of the military reflects the contrast between two eras. I will not repeat what I have expounded elsewhere in a more detailed fashion,[39] namely how often in the traditional world we encounter the interpretation of life as a perennial struggle between metaphysical powers, between Uranian forces of light and order, on the one hand, and telluric, dark forces of chaos and matter on the other. Traditional man yearned to fight this battle and to triumph in both the inner and outer worlds. A true and just war on the external plane reproduced in other terms the same struggle that had to be waged within: it was a struggle against forces and people that in the external world presented the same traits as the powers the single individual needed to subjugate and dominate internally, until a *pax triumphalis* was achieved.[40]

From this follows an interdependence between the warrior idea and that of a certain "asceticism," inner discipline, and superiority toward or control of one's self that appears in various degrees in the best warrior traditions and remains on the military plane (in the specific sense of the term) with the authentic value of a *culture*, in the anti-intellectualist sense of development and mastery of one's self. Contrary to what the bourgeois and liberal polemics claim, the warrior idea may not be reduced to materialism, nor it is synonymous with the exaltation of the brutal use of strength and destructive violence. Rather, the calm, conscious, and planned development of the inner being and a code of ethics; love of distance; hierarchy; order; the faculty of subordinating the emotional and individualistic element of one's self to higher goals and principles, especially in the name of honor and duty—these are all elements of the warrior idea, and they act as the foundations of a specific "style" that has largely been lost. This loss occurred with the shift from the States that are regarded as "militaristic," in which all this corresponded to a long and stern tradition, to the democratic and nationalistic States, in which the *duty* of serving in the armed forces has replaced the *right* to bear arms. Thus, the real antithesis is not between the "spiritual values" and "culture," on the one hand, and "militaristic materialism," on the other; the antithesis is between two ways of conceiving what spirit and culture really are. We must resolutely oppose the democratic, bourgeois, and humanistic view of the nineteenth century, which, in correspondence with the advent of an inferior human type, has presented its interpretation as the only legitimate and unquestionable one.

The truth is that there has been an entire cycle of civilization, especially in the Indo-European areas, in which elements, feelings, and structures of an analogous warrior type were determinant in all the domains of life, up to and including the domain of familiar and patrician right, whereas the factors of a naturalistic, sentimental, and economic character were limited. The hierarchical idea is certainly not exhausted in the hierarchy of a military or warrior type. The more original form of hierarchy is defined with essentially spiritual values (the Greek word for *hierarchy* means "sovereignty of the sacred," *hieros*). However, it must be pointed out that in many civilizations even the hierarchies with a spiritual foundation either relied on hierarchies that were more or less warrior and military or reproduced their form, at least externally. Thus, when the original spiritual level could not be maintained, hierarchical structures of a warrior type constituted the armature of the major States, especially in the West.[41]

The Prussian spirit, the *bête noire* of democracies, should not be regarded as the anomaly of a certain people; on the contrary, in it we must see the same style that, thanks to a set of favorable circumstances, was preserved until recent times in German-speaking countries (as an "intolerable obscurantist residue," according to the progressive representatives of the modern era). The Prussian style did not apply only to the military: by defining itself as "Frederickianism," it shaped one of the most austere and aristocratic European military traditions, but also manifested its influence in everything that is service to the State, loyalty, and anti-individualism. This style educated a class of government officials according to principles very different from mere bureaucracy, petty clerical spirit, and the irresponsible and lazy administration of the affairs of the state.[42] Moreover, this style never failed to act in the economic sector, ensuring, at the onset of the industrial era, an intimate cohesion to great industrial complexes led by quasi-dynastic lines of entrepreneurs who were respected and obeyed by the workers almost in terms of military loyalty and solidarity.

Thus, the antithesis between two eras is reflected in the polemics concerning the meaning of the military and warrior element: moreover, in it we see the polemics between the two components of a collective organism—the *social* and the *political*. Antimilitaristic democracy is the expression of "society," which, with its material ideals of peace or, at most, of wars waged to maintain peace, is opposed to the political principle—that is, to the principle of the *Männerbund*, the shaping force of the State that has always depended on a warrior or military element, that cherished less material ideals, such as honor and superiority. Thus, what has transpired at an international level in the democratic ideology upheld during the two world wars is yet another aspect of the regressive phenomena and of the aggressive emergence of an inferior element.

Aside from this, from a practical point of view we must acknowledge that in modern times, since the sensibility for purely spiritual values and dignities has become mostly atrophied among Western populations ("spiritual" in a traditional sense, not an "intellectualist" or "cultural" one), the model of a military hierarchy, though it is not the highest nor the original one, is almost the only one that can still supply the basis and act so as to emphasize hierarchical values in general, and thus save what can still be saved. That model still retains a certain prestige, and exercises a certain attraction on every human type that is not yet entirely disintegrated and "socialized." Despite any antimilitaristic propaganda culminating in the shallow, spineless, and gutless "conscientious objectors," there is a heroic dimension in the Western soul that cannot be totally extirpated. Maybe it is still possible to appeal to this dimension through an adequate view of life.

In relation to this, a further consideration concerns a general attitude and a certain level of tension, which in many sectors of contemporary life become necessary, with the effect of minimizing the distinction between times of peace and times of war. I am not alluding to the political struggles among political parties, which are phenomena that relate only to a period of decadence and an absence of the idea of the State: I am alluding to all those aspects of modern life that, in order to be mastered and not to have destructive consequences on the individual, require a complete assumption of one's own position, so as not to refrain from turning risk and discipline into an integral part of one's way of being. In this case, too, we have an attitude opposite of the bourgeois man's. Obviously it cannot be required that such a climate of tension last permanently and remain in everybody, in the same degree: however, at the present time, in certain instances there is no other choice. It is on the basis of various capabilities of the individuals to conform to such a climate, *to love* such a climate, so that in every domain new selections and real, existential hierarchies can be determined; these hierarchies are such as to find a natural acknowledgment from every healthy human being.

It is obvious that the nations in which such premises are sufficiently realized will be not only the ones better prepared for war, but also the ones in which war will acquire a higher meaning. Concerning the first point, it is the equivalent of what applies on the material plane, where the wartime efficiency of a nation is measured by the virtual potential for industries and peacetime economy to be suddenly converted into wartime industries and economy. There will be a certain continuity of spirit and attitude, a common moral denominator in peace and in war that facilitates the shift from one state to the other. It has rightly been affirmed that war shows a nation what peace has meant for it. The "military" education of the spirit has an independent value from "militarism" and from war; however, it creates the necessary potential so that, when a war breaks out, a nation is ready for it, and fights it with a sufficient number of men who reproduce in a new form the warrior type, rather than that of the "soldier."

The entire order of ideas that has been discussed so far is thus ignored or falsified by the polemics against "militarism," just as in other cases (e.g., "totalitarianism") a false target is created. In reality, what is meant to be effaced and discredited is a world that the merchant and the bourgeois type abhor, hate, and regard as intolerable, even when it does not directly threaten democracy. Thus, it is convenient to focus on that which is only a degeneration of militarism, namely those situations in which a certain class of professional soldiers, of rather narrow views and limited competence, exercises an artificial influence on the politics of a nation, pushing it to the brink of war with the support of warmongering elements. Such situations can be definitely condemned without thereby compromising the value of the overall warrior view that I have discussed so far. However, this does not amount to espousing the democracies' theoretical pacifism and sharing their totally negative view concerning war and the meaning of battle.

Contemporary democracies are caught in a contradiction that undermines their very physical existence. After trying to persuade the world that their last anti-European crusade was a "war against war," or the last war, now they need to rearm themselves, since they cannot defend their interests against the new "aggressors" with mere prayers and solemn proclamations issued by their leadership. Thus, this is the situation we are facing today: democracies theoretically continue to deprecate war; to conceive of war only in terms of "defense" and "aggression"; to abhor "militarism"; and almost to perceive the warrior as a criminal—and yet with such demoralizing and self-defeating ideological views, they arm themselves in order to confront their new opponents, namely the world of the Fourth Estate, organized by communism into one powerful bloc. The ideal for these democracies would be to find someone else to wage a war for them, as their "soldiers," limiting themselves to supplying weapons, ammunition, financing, and well-tested propaganda employing slogans such as "defense of the free world" and "defense of civilization." But such propaganda loses credibility day by day; moreover, we should not harbor too many illusions concerning the value of a technical and industrial superiority (unless it is totally overwhelming) when the counterpart of a moral factor and the warrior spirit is lacking in the fighting troops.

Finally, it is not easy to find somebody naive enough to believe that he is fighting in the "last war" and to be so selfless as to risk or sacrifice his life for those who will come after him in the hypothetical, idyllic democratic age without wars. And so the situation arises in which one is forced to fight, while his entire bourgeois and democratic education makes him hate war and conceive it as the worst scourge or as something ushering in ruin and all sorts of miseries. The best possibility will be to fight out of desperation in order to save one's life or wallet, since plutocratic democracies today remind us of the situation of one who, confronted with the choice between his wallet and his life, prefers to risk his life rather than surrendering the wallet. We can see up what blind alleys the democratic "antimilitarism" leads today, when those who are fighting are the elements more or less directly threatened and pushed against the wall. The civilization of the merchant and the bourgeois who extols only the "civic virtues" and who identifies the standard of values with material well-being, economic prosperity, a comfortable and conformist existence based on one's work, productivity, sports, movies, and sexuality causes the involution and extinction of the warrior type and the hero; what remains is the military man as "human material," whose performance on the battlefield is very problematic due to the above-mentioned absence of the inner factor—namely, a corresponding tradition and warrior view of life.

However, we may wonder if, after the recent experiences, one has had enough, or if one should forget what a modern "total war" entails; moreover, we may recall the extreme technical nature of such a conflict, seeing it not as a war of man against man, but rather as a war of the machine, *matériel*, and everything devised by science harnessed for purposes of radical destruction against man. We may wonder, in such a war, what margin is left to the traditional type of the warrior and the hero. The reply is that what is at work here is what Asians call *karma*. Modern man has no other choice. We may well agree with Ernst Jünger's views, according to which modern man, by creating the technology to dominate nature, has signed a promissory note that is now due; for instance, this is the type of war in which technology turns against him and threatens to destroy him not only physically, but spiritually as well.[43] Thus, mankind must come to terms with its creation and compete with it. This is impossible unless a new inner dimension is created, which, in the case of war, will manifest itself in the form of a cold, lucid, and complex heroism in which the romantic, patriotic, instinctive element is absent, and in which, beside a more specific technical preparation, we find a sacrificial disposition: man's capability to face, and even to love, the most destructive situations through the possibilities they afford. These possibilities, in their elementary character, offer him the chance to grasp what may be called the "absolute person." All this, to a certain degree, will have to be applied to an entire nation, as in the modern "total war" the distinction between combatants and noncombatants is a relative one.

It may be said that modern war will lead only to the transformation of the heroic disposition and that its increasingly technical nature will constitute a real test, so that this disposition may assume a quintessential form, be purified and almost deindividualized, joining particular and complex forms of control, lucidity, and dominion. This purely spiritual and naked assumption of heroism is probably the only one that is still possible.

Obviously, in these terms heroism assumes an *autonomous* value as pure experience and individual realization. The circumstances of modern times seem such that those who still yearn to be warriors and heroes must place this value at the forefront. In a novel written during World War II, a character says: "It is a luxury to be able to fight for a just cause." This is a significant testimony concerning the deep, widespread mistrust toward the ideological background of the recent wars, a background shaped by many lies and much propaganda. Thus, wars will increasingly display the traits attributed to them by certain sociologists; such traits are similar to those of elementary and unavoidable natural phenomena, and the result is the relativization of the meaning and value of the "cause" in the name of which people fight on both sides. We might be inclined to suspect that to think in these terms may promote a demoralizing and defeatist attitude. This may be the case, but only in those who have a passive attitude toward the phenomenon of war and who are bourgeois in spirit. In other instances, it will be a matter of inverting the relationship from means to end: the value of the "cause" will consist in its susceptibility to become a mere means for the realization of the experience as "autonomous value." Beyond any destruction, ideology, and "ideals," this realization will remain as an intangible and inalienable thing. However, it is not the view of life endorsed by modern democracies that will propitiate this eventual inversion of perspectives. The times ahead of us, despite the euphoria for the "second industrial revolution," make it very likely that to remain spiritually upright and to endure even after extreme trials and destructions will be possible only on such conditions.

As a last point, I will note that the above-mentioned situation could somewhat propitiate a return to the style that was proper to the warrior States and was lost in the age of democracies, revolutions, and nationalism. A warrior tradition and a pure military tradition do not have *hatred* as the basis of war. The need to fight and even to exterminate another people may be acknowledged, but this does not entail hatred, anger, animosity, and contempt for the enemy. All these feelings, for a true soldier, are degrading: in order to fight he need not be motivated by such lowly feelings, nor be energized by propaganda, smoky rhetoric, and lies. All these things have come into play with the plebeianization of war, since men who were shaped by an aristocratic warrior tradition have been collectively replaced by the "nation in arms," that is, the masses recruited indiscriminately through a mandatory draft. This happened right at the time when the traditional State began to decline and the national States arose, the latter animated by passions, hatred, and pride. In order to mobilize the masses, it is necessary to intoxicate or deceive them, with the consequence of introducing emotional, ideological, and propaganda factors into the war that have conferred and continue to confer on it a most heinous and deprecable character. Traditional States did not need all this. They did not create a chauvinist pathos and near psychosis in order to mobilize their troops and boost their morale. This was obtained by the pure principle of the *imperium* and by the reference to principles of loyalty and honor. Clearly defined goals were established for a necessary war, which was waged in a detached manner, hence without any room for hatred and contempt among combatants.

We can see that in this regard the perspectives are inverted: in the age of democracies, even war is degraded and accompanied by an exasperation and radicalism that were unknown in the age of alleged "militarism" and the "military States." Moreover, wars appear increasingly unleashed by uncontrollable factors, precisely because of the passions and interests that predominate in democratic States, lacking a principle of pure sovereignty. The unavoidable consequence of this is that conflicts acquire an increasingly irrational character, they lead to what was least foreseen and willed, and their tragic balance is often negative, in terms of a "useless slaughter" or a further contribution to universal disorder.

However, the extreme technical level of modern war and the growing dissolution of the fabric of the democratic myths may lead to a purification of war in those who, despite all, will be unable to avoid it. Where corresponding political factors are at work, we cannot exclude the possibility that the overall effect will be a partial return to normalcy.

I have not discussed "nuclear war" in this context, for various reasons. First of all because it seems that thermonuclear weapons will have the long-term effect of a "deterrent," keeping opposing blocs from taking the initiative, the consequence of which would be most severe and unforgiving. Second, the partial use of these weapons will necessarily entail, as a complement, the need for a war waged with conventional weapons; thus, the considerations I have made so far are still valid. The extreme case of a total nuclear war, which is usually depicted with apocalyptic overtones, may be ignored, because it would seal the destiny of a whole civilization, doomed in the cosmic balance.

Nor should we consider here the alternative and utopian idea of a "Global" or "Universal Government" that precedes the point when, after further collapses, the complete leveling of mankind has become a *fait accompli*.

Ten

TRADITION
CATHOLICISM
GHIBELLINISM

In the previous chapters I have made numerous and explicit references to tradition and the traditional spirit. I have also given the term *tradition* a spiritual meaning, and not an empirical or factually historical one. Thus, some readers may be inclined to think that when I talk about tradition I am referring to religious traditions in general or to the Catholic-Christian tradition in particular.[44] This is incorrect. I do acknowledge that some traditional and conservative forces have been inspired by Catholicism, especially in the Latin countries, and that there was a time when Catholicism gave a special chrism to the principles of authority and sovereignty. However, when I am discussing tradition I refer to something wider, more austere, and more universal than mere Catholicism; only by being integrated into it could Catholicism claim a character of authentic traditionality. It must be made clear that being a traditionalist and being a Catholic are not at all the same thing. Paradoxical as it may seem to some, one who is a traditionalist only by virtue of being Catholic in the current, confessional sense of the term *is only half a traditionalist*. Let me repeat: the true traditional spirit is a category wider than what is merely Catholic. The development of this point would lead us away from the order of considerations I intend to pursue here: besides referring readers to what I have said in other works,[45] I will limit myself to some considerations related to the political dimension and to recent times, in order to supply the reader with a general orientation.

First of all, the true traditional spirit acknowledges a superior, metaphysical unity beyond the individual religious traditions, a unity of which they represent various historically conditioned expressions, more or less complete and "orthodox" (hence, a higher standard for "orthodoxy"). Despite the fact that

204

every religious form has the right to claim a certain exclusivity in the area of its pertinence, the idea of this higher unity (although it is an "esoteric" truth— that is, not reserved for ordinary people, to whom it may be confusing) should be acknowledged by its most qualified representatives. Without it we would be stuck in a schismatic atomism and thus in such a relativism that the individual religious traditions would be utterly unable to establish the principle of their own authority.

On the one hand, we must acknowledge that Catholicism has been one of the most exclusivist and not to say partisan traditions that ever existed, and thereby further removed from this super-traditional awareness; on the other hand, we must admit that the development of civilization and our knowledge in matters of the history of religions is such that this exclusivist position may not be maintained without the danger of discrediting the traditionalist Catholics who rigidly adhere to it. In effect, nobody with a higher education can really believe in the axiom "There is no salvation outside the Church" *(nulla salus extra ecclesiam)*, meaning the great civilizations that have preceded Christianity (the still existing millennia old non-European traditions, such as Buddhism and Hinduism, and even relatively recent ones such as Islam) have not known the supernatural or the sacred, but only distorted images and obscure "prefigurations" and that they amount to mere "paganism," polytheism, and "natural mysticism." In the recent Catholic council called Vatican II, this point of view has been somewhat revised—although with a certain reticence—and mention was made of "ecumenism." More specifically, it is difficult to find someone who still believes the Jewish people have been God's chosen people, and the only repository of true and perfect revelation, and who thus considers everything belonging to the luminous cycle of the great Indo-European civilizations and religions as nonexistent or relegated to a lower sphere. This is a matter not of "faith," but of either knowledge or ignorance. For a modern Catholic, to persist in the sectarian and dogmatic exclusivism about this matter would amount to being in the same predicament of one who wished to defend the views of physics and astronomy found in the Old Testament, which have been made obsolete by the current state of knowledge on these matters. The current state of knowledge in matters of comparative religion, mythology, and even ethnology requires a revision and an adequate widening of the intellectual horizons. Thus, everything I say in relation to "tradition" and to "traditional spirit" may or may not refer to Catholicism; if it does, it is only *sub conditione* [conditionally]. In general, the contemporary "traditional man" should be freer toward external bonds and forms, but also more firmly rooted in what is the common, unchanging, perennial foundation of every great historical tradition.

Let us now turn to the particular problem of the relation between Catholicism and the political idea, and to the relationship between Catholicism and so-called Ghibellinism. The latter term has reemerged in Italy as well, in some political polemics, to designate the attitude of one who takes a position against a certain political Catholicism and clerical interferences in secular affairs, defending the authority and right of the political-State idea vis-à-vis the Church. However, considering the low level of contemporary politics, in this usage there is an unavoidable degradation of the meaning of "Ghibellinism." To denounce the abuse of this word is important for the entire order of ideas that I am expounding. This order of ideas would lack its own sufficient reason if the spiritual nature of the foundation of the true State and the system of its hierarchies were not adequately acknowledged; however, this would be impossible without facing the problem of the relationships between the principle of sovereignty and the religious principle in general. This is the problem of Ghibellinism. Concerning the nature of this tendency, it is sufficiently clarified only if we refer to the period in which it originally defined itself, the Middle Ages; during this period what mattered was to defend not the right of a political organization of a secular, lay, and national type such as those that exist today, but rather the right of the Empire, which at that time meant something else.

According to the Ghibelline theology, the Empire was an institution of supernatural origin and character, like the Church. It had its own sacred nature, just as, during the Middle Ages, the dignity of the kings themselves had an almost priestly nature (kingship being established through a rite that differed only in minor detail from episcopal ordination). On this basis, the Ghibelline emperors—who were the representatives of a universal and supernational idea, embodying a *lex animata in terris* [a living law on earth]—opposed the hegemonic claims of the clergy and claimed to have only God above themselves, once they had been regularly invested with their function. The Ghibelline emperors did not oppose the clergy on the plane of mere political rivalry, as is claimed by the shortsighted historiography that has shaped ordinary education. The political contention was only consequential and occasional in regard to the conflict among *dignitates* [those in high-ranking offices] that referred to a spiritual plane.

During the Middle Ages, the realization of the human personality was be-lieved to consist either in the path of *action* or in the path of *contemplation;* the two paths usually referred to the Empire and to the Church, respectively. As is well known, this was Dante's view. In its deeper aspect, Ghibellinism more or less claimed that through the view of earthly life as discipline, militia, and ser-vice, the individual can be led beyond himself and reach the supernatural cul-mination of human personality through action and under the aegis of the Em-pire. This was related to the character of a nonnaturalistic but "providential" institution acknowledged in the Empire; knighthood and the great knightly Orders stood in relation to the Empire in the same way in which the clergy and the ascetic Orders stood in relation to the Church. These Orders were based on a idea that was less political than ethical-spiritual, and partially even ascetic, ac-cording to an asceticism that was not cloistered and contemplative, but rather of a warrior type. In this last regard, the most typical example was constituted by the Order of Knights Templar, and in part by the Order of the Teutonic Knights.[46]

It is important to keep in mind that medieval Ghibellinism merely revived a preexisting and more ancient tradition. Elsewhere, I have discussed the sub-ject matter extensively and produced a body of evidence. Here I will limit my-self to emphasizing a single point. *Pontifex maximus* is a title assumed by the supreme head of the Catholic Church. However, it had previously been an imperial and regal title; this is what the leaders of early Rome and later the emperors, from Augustus on, were called, and therefore this title is often found on Roman coins. *Pontifex* means "maker of bridges." Obviously that was no reference to material bridges, but instead to the function of establishing a con-nection (a symbolic "bridge") between the human and supernatural worlds. A similar function was originally attributed to leaders. A Nordic saying goes: "He who is our leader should also be our bridge." The popes, wishing to exer-cise the same function, again took up that title of ancient imperial Roman tra-dition; therefore, this is a usurpation of some sort. In any event, both the sym-bol and the "pontifical" function preexisted Christianity and were intimately associated with the Roman, pre-Christian idea of sovereignty. In *The Mystery of the Grail* I have shown that what was proper to ancient Rome was equally proper to many other non-Christian or pre-Christian civilizations.

The conflict between the Ghibelline and Guelph views existed at an incu-batory stage during the growth of Christianity, through the contrast of two general views that were clearly irreconcilable. The first was a dualistic view characterized by the formula "Render unto Caesar what is Caesar's and unto God what is God's," namely by a separation between human institutions and supernatural order. The second view, the Roman and traditional one, was a hierarchical view that saw the leaders as representatives of a power from above, since, as St. Paul had said, "every power comes from God" *(non est potestas, nisi a Deo):* the consequence was to confer a spiritual and religious value upon every loyalty and every political discipline.[47] In this case, too, common historiography has distorted the truth when dealing with the "persecutions" against Christianity. What the representatives of the ancient Roman tradition, such as Celsus and the emperor Julian, reproached Christians for was their upholding of an anarchical doctrine; with the excuse of paying homage to God alone, they refused to give him homage in the person of those who, as legitimate leaders of men, were his representatives on earth and drew from him the principle of their power. This, according to Celsus, was an example of impiety. The starting point was a metaphysics or theology of the *imperium* with a non-dualistic character, and not a "pagan idolatry" that was opposed by a "true faith," as the common historiography claims.

The original tension between the two attitudes eventually decreased, but at first, especially in the Christianized Empire, was far from leaning toward Guelphism. In fact, in the first few centuries of the current era, as well as in the Byzantine Empire, the clergy was subjected to the emperor not only in the temporal and administrative domain, but in the theological one as well, as is proved by the fact that it was to the emperor that the formulas of the councils were submitted for their final decision and ratification.[48] It was only during the Middle Ages that the priest nourished the ambition, not of being king, but of being the one to whom kings are subject. At that time, Ghibellinism arose as a reaction, and the rivalry was rekindled, the new reference point now being the authority and the right reclaimed by the Holy Roman Empire.

Coming back to my original starting point, a similar antagonism is totally misunderstood in its true nature when only a political, secular view of the State is considered or, worse yet, when such a principle is deified or made absolute. This was not at all the case with the Ghibelline emperors; that was rather the policy first pursued by Philip the Fair [1268–1314], one of the most sinister figures in European history. The line, beginning with him and continuing through various examples of secular States with a Masonic, anticlerical character, leads to those "totalitarian" forms where religion is eventually tolerated only if it is at the service of the State, which in this context corresponds to the total subjugation of the spiritual element to the temporal, material, and collective element.

All this represents an almost diabolical inversion of Ghibellinism, in which we must also acknowledge a sort of boomerang reaction to the Church's anti-Ghibelline polemics. The Christian formula of "Render unto Caesar," while it did not sanction political insubordination, started from a very degraded and secular notion of Caesar, a notion that was unknown to the Roman theology of the State; this notion reduced loyalty to mere acquiescence, almost like telling a woman to give to her man her body but not her soul. From the late Middle Ages onward, the Catholic Church, in order to gain the exclusive monopoly in the domain of the supernatural, increasingly attempted to eliminate any spiritual character from the political idea, to interpret sovereignty as a mere "natural right," using various States as its secular arm and as compliant administrators of Catholic morality. After the Counter-Reformation it was only in this fashion that the Church promoted and upheld the absolutism of rulers who, despite the formula of "divine right," were nothing less than atheists imbued with the enlightened ideas that paved the way to the French Revolution. Things did not change much in the period of the Holy Alliance. For both sides the so-called alliance of throne and altar had purely tactical considerations, and thus supplied arms to the antitraditional, nationalist, and revolutionary front.

The secularized State, however, after leaving freedom to the Church in spiritual matters, shifted to an aggressive attitude toward Catholicism, which should not be confused with the Ghibelline opposition. Ghibellinism did not pursue the subjection of spiritual authority to temporal powers, but rather upheld, vis-à-vis the exclusivist claim of the Church, a value and a right for the State, different from those that are proper to an organization with a merely human and material character.

Thus, these were two very distinct attitudes toward the Church. It is therefore inappropriate today, to say the least, to talk of "Ghibellinism" in the context of anticlerical and secular-liberal political polemics. To really revive Ghibellinism would amount to revisiting the problem of the ultimate foundation of the principle of sovereignty in its relation to Catholicism in general. I do not see how this problem can be posed today, considering the overall historical conditions. The following considerations will provide an orientation.

First of all, we must firmly uphold the idea that a secular State, in any form, including that of the "Ethical State," contradicts every higher political ideal. A clerical or pseudo-clerical State is also unacceptable.

The religious factor is an indispensable element in the view of life that can bring about a restoration through the heroic dimension that is essential to it. Generally speaking, it must be felt as evident that beyond earthly life there is a higher life, as only those who feel this way have an intangible and unconquerable strength and are capable, when necessary, of active sacrifice and absolute élan. In the opposite case, to have little regard for one's life is possible only in moments of exaltation and when irrational forces are unleashed, while disciplines that aim beyond an individual's life cannot be endowed with a higher meaning. I have already discussed this in chapter 3; without a similar direct reference to a reality that is more than human, there can be no overcoming of the solutions advanced by a utilitarian and contractual sociology, nor a climate of high political tension.

However, a given religious confession may be used only as a support for such an orientation, and merely in terms of an arousing action. In Catholicism, specific reservations should be made. Concerning the political dimension, if Catholicism, feeling that decisive times were approaching, had the strength to rise above the contingent plane and to follow a line of high asceticism; and if, on such a basis, Catholicism, almost as in a revival of the medieval Crusades, had not hesitated to fortify faith with the soul of an armed, united, and inexorable bloc of powers, set against the currents of chaos, compromise, and the political materialism of the age—in that event there would have been no doubts as to its value. However, things happened otherwise.

Aside from the relativist Catholic view that no particular political regime may be regarded as "willed by God" or even accorded special acknowledgment; and after the times of De Maistre, Bonald, Donoso Cortès, and the *Syllabus* have passed, Catholicism has been characterized by political maneuvering and by its taking advantage of various situations, avoiding any stance that is too committed. Inevitably, the Church's sympathies must gravitate toward a democratic-liberal political system. Moreover, Catholicism had for a long time espoused the theory of "natural right," which hardly agrees with the positive and differentiated right on which a strong and hierarchical State can be built. Nowadays things have deteriorated in the sense of a rapid, disturbing collapse of every valid element in Catholicism, and in the sense of a desire to "be in tune with the times," with the modern world, and with the direction of history.

Militant Catholics like Maritain had revived Bergson's formula according to which "democracy is essentially evangelical"; they tried to demonstrate that the democratic impulse in history appears as a temporal manifestation of the authentic Christian and Catholic spirit. But this is not the end of it: in the climate of "opening to the Left" it seems that not only isolated intellectuals, but the highest Catholic hierarchies as well, do not hesitate to bestow this consecration on Marxism itself, and to engage in "dialogue" with communism, in order not to be "left behind." By now, the categorical condemnations of modernism and progressivism are a thing of the past. Teilhard de Chardin, with his updated version of Catholicism in regard to science and evolutionism, is about to be rehabilitated. This may also be the case for Ernesto Bonaiuti, the modernist apostle of a purely social view of Catholicism; and of Mounier, who, while opposing both capitalism and communism, does not conceal his sympathies for the latter, deploring the Church for not being the first to take an initiative analogous to the proletarian-communist revolution (Maritain's own view). When today's Catholics reject the "medieval residues" of their tradition; when Vatican II and its implementations have pushed for debilitating forms of "bringing things up to date"; when popes uphold the United Nations (a ridiculous hybrid and illegitimate organization) practically as the prefiguration of a future Christian ecumene—this leaves no doubts as to the direction in which the Church is being dragged. All things considered, Catholicism's capability of providing adequate support for a revolutionary-conservative and traditionalist movement must be resolutely denied. We shall more likely be able to witness some return of the Church to its origins, namely to that climate of early Christianity that displayed very "modern," socialist, and communitarian traits, almost as a "white communism"; the direction being pursued enables today's Catholics to be in tune with the "march of history" (as it is envisioned by subversion), avoiding any "reactionary" and "integralist" attitude.

If this deviation of modern Catholicism originated from strategic considerations, as if a policy of "opening up" were pursued in order to win over various left-wing movements to Christianity, we should regard this as a serious shortsightedness on the part of those who are allegedly enlightened by that Holy Spirit they profess to believe in. The presupposition of this tactic is that left-wing movements have a merely social and economic character, the truth being that in their deeper dimension they amount to an inverted religion. However, it is a perennially valid lesson of history that one should not make deals with subversion; those who follow its course, thereby presuming to outmaneuver it, soon or later will be swept away by it. The situation of the modern world is such that it is irresponsible to pursue similar experiments, even as a mere tactic and not a willing surrender.

Besides these political aspects, or better, in relation to them, the decline of the modern Church is undeniable because she gives to social and moral concerns a greater weight than what pertains to the supernatural life, to asceticism, and to contemplation, which are essential reference points of any higher form of religiosity. When somebody like Don Bosco is made a saint, we are not far from a liberal Protestant spirit, according to which the value of religion consists exclusively in social service, while anything authentically transcendent is more or less put aside. We could make similar remarks about many recent canonizations. For all practical purposes, the main concerns of Catholicism today seem to turn it into a petty bourgeois moralism that shuns sexuality and upholds virtue, or an inadequate paternalistic welfare system. In these times of crisis and emerging brutal forces, the Christian faith should devote itself to very different tasks.

Today's catechism is of a parochial quality; its fitting counterpart is the figure of those popes who, yearning to be popular, travel here and there, totally losing the higher prestige that only distance and unapproachability can confer.

But we can and should go beyond these contingent examples and examine, independently from a specific time frame, a fundamental problem concerning those typical values that must shape a given human type. Since this formulation is claimed by the Church and by every true State, I must ascertain if there are indeed incompatibilities with the point of view I have espoused. In regard to those values, we must distinguish between original Christianity, based on the Gospel, and Catholicism, and express the necessary reservations concerning the formulas of "Christianizing politics" and "giving a Christian foundation to the State." While the principles of pure Christianity are obviously valuable on the plane of a special type of asceticism, nevertheless they exercise a problematic influence, to say the least, in the political domain. On the one hand, they could mitigate the harshness of life by promoting public assistance or by fostering a mystical, brotherly spirit; but on the other hand, they could not promote the most fitting ethos that is expected from those who engage in combat.

We should not try to dissimulate the antithesis existing between, on the one hand, the pure Christian morality of love, submission, humility, and mystical humanism and, on the other hand, ethical-political values such as justice, honor, difference, and a spirituality that is not the opposite of power, but of which power is a normal attribute. The Christian precept of returning good for evil is opposed by the principle of striking the unjust, of forgiving and generosity, but only to a vanquished foe, and not to an enemy who still stands strong in his injustice. In a virile institution, as is contemplated in the ideal of the true State, there is little or no room for love (conceived as the need to communicate, to embrace others, to lower oneself, and to take care of those who may not even ask for it or be worthy of it). Again, in such an institution there can be relationships among equals, but without a communitarian-social and brotherly tint, established on the basis of loyalty, mutual acknowledgment and respect, as everyone retains his own dignity and a healthy love for distance. I will not discuss here what consequences would ensue on the political plane if we were to take literally the evangelical parables concerning the lilies of the field and the birds of the air, as well as all the other nihilist teachings that are built on the overthrow of earthly values and on the idea of the imminent advent of the *Regnum*.

Historically speaking, Christianity has been largely corrected and mitigated in Catholicism through the aggregation and assimilation of principles from various origins (especially Roman and Classical), as can be seen in the theological domain of Thomism, which would be inconceivable without Aristotelianism. This is precisely the reason that in the past, and especially during the Middle Ages, the Roman Church was able to exercise a certain traditional and formative influence. But this was not achieved, nor could it have been, without neutralizing the original premises of the Christian religion. Even in the best Catholicism there is still a residue large enough to ensure ambiguous and problematic traits for any ideal of a "Christian State" and a "Christianized politics." In this regard, a dualism will always invalidate the proper synthesis of the Ghibelline tradition and of the above-mentioned universal tradition, in which there is no room for such a view. This is not because the Christian values are "too noble" for real life, but rather because of their special nature. This nature allows only in part for a spiritual recovery of political values, and then according to the compromise found in the formula "Render unto Caesar."

This is all I have to say from the point of view of principles. If we also consider the role Catholicism plays in the current militant parties such as the faction of the Christian Democratic Party which makes overtures to the Left, and the aforementioned moralistic-bourgeois and partisan level to which Catholicism is reduced (in virtue of exercising the "care of the souls" and a deplorable modernist "keeping up with the times")—then it becomes apparent that we should distance ourselves from Catholicism when it comes to a worldview and a lifestyle on the basis of which we must act. In regard to these values, it will suffice to refer to a transcendent reality and order, beyond that which is merely human and which amounts to a mere earthly individual existence; this reference should not encourage pietistic evasions and humanitarian alibis, but instead be used to graft another force onto human strength, in order to draw an invisible consecration upon a new world of men and leaders of men. Wherever Catholicism in general promotes all this, or wherever in order to attain this ideal situation some categories of people resort to Catholicism and are not affected by its negative factors, Ghibellinism will not need to oppose this particular religion that has become predominant in the West and which has grown deep roots in Italy.

However, this exclusively concerns a personal problem for single individuals; for a nation such as Italy, it is justifiable due to the lack of a concrete historical tradition of men and groups who have been and still are the defenders of a precise Ghibelline doctrine in the nonsecular and nonliberal terms I have outlined.

Today in Italy it seems that some small groups have not been insensitive to the problem I have mentioned earlier on, that of the integration of those aspects of Catholicism that are susceptible to it, into the wider reality of Tradition (this is the task Guénon pointed out, though he once confessed to me that he did not believe at all that it could be achieved); these elements likewise incline toward the revival of a line of thought analogous to that which in the past led some Catholics to defend the idea of Authority and order, and to fight against revolutionary ideas. In this regard we need to discuss two precise reservations.

The first reservation concerns the doctrinal plane. In these people we can always see an inversion of the legitimate way of proceeding: instead of starting from Tradition as a super-ordained reality, the opposite attitude is chosen. The basis and the primary element adopted is that of Catholicism and its exclusivist claim of being the only true revealed religion; then an attempt is made to attribute value to Catholicism through fleeting references to this or that traditional idea, which is used as a means and almost as an ingredient, thus placing the universal at the service of the particular. Such perversion must be denounced.[49]

Second, these people, even when they proceed in the right direction in the doctrinal domain, should be aware of the "private" character of their initiatives. If these initiatives were to be taken seriously enough for me to modify my negative opinion about them, they should be taken not by these people, but by the higher elements in the Church. Obviously, this is not the case at all; the direction taken by the Church is a descending and antitraditional one, consisting of modernization and coming to terms with the modern world, democracy, socialism, progressivism, and everything else. Therefore, these individuals are not authorized to speak in the name of Catholicism, which ignores them, and should not try to attribute to Catholicism a dignity the latter spurns. The "eternal Church," to which some would like to refer, distinguishing it from the Church that is active in history, is nothing but a fantasy with heretical tinges.

Thus, regardless of how a certain belief may be valued by an individual, the norm that must be followed, for both extrinsic and intrinsic reasons, is to travel an autonomous way, abandoning the Church to her destiny, considering her actual inability to bestow an official consecration on a true, great, traditional and super-traditional Right: this course of action should be pursued when we think in terms of a movement, rather than of how a certain belief may benefit a single individual personally and pragmatically.

If we decide to take this course, we should be aware that in our day and age there is a great danger that where the political world appeals to forces that are usually awakened by religions, these forces may be degraded in order to create a sort of mysticism around things that are essentially rather profane: to this effect there exist many sad and deprecable examples, such as various "totalitarianisms." I have already denounced the gap between the situation in which human reality receives a spiritual chrism (which then changes its nature) and the one in which it replaces the spiritual, usurping its place and right. Even by upholding this, the above-mentioned danger must be confronted, because there is no other choice. As I have said repeatedly, a State that lacks a spiritual dimension and a legitimization from above cannot be called a State; not to mention that it is powerless against the arguments advanced by the rationalist, revolutionary, social, and subversive polemics. The problem that needs to be solved is particularly difficult, considering that today the continuity of dynastic and traditional lineages is broken, and that, in the case of a purely Ghibelline orientation, we must begin from a pure idea, without the basis of a proximate historical reference.

As in many other domains, here too we will have to settle for provisional solutions. On the one hand, we will have to uphold principles that have been rigorously formulated; on the other hand, practically speaking, we must be strong enough to follow and to assert them even when the basis they may now have is inadequate. This is what happens, more or less, in the institutional context, as in an interregnum or a regency. Thus, the symbol remains, preserves its prestige and authority, is acknowledged, even if temporarily there is no one who can embody it fully and the real leader has only a vicarious position. In our case, the reference concerns in general the spiritual center of gravity of a political organism: what is needed is to define well and to acknowledge its dignity and function in the previously mentioned terms, as we wait for its effective actualization. Throughout history this has always corresponded to a mysterious fact of a nature that is not merely human, and which a given general disposition and a collective climate may favor but never determine.

Eleven

REALISM
COMMUNISM
ANTIBOURGEOISIE

One of the reasons we see some intellectuals sympathizing today with communism (which is paradoxical, as it is well known that communism harbors contempt toward intellectuals) is related to the antibourgeois stance communism has assumed. Among other things, communism claims to represent the overcoming of the "bourgeois era" and to lead mankind toward a new realism, beyond subjectivism, individualism, the cult of the ego, and the various types of Idealist rhetoric. If the materialistic and exclusively economic plane on which communism contextualizes these issues is not recognized, they are likely to exercise a certain power of suggestion on those intellectuals.

There is no doubt that in the present age multiple processes are acting in this direction. Following World War I, this direction displayed typical traits: we may recall in Germany the movement called *Neue Sachlichkeit*, or New Objectivity;[50] in France, the current inspired by the *Esprit Nouveau* (of communist leanings) was destined to exercise a considerable influence, especially in the field of architecture. Today communism finds solidarity with similar issues that are formulated in certain milieus; thus, it is no surprise that some unprincipled intellectuals, who fail to understand the ultimate and contaminating meaning of communism (known only from afar and in theory), side with it, thereby deluding themselves about being in an avant-garde position.

This is a serious mistake. However, we must concede that, per se, an antibourgeois stance has a reason for existence. I do not mean bourgeois so much in the sense of an economic class, but rather its counterpart: there is an intellectual world, an art, custom, and general view of life that, having been shaped in the last century parallel to the revolution of the Third Estate, appear as empty, decadent, and corrupt. A resolute overcoming of all this is one of the conditions required to solve the present crisis of our civilization.

Thus, those attempts to react against the most extreme aspects of world subversion are very dangerous indeed, when they aim only at ideas, habits, and institutions of the bourgeois era. This amounts to supplying ammunition to the enemy. A bourgeois mentality and spirit, with its conformism, psychological and romantic appendices, moralism, and concerns for a petty, safe existence in which a fundamental materialism finds its compensation in sentimentality and the rhetoric of the great humanitarian and democratic words—all this has only an artificial, peripheral, and precarious life, no matter how resolutely it survives due to the inertia in wide social strata of many countries of the "free world." Therefore, I claim that to react in the name of the idols, the lifestyle, and the mediocre values of the bourgeois world, as is the case with the great majority of modern supporters of "law and order," means the battle is lost from the start.

However, just as the bourgeoisie in previous civilizations was a socially intermediate class, situated between the warriors and the political aristocracy on the one hand, and the mere "people" on the other hand—likewise, there is a double possibility (one positive, the other negative) of overcoming the bourgeoisie in general—that of taking a resolute stand against the bourgeois type, the bourgeois civilization, and its spirit and its values.

The first possibility corresponds to a direction that leads even lower, toward a collectivized and materialist subhumanity, under the banner of Marxist realism—to social and proletarian values against the "bourgeois decadence." It is indeed possible to conceive a liquidation of everything that pertains to the conventional, subjectivist, and "unrealistic" world that was generally bourgeois, leading not higher but lower than what is proper to the normal ideal of the personality. This happens when the final result is the mass individual, the "collective" of Soviet ideology, in the mechanized and soulless climate that accompanies it. In this case, the result of the liquidation of the bourgeois world may amount only to a further regression: we go toward what is below rather than above the person. It is the opposite of what happened in the great "objective" civilizations (to use Goethe's expression), which fostered anonymity and disdain for the individual, though against the background of superior, heroic, and transcendent values.

Likewise, if the striving toward a new realism is right, we can clearly see the mistake of those who regard only the inferior degrees of reality as real. This is when realism is essentially formulated in economic terms (as happens in communism). The same applies to some trends that have emerged in the arts or at the margins of philosophy, and that have sided with left-wing movements, assuming an anticonformist stance toward the actual society. One of these trends calls itself "neo-realism," while another is the radical existentialism inspired by Sartre and his coterie. In this philosophy, "existence" is identified with the most shallow forms of life; this kind of existence is separated from any superior principle, made absolute, and cherished in its anguished and lightless immediacy. This type of existentialism has its counterpart in psychoanalysis, a doctrine that divests and brands as unreal the conscious and sovereign principle of the person, considering instead as "real" the irrational, unconscious, collective, and nocturnal dimension of the human being: on this basis, every higher faculty is seen as derived and dependent. This also happens on the social and cultural plane, where Marxism endeavors to portray as mere "superstructure" everything that cannot be counted as social and economic processes. We are obviously in the same line of thought when existentialism proclaims the primacy of "existence" over "being," instead of acknowledging that existence acquires a meaning only when it is inspired by something beyond itself. Thus, there is an exact, visible parallel between such intellectual currents and revolutionary, sociopolitical movements, because what we are dealing with is the manifestation, in the individual domain, of what in the social and historical domain manifests itself as a subversive shift of power toward the masses, replacement of the superior with the inferior, and the removal of every principle of sovereignty that does not originate "from below." The existentialist and psychoanalytical "realism," together with similar trends, points to a human image that reflects such relationships in the individual; such an image appears as mutilated, distorted, and subversive. Thus, we may regard it as the result of some congeniality when many intellectuals of similar leanings sympathize with the social left-wing currents, even when the political leaders of these currents do not have the same feelings for them.

However, there is a second possibility: one may conceive a realistic view and a struggle against the bourgeois spirit, individualism, and false idealism that is more radical than the struggle waged against them by the Left, and yet oriented upward, not downward. As I have said in a previous chapter, this different possibility is contingent upon a revival of the heroic and aristocratic values when they are assumed naturally and clearly, without rhetoric or pomposity: in retrospect, typical aspects of the Roman and Germanic-Roman world have already exemplified it. It is possible to keep a distance from everything that has only a human and especially subjectivist character; to feel contempt for bourgeois conformism and its petty selfishness and moralism; to embody the style of an impersonal activity; to prefer what is essential and real in a higher sense, free from the trappings of sentimentalism and from pseudo-intellectual superstructures—and yet all this must be done *remaining upright*, feeling the presence in life of that which leads beyond life, drawing from it precise norms of behavior and action.

Everything that is antibourgeois in this sense does not converge toward the communist world; on the contrary, it is the premise for the emergence of new men and leaders, capable of erecting true barriers against global subversion, in correspondence with the establishment of a new climate, one that will be endowed with its own unique expressions even in terms of culture and civilization.

It is therefore paramount to recognize clearly the opposition between the two above-mentioned possibilities or directions of the antibourgeois stance. This is especially true in Italy. In the past, Fascism adopted an antibourgeois stance and, as part of the renewal that it was supposed to usher in, desired the advent of a new man, who was supposed to break with the bourgeois style of thinking, feeling, and behaving. Unfortunately, this was one of the cases where Fascism never got past its own sloganeering; those elements in Fascism that, despite all, remained bourgeois or became bourgeois by contagion constituted one of its weaknesses. As far as the present is concerned, with rare exceptions the average Italian communist is nothing but a bourgeois who takes to the streets (Lenin himself said that a proletarian, left to himself, tends to become a bourgeois), just as a false Christian and a member of the Christian Democratic Party represent nothing more than the bourgeoisie in the temple. Even those who call themselves monarchists can only conceive of a bourgeois king. The worst evil for Italy is the bourgeoisie: the bourgeois-priest, the bourgeois-worker, the bourgeois-"noble," the bourgeois-intellectual. This type is inconsistent, a substance without form, in which there is no "above" and no "below." The watchword or rallying cry should be: "Wipe the slate clean!" Only by following this dictum will the shift toward the wrong direction be averted.

After mentioning intellectuals and realism, it is still necessary to make one point. I have suggested that the flirtation of some intellectuals with communism is paradoxical, since communism despises the figure of the intellectual, whom it regards as a member of the hated bourgeois. Incidentally, a similar attitude may be shared even by those who are on the opposite front to communism. It is indeed possible to be opposed to any exaggerated appreciation of culture and intellectualism, considering what they amount to in the contemporary world. To make a cult of them, to define their representatives as a higher social stratum, almost an aristocracy—the "aristocracy of thought," which is believed to be the true one, legitimately replacing the previous forms of the elite and the nobility—is a characteristic prejudice of the bourgeois era in its humanistic or liberal sphere. The truth is that this culture and intellectualism are nothing but the products of dissociation and neutralization within a wider order of things. As this has not gone unnoticed, anti-intellectualism has been almost a biological reaction, playing a relevant part in recent times: unfortunately it has pursued false or problematic directions.

I will not, however, dwell on this last point, as I have already discussed it in another context, when dealing with the error of anti-rationalism.[51] Here I only want to point out that if we desire to overcome bourgeois "culture," there is a third possible reference point beyond both intellectualism and anti-intellectualism: a *worldview* (the German *Weltanschauung*). A worldview is based not on books, but on an inner form and a sensibility endowed with an innate, rather than acquired, character. It is essentially a disposition and an attitude, instead of a culture or a theory—a disposition and an attitude that do not merely concern the mental domain, but also affect the domain of feelings and of the will, forge one's character, and manifest themselves in reactions having the same instinctive certainty, giving evidence of a sure meaning of life. Usually, a worldview, rather than being an individual affair, proceeds from a tradition and is the *organic* effect of forces that have shaped a certain type of civilization; at the same time, *a parte subiecti* [from the subject's perspective] the worldview manifests itself as a sort of "inner race" and an existential structure. In every civilization but the modern one, it was a "worldview" and not a "culture" that permeated the various strata of society; where culture and conceptual thought were present, they never enjoyed primacy, for their function was as simple expressive means and organs in service of the worldview. Nobody believed "pure thought" was supposed to reveal truth and to supply meaning to life: the role of thought consisted in clarifying what was already possessed and what preexisted as direct feeling and evidence, before any speculation was formulated. The products of thought had only a symbolic value, acting as signposts—thus, conceptual expression did not have a character privileged over other forms of expression. In previous civilizations the latter consisted of evocative images, symbols, and myths. Today things may go otherwise, considering the growing, hypertrophic cerebralization of Western man. However, it is important not to mistake the essential for the accessory, and that the above-mentioned relationships are acknowledged and retained; in other words, wherever "culture" and "intellectualism" are present, they may play an only instrumental role, expressing something deeper and more organic, namely a worldview. The worldview may find clearer expression in a man with no formal education than in a writer, just as it may be more strongly represented in a soldier, an aristocrat, or a farmer who is faithful to the earth than in the bourgeois intellectual, the typical "professor," or the journalist.

Concerning all this, Italy is at a disadvantage, as those with all the power in the media, academic culture, and in critical journals, and who thereby organize real, monopolizing, quasi-Masonic societies, are the worst type of intellectual, who knows nothing of the meaning of spirituality, human wholeness, or thinking that reflects strong principles.[52]

"Culture" in the modern sense ceases to be a danger only when those who deal with it already have a worldview. Only then will an active relationship toward it be possible, because one will already have an inner form enabling him to discern confidently what may be assimilated and what should be rejected—more or less as happens in all the differentiated processes of organic assimilation.

All this is rather evident, and yet it has been systematically misjudged by liberal and individualistic thought: one of the calamities of "free culture" made available to everybody and expounded by this ideology is the fact that in this way many whose minds are incapable of discrimination according to proper judgment, and who still lack their own form and worldview, find themselves at the mercy of similar influences. This deleterious situation, which is flaunted as a triumph and as progress, proceeds from a premise that is exactly the opposite of the truth: it is assumed that, unlike men who lived in the "obscurantist" epochs of the past, modern man is spiritually mature, and thus capable of judging for himself and of being on his own (this is the same premise of modern "democracy" in its polemics against any principle of authority). But this is sheer illusion: never before as in modern times was there such a number of men who are spiritually formless, and thus open to any suggestion and ideological intoxication, so as to become dominated by psychic currents (without being aware of it in the least) and of manipulations belonging to the intellectual, political, and social climate in which they live. But these considerations would take us too far.

My comments concerning the "worldview" supplement the aspects of the problem I have dealt with when I mentioned the new realism; they specify where this problem must be situated and resolved, in an antibourgeois mode—for there is nothing worse than a merely intellectual reaction against intellectualism. If the fog will lift, it will become clear that the "worldview" must be the unifying or dividing factor, staking out spiritually insurmountable barriers. Even in a political movement it constitutes the primary element, because only a worldview has the power to produce a given human type and thus to impart a specific tone to a given community.

With communism there have been situations in which something began to reach such depths. Quite correctly, a contemporary politician spoke of an inner and deep change that, by manifesting itself in the form of an obsession, is produced in those who truly adhere to communism; their thinking and conduct are altered by it. In my view, it is an alteration or a fundamental contamination of the human being: *in such cases it affects the plane of existential reality*, which is not what happens with those who react from bourgeois and intellectualist positions. The possibility of revolutionary-conservative action depends essentially on the measure in which the opposing idea, namely the traditional, aristocratic, anti-proletarian idea, is able to reach such existential levels—thereby giving rise to a new realism and allowing Tradition, as a worldview, to give form to a specific type of antibourgeois man as the nucleus of new elites, beyond the crisis of all individualistic and unrealistic values.

*the problem is the way we view
the entire process. it will not be
fixed by simply switching econo-
systems. ie. change from Capitali
to Communism. The same inherant
problems still exsist. Must Alter
economic
Approach
Completely

Twelve

ECONOMY AND POLITICS

CORPORATIONS

UNITY OF WORK

In chapter 6 I stated that one of the fundamental premises for the return to a general condition of normalcy is to break the control exercised by the economy ✴ on the modern Western world. I have also briefly indicated the change of inner attitude necessary for this to happen. However, in the actual state of things, due to the pressure of forces that are spiraling the socioeconomic domain downward, it is impossible to rely solely on inner factors, although they will always remain the ones that really matter. Moreover, it is necessary to consider those forms through which the economy can be restrained and organized, and through which the factors of disorder and subversion intrinsic to the most recent developments may be limited.

It is rather obvious that it is not possible to achieve this today through a spontaneous process; rather, a political intervention is required. The following are the two fundamental premises: *the State, incarnation of an idea and a power, is a higher reality with respect to the world of the economy; political necessity always takes precedence over economic, and one might add, socioeconomic necessity.* As far as the second point is concerned, considering what I previously said, it is not necessary to repeat that according to the traditional view, the political domain is legitimized with spiritual and super-individual values. The State is the power that gives such values the weight they deserve within an overall normal institution, thus implementing the idea of "justice" in the higher sense of the word.

Having said that, the first step to normalize the economy is to overcome classism, which is the principal cause of the disorder and crisis of our time. For this purpose, we need not invent new ideas; all we must do is to borrow from the traditional legacy, which in the *corporative principle* offers the leading idea that may serve as the best reference point, provided it is opportunely adapted.

The fundamental spirit of corporativism was that of a community of work and productive solidarity, based on the principles of competence, qualification, and natural hierarchy, with the overall system characterized by a style of active impersonality, selflessness, and dignity. This was very visible in the medieval artisan corporations, guilds, and craft fraternities. Going further back in time, we have the example of the ancient Roman professional corporations. These, according to a characteristic expression, were modeled *ad exemplum rei publicae*—that is, in the image of the State; on their own level, the corporations' designations (e.g., *milites* or *milites caligati*) for their members in contrast to the *magistri* also reflected the institution of the military. As far as the corporative tradition that flourished in the Romano-Germanic Middle Ages is concerned, we know that members of a corporation enjoyed the status of *free* men and were also very proud of belonging to the association; they felt love for their work, which was regarded not as a mere source of profit, but rather as an art and an expression of one's vocation. The commitment of the workers was matched by the master of the art's competence, care, and knowledge; by their effort to strengthen and to raise the quality of the overall corporate unit; and by their protecting and upholding the code of honor of their corporation.[53] The problems of capital and the ownership of the means of production were almost never an issue, due to the natural convergence of the various elements of the productive process in view of the realization of the common goal. After all, these were organizations that "owned" the instruments of production; nobody thought about monopolizing these instruments for exploitation, as they were not tied to financing extraneous work. The usury of "liquid assets"—the equivalent of what today is the banking and financial employment of capital— was regarded as a Jewish business, far from affecting the whole system. Anybody endowed with an average sense of discernment will be able to understand that all this is found in conditions of normalcy, and that the problem today lies in the quest for forms and conditions capable of restoring the basic ideas of the corporative world in the modern age, which has been turned upside down by the "industrial revolution" (paralleling the revolution of the Third Estate and the Judaization of the economy). For this purpose, the main problem is to overcome classism. Fascist corporativism pursued this goal too, though it achieved it only incompletely, mainly because of two reasons. First, because in Fascist corporativism there was still the basic idea of a double align-ment outside the companies—the trade union alignment and the owners' align-ment. Trade unions continued to be recognized as class organizations, although following the so-called unfreezing of the General Confederation of Workers they were fractioned and distributed according to the various corporations. Second, in Fascist corporativism the unity of work was not re-constituted where both capitalism and Marxism had broken it—within *every company or aggregate of companies*—rather, it was reconstituted on the outside, in the context of a bureaucratic-government system, with organs that often amounted to nothing more than a larger superstructure.

The German National Socialist work legislation came closer to this goal, because it understood that what mattered most was to achieve that organic solidarity of entrepreneurs and workers *within the companies*, promoting a down-sizing that reflected to a certain degree the spirit of traditional corporativism. In this German system, the company managers took on the figure and the responsibility of "leaders" *(Betriebsführer)* and the workers that of their follow-ers *(Gefolgschaft)*, within a solidarity that was guaranteed and protected by vari-ous measures, with a great emphasis placed on ethics. Both managers and work-ers were asked to rise above the purely individual interest (maximizing profits and surpluses in the case of management, and the highest possible salary in the case of the workers, regardless of the company's financial status, the country's economy, and the situation in general), and thus to place a limit on the mere economic interest (a "tribunal of honor" was supposed to rule in times of con-flict). Thus, even during the period of rapid economic recovery following World War II, we can say the German workers worked with the same spirit of sacri-fice as a soldier; despite harsh life conditions, strikes for higher pay and more benefits were almost nonexistent during this period, in which a wide degree of free-market economy, and thus of non-protectionism, was severely testing the responsible initiative of any company owners who wanted to do well for them-selves. In Austria, Spain, and Portugal, organic-corporative models were also experimented with.

Thus, the basic conditions for the restoration of normal conditions are, on the one hand, the *deproletarization* of the worker and, on the other hand, the elimination of the worst type of capitalist, who is a parasitical recipient of prof-its and dividends and who remains extraneous to the productive process. In this last regard, we can rightly speak of the recent twofold defection on the part of the capitalist. At first, the figure of the capitalist-financier or speculator, who is extraneous to the day-to-day management of the businesses he owns, has emerged from the earlier figure of the capitalist-entrepreneur. In the second phase, what emerged was the type of capitalist who is not even a speculator, but someone who merely cashes in the dividends, barely knowing where they come from, employing them to support a vain and mundane lifestyle. It is evident that against these types, subversive propaganda has an easy time; nor is it possible to defeat the latter's arguments without removing the cause of the scandal—that is, without opposing the representatives of such a deteriorated form of capitalism. In a new corporative system, the capitalist, or the owner of the means of production, should instead assume the function of responsible leader, technical manager, and capable organizer of the businesses he owns, maintaining close personal ties with the most trusted and qualified elements of his companies, almost as if they were his headquarters, and being surrounded by loyal workers who are free from trade union control and are proud to belong to his company. The authority of such a type of capitalist-entrepreneur should be based not only on his specialized technical competence, control of the means of production, and a particular initiative and organizational skills, but also on some sort of political consecration, as I will suggest further on.

This point leads to the consideration of the relationships between economy and State, a consideration that should be prefaced by some remarks.

On of the main obstacles to the revival of the corporative spirit and to the overcoming of the proletarian spirit certainly lies in the change that the industrial revolution has brought about in the area of work conditions. In the varieties of what is essentially mechanical work it is very difficult to retain the character of "art" and of "vocation," and for the results of production to show any signature of the personality of those who worked to manufacture them. Hence the danger for the modern worker to be inclined to regard his work as mere necessity and his performance as a product sold to a third party in exchange for the highest possible remuneration. What is missing are the living, personal relationships that existed between workers and owners in the ancient corporations and even in many companies during the earlier capitalist era. The only thing that could help overcome this difficulty is the emergence of a new type, characterized by a certain kind of impersonality; this is no different from what may characterize the new type of fighter I talked about before. What is needed is the reemergence, within the world of technology and economy, of new forms of the anonymity and unselfishness that characterized ancient corporativism. In this regard it would be decisive to have an attitude that is no different from the one exhibited by those who know how to endure even through a war of attrition. In many regards, the test taking place amid machines and industrial conglomerates may turn out to be more difficult for the average man than the experiences of wartime. Whereas in war, physical annihilation is a constant possibility, nevertheless a body of moral and emotional factors supply man with a support that is for the most part lacking in the dull, monotonous front of modern work.

Coming back to the specifically economic domain, it is necessary to consider some modern instances of the organic reintegration of companies, which still pursue the wrong course. I will briefly mention the so-called "socialization," the name given to an economic system in which (unlike what is typical of nationalization and the collectivist centralization of the economy) the companies retain their autonomy, as their inner unity needs to be forged by the involvement of the workers in management (the right of co-direction, co-management, and co-determination) and by the distribution among them of the profits of the venture, with the exception of a certain amount that is the rightful interest of the capital.

The first thing to consider in this regard is that, as far as profit sharing is concerned, this type of system could represent something right only in the context of a wider principle of solidarity. Thus, if we want to implement profit sharing, we should also talk about a distribution among the workers of an eventual deficit of the company; this factor alone would deprive the formula of socialization of the mystique it exercises on the plane of a certain demagogy. After all, in big companies the amount of profit sharing will never be more important than base salaries, which suggests the political rather than social goal of this trend. It would be much more important to implement a differentiated determination of salaries, freed from the trade unions' imposed uniformity and commonly agreed upon in every company, depending on its conditions.

As far as co-participation with finalities that are not utilitarian-individualistic but rather truly *organic*, instead of the distribution of the dividends we should implement co-participation in the property. Ways should be devised through which the worker could gradually become a small owner (this is the only way to deproletarize him and thus to break the backbone of Marxism) by making him owner of nontransferable stocks of his company-corporation, although not beyond the measure necessary for the maintenance of the right hierarchical relations. This would be the best way to "integrate" the individual worker into his company, motivate him, and raise him above his most immediate interest as a mere rootless individual. In this way we could reproduce in a company's life the type of organic belonging that was proper to the ancient corporative formations.

As far as co-management and co-direction through "committees" and "internal commissions" are concerned, they represent a total absurdity when they occupy themselves with anything beyond the more immediate and personal interests limited to working conditions, and, in general, to what is expected from the subordinated, administrative part of a company. As far as the true direction and ultimate issue is concerned, trying to establish a type of "economic parliamentary system" in a company would entail ignoring the extremely differentiated and almost "esoteric" character played by the technical and managerial functions in contemporary high industry, a character for which every interference from below has a damaging, or at least disorganizing, effect. It would also be absurd to think that committees of soldiers could have an input in matters of high strategy, general mobilization, conduct, and organization in a modern war.[54] Besides the economic consideration, there is another one, no less important, that militates against the idea of co-management. In the system of an integrated company, what must be imposed, starting from the top of the hierarchy, are considerations that are not merely utilitarian, but political as well, on the basis of an equally superior and unquestionable authority. However, it is unavoidable that the control of the workers would cause the predominance of considerations that are purely economic and utilitarian, or political in the worst Marxist and classist sense of the word.

In fact, the spirit of "socialization" is a form of crypto-Marxism; it is almost a Trojan horse introduced into a noncommunist economic system, as the beginning of that conquest of the companies which in its declared and complete form corresponds to the tendency of a radical "trade unionism." The final phase of this process is the communist economy, through which the attack is launched not only on the company but on the State as well.

Similar radical demands were already loudly expressed at the margins of Fascist corporativism. According to some, the dualism inherent in this system needed to be overcome, as well as the corresponding "mobility" of the representatives of the workers and the owners, through a rigorous system of responsibilities. Technicians, differentiated as "directing" rather than "perform-ing" work, should have ceased to be the organs of capital and become the only leaders and managers in the organic unity of the corporation controlled by the trade unions. According to others, not only the "proletarian corporation" (an idea that could be considered up to a point and in certain circumstances) had to be instituted, but also the full incorporation of the State's bureaucracy into the corporative organs, and the identification of political representatives with cor-porative representatives, in the name of the "integral State based on Work." To this effect, the slogan "Introducing the worker into the citadel of the State" was proclaimed. This represented the path of the degeneration of politics into the economy, which was here indicated as the goal of true corporativism, or of a "radical and revolutionary corporativism."

I have briefly mentioned these tendencies in order to make it clear that wherever one leans toward organic and anti-dualistic forms, there can be only two possibilities or directions: we can proceed "from above" or "from below." We can allow the center of gravity of the structures, which are reorganized in a corporate manner according to the principle of competencies, to fall either on the inferior, material and trade union plane or on the superior, properly political plane.

Thus, it is necessary to reexamine the relationships between State and economy that must exist in a normal system. The conditions of the present era are such that a totally autonomous activity on the part of companies is virtually impossible. No matter how powerful and wide-ranging they are, these compa-nies must deal with forces and monopolies that control to a large degree the fundamental elements of the productive process. Thus, some have rightly no-ticed that today the truly relevant and serious problem is no longer a classist one, but rather the problem of the restraint that needs to be placed on the wild and unscrupulous struggle among various monopolies, and especially among the monopoly of goods and materials (cooperatives), the monopoly of money (banking, finance, stock speculations), and the monopoly of labor (trade unions).[55] Considering the way things are in modern society, only the State can effectively avoid the destructive results of this struggle, limit the power of these groups that exist outside and above the companies, and thus ensure the latter conditions of security and regulated production. This could happen only where the State appears as a super-ordained power, capable of facing and defeating any subversive force, no matter how powerful it may be.

The only realistic way to redistribute wealth is by a forceful action by the state.

In the contemporary era it is absolutely important that *the struggle against a degenerate and arrogant Capitalism be waged from above*—in other words, that the State will be the one to assume the initiative of mercilessly fighting this phenomenon and restoring normal conditions, rather than leaving to the Left alone the right of accusation and protest (which then are used to justify subversive actions). Today a modern State, integrated in this way, would have sufficient powers for such an action. The situation of the contemporary economy is such that a rigorous ostracism on the part of the State would prove deadly for any capitalist group, no matter how powerful. The preliminary condition would naturally be the overcoming of the typical situation in democracies, where the political element makes promiscuous alliances with the plutocratic element, opening itself to corruption and pretending to represent a "Right" in opposition to Marxism. Again, the pure political power must be released from every bond—first from the bonds of capitalism, and then from those of the economy. Even from a practical point of view, when we take into account what is "all too human," there is no reason the representatives of the pure political principle should prostitute themselves and be enslaved to the representatives of capitalism, as now they hold power in their hands and *could* have the power by which to determine the possibility to dominate wealth and dictate orders to the lords of capital. The regime of corruption is possible, and even unavoidable, where a strong traditional State does not exist and where the State is reduced to an instrument that the ambitious and unscrupulous politician exploits individually in order to benefit from the advantages connected to various political offices. But if a strong traditional State were to arise in opposition to degenerate and arrogant capitalism, the polemics of the Left would thereby be nullified. This would also frustrate any attempt on the part of the economy to gain control in the State, in a Marxist or semi-Marxist sense (trade unionism, labor movements, etc.) with the pretext of setting things right and of promoting an alleged "social justice." Thus, it is decisive whether a really sovereign State is capable of preventing the subversive forces and replacing them with an appropriate *revolution from above*.[56]

The main problem, then, is to establish organic though not totalitarian relations between the State and companies-corporations, excluding or greatly reducing any power, front, monopoly, and foreign interest that is extraneous to a healthy economy and a pure political approach.

To this effect, the traditional legacy can again be an inspiration: we could refer to the *feudal system*, after it has been adequately translated into and adapted to modern categories. That which in the feudal system was the bestowal of a particular land and the corresponding jurisdiction or a partial sovereignty, in an economic context would amount to the State's acknowledgment of private economic complexes responsible for certain productive functions, and enjoying a wide degree of initiative and autonomy. This bestowal would imply economic protection in time of need, but also the counterpart of a bond of "loyalty" and accountability to the political power, or the acceptance of an "eminent domain" proper to the latter, even though limited to situations of emergency and particular tension. On such bases a system could be built that incorporates both unity and plurality, the political and the economic factors, planning, and a range of free initiative and personal responsibility. Therefore, there would be no totalitarian centralization on the part of the State, nor measures that disturb or pressure economic groups and processes, as long as the latter act in an orderly fashion. General directives and overall schemes may be issued, but as far as their execution is concerned, maximum room must be given to the spirit of initiative and of organization.[57] Within the overall system will be a hierarchical system. This system consists of "work units"—that is, organically integrated companies, with a work force gathered around their managers, who in turn rally around the State, in the context of a rigorous regime of competencies and of production, with the elimination of every form of "poisonous" classist ideology and irresponsible activism. Moreover, to proceed even partially in such a direction would amount to going beyond the climate of the "economic era," thanks to the special antiproletarian and anticapitalist ethos that all this presupposes. The ultimate goal of the corporative idea, understood in this fashion, is to effectively elevate the lower activities connected with production and material concerns to the plane that in a qualitative hierarchy comes immediately after the economic one in an ascending direction; in the system of ancient or functional castes, this plane was that of the warrior caste, which ranked higher than the merchant caste and the workers' caste. It becomes evident that if this system were to take effect, the world of the economy too would reflect the clear, virile, and personalized ethos that is proper to a society based on the general type of the "warrior" (in terms of character and of general disposition) rather than of the "merchant" and "worker." This would mark the beginning of a revival.

These brief mentions concerning an overall orientation will suffice here, as the study of the concrete formulas in which the aforementioned issues could be actualized falls outside the scope of this book. I want to reiterate that the economic order should never be anything more than an *order of means:* thus, in principle, it must be subjected to an order of ends that transcend the economic plane and stand in the same relationship to it as the higher goals and even the emotional life of the individual stand in relation to the elementary requirements of his physical existence.

This is why the formula of a "State based on work" represents a pure aberration, or something turned upside down, degrading, and degenerated; it is the opposite of the traditional view. To this regard, I will add the following considerations.

The Fascist reform that led to the constitution of the House of Corporations, in opposition to the party-based democratic parliamentary system, certainly had various legitimate features. What was meant to be established was a regime of competence in opposition to the political incompetence that is rampant in a democratic regime and thus exercises disturbing influences in the economic domain. Such a line may be developed once again, first by revising the Fascist system of corporative representation in view of a different institution. Such an institution will not include the corporation in the Fascist bureaucratic sense, but rather the corporations in the aforementioned sense of organic units and complexes variously coordinated and arranged in a hierarchical fashion.

As a foundation, what must be implemented here is the above-mentioned principle of the depoliticization of the socioeconomic forces. The rigid application of the principle of competency should deprive any corporative representation of what may be called its "political surplus value." The Corporative House of Representatives should not have the traits of a political assembly. It should merely constitute the Lower House; political concerns would be dealt with in an Upper House, ranked above the former. Once the economy is brought back within its normal limitations, something becomes evident. When, within the context of corporativism, the economy affects the legislative order and when the need arises to deal with those problems of organization on a large scale (which have become fundamental in a modern economy, and concern the power of the State), then it becomes necessary to adequately implement higher criteria through a distinct and more complex organ, endowed with a higher authority and representing the supreme and final authority in controversial cases.

This organ should be the Upper House. While in the Corporative House the economy and everything that concerns the professional world would be represented, the political concerns should be concentrated and addressed in the Upper House through men who represent and defend not only interests that are economic and material, but also spiritual and national interests of prestige and power; these men are responsible for ensuring that a constant, overall direction be maintained in the solution of all the main problems concerning the physical-material component of the political organism.

A mixed system of elections and appointments, not dissimilar from the one devised for the Fascist political-corporative representations, could also be allowed in the Lower House. However, analogously to what was proper in the representations that existed in the past in other nations, the democratic principle should be excluded in the case of the Upper House; one should belong to it not by being voted into office or on a contingent and temporal basis, but by designation from above and for life, almost as it were an Order, on the basis of one's natural dignity and inalienable qualification. In fact, it is necessary to ensure stability and continuity not only at the top, where the stable, pure principle of the *imperium* resides, but almost as if by participation, too, in a selected group that has the characteristics and functions of a political class, as was once the legacy of the traditional nobility. Institutionally, this would be actualized in the Upper House. And when those who are part of the Upper House exemplified the same severe impersonality, the same distance from mere necessities and contingencies of the time, the same neutrality toward every particular and partisan interest (obviously in such a system there would be no room for "political parties" in the current ideological sense), which the pure symbol of sovereignty eminently embodies—then there would be no doubt about the monolithic character of a structure that is really able to assert itself against every action of the subversive forces of the "economic era."

Thirteen

OCCULT WAR
WEAPONS OF
THE OCCULT WAR

I

Various causes have been adduced to explain the crisis that has affected and still affects the life of modern peoples: historical, social, socioeconomic, political, moral, and cultural causes, according to different perspectives. The part played by each of these causes should not be disputed. However, we need to ask a higher and essential question: are these *always* the first causes and do they have an inevitable character like those causes found in the material world? Do they supply an ultimate explanation or, occasionally, is it necessary to identify influences of a higher order, which may cause what has occurred in the West to appear very suspicious, and which, beyond the multiplicity of individual aspects, suggest there is the same logic at work?

The concept of *occult war* must be defined within the context of the dilemma. The occult war is a battle that is waged imperceptibly by the forces of global subversion, with means and in circumstances ignored by current historiography. The notion of occult war belongs to a three-dimensional view of history: this view does not regard as essential the two superficial dimensions of time and space (which include causes, facts, and visible leaders) but rather emphasizes the dimension of *depth*, or the "subterranean" dimension in which forces and influences often act in a decisive manner, and which, more often not than not, cannot be reduced to what is merely human, whether at an individual or a collective level.

Having said that, it is necessary to specify the meaning of the term *subterranean*. We should not think, in this regard, of a dark and irrational background that stands in relation to the known forces of history as the unconscious stands to consciousness, in the way the latter relationship is discussed in the recently developed "Depth Psychology." If anything, we can talk about the unconscious only in regard to those who, according to the three-dimensional view, appear to be history's *objects* rather than its *subjects*, since in their thoughts and conduct they are scarcely aware of the influences they obey and the goals they contribute toward achieving. In these people, the center falls more in the unconscious and the preconscious than in the clear reflected consciousness, no matter what they—who are often men of action and ideologues—believe. Considering this relation, we can say the most decisive actions of the occult war take place in the human unconscious. However, if we consider the true agents of history in the special aspects we are now discussing, things are otherwise: here we cannot talk of the subconscious or the unconscious, for we are dealing with intelligent forces that know very well what they want and the means most suited to achieve their objectives.

The third dimension of history should not be diluted in the fog of abstract philosophical or sociological concepts, but rather should be thought of as a "backstage" dimension where specific "intelligences" are at work.

An investigation of the secret history that aspires to be positivist and scientific should not be too lofty or removed from reality. However, it is necessary to assume as the ultimate reference point a dualistic scheme not dissimilar from the one found in an older tradition. Catholic historiography used to regard history not only as a mechanism of natural, political, economic, and social causes, but also as the unfolding of divine Providence, to which hostile forces are opposed. These forces are sometimes referred to in a moralistic fashion as "forces of evil," or in a theological fashion as the "forces of the Antichrist." Such a view has a positive content, provided it is purified and emphasized by bringing it to a less religious and more metaphysical plane, as was done in Classical and Indo-European antiquity: forces of the *cosmos* against forces of *chaos*. To the former corresponds everything that is form, order, law, spiritual hierarchy, and tradition in the higher sense of the word; to the latter correspond every influence that disintegrates, subverts, degrades, and promotes the predominance of the inferior over the superior, matter over spirit, quantity over quality. This is what can be said in regard to the ultimate reference points of the various influences that act upon the realm of tangible causes behind known history. These must be kept into account, though with some prudence. Let me repeat: aside from this necessary metaphysical background, let us never lose sight of concrete history.

Today more than ever it is necessary to refer to these perspectives, which should not be confused with mere speculations and which, besides having a value for knowledge, can supply weapons for the right course of action. In a document that I will soon discuss, it is written:

> Because the mentality of Gentiles is of a purely animal nature, they are unable to foresee the consequences to which a cause may lead, if it is portrayed in a certain light. It is precisely in this difference between Jews and non-Jews that we can easily recognize God's election, as well as our super-human nature, in comparison with the instinctive and animalistic mentality of the Gentiles. The latter see the facts, but do not foresee them and are unable to invent anything other than material things.

Apart from the reference to Jews, who this document purports are the only secret agents of world subversion (we shall see later if this is so), such considerations are true in general only for those whom I have called history's "objects." When measured against that of their disguised opponents, the mentality of the great majority of modern men of action appears to be quite primitive. The latter concentrate their energies on what is tangible and "concrete," and are unable to perceive the interplay of concordant actions and reactions, causes and effects, beyond a very limited and almost always coarsely materialistic horizon.

The deeper causes of history—here we can refer to both those that act in a negative sense and those that may act in an equilibrating and positive sense—operate prevalently through what can be called "imponderable factors," to use an image borrowed from natural science. These causes are responsible for almost undetectable ideological, social, and political changes, which eventually produce remarkable effects: they are like the first cracks in a layer of snow that eventually produce an avalanche. These causes almost never act in a direct manner, but instead bestow to some existing processes an adequate *direction* that leads to the designated goal. Thus, men and groups who believe they are pursuing something willed by themselves become the means through which something different is realized and made possible: it is precisely in this that a super-ordained influence and meaning are revealed. This was noticed by Wundt, who talked about the "heterogeneity of the effects," and by Hegel as well, who introduced the notion of the *List der Vernunft* [Cunning of Reason] in his philosophy of history; however, neither of these thinkers was able to fruitfully develop his intuitions. Unlike what happens in the domain of physical phenomena, an insightful historian encounters several instances where the "causal" explanation (in the deterministic, physical sense) is unsatisfactory, because things do not add up and the total does not equal the sum of the apparent historical factors—almost as if someone adding five, three, and two ended up not with ten, but with fifteen or seven. This differential, especially when it appears as a differential between what is willed and what has really happened, or between ideas, principles, and programs on the one hand and their effective consequences in history on the other, offers the most valuable material for the investigation of the secret causes of history.

Methodologically speaking, we must be careful to prevent valid insights from degenerating into fantasies and superstition, and not develop the tendency to see an occult background everywhere and at all costs. In this regard, every assumption we make must have the character of what are called "working hypotheses" in scientific research—as when something is admitted provisionally, thus allowing the gathering and arranging of a group of apparently isolated facts, only to confer on them a character not of hypothesis but of truth when, at the end of a serious inductive effort, the data converge in validating the original assumption. Every time an effect outlasts and transcends its tangible causes, a suspicion should arise, and a positive or negative influence behind the stages should be perceived. A problem is posited, but in analyzing it and seeking its solution, prudence must be exercised. The fact that those who have ventured in this direction have not restrained their wild imaginations has discredited what could have been a science, the results of which could hardly be overestimated. This too meets the expectations of the hidden enemy.

This is all I have to say concerning the general premises proper to a new three-dimensional study of history. Now let us return to what I said earlier on. After considering the state of society and modern civilization, one should ask if this is not a specific case that requires the application of this method; in other words, one should ask whether some situations of real crisis and radical subversion in the modern world can be satisfactorily explained through "natural" and spontaneous processes, or whether we need to refer to something that has been concerted, a still unfolding plan devised by forces hiding in the shadows.

In this particular domain, many red flags have gone up: too many elements have concurred to alarm the less superficial observers. In the middle of the past century, Disraeli wrote these significant and often quoted words: "The world is governed by people entirely different from the ones imagined by those who are unable to see behind the scenes." Malinsky and De Poncins, when considering the phenomenon of revolution, have remarked that in our age, where it is commonly acknowledged that every disease of the individual organism is caused by bacteria, people pretended that the diseases of the social body—revolutions and disorder—are spontaneous, self-generated phenomena rather than the effect of invisible agents, acting in society the way bacteria and pathogenic germs act in the organism of the individual. Disraeli, in the mid-nineteenth century, wrote:

> The public does not realize that in all the conflicts within nations and in the conflicts between nations there are, besides the people apparently responsible for them, hidden agitators who with their selfish plans make these conflicts unavoidable. . . . Everything that happens in the confused evolution of peoples is secretly prepared in order to ensure the dominion of certain people: it is these people, known and unknown, that we must find behind every public event.[58]

In this order of ideas, there is an interesting document known as *The Protocols of the Learned Elders of Zion*. I have discussed the nature and scope of this document in the introduction to its last Italian edition (Rome, 1937). Here I will only mention some fundamental points.

This document was purported to be a protocol stolen from a secret Judeo-Masonic organization and allegedly reveals a plan that was devised and implemented with the subversion and the destruction of traditional Europe in mind. Regarding the authenticity of the *Protocols* a rabid and complex debate has erupted, which can be dismissed, however, by Guénon's correct observation that a truly occult organization, no matter what its nature, never leaves behind written documents or "protocols." Thus, in the most favorable hypothesis, the *Protocols* could have been the work of someone who had contacts with some representatives of this alleged organization. However, we cannot agree either with those who wish to dismiss this document as a vulgar mystification, forgery, and work of plagiarism. The main argument adduced by the latter is that the *Protocols* reproduce and paraphrase in many parts the ideas found in a short book written by a certain Maurice Joly during the period of Napoleon's Second Empire.[59] Allegedly, mysterious provocateurs of the Czar's secret police were responsible for writing the *Protocols*. This argument is truly irrelevant: those who decry plagiarism should keep in mind that this is not a matter of a literary work or of copyright. For example, when a general writes a plan, he could employ previous materials and writings as long as they contain ideas fit for his purpose. This would be a case of plagiarism, but it would not affect at all the question of whether or not this plan has really been conceived and carried out. Cutting short all this—that is, leaving aside the issue of the "authenticity" of the document in terms of real protocols stolen from an international secret organization—the only important and essential point is the following: this writing is part of a group of texts that in various ways (more or less fantastic and at times even fictional) have expressed the feeling that the disorder of recent times is not accidental, since it corresponds to a plan, the phases and fundamental instruments of which are accurately described in the *Protocols*. Hugo Wast wrote: "The *Protocols* may well be a fake, but their predictions have been fulfilled in an amazing way." Henry Ford added: "The only comment that I can make about the *Protocols* is that they perfectly correspond to what is happening today. They were published sixteen years ago, and ever since then they have corresponded to the world situation and today they still dictate its rhythm."[60] In a sense, we can speak of a prophetic premonition. In any event, the value of the document as a working hypothesis is undeniable: it presents the various aspects of global subversion (among them, some aspects that were destined to be outlined and accomplished only many years after the publication of the *Protocols*) in terms of a whole, in which they find their sufficient reason and logical combination.

As I have said, this is not the place to engage in a detailed analysis of the text; it will suffice to recall the main points. First of all, the primary ideologies that are responsible for the modern disorder did not arise spontaneously, but have been evoked and supported by forces that knew they were false[61] and had in mind only the latter's destructive and demoralizing effects. This would apply to democratic and liberal ideas; the Third Estate had purposely been mobilized to destroy the previous feudal and aristocratic society, while in a second phase the workers were mobilized to undermine the bourgeois. Another basic idea of the *Protocols* is that, despite all, the capitalist and the proletarian Internationals are in agreement, being almost two columns with distinct ideas but which act in unison at a tactical level in order to achieve the same strategy. Likewise, the economization of life, especially in the context of an industry that develops at the expense of agriculture, and a wealth that is concentrated on liquid capital and finance, proceeds from a secret design. The phalanx of the modern "economists" followed this design, just as those who spread a demoralizing literature attack spiritual and ethical values and scorn every principle of authority. Among other things, mention is made of the success that the secret front achieved not only for Marxism, but for Darwinism and Nietzsche's nihilism as well.[62] The *Protocols* at times even encourage the spread of anti-Semitism, while in other cases mention is made of the secret monopoly of the press and of the media in democratic countries as well as the power to paralyze or destroy the most prestigious banks. This power concentrates the rootless, financial wealth in a few hands, and through it controls peoples, parties, and governments. One of the most important objectives is to remove the support of spiritual and traditional values from the human personality, knowing that when this is accomplished it is not difficult to turn man into a passive instrument of the secret front's direct forces and influences. The counterpart of the action of cultural demoralization, materialization, and disorganization causes unavoidable social crises to grow increasingly worse and collective situations to grow increasingly desperate and unbearable; in this way, a final conflict will eventually be considered as the means to finally sweep away the last residual resistance.

It is difficult to deny that such a "fiction" exposed at the beginning of this century has indeed reflected and anticipated much of what has taken place in the modern world, not to mention the predictions of what is in store for us. It is therefore no surprise that the *Protocols* received so much attention from those movements of the past that intended to react against and stem the currents of national, social, and moral dissolution in their own day and age. However, these movements often upheld dangerously unilateral positions, due to the lack of adequate discernment; this was a weakness that, again, has played into the enemy's hands.

In relation to this, we must deal with the issue raised by this document concerning the leaders of the occult war. According to the *Protocols*, the leaders of the global plot are Jews who planned and undertook the destruction of the traditional and Christian European civilization in order to achieve the universal rule of Israel, or God's "chosen people." This is obviously an exaggeration. At this point we may even wonder whether a fanatical anti-Semitism, which always sees the Jew as a *deus ex machina*, is not unwittingly playing into the hands of the enemy. One of the means employed by the occult forces to protect themselves consists of directing their opponents' attention toward those who are only partially responsible for certain upheavals, thus concealing the rest of the story, namely a wider sequence of causes. It could be shown that even if the

Protocols were a forgery perpetrated by provocateurs, nonetheless they reflect ideas very congenial to the Law and spirit of Israel. Second, it is true that many Jews have been and still are among the promoters of modern disorder in its more radical cultural expressions, whether political or social. This, however, should not prevent a deeper analysis, capable of exposing forces that may have employed modern Judaism merely as an instrument. After all, despite the fact that many Jews are among the apostles of the main ideologies regarded by the *Protocols* as instruments of global subversion (i.e., liberalism, socialism, scientism, and rationalism), it is also evident that these ideas would have never arisen and triumphed without historical antecedents, such as the Reformation, Humanism, the naturalism and individualism of the Renaissance, and the philosophy of Descartes. Such phenomena cannot be attributed to Judaism, but rather point to a wider web of influences.

In the *Protocols* the concepts of Judaism and Masonry are interwoven; therefore, in the literature that this text spawned, mention is often made in careless terms of a Jewish-Masonic plot. Here caution must be exercised. While recognizing the Jewish predominance in many sectors of modern Masonry, as well as the Jewish origin of several elements in the Masonic symbolism and rituals, the anti-Semitic thesis, according to which Masonry has been the creation and tool of Israel, must be rejected. Modern Masonry (with this designation I allude essentially to the Freemasonry that developed since the creation of London's Grand Lodge in 1717) has undoubtedly been one of the societies that promoted the modern political subversions, and especially their ideological background. However, here too the danger is to be distracted by explaining everything with the action of ordinary Masonry.

Among those who regard the *Protocols* as a forgery, there are some who have noticed that various ideas in this text are similar to those that have been implemented by centralizing and dictatorial regimes, so much so that the *Protocols* can be an excellent manual for those who wish to install a new Bonapartism or totalitarianism. This view is partially correct. This amounts to saying that the "occult war" should be conceived, from a positive point of view, within a wide and elastic context, and we should expose the part played in it by phenomena that are apparently contradictory and hardly reducible to the simplistic formula of a Jewish-Masonic global plot.[63]

Regardless of the role played by Jews and Masonry in the modern subversion, it is necessary to recognize clearly the real historical context of their influence, as well as the limit beyond which the occult war is destined to develop by employing forces that not only are no longer those of Judaism and of Masonry, but that could even totally turn against them. To realize this, consider the *law of the regression of the castes*, which I have employed as a hermeneutic tool in my *Revolt Against the Modern World* in order to assess the effective meaning of history. From a civilization led by spiritual leaders and by a sacred regality, a shift occurred to civilizations led by mere warrior aristocracies; the latter were eventually replaced by the civilization of the Third Estate. The last stage is the collectivist civilization of the Fourth Estate. When we reflect carefully on things, modern Judaism as a *power* (quite apart from the concomitant, widespread, and instinctive action of individual Jewish thinkers and writers) is inseparable from capitalism and finance, which fall within the civilization of the Third Estate. The same applies to modern Masonry, which prepared ideologically for and supported the advent of the Third Estate. Masonry still presents itself today as the custodian of the principles of the Enlightenment and the French Revolution, its doctrines acting as a kind of secular religion of modern democracy; its militant action has revealed and continues to reveal itself along this line, openly or in semisecret ways. All this falls within the penultimate phase; this phase, the overall cycle of democratic and capitalist civilization of the Third Estate, will eventually usher in the last collectivist phase, to which it has inadvertently opened the way. It is therefore logical that the role of a central guiding force of global subversion in this last period will no longer be played by Judaism or Masonry and that the main current may turn against both of these groups, as if they were residues to be liquidated once and for all; after all, this can be seen in countries in which regimes controlled by the Fourth Estate (i.e., Marxist regimes) are beginning to be consolidated, even though Jews and Masons contributed to their advent.

But then again, as far as the general radical Jewish-Masonic conspiracy thesis upheld in some milieus is concerned, the actual situation shows its inconsistency. It would be a real abandonment to fantasy to suppose that the leaders of the great conflicting powers—the United States, the USSR, and Red China—receive orders from an international center of Jews and Masons (almost nonexistent in China), and act accordingly in view of the same goal. Again, it is necessary to refer to a wider horizon of influences and to look elsewhere.

II

For practical purposes, too, it is very important to recognize the instruments of the occult war, namely the means employed by the secret forces of global subversion to conceal their action, prevent their opponents' action, and continue to exercise their influence. I will now say something in this regard, drawing inspiration from some of the points developed by René Guénon, who was one of the most perceptive people in reference to the secret backgrounds of many upheavals of modern times.

Let us begin with the tool of *scientific suggestion.* I believe the "scientific" method of considering events and history is more the consequence of a suggestion spread in modern culture by antitraditional forces in order to conceal their action than the natural orientation of a shortsighted mentality. Those who believe that history is made only by the men on the stage and determined by the most evident economic, social, political, and cultural factors do not see and do not seek any other explanation; and yet this is exactly what every force operating in secret desires. A civilization dominated by the positivist prejudice offers the most fertile ground to an action arising from what I have called the "third dimension." In great part this is the case with modern civilization. It is a civilization rendered myopic and defenseless by the positivist, rationalist, and scientist prejudice. We have scarcely begun to expose all the ideas that remain as the basis of the modern mentality and education; these ideas are not so much errors and limitations as they are suggestions spread and promoted for precise reasons by antitraditional forces.

I have already mentioned some nonpositivist views of the course of events that introduce various entities, such as the "absolute Spirit," or the *élan vital,* or "History." In this we can see an example of the possible application of a second instrument of the occult war, the *tactic of replacement.* This tactic is employed every time there is the danger of an awakening on the part of "history's objects," or when some ideas that facilitate the occult game of the forces of global subversion have lost their power of suggestion. In the above-mentioned case, such confused philosophical views act as a sort of bait for those who are unsatisfied with positivist views, so that their eyes may not look in the direction where they should. Due to the vagueness of these notions, the field is not any less concealed than by positivist blindness. People will play around with "philosophical ideas" while the plan continues to unfold.

Often the tactic of replacement develops efficaciously in the form of a *tactic of counterfeits.* It may happen that after the effects of the destructive work reach the material plane, they become so visible as to provoke a reaction, and thus ideas and symbols are employed for a defense and a reconstruction. In the best scenario they are values of the traditional past, which come back to life thanks to this existential reaction of a society or civilization threatened by dissolution. Then the occult war is not waged in a direct manner; often attention is paid to promoting only distortions and counterfeits of these ideas. In this way, the reaction is contained, deviated, or even led in the opposite direction.

Such a tactic may be employed in various domains, from the spiritual and cultural to the political. An example is given by "traditionalism." I have already discussed what the term *tradition* signifies in the higher sense of the word: it is the form bestowed by forces from above upon the overall possibilities of a given cultural area and specific period, through super-individual and even antihistorical values and through elites that know how to derive an authority and natural prestige from such values. In the present day it often happens that a confused desire to return to "tradition" is purposely channeled to the form of "traditionalism." The content of this "traditionalism" consists of habits, routines, surviving residues and vestiges of what once was, without a real understanding of the spiritual world and of what in them is not merely factual but has a character of perennial value. Thus, such nontraditional or, should we say, "traditionalist" attitudes offer an easy target to the enemy, whose attack mounted against traditionalism is only the opening barrage preceding an attack against Tradition itself: to this purpose the slogans of "anachronism," "anti-history," "immobilism," and "regression" are employed. Thus, reaction is paralyzed as the maneuver leads successfully to the preestablished goal.

From the general plane it is easy to shift to particular cases, since recent history is full of them. Thus, in the political context, the Roman idea with its symbols, the "Aryan" idea, and the idea of the Empire or Reich—to all this the tactic of misleading substitutions and counterfeits has been applied with deprecable effects that cannot elude an attentive observer. Therefore, it is possible to understand the validity of the points I made in the first chapter.

Fourth, we must point out the *tactic of inversion.* Let us take a typical example. The secret forces of global subversion knew exactly that the basis of the order to be destroyed consisted in the supernatural element—that is, in the spirit—conceived not as a philosophical abstraction or as an element of faith, but as a superior reality, as a reference point for the integration of everything that is human.

After limiting the influence that could be exercised in this regard by Christianity, through the spread of materialism and scientism, the forces of global subversion have endeavored to conveniently divert any tendency toward the supernatural arising outside the dominant religion and the limitation of its dogmas. So-called "neo-spiritualism,"[64] not only in its more deleterious spiritualist forms, but also in its pseudo-Eastern and occultist forms (not to mention the theories concerning the unconscious, the irrational, and so on), is greatly influenced by the tactic of inversion. Instead of rising toward what is beyond the person as a really supernatural element, here we remain in the subpersonal and in the infrarational, according to an inversion that quite often has sinister characteristics.

The results achieved in this way are twofold. First, it was easy to extend the discredit that in numerous cases rightly affected these ideas to different ideas that might appear related, even though in their innermost essence they have nothing in common; thus, the latter genuine ideas are put in a condition to no longer pose a threat. A good part of what the West has learned about the East, outside the dry and sterile domain of philology and academic specialization, is often affected by this maneuver. The results seem to be for the most part something distorted; this severely limits the positive influence that various aspects of the legacy of ancient Eastern spirituality are liable to exercise, provoking the reaction of the most obtuse and inappropriate "defenses of the West." Another example lies in the milieus that, when it comes to symbols and esotericism, can think only of Masonry or Theosophy, even when the reference goes back to ancient and noble traditions that have nothing to do with the latter; the positivist and rationalist prejudice of a certain critical "culture" identifies all this as superstition and fantasy, thus completing the smear campaign. This is the case with examples of some militant Catholic apologetics that see only naturalism and pantheism in everything outside their perspective; these are misunderstandings and effects of an interplay of concordant actions and reactions, to which several representatives of Catholicism are liable.

The second result does not concern the domain of ideas but rather the practical and concrete domain. The inverted tendencies toward the spiritual and the supernatural can favor the emergence of dark forces, and be resolved in a deceitful action against the human personality. Many reactions against rationalism and intellectualism lead exactly to this, especially the theories of the unconscious, which through psychoanalysis have either generated a well-established practice or encouraged various forms of morbid fascination.

Another method is the *tactic of ricochet*. This occurs when the traditional forces being targeted take the initiative through an action against other traditional forces, an action that eventually ricochets back at its promoters. For instance, the secret forces of global subversion, through opportune infiltrations or suggestions, may induce the representatives of a certain tradition to believe that the best way to strengthen it consists of either undermining or discrediting other traditions. Those who do not realize what is going on and who, because of material interests, attack Tradition in like-minded people sooner or later must expect to see Tradition attacked in themselves, by ricochet. The forces of global subversion rely very much on this tactic; thus, they attempt in every possible way to cause any higher idea to give in to the tyranny of individual interests or proselytizing, prideful, and power-hungry tendencies. They know perfectly well that this is the best way to destroy every unity and solidarity and to favor a state of affairs in which their overall scheme will be implemented. They know well that there is an objective law of immanent justice and that "the mills of God grind slowly, but they grind exceeding fine," and thus they act accordingly; they wait for the fruits of these inconsiderable initiatives to mature and then they intervene.

In the political domain, the case of every Machiavellian employment of revolutionary forces falls within this category. Shortsighted political leaders have often believed that to arouse or to support revolution in hostile nations is, in certain circumstances, an excellent means to benefit their own people. Without realizing it, or in becoming aware of it too late, they have obtained the opposite result. While they thought they were using the revolution as a means, it was the revolution that used them as tools; eventually, the revolution spread to other countries, catching up with the politicians who unleashed it and wiping them out. Modern history has been in part the theater of a subversion that has tragically spread in this way.

Thus, we can never emphasize too much that unconditioned loyalty to an idea is the only possible protection from occult war; where such loyalty falls short and where the contingent goals of "real politics" are obeyed, the front of resistance is already undermined. The ricochet should be seen in an analogous context, in the case of "peoples' right to self-determination." This principle, after having been employed by modern democracies as an ideological instrument during World War II, eventually affected white peoples, thus putting an end to Europe's prestige and preeminence.

When the secret forces of world subversion are fearful of exposure or realize that, due to special circumstances, the direction imparted from backstage
has become obvious, at least in its major effects, they employ the *scapegoat tactic.* They try to shift the enemy's attention onto elements that are responsible
only partially, or in a subordinated fashion, for their own wrongful deeds. A
reaction is unleashed against those elements, which then become the scapegoats. Thus, after a pause, the secret front may resume its work, because its
opponents believe they have identified the enemy and dealt with it. Talking
about the *Protocols*, I have mentioned a possible example of such tactics in reference to the part attributed to Jews and Masons. Thus, we must beware of any
unilaterality and never lose sight of the overall picture of the secret front.

Let us now discuss the *tactic of dilution*, which constitutes a particular aspect
of the "tactic of surrogates." The main example that I will now introduce must
be prefaced with the following: the process that has led to the current crises
has remote origins and has developed in several phases.[65] In each of these phases
the crisis was already present, though in a latent or potential form. The theory
of "progress" may be regarded as one of the suggestions spread by the secret
forces of world subversion so that attention would be diverted from the origins
and the process of dissolution could proceed, carried forth by the illusion of
the triumphs of technological-industrial civilization. The tragic events of recent times have provoked a partial awakening from this hypnosis. Many people
have begun to realize that the march of so-called progress paralleled a race
toward the abyss. Thus, to stop and return to the origins as the only way to
restore a normal civilization has been the inspiring vision for many. Next, the
occult front employed new means to prevent any radical reaction. Here, too, it
employed the slogans of "anachronism" and "reactionary and retrograde forces";
then it caused the forces that aimed at a return to the origins to be led toward
stages in which the crisis and the disease were present in less extreme forms,
though still clearly visible. This trap worked as well. The leaders of world
subversion naturally know that, once this is done, there is no longer a real
danger: it is enough to wait and soon we will be back at the starting point, by
following processes analogous to the ones that have already occurred, but now
without the possibility of any resistance to the dissolution.

There are many historical examples of this tactic, which should be rather
instructive for those who hope to assume the initiative of a reconstructive
action. As a first example, we should examine closely some traits of modern

nationalism. We know about the revolutionary, subversive, and antihierarchical function that the collectivist-demagogic concept of "nation" has played against the previous forms of European civilization and political organization. The reference point of many people who have fought against the various internationals (especially against the communist International) has been the concept of the nation; care was rarely taken to define such a concept in a way that would no longer represent what needed to be opposed.

In this regard, it will suffice to recall what I have said earlier about the opposition existing between popular nationalism and the spiritual nation, between national State and traditional State (see chapter 3). In the first case, nationalism has a leveling and antiaristocratic function; it is like the prelude to a wider leveling, the common denominator of which is no longer the nation, but rather the International. In the second case, the idea of the nation may serve as the foundation for a new recovery and an important first reaction against the internationalist dissolution; it upholds a principle of differentiation that still needs to be further carried through toward an articulation and hierarchy within every single people. But where the awareness of this opposition is lacking, as in indiscriminate nationalism, there is a danger of being subjected to the tactic of dilution: this danger, incidentally, has already occurred. It is in view of this—that is, of such a possible meaning of nationalistic orientation—that Soviet communism, while opposing nationalism as a counterrevolutionary phenomenon, favors and supports it in the non-Marxist areas inhabited by the "underdeveloped" peoples, who are the alleged victims of colonialism, waiting for further developments to lead to the stage in which it will be able to reap its fruits.

I will mention here two more examples of the tactic of dilution. The first concerns the socioeconomic domain and is connected to all the "national" and social-conformist versions of Marxism; it is the same disease in diluted form. This is also the case with "socializing" theories, which are Trojan horses to be introduced into the citadel, in order to conquer it not with a direct attack, but rather through a natural and inevitable inner development. The second example concerns the cultural domain. I have already discussed the meaning of psychoanalytical theories in the context of the modern subversion. Among those who are capable of a healthy discernment there has been a reaction against the coarsest forms of this pseudo-science, which correspond to pure or "orthodox" Freudianism. The tactic of dilution was employed again; the formulation and spread of a spiritualized psychoanalysis for more refined tastes was furthered.

The result was that those who react against Freud and his disciples no longer do so against Jung, without realizing that what is at work here is the same inversion, though in a more dangerous form because it is subtler, and a contaminating exegesis ventures more decidedly into the domain of spirituality than in the case of Freud.

Another tactic is the *deliberate misidentification of a principle with its representatives.* In many regards the decay of traditional institutions began with the corruption of their worldly representatives. The effective dissolution and destruction has been made possible by the confusion between principles and people; this is another weapon of the occult war. When the representatives of a given principle prove to be unworthy of it, the criticism of them extends immediately to the principle itself and is especially directed against it. Instead of acknowledging that some individuals are not at the level of the principle, and instead of requiring that they be replaced by qualified individuals, in order to restore a situation of normalcy, it is claimed that the principle itself is false, corrupt, or passé, and that it should be replaced with a different principle. In almost every revolution this tactic has played a major role. It may also be characterized as that of portraying a crisis *in* the system as a crisis *of* the system. Examples of this kind are so prevalent that I hardly need mention them. The attack against monarchies and aristocracies has followed this path. Marxism has applied the same device, using the injustices of capitalism as a pretext in order to attack free-market economy and to proclaim a collectivist economy. In the spiritual domain the examples are numerous. The Lutheran Reformation used the corruption of the representatives of the Roman Church in order to question the principle of authority and many fundamental beliefs of the Catholic tradition, thus shifting over from people to principles.

Finally, I wish to mention one more instrument of the secret war, though it refers to a very particular domain: the tactic of the *replacing infiltrations.* It is when a certain spiritual or traditional organization falls into such a state of degeneration that its representatives know very little of its true, inner foundation, or the basis of its authority and prestige. The life of such an organization may then be compared to the automatic state of a sleepwalker, or living body deprived of its soul. In a sense a spiritual "void" has been created that can be filled, through infiltrations, by other subversive forces. These forces, while leaving the appearances unchanged, use the organization for totally different purposes, which at times may even be the opposite of those that were originally its own. We should also not rule out the case where such infiltrated elements work for the destruction of the organization that they now control—for example, by creating new scandals, liable to give rise to serious repercussions. In this particular instance what is employed on the outside is the previously mentioned tactic of mistaking the representatives for the principle. Even the knowledge of this can cast light on many phenomena of the past and present. Having mentioned Masonry, it must be stated that the genesis of modern Freemasonry as a subversive force is due to this tactic of replacement and inversion that is exercised within some of the oldest organizations, which Masonry retained as mere vestiges, structures, symbols, and hierarchies, while the effective guiding influences have a different nature altogether.

⟫•⟪

I hope that having limited myself to only a few examples and having primarily discussed principles will not prevent the reader from recognizing the multiple possibilities of application of those same principles in various spheres, for there is no sphere in which the occult war has not in some manner been undertaken and is not still being waged today. The most important sphere for the application of the knowledge of the weapons of the occult war is the inner one: the world of one's own thoughts. It is here that one needs to be on guard; it is here one should be able to recognize the subtle influences that try to suggest ideas and reactions to us in certain situations. If this can be accomplished, even if it is still not possible to identify the enemy in our midst, it would at least bar to him the main paths of his secret action.

In what I have expounded there is no philosophical speculation nor flight of fancy, but rather serious and positive ideas. I am firmly convinced that no fighter or leader on the front of counter-subversion and Tradition can be regarded as mature and fit for his tasks before developing the faculty to perceive this world of subterranean causes, so that he can face the enemy on the proper ground. We should recall the myth of the Learned Elders of the *Protocols:* compared to them, men who see only "facts" are like dumb animals. There is little hope that anything may be saved when among the leaders of a new movement there are no men capable of integrating the material struggle with a secret and inexorable knowledge, one that is not at the service of dark forces but stands instead on the side of the luminous principle of traditional spirituality.

Fourteen

LATIN CHARACTER
ROMAN WORLD
MEDITERRANEAN SOUL

I

In a previous chapter I mentioned the part played by anti-German prejudice in some patriotic Italian historiography influenced by Masonic and democratic-liberal ideology. This prejudice is also found in the cultural domain, and especially among those who cherish the myth of the Latin world. For these people, the catch phrase is "We are Latin and Mediterranean"; in their view, the natural tendencies and elective affinities of the Italians lean toward other nations of Latin culture, while spiritual barriers allegedly separate us from everything that is Germanic. Italians and Germans, it is claimed, will never understand each other. Our Latin civilization and mind-set stand in contrast with anything German. Some people have emphasized the religious domain, pointing to the Protestantism of Germanic populations versus the Catholicism of Latin peoples. The fact the German Rhineland, Austria, and Bavaria are Catholic is conveniently ignored.

In all this there is a misunderstanding, for the most part caused by stereotypical phrases and superficial ideas, but also by the Italian people's instinctual antipathy, which is motivated by questionable racial factors. It is very important for those who want to promote a revolutionary-conservative action to be able to acknowledge this.

Let us begin by asking: What is meant by the term "Latin"? To what domain does this word apply?

It is not a coincidence that in Italy the myth of the "Latin spirit" is cherished especially in literary and intellectual circles. In reality, the "Latin spirit" may be defined almost exclusively on the plane of letters and the arts, or of culture in the most external and decadent sense of the term. However, it would be more appropriate to talk about a "Romanic element," since it consists of reflections of late Classical civilization, which were preserved among populations already included in the orbit of the Roman empire; these populations appropriated Rome's language (i.e., Latin) and retained various forms of that late civilization. The fact is that this "Latin spirit" is just a facade, behind which deep ethnic and spiritual differences quite often provoked bitter controversies.

What matters to us is to notice that the "common Latin legacy" cannot be identified at all or characterized as "Roman"; in the above-mentioned aesthetic and humanistic traits and even in some juridical forms, what is "Latin" derives from a world that is "Roman" in name only—a world that the ancient, heroic, patrician Rome of Cato would probably have despised.

At this point we must make some general considerations about values, since we need to specify the meaning of that "Classical," Greco-Roman world that was the object of adoration for the humanists of the Renaissance. Without discussing this problem at great length, I will limit myself to saying that the "Classical" myth is very similar to the Enlightenment myth, according to which true civilization began only with the "triumphs" and the artistic creations of the Renaissance, following the dark Middle Ages. Even in the Classical myth, as it was formulated by the people I have mentioned before, we find this aesthetic and antitraditional mentality. What is portrayed as "Classical," in relation to Greece and Rome, is a period of civilization that, despite its external splendor and refinement, represented a decadence; in many regards this was the civilization that arose and prevailed when the cycle of the previous civilization, a heroic-sacred type of both Hellenic and Roman origin, was in its declining phase.

If we refer to the origins, the Latin myth is relativized and the "Latin spirit" appears unrelated to the fundamental creative forces of the peoples that it encompasses. From a philological perspective, we may note that if the Romance languages are essentially inspired by the ancient language of Rome, namely Latin, the Latin language, in turn, notoriously belongs to the general family of Indo-European languages, to which the German language legitimately belongs; it is a fact that the ancient Latin language (as far as words, articulation, syntax, and declensions are concerned) is more similar to German than to the other Latin Romance languages.

Things are similar in the ethnic domain, since it has long been established that both the early Roman world and early Hellas were the creations of forces belonging to the same Indo-European stock, from which later on the properly Germanic populations separated themselves. There is more. It is important to note that when we refer to the world of the origins, the expression "Latin" assumes a meaning that eventually undermines the thesis of today's zealous supporters of the anti-Nordic, Latin spirit. One of the results of recent studies concerning pre-Roman and prehistoric Rome is that the forefathers of the "Latins" were a people whose ethnic and spiritual kinship with the family of Nordic-Aryan peoples is unquestionable. These forefathers were a splinter group from the "battle-ax people," who practiced the ritual of cremation; this people, after traveling to central Italy, opposed the local Oscan-Sabellian civilization characterized by the funeral ritual of burial. The relationship of the latter civilization with the pre- and non-Indo-European Mediterranean and Asian-Mediterranean civilizations is also apparent.

Among the oldest traces left behind by these Nordic stocks, we should mention those discovered in Val Camonica. These traces have an interesting correspondence with the prehistoric traces of primordial races, both Northern-Atlantic (Franco-Cantabric civilization of the Cro-Magnons) and Northern-Scandinavian (Fossum culture). There we find the same symbols of a "solar" spirituality, the same style, the same absence of traces of feminine (telluric-maternal) cults that instead are abundant in non-Indo-European civilizations or in degenerated Mediterranean paleo-Indo-European civilizations (Pelasgians, Cretans; in Italy, the civilization of Maiella, the Etruscans, etc.) Moreover, there is an affinity among the traces of Val Camonica and the civilization of the Dorians, people who arrived in Greece from the North and created Sparta, and who worshiped Apollo as the Hyperborean god of light. Thus it was said that the migration of the peoples from whom the Latins descended (the final destination of their migration in Italy being Rome) was analogous to the Achaean-Doric migration that in Greece ended with the creation of Sparta; Rome and Sparta are both corresponding manifestations related to those that are properly Northern.[66]

With the early Roman spirit and with Sparta we find a heroic-sacred world that was characterized by a strict ethos, love of discipline and of a virile and dominating spiritual attitude. This world was not perpetuated in the following "Classical"[67] civilization from which, in turn, the "Latin spirit" and the "unity of the peoples of Latin civilization" derived. Instead, if by using the term *Latin* we refer to the origins, we see a complete overthrow of the "Latin" thesis. The Latins were among the peoples who bore the influences to which the early Roman world owes its greatness and its specific traits. The Latins had forms of cult, civilization, and life that were not opposed, but instead similar to those exhibited by the German peoples before a decadent world that rather than being "Latin" was only "Romanic" and largely Byzantinized. The later "Latin world," beyond the external facade and mere vestiges, included heterogeneous forces that were susceptible to convergence only when nothing more serious than "the world of letters and the arts" was to be found (with the exception of Catholicism and some ways of feeling to which the term *Mediterranean*, rather than *Latin* should be applied).[68]

I would like to underscore the importance of what I have briefly stated, not only from a historical and retrospective point of view, but also from a normative one; the similarities between the early Roman and Spartan lifestyles are obvious and well acknowledged, as are the similarities between both of them and some characteristic traits displayed by Germanic peoples; these traits, due to a number of circumstances, were retained by Germanic populations longer than by other nations of the same Indo-European stock. If those who are mere "Italiots" and who also want to feel "Latin" and "Mediterranean" could meet face-to-face with the Romans of the heroic period, their intolerance for the latter's discipline, honor, hierarchy, straightforwardness, and anonymous and anti-exhibitionist virility would not be any less than the intolerance provoked in them by their anti-German and especially anti-Prussian animus (it is significant that L. Aldington called the Romans "the Prussians of their times").

In such an animus there are certainly suspicious racial influences at work. This is an example of what is wrong with too many Italians, who employ the thesis of the "Catholic Latin spirit" or the "Mediterranean civilization" as a specious alibi.

This alibi has often been associated with the polemic proper to a militant Guelphism, which conveniently identified the Roman and Latin spirit with the Catholic Church, in an anti-German and anti-Ghibelline function. Thus, there have been people who ventured to speak of the antithesis between "temple" and "woods"; the "temple" representing the Latin-Catholic view of life, with its principles of authority, order, and transcendence, while the "woods" represent the chaotic, "Nibelungen-like," individualistic, and Protestant Germanic world. This is pure amateurishness typical of partisan pseudo-intellectuals, who are obviously acquainted only with Wagner and some German Romantic philosophers and who are ignorant, or pretend to be, of everything that remained in many social strata of the Central European States as an inner attitude until recent times, before the catastrophe of the two world wars. In regard to the external domain, Pareto rightly remarked that in Germany, despite its being mostly Protestant, the feelings of order, hierarchy, and discipline are very strong, while in Italy, despite its being a Catholic country, all this is present to a negligible degree, while individualism, disorder, instinctiveness, and lack of discipline tend to prevail.[69]

Here lies the true root of the intolerance that a certain Italian type harbors toward the Germanic element. It does not have to do only with another way of life, but also with another ethical conception. For example, in a Germanic heroic saga there is a characteristic episode: a prince, having been invited to the court of King Etzel, is warned that a trap is probably being set for him. That prince replied: "I will go anyway, and if that is true, that is too bad for King Etzel." He meant to say that he could have lost his life, but Etzel would have lost his honor. On the contrary, according to a certain "Mediterranean" mentality, one who is able to deceive others enjoys a higher standing, though in so doing he has no care or respect for himself.

Here another example comes to mind, concerning one of the most zealous supporters of the Latin, Catholic, anti-Germanic myth, namely Guido Manacorda. In one of his lectures, he thought it was in good taste to poke fun at the "gloomy" Germanic notion of loyalty. He reported on one of the legends concerning Faust, according to which the latter sealed his famous pact with the devil with his word of honor. Faust learns from a hermit that he is being led to the abyss and that he needs to rescind the deal. As soon as Faust becomes aware of it and is about to act accordingly, he remembers he has given his word. At that point, he feels that he cannot break his promise. Manacorda, with a sinister spirit, commented: "One of us Latins would have found a way to screw the devil too!" I have no doubt about that.

I will later return to the problem of ethics and style. For now I want to note that the myth of the Italian-German "Axis" could have had a particular meaning, not only from a political perspective, but also from a moral and spiritual one, in view of a reciprocal integration of the two peoples and cultures.[70] This is one of the reasons that the "Axis" was sabotaged and regarded as "unpopular";

the contrast between the confused nationalistic and patriotic myth connected to residual ideas of the Risorgimento on the one hand, and the yearning for a strong and "Roman" State on the other, played its own part in such a dislike, which was harbored even by many people who claimed to be Fascist. All these people can be happy again, now that Italy has returned to be itself—the petty Italy of mandolins, museums, "O Sole Mio," and the tourist industry (not to mention the democratic quagmire and the Marxist infection), having been "liberated" from the difficult task of forming itself on the inspiration of its highest traditions, which must be described not as "Latin," but as "Roman."

II

When we talk about racism, most people think of anti-Semitism; in other words, they refer to the mere anthropological and biological domain: only a few have an idea of the meaning that this doctrine may have from a practical and formative point of view and even of its political importance. However, here I will state only what is relevant to the specific order of ideas that we are discussing.

First of all, we must note that in modern racism the race is not considered within the context of those general classifications that school textbooks refer to as the white, yellow, and black races. The race is conceived as a more elementary and specialized unit; thus, within the white race there are several races. These elementary races are defined in terms that are not merely biological and anthropological, but psychological and spiritual as well. To each of the racial components there correspond various dispositions, forms of sensibility, values, and views of life which are also differentiated.[71]

There are actually no civilized peoples or nations composed of pure individuals belonging to the same single race. All peoples are composed of more or less stable racial mixtures. We go from the theoretical domain to the practical one, or to "active racism," whenever we take a position before the racial components of a given nation, refusing to acknowledge to all of them the same value, the same dignity, and the same right to impart the tone and form to the whole. At that point a choice, an election, and a decision are necessary. One of the components must be given preeminence, by referring to the typical values and the human ideals that correspond to it.

In the case of German populations, the racial component that is superior to the other ones with which it is mixed has usually been identified with the Nordic element. When we consider Italy, the superior component is identified with the Roman element.

First of all it is necessary to overcome the frivolous pride of some nationalists, according to whom the ultimate criterion consists of having the same fatherland and a common history; hence the Italian habit of indiscriminately exalting everything that is "ours." The truth is that just as with any great historical nation, and likewise with Italy, despite a certain uniformity of the common type, there are different components. It is important not to create illusions but to objectively recognize that which, although being "ours," hardly corresponds to a higher calling. As we can see, this is the counterpart of what I discussed in chapter 8 about the political-cultural domain, in regard to a "choice of traditions."

The creation of a new State and of a new civilization will always be ephemeral unless their substratum is a new man. In Italy, if this problem were to be addressed by a revolutionary-conservative movement, the differentiation of such a man would appear as a difficult and even problematic affair, due to the presence of suspicious ethnic components, chaotic and anarchic inclinations, weakness of character, unfavorable atavisms, and false values.

Having already discussed the myth of the Latin spirit, I will now focus on another element, which is less intellectual and more concrete than the "common Latin civilization." This element may be designated as "Mediterranean." Italians oscillate between the two poles constituted by the Roman and the Mediterranean elements; they represent, respectively, the superior and inferior limits of the possibilities that Italians have in themselves and of a legacy transmitted through the centuries. The main task, at both an individual and a social level, consists of maturing an inner decision, and in promoting a greater crystallization and formation in the direction of the first element. This task requires a double analysis. On the one hand, it would be necessary to emphasize the traits of style and character that are typical of the Roman component, independently from any form of expression tied to the past. On the other hand, we should identify the undesirable qualities of the "Mediterranean" type that are also present, if not prevalent, in the Italian people, and determine how it would be possible to rectify them.

Concerning the first issue, we should be able to extract from the Roman spirit a living content that has nothing to do with rhetorical assumptions or with museums and scholarly dissertations, such that even a simple man could understand it without the need of erudition and historical notions. To this effect, I have spoken about "elements of style." These elements have to be drawn from what we know about the Roman tradition and customs; in this case too, we need to discriminate among various types of Roman spirit. Alongside the Roman spirit of the origins, which reproduced in a special and original form a type of culture and custom common to the main, higher Indo-European civilizations, there were a Hellenized (in the negative sense of the term), a "Punicized," a "Ciceronian," an "Asiaticized," and a Catholic Roman spirit. The reference points should *not* be sought in these cases. Everything that is valid in them can be reduced to the first Roman spirit.

This original Roman spirit was based on a human type characterized by a group of typical dispositions. Among them we should include self-control, an enlightened boldness, a concise speech and determined and coherent conduct, and a cold dominating attitude, exempt from personalism and vanity. To the Roman style belong *virtus*, in the sense not of moralism, but of virile spirit and courage; *fortitudo* and *constantia*, namely spiritual strength; *sapientia*, in the sense of thoughtfulness and awareness; *disciplina*, understood as love for a self-given law and form; *fides*, in the specifically Roman sense of loyalty and faithfulness; and *dignitas*, which in the ancient patrician aristocracy became *gravitas* and *solemnitas*, a studied and moderate seriousness.[72] The same style is characterized by deliberate actions, without grand gestures; a realism that is not materialism, but rather love for the essential; the ideal of clarity, which eventually turned into rationalism in only some Latin peoples; an inner equilibrium and a healthy suspicion for every confused form of mysticism; a love for boundaries; the readiness to unite, as free human beings and without losing one's identity, in view of a higher goal or for an idea. We may also add *religio* and *pietas*, which do not mean "religiosity" in the Christian sense of the word, but instead signify for a Roman an attitude of respectful and dignified veneration for the gods and, at the same time, of trust and re-connection with the supernatural, which was experienced as omnipresent and effective in terms of individual, collective, and historical forces. Obviously, I am far from suggesting that every Roman man and woman embodied these traits; however, they represented the "dominant factor" and were embodied in the ideal that everybody perceived to be specifically Roman.

Likewise, these elements of style are self-evident. They are not connected to past times; they may act in every period as character-forming influences and effective values as soon as a corresponding calling is awakened. They have a *normative* value. In the worst case, they might have only the value of a *measure*. Moreover, we should not think they must be adopted by every individual; this would be absurd and even unnecessary. It would suffice if only a certain social stratum, called to inspire the others, could embody them.

Now we need to characterize the second pole, namely the "Mediterranean" style.

The way in which I employ the term *Mediterranean* requires a further clarification. I have often spoken of Mediterranean civilization, the Mediterranean spirit, and even a Mediterranean race, taking little care to indicate what these vague and elastic designations meant.[73]

"Mediterranean" merely designates a space, or a geographical area in which very different cultures and spiritual and racial powers often clashed or met, without ever producing a typical civilization. In anthropology, the "Mediterranean" myth was promoted by Giuseppe Sergi in the past century. Sergi believed in the existence of a Mediterranean race of African origin to which many Italic populations belonged, including the Pelasgians, the Phoenicians, the Levantines,[74] and other half-Semitic populations: these are hardly flattering kinships, which should rather be referred to as "bastard brothers," an expression Mussolini once used to refer to the myth of the Latin spirit. The theory of Sergi is now passé. I believe it is fitting to use the term *Mediterranean* to designate some suspicious spiritual and ethnic components. These components, which are found in other Mediterranean and "Latin" more or less mixed populations, are also present in various strata of the Italian people, in opposition to its more noble and original nucleus (which should not be called "Mediterranean") reflecting the "Roman" element.

Some psychologists have tried to define the Mediterranean type, not so much anthropologically, but in terms of character and style.[75] In these descriptions we can easily recognize the other pole of the Italian soul, namely negative aspects likewise found in the Italian people, that need to be rectified.

The first "Mediterranean" trait is love for outward appearances and grand gestures. The Mediterranean type needs a stage, if not for the sake of vanity and exhibitionism, at least in the sense that he often draws the impulse and motivation even for noble, remarkable, and sincere things from his main concern to be noticed by others and to make an impact on them. Hence the inclination for a "gesture"—that is, to do something to draw attention and curiosity, even when the person knows he is the only one to witness it. In the Mediterranean man there is a splitting between an "I" that plays the role and an "I" that regards his part from the point of view of a possible observer or spectator, more or less as actors do.[76]

Let me repeat: what is problematic here is the style, as the action or the work per se could have a positive value. But this has very little to do with

Roman style, and it marks a disintegration and an alteration; it is the antithesis of the ancient saying *esse non haberi* [to be and not appear to be], or of the style due to which, among other reasons, ancient Roman civilization was characterized by anonymous heroes. In a wider context, the opposition could be formulated in these terms: the Roman style is monumental, monolithic, while the Mediterranean style is choreographic-theatrical and spectacular (see also the French notions of *grandeur* and *gloire*). Thus, if this "Mediterranean" component of the Italian man were to be rectified, the best model to follow would be that of the ancient race of Rome—the sober, austere, active style, free from exhibitionism, measured, endowed with a calm awareness of one's dignity. To have the sense of what one is and of one's value independently of any external reference, loving distance as well as actions and expressions reduced to the essential, devoid of any exhibition and cheap showmanship—all these are fundamental elements for the eventual formation of a superior type. And even if the Italian man had in common with the Mediterranean type the above-mentioned "splitting" (as simultaneous actor and spectator), this splitting should be utilized for a careful supervision of one's conduct and expressions. This supervision should prevent every primitive spontaneity; one should carefully study one's own demeanor, not with the purpose of making an "impression" on others, or with great concern for their opinion, but for sake of the style that one intends to display to oneself.

The propensity toward outward appearances is easily associated with a personalism that degenerates into individualism. This is another typical negative trait of the Mediterranean soul: the tendency toward a restless, chaotic, and undisciplined individualism. Politically speaking, this is the tendency that, after asserting itself by fomenting struggles and constant quarrels, led the Greek city-states to ruin, although it had previously contributed in a positive manner to their articulated formation. We find this trait in the turbulent times of the early empire; it finally erupted in medieval Italy, degenerating into particularisms, schisms, struggles, factions, and all kinds of rivalries. And although the Italian Renaissance has splendid features, they are nevertheless problematic features that derive from this Mediterranean individualism, which does not tolerate any general and strict law of order; and valuable possibilities dissipated in purely personal positions and in the fireworks of a creativity disjoined from any higher meaning and tradition. Here the author, rather than the work itself, is at center stage.

Thus, descending even lower, the same "Mediterranean" component is found in the contemporary pseudo-genial type, who is ever critical and always ready to uphold the opposite thesis in order to make a show of himself, being very clever in finding ways to get around an obstacle and in eluding a law. Even lower we find the maliciousness and the shrewdness (i.e., knowing how to "fool" others) that the Mediterranean type regards as synonyms for intelligence and superiority, whereas the "Roman" type would feel in this a degradation, a betrayal of one's dignity. I have discussed this attitude earlier on, when speaking of Manacorda.

The Roman chastity or sobriety of speech, expression, and gesture is contrasted by the gesticulating, noisy, and disordered exuberance of the Mediterranean type, by his mania for communication and effusiveness, and by his feeble sense of boundaries, hierarchy, and silent subordination. The counterpart of these traits is often a lack of character, the tendency to get excited and become drunk with words: verbosity, a flaunted and conventional sense of honor, susceptibility, concern for appearances but with little or no substance. The expression *"Pobre in palabras pero in obras largo"* [Poor of words but rich in deeds], which characterized the ancient Spanish aristocratic type, should be compared with Moltke's characterization: "Talk little, do much, and be more than you appear to be"; all this points to the "Roman" style.

The Mediterranean man often shares with the so-called "desert race" (a psychological-anthropological classification by Clauss, probably the effect of the presence within him of some elements of this race) an intense, explosive, and changeable temperament, tied to circumstances and also flaring up; an immediacy and the power of desire or affection in the emotional life; and random intuitions in the intellectual life. A style of psychological equilibrium and a sense of measure are not his strength. Although he is always cheerful, enthusiastic, and optimistic in appearance, especially when he is in the company of other people, in reality the Mediterranean type experiences sudden psychological lows, and discovers dark and hopeless inner visions that make him anxiously shun solitude and return to exteriority, noisy social interactions, effusions, and passionateness.

While acknowledging this, in an eventual rectification we should not proceed by mere antitheses. Nietzsche's saying: "I evaluate a man by his power to delay his reactions" may certainly act as a general basic principle against disorderly impulsivity and "explosiveness." Nietzsche himself warned against every morality that tends to dry up every impetuous current of the human soul instead of channeling it. The capability of control, equilibrium, continuity in feeling and in willing must not lead to a withering and mechanization of one's being, as seems to be the case with some negative traits of the central-European and Anglo-Saxon man. What matters is not to suppress passion and to give to the soul a beautiful, regulated, and homogeneous, though flat form; but rather to organize one's being in an integral way around the capability of recognizing, discriminating, and adequately utilizing the impulses and the lights that emerge from one's deep recesses. It cannot be denied that passion is predominant in many Mediterranean Italian types, but this disposition does not amount to a defect, but rather to an enrichment, provided it finds its correlative in a firmly organized life.

A more negative element of the Mediterranean type is sentimentality. Here we should distinguish between sentimentality and true feeling, the former being a degeneration and rhetorical form of the latter. The former plays a predominant role in various expressions typical of the Mediterranean soul. As an example we could adduce a number of sugary songs; the success and the echo they have in the popular soul, despite their patent insincerity, are significative.

The Mediterranean man is always inclined to defend himself, just as the Nordic man tends to judge himself. The former is alleged to be more indulgent with himself than with others, and to be reluctant to examine the hidden motives of his inner life under a clear and objective light. This opposition is rather unilateral. Generally speaking, we should not ignore the dangers inherent in morbid introspection: I am thinking here of the line that leads to psychoanalysis and to the psychology of some of Dostoyevsky's characters on the one hand, and to certain complexes of guilt or existential anguish on the other. A style of simplicity and sincerity, first of all toward one's soul, is essential for a superior human type, as is the natural precept of being strict with oneself but understanding and cordial with others. Specific connections with the racial factor subsist only in part in this regard.

We should instead consider the importance that sex has for the Mediterranean type. The sexualization of morality on the one hand, and the turning of women and sex almost into an obsession on the other, are not just typically "Mediterranean" traits, since in the latter we can recognize one of the general phenomena of every degenerating civilization. We cannot deny, however, the emphasis that this inclination receives in the average Mediterranean-Southern type, in contrast with what was proper to the best Roman ethics, which assigned to women and to love their rightful place, neither too high nor too low. Roman ethics pointed to the really fundamental values for a clear and virile formation of character and life, without adopting puritanical moralisms.[77] Generally speaking, in Italy the relationships between the two sexes present a far from satisfactory aspect. Southern "temperament" with its primitive features, or with its up-to-date type of the *Latin lover;* an existing complex of bourgeois prejudices, with hypocrisies, inhibitions, conventionalisms; and a cheap and widespread corruption—all this is far from a line of clarity, sincerity, freedom, and courage. This theme would require a special analysis, but this is not the proper context for it, as it affects more general problems than those of the Mediterranean typology.[78]

Having briefly outlined these opposite elements of style, we should recall that they represent two limits. The qualities of the "Roman" type represent the *positive limit* of dispositions hidden in the best parts of our people, just as the qualities characterized as "Mediterranean" correspond to the *negative limit* and the less noble part of it; these limits are also found as components in other peoples, especially in the "Latin" group. However, we must realize that too many times behaviors resembling the "Mediterranean" type have been identified, especially abroad, as typically Italian, and that the "Mediterranean" component appears to have prevailed overall in Italian life following World War II.

And yet, a trend in the opposite direction would not be inconceivable under certain conditions. Only this trend could create the basis for a new State and a new society, for there is no doubt that formulas, programs, and institutions are of little help when there is no human substance, at least in the dominating elite. In every man there are various possibilities, at least in principle, that can be traced to primordial legacies. While in the best moments of our history we recognize the Aryan-Roman component, in periods of crisis and concealment we can detect the emergence and prevalence of what we have conventionally called the "Mediterranean" component; I said "conventionally" because it consists rather of Mediterranean debris and residues, influences of non-European races that have almost no history, or products of ethnic decay and erosion.

In the rectifying and formative action the key role will always be played by the political myth, in Sorel's sense of a galvanizing idea-force. The myth reacts on the environment, implementing the law of elective affinities: it awakens, frees, and imposes those possibilities of single individuals and the environment to which they correspond, while the others are silenced or neutralized. The selection can obviously take place in reverse, according to the nature of the myth. Thus, the communist and democratic myths appeal to what is most promiscuous and degraded in modern man; the corresponding movements owe their success to the mobilization of such elements through the inhibition of every different, higher possibility and sensibility.

If a rectification occurred, obviously we would not be able to see results overnight. Besides the above-mentioned condition, consisting of the presence of a political myth capable of creating a given climate, and a specific human ideal, what is needed is a persistent action for a sufficiently long period, stronger than the relapses and eventual reemergences of the opposite possibilities. As is well known, during the Fascist era Italy attempted to start similar developments, whose most serious concern, though it was felt only by a minority, was to increasingly transform a "Mediterranean" Italy into a "Roman" Italy. An adequate integrating counterpart could have been the initial separation of Italy from her "Latin sisters" and a reapproach to the German people, beyond the plane of mere political concerns.

It goes without saying that considering the contemporary climate in Italy, with its democratic nadir and its Marxist intoxication, it would be purely utopian to suggest similar ideas again. This obviously does not affect their intrinsic and normative value, as well as the value of other "outdated" ideas. Their "outdatedness" could disappear only at the point of a rupture and a reaction from within, which quite often take place in almost organic terms at the end of dissolutive processes.

Fifteen

THE PROBLEM OF BIRTHS

Among the factors of the disorder and crisis of modern times, besides those caused by processes of subversion that cannot be regarded as spontaneous, there are unquestionably others that have a natural character and wreak havoc only because a stand is not made against them. A particularly important factor of this latter type is the *world's population growth*. There is no doubt that if it were possible to reduce the world's population density to that of three centuries ago, while also retaining the current degree of material civilization, the social and economic problems that afflict the world population today would basically be irrelevant. In that event, we would eliminate for the most part situations that revolutionary forces exploit to their advantage; we could head toward a relaxation and a decongestion that would limit every activist frenzy (first among them, those that pertain to the overall power of the economy) and greatly propitiate the return to normalcy, thanks to a new, wider, and freer space.

However, it is well known that we are proceeding in the opposite direction at an accelerated pace. The alarm that was launched in the past, with the cry "The races are dying," turned out to be false. Not even the destructions of a "total" war, which spared neither defenseless cities nor women and children, were able to stop the demographic growth even in the Central European countries (with the exception of Italy) in comparison to prewar conditions. It is like standing before an avalanche that, as it continually gains ground, grows irresistibly, exacerbating all kinds of crises and disorders; we cannot help but reject the idea that this is not a matter of fate, but rather something that human beings could easily control. What we have here is a case of disproportion that exists in modern Western people, between the control of the external domain and the control of the inner domain. Elementary forces of nature are controlled by technology so that they may serve man's wishes, or in order to prevent them

THE PROBLEM OF BIRTHS   267

from being harmful; and yet nothing is done about the population explosion, because then man would have to act upon himself, his prejudices and instincts. Modern man is increasingly losing this vocation, and the only domain he can flaunt is the ephemeral control he exercises on matter.

It is well known, too, that the danger of overpopulation was warned of in the last century by Malthus. However, his starting point was totally materialistic and only relatively consistent. In any case, it is *not* the one I regard as decisive for the final solution of the problem. The real danger is not, as Malthus believed, that the means of subsistence and food supply may become insufficient for an overly increased world population. Considering all the measures that could be taken before we got to that situation, this danger would occur only in a distant future. Before reaching this point, many unpleasant things could happen that were not considered by the zealous apostles of continuous and uninterrupted progress. Even considering only the material plane, the crisis caused by overpopulation in our age and in the future appears in different terms. Overpopulation exacerbates the problem of how to employ the workforces; it also unavoidably intensifies production processes, which in turn, due to their determinisms, strengthen the demonic nature of the economy. The result is an increasing enslavement of the individual and the reduction of free space and of any autonomous movement in modern cities, swarming as though in putrefaction with faceless beings of "mass civilization." This is the most important aspect of the problem.

Sombart correctly saw that the decrease of population would have been one of the few ways of dealing a deathblow to high capitalism (which he compared to a wild and destructive giant) without proceeding to disastrous modifications in every normal socioeconomic institution. Sombart believed that this was where we were headed. However, the current, after some slowing down, continued to flow in the opposite direction; thus, the above-mentioned perspectives are the ones that the near future has in store for us, unless we decide to react.

For a proper reaction we need first of all to clear the path of the mistakes and prejudices that still foster a passive attitude toward the scourge of overpopulation.

In the political domain we need to take a stand against the myth expressed in the formula: "There is power in numbers." Attempting to base an imperialistic policy on a demographic campaign was one of the serious mistakes of the Fascist ideology that must be denounced without hesitation. The power of numbers is the power of the mere brute masses; this power is in itself very relative, because even herds need to be guided. Every true empire is born from a race of conquerors who conquered lands and peoples, not because they suffered from overpopulation or did not have "a place in the sun," but on the basis of a higher calling and qualification, which allowed them to rule as a minority in foreign lands. Was it an impulse resulting from a complex and intolerable overpopulation that led the Romans, Achaemenids, Franks, Spaniards, early Islamic hosts, and the British of yesterday to conquest? Moreover, when we consider the phase in which the material dominion is integrated with spiritual factors, an even greater emphasis should be given to factors that cannot be reduced to mere numbers and to the power of numbers.

There is more to say concerning the inner problems of a people. Wherever indiscriminate demographic growth is promoted or allowed to go unchallenged, we can expect the harmful effects of the law of natural counter-selection. The fact is that the inferior races and the lower social strata are the most prolific ones. Thus, we can say that while the number of superior, more differentiated elements grows in arithmetic proportion, the number of inferior elements grows in geometric proportion, the result being a fatal involution of the human race. The collapse and disintegration of the great imperial organisms has often occurred for that reason: as if it were due to a low tide, because of a monstrous expansion of the basis constituted by the promiscuous and "proletarian" element. We should recall here that the term *proletarian* comes from the Latin *proles* and suggests the idea of an animalistic fertility. As Mereshkovski rightly noted, this term was applied especially to those whose only creative skill consisted of begetting children—these were men in body but eunuchs in spirit. In its logical development, this trend leads toward that "ideal" society in which there are no more classes, no men or women, but instead comrades, or asexual cells belonging to the same immense anthill.

Politically speaking, the demographic explosion is doomed to create a congestion that in turn produces critical international solutions, resulting in wars that cannot be justified by any higher right or idea: here the mere quantity and condition of a "proletarian nation" do not correspond to a right or an idea. In regard to military solutions, we should also keep in mind that the importance of the numerical factor has become relative due to the increasingly technical nature of recent wars. Aside from war, the population overload can only lead some countries to seek "space" among other peoples as an emigrating exportation of "cheap labor" who are eventually destined to lose their identity and be scattered among other peoples. As the congestion continues, the fatal effects will be inner crises and social tensions representing manna from heaven for the leaders of Marxist subversion.

Again, anyone can see what negative consequences come from an indiscriminate population increase (as I said, this increase results in a numeric superiority of the inferior, "proletarian" strata) when a democratic regime is in power: in a democracy it is numbers that ensure power, through "universal suffrage," destroying the limits through which, in other regimes, the numerical growth of the "base" did not concern the minority or the elite that was in firm control of key positions in the State.

After these considerations of a political order, I will now make some comments about the prejudices of a religious and bourgeois nature that shun birth control.

The Catholic religion has embraced the biblical principle concerning the multiplication of the human species. This is one of the cases in which the Church has bestowed an ethical value on things that have only a practical, relative value that is quite outdated today. The Jewish precept was justified only considering the patriarchal conditions of the ancient Jewish tribes, composed of farmers and herdsmen, in which (as still happens today in those few rural areas where analogous situations are found) a plentiful offspring was regarded as desirable and providential because of the need for able bodies. All this has nothing to do with religion or ethics. From a specific point of view—that of asceticism—it is possible to condemn the pleasures of sex in general, as was the case of the original ascetic Christian tradition. But in ordinary life, and in general, wherever there are no ascetic vocations it is extremely unreasonable to legitimize and sanctify sexual union and marriage only when they are aimed at procreation, declaring them to be sinful in every other instance. For practical purposes, what does this mean, other than that the religious perspective here approves and even encourages the most primitive and animalistic expression of an instinct? Conception essentially implies a state of complete abandonment of man to the sexual passion, just as one of the most natural means to avoid conception implies a certain renunciation, predominance of will, and self-control vis-à-vis the most primitive impulse of instinct and desire. In every other instance besides sex, the Church praises and formally approves the latter disposition—that is, the predominance of the intellect and will over the impulses of the senses. But when it comes to sexual union, because it obtusely maintains the outdated precept of the Jewish law, either out of hypocrisy or from a theological hatred of sex per se, Catholic morality has endorsed the opposite attitude: the attitude of those who passively play into the hands of Schopenhauer's "genius of the species," through couplings that are really *more ferarum* [after the manner of beasts].

Let me repeat: I could understand the precept of celibacy and chastity and the total condemnation of the pleasures of sex and the use of women from the point of view of an ascetic morality with supernatural objectives. However, it is incomprehensible to endorse the use of women and sexuality only in terms of procreation, as this amounts to degrading every relation between the sexes to an animal level. Even a libertine, who elevates pleasure to an art (not to mention a certain "Dionysism" that in antiquity enjoyed a religious sanction), is undoubtedly superior to those who follow the Catholic view to the letter.

However, it seems that the Church has recently been willing to make some concessions. While the concern of Vatican II to keep up with the times has had several deprecable consequences, we can still recognize as a positive thing the council's explicit acknowledgment that not only procreation, but "love" as well, may be the legitimate foundation of marriage. Moreover, revisionist tendencies have gained momentum even in matters related to "birth control": nowadays the issue for the Church is not birth control as such, but whether or not the methods employed are legitimate. However, we need only look at the reactions of Catholic philosopher Gabriel Marcel, who wrote with indignation about measures to limit the birthrate as "blasphemies against Life," in order to realize the tenacious persistence of prejudices among Catholics even outside the official doctrine.

Besides these religious prejudices, the anti-birth-control position derives from a mentality in which a great role is played by slogans and conventional feelings, marked by a large degree of hypocrisy and lies. For instance, there is meaningless bourgeois rhetoric about children, the cult of children, and the desire to have children. In the great majority of cases, it is not true at all that children are desired and are the main reason why a man and woman get married. Children just "come." A poll taken in Central Europe has yielded these results: of those interviewed, 45 percent never really gave thought to having children or not when they got married; 30 percent did *not* want them; only 25 percent expressly wanted to have some.

As far as a revolutionary-conservative movement is concerned, there is a need for men who are free from these bourgeois feelings. These men, by adopting an attitude of militant and absolute commitment, should be ready for anything and almost feel that creating a family is a "betrayal"; these men should live *sine impedimentis*, without any ties or limits to their freedom. In the past there were secular Orders where celibacy was the rule. We should also appreciate the validity of Nietzsche's dictum: "Man should be trained for war and woman for the recreation (or rest, *Erholung*) of the warrior: all else is folly!" In any event, the ideal of a "warrior society" obviously cannot be the petit-bourgeois and parochial ideal of "home and children"; on the contrary, I believe that in the personal domain the right to an ample degree of sexual freedom for these men should be acknowledged, against moralism, social conformism, and "heroism in slippers."

We should consider one more thing. Without successors, this elite would begin and end without leaving anything for posterity: it would seem only natural that it should take care to create offspring, and through its own propagation work as much as possible against the threatening growth of the inferior social strata. I have several reservations about this idea. First of all, the example of those centuries-old religious orders that embraced celibacy suggests that a continuity may be ensured with means other than physical procreation. Besides those who should be available as shock troops, it would certainly be auspicious to form a second group that would ensure the hereditary continuity of a chosen and protected elite, as the counterpart of the transmission of a political-spiritual tradition and worldview: ancient nobility was an example of this. But to pursue this goal today would be rather utopian, and would amount to closing one's eyes to reality, failing to consider the general social and existential conditions that are now prevalent. In this context it would be possible to begin the adventure of fatherhood, where something of the meaning and dignity of fatherhood may subsist in the modern family, *making sure first, however, through a deep examination of one's conscience, that the higher goal is not a pretext to unleash one's procreative incontinence.* It is obvious that, in any event, in a family that is not inspired by the traditional, "Roman" model, there is little hope of exercising a formative influence on one's progeny; this necessary counterpart, which is almost nonexistent, is very difficult to realize in the West.

But even in the best hypothesis, we cannot reasonably expect to compete in fertility with the lowest strata in order to contain them: no matter how much we try, and always assuming that the progeny inherits more than the blood, it will never be possible to counterbalance the demographic growth of inferior stocks and social strata. Other means should also be employed: the elimination of the democratic and egalitarian system being the first, necessary presupposition. Another means would be the adoption of an adequate attitude toward the so-called Third World.

Ancient Indo-European traditions regarded the procreation of a son as a "duty" (in general, the norm did not apply to those who followed an ascetic calling): because of this, the firstborn was called the "son of duty," in distinction from any subsequent children. It goes without saying that an analogous precept would automatically produce the desired descending direction in the demographic curve, while safeguarding the principle of patrilineal descent and what in it can still be salvaged.

Having discussed the group that should remain free from all bonds, and the second group that attempts, by procreating, to form a posterity, and thus to supply a biological basis to a spiritual legacy and to the structure of an Order, we should now consider something else. When talking about the great majority of our contemporaries, it is absolutely irresponsible, considering the collective consequences that result from it, to beget other beings who will repeat the same inconsistency, the same vacuity of a life lacking any real meaning; in other words, it is absolutely irresponsible to feed the threatening avalanche of the formless world of quantity only because one is passive toward the natural part of himself and toward the most primitive sexual urge, or because one is enslaved to prejudices. The truth is, therefore, the opposite of what is alleged by those who accuse people who refuse to procreate of selfishness and of individualism: it is the former who think only of themselves, without thinking about the contribution they unwillingly make to the general disorder; therefore, fundamentally these people do not even think about themselves, other than in a most obtuse and immediate way. When considering the effects of the scourge of overpopulation, one could easily say "They got what they deserved," except the consequences also affect those who do not follow the herd. Thus, it would be desirable for the State to take rigorous, systematic, prophylactic, repressive, and encouraging measures in this regard, despite the fact that in any other situation such interventions in the private domain are intrusive and oppressive (as was the situation with the absurd "campaign for population growth" during the Fascist era). For my part, I think that one can never stress too heavily the need for an anti-demographic policy, especially because, due to an inner inhibition found even among qualified milieus, it is not possible to see the numerous and heavy contributions, whether direct or indirect, that growth in population has made and still makes to the crisis of the modern world.

Thus, in a new movement, the anti-demographic orientation will necessarily be part of the overall struggle against the world of quantity and against the already mentioned processes of counter-selection. In the context of a real State, in modern times, the task will be twofold: to stem the cancerous proliferation of a faceless and promiscuous mass and to realize the presuppositions for the nucleation and consolidation of a stratum in which some qualifications are stabilized so as to make some individuals worthy and capable of holding power. In all this, the need for an equilibrium or for a limit is paramount, not least in the struggle against the global power of the economy, since these two things, as I have suggested, are complementary.

Sixteen

FORM AND PRESUPPOSITIONS OF A UNITED EUROPE

The need for a united Europe is strongly felt in various milieus today. It is necessary to distinguish where this need is upheld on a merely material and pragmatic level from those situations in which the issue is posited at a higher level, emphasizing spiritual and traditional values.

In the best case, similar needs arise from an inner rebellion against the existing situation, due to the sight of Europe, which, following concomitant actions and reactions (in which we should also recognize the part played by the "occult war"), has been thrown from its role as a great subject in world politics and become an object conditioned by foreign interests and influences. Today Europe has to live between two superpowers struggling for control of the world (USA and USSR), and eventually accept an American and "Atlantic" protection in order to avoid a worse scenario yet—total enslavement to communism.

Obviously, the discord among European nations can only maintain and strengthen this situation. However, when it came to concrete initiatives leading to a possible unification, the creation of the European Economic Community was the only tangible achievement: a partial initiative, limited to the economic plane and lacking a binding political counterpart. Other than that, nothing else exists, and the situation is such as to eliminate any illusion. The disastrous consequences of two world wars, which were themselves in great part the effect of the lack of union and the selfishness of European nations, cannot be easily eliminated. The true measure of concrete freedom, independence, and autonomy is first of all *power*. Europe could have been the third greatest world power, retaining all the vast resources of materials and the vast extra-European markets, if only a principle of strict solidarity had succeeded immediately and absolutely in causing *every* European nation to rally to the

side of any one of them in the event of a threat. This line has not been followed, which, after all, has few precedents even in more recent European history (i.e., aside from the Roman period and, in part, from the Ghibelline Middle
Ages and the Holy Alliance). Thus, one capitulation was followed by another.

Today there are those who speak of Europe as a potential empire of more
than 400 million people, and thus capable of facing the United States (179
million) and the USSR (225 million).[79] That number, however, includes countries that could hardly be won back, as they are located behind the Iron Cur-
tain. Even if we were to limit ourselves to Western Europe, with its 364 million, it would constitute a sufficiently strong bloc if we did not also have to
consider the industrial potential that affects the military potential. The non-
European countries that produced these materials, which were once under European control, have been lost; now those areas are the theater of Russian,
American, and even Chinese intrigues.

In order to head toward a united Europe, the first step should consist of a
concerted exit of all European nations from the United Nations, which is an
illegitimate, promiscuous, and hypocritical association. Another obvious imperative should be to become emancipated in every aspect and in equal measure from both the United States and the USSR. However, this would require
a very subtle and prudent political art, for which today's politicians are hardly
qualified. The reason is that a significant interval between the rejection of the
American and "Atlantic" tutelage and the effective organization of Europe into
a united bloc capable of defending itself (where possible) could cause Europe,
which is still materially and spiritually weak, to fall prey to communism and
the USSR as a result of inner upheavals and external aggressions. Thus, a work
of preparation should precede such initiatives.

These problems of concrete politics fall outside the context of this book.
Here I will only hint at what concerns the form and the spiritual and doctrinal
presuppositions of a united Europe. The vaguely federalist and aggregative
solutions can have only a contingent character, and even a political and economic defensive unity should be only a consequence. The only genuine solution must have an *organic* character; the primary element should be a shaping
force from within and from above, proper to an idea and a common tradition.
Some milieus have upheld a pragmatic and activist point of view. Reference has
been made to the idea that nations have not fallen from the sky, already made,
but instead have been forged on the basis of a common task that confronted

scattered forces, and even as a consequence of some historical challenge, due to the initiative of an energetic and central group that eventually led to the unity of this or that historical nation. It is believed that things could be the same in regard to the "Nation Europa" that needs to be born, and that it is enough to refer to a myth and to the idea of a common destiny, defended by a revolutionary European front. I think this point of view is insufficient; even in the interpretation of the genesis of historical nations, we should not forget what was essentially due to dynasties representing a tradition and to the loyalty that was created around them (as in the birth of Prussia). These presuppositions for a united Europe are absent. We can refer only to a situation of necessity, which would generate a unitary impulse and an élan that in European history—let us admit it—finds scant antecedents. It is superfluous to remember the obvious phenomena of European disunion (rather than union) such as the Hundred Years' War, the wars of religion, the wars of succession, all the way down to the last two world wars.

We must also note, among the champions of a united Europe, the oscillation between the notion of empire, though in an approximative sense (an expression employed by Thiriart and by Varange[80]) and that of "Nation Europa" (which is also the title of a German periodical). This requires a more precise explication. The concept of the nation can never be applied to an organic, supernational type of unity. By rejecting the formula of a "Europe of Fatherlands" and a mere federation of European nations, we must be careful not to be misled. As I have indicated in another chapter, the concepts of fatherland and nation (or ethnic group) belong to an essentially naturalistic or "physical" plane. In a united Europe, fatherlands and nations may exist (ethnic communities have been partially respected even in the totalitarian Soviet Union). What should be excluded is nationalism (with its monstrous appendix, namely imperialism) and chauvinism—in other words, every fanatical absolutization of a particular unit. Thus "European Empire," and not "Nation Europa" or "European Fatherland" should be the right term, in a doctrinal sense. In the Europeans we should appeal to a feeling of higher order, qualitatively very different from the nationalistic feeling rooted in other strata of the human being. We cannot claim to be "Europeans" on the basis of an analogous feeling due to which one feels Italian, Prussian, Basque, Finnish, Scottish, Hungarian, and so on, or believe that a unique feeling of the same kind may become widespread, thereby erasing and leveling these differences and replacing them in a "Nation

Europa." However, some problems arise even if the mere term *empire* does not immediately suggest an anachronistic and unrealistic fantasy, and even if we were to consider some adaptations of the principle to the times we live in.

The scheme of an empire in a true and organic sense (which must clearly be distinguished from every imperialism, a phenomenon that should be regarded as a deplorable extension of nationalism) was previously displayed in the European medieval world, which safeguarded the principles of both unity and multiplicity. In this world, individual States have the character of partial organic units, gravitating around a *unum quod non est pars* ("a one that is not a part," to use Dante's expression)—namely, a principle of unity, authority, and sovereignty of a different nature from that which is proper to each particular State. But the principle of the Empire can have such a dignity only by transcending the political sphere in the strict sense, founding and legitimizing itself with an idea, a tradition, and a power that is also spiritual. The limitations of the sovereignty of the single national units before an eminent right of the Empire have as their sole condition this transcendent dignity of the Empire; as far as structure is concerned, the whole will appear as an "organism composed of organisms," or as an organic federalism similar to that realized by Bismarck in the second German Reich, which was not acephalous. These are the essential traits of a true Empire.

What are the conditions and the opportunities for the realization of such an idea in Europe today? Obviously, it would be necessary to be willing and able to go against the current. As I have said, we need to discard the idea of a "Nation Europa," which is almost as if the ultimate goal were the amalgamation of the individual European nations in one and the same nation, in a sort of promiscuous European communitarian substance that erased linguistic, ethnic, and historical differences. Because what is needed is an organic unity, the premise should rather be the integration and consolidation of every single nation as a hierarchical, united, and well-differentiated whole. The nature of the parts should reflect the nature of the whole. Once the individual nations are arranged hierarchically in the stable form of single units, and after breaking the nationalist hubris or Vico's "pride of the nations" (which is almost always parallel to a demagogic and collectivizing element), a virtual direction would be imparted that is susceptible to being continued beyond the individual national areas and leading to a superior unity. This, due to its super-ordained nature, would be such as to leave wide room for nationalities according to their natural and historical individuality. It is a well-known principle of the organic view that the more the higher unity is steady and perfect, the more the single parts are differentiated and enjoy autonomy. What matters is the synergy and the opportunity for every common action.

Every organic unit is characterized by a principle of stability. We should not expect a stability of the whole, where there is no stability guaranteed in its very components. Even from this point of view, the elementary presupposition of an eventual united Europe appears to be the political integration of the single nations. European unity would always be precarious if it leaned on some external factor, like an international parliament lacking a common, higher authority, with representations from various democratic regimes; such regimes, because they are constantly and mutually conditioned from below, cannot in any way ensure a continuity of political will and direction. In a democratic regime the sovereignty of the State is ephemeral, as a nation does not represent a true unity; the political will is conditioned from one day to the next by the mere numbers gained by this or that party through political maneuvers within the absurd system of universal suffrage. What is lacking here is the character of an organic "partial whole."

What is required is not to impose a common regime on every European nation; however, an organic, hierarchical, anti-individualistic, and antidemocratic principle should be adequately implemented, even though in various forms adopted to different circumstances. Thus, the preliminary condition is a general antidemocratic cleansing, which at the present appears to be almost utopian. Democracy, on the one hand, and a European parliament that reproduces on a larger scale the depressing and pathetic sight of the European parliamentary systems on the other hand: all this would bring ridicule upon the idea of a united Europe. In general, we should think of an organic unity to be attained from the top down rather than from the bottom up. Only elites of individual European nations could understand one another and coordinate their work, overcoming every particularism and spirit of division, asserting higher interests and motives with their authority. In other times, it was royalty and the leaders who could make the great European policy; they regarded each other almost as members of the same family (which in part they were, due to dynastic inter-marriages), even when grave conflicts temporarily arose between their peoples. A well-established "center" should exist in every nation; as a result of the harmony and the synergy of such centers, the higher European unity would organize itself and operate.

Overall, what should be promoted is a twofold process of integration: on the one hand, national integration through the acknowledgment of a substantial principle of authority that is the basis for the organic, anti-individualistic, and corporative formation of the various sociopolitical national forces; on the other hand, supernational European integration through the acknowledgment of a principle of authority that is as super-ordained toward that which is proper to single units (individual States), as it is toward the people included in each of these units. Without this, it is useless to talk about an organically united Europe.

Having put the problem in these terms, there are serious difficulties regarding the spiritual, not merely political, foundations required to implement this European unity. Where should we find these foundations? Little can be done on the higher and proper plane, which is the religious one. We cannot refer to Catholicism, asking it to become the sanction and the anointer of a super-ordained principle of authority, first of all because Catholicism is the faith of only some European nations; second, due to the democratic and modernizing collapse of the contemporary Church (which I discussed in chapter 10); and third, due to the effects of the general processes of desacralization and secularization that have occurred in Europe. Least of all can an appeal be made to a generic Christianity, since this would be weak, insubstantial and formless, not specifically European and not liable to be monopolized for European civilization alone: after all, even American blacks are Christians. The reader should also refer to what I have said in chapter 10 about the irreconcilability between pure Christianity and a "metaphysics of the State."

From this plane, let us move to an even lower one. Mention is often made of "European tradition" and of "European culture." Unfortunately, these are mere words. As far as "tradition" is concerned, it has been a long time since Europe was acquainted with its highest meaning. We could say that "tradition" in an integral sense, which is very different from mere "traditionalism," is a category that belongs to a world that has almost disappeared, or to periods in which the same formative force was manifested both in customs and in faith, in rights and in political and cultural forms: in other words, in every domain of life. Nobody can claim that today in Europe there is one tradition in this sense, which could be used to legitimize the European idea—while, at the same time, we must recognize the absence of an animating center that should be its necessary presupposition. For all practical purposes, in Europe there are only some historical vestiges of "tradition," understood in this deeper sense.

As far as "European culture" is concerned, it is the focus of liberal and humanistic amateur intellectuals who like to blabber on about "personality," "freedom," and the "free world" in a tone that conforms totally to the disintegrated democratic postwar climate, at the same time flirting with UNESCO and other shallow organizations. Generally speaking, I do not believe that anything serious can be gained from the encounter and interaction of representatives of what today goes by the name of "culture," which is really just an appendix of the bourgeois civilization of the Third Estate. This "culture" is characterized by the myth of the "aristocracy of thought," which is rather the aristocracy of the *parvenu*, with an antitraditional liberal and secular slant. Thus, in my view, "intellectuals," with or without European leanings, should be regarded with the same disdain as early communism displayed for them. We cannot entrust to the representatives of "culture" the authority proper to the bearers and representatives of a superior idea. Goethe, Von Humboldt, and all the other representatives of a sophisticated culture should be paid high honors, but it would be absurd to believe that their world could supply an arousing and animating strength to the forces and revolutionary elites that are struggling to unify Europe: their contribution belongs to the mere domain of a dignified "representation," with an essentially historical character.

After all, every time we leave generalities and try to give a concrete and important content to the notion of a "common European culture," we are immediately confronted by a difficult task. Years ago, a conference sponsored by the Italian Academy on the topic "Europe" and attended by well-known representatives from many nations showed how difficult this task is, since no conclusions could be drawn, due to the many personal interpretations that were more or less in conflict. But this was not the most important thing. The problem is that no importance was attached to the guilt complex that Europe should have, especially in regard to its "culture." Besides the fact that culture has only a peripheral literary and humanistic value, lacking any relation with the deeper historical forces (in regard to which I have mentioned that European history more often presents the spectacle of a worn-down disunion than one of union and synergy), how can we ignore that Western culture and civilization on the one hand and the antitraditional spirit on the other have converged from the time of the Renaissance? How can we ignore that almost everything that the liberal and progressive defenders of European culture, civilization, and tradition uphold as a European achievement, starting from the Renaissance, has been the greatest factor of Europe's spiritual crisis? How can we ignore that the Europeanization of the world has contributed to spreading germs of decomposition and subversion, and to the arousal of forces that were destined to have negative repercussions in Europe? Europe was the original hotbed of the Enlightenment, liberalism, democracy (the prior American experiment with democracy had little influence on the European continent), and finally, Marxism and communism. Unfortunately, in modern history this has been the most relevant contribution of "European culture": the contribution given by intellectuals, humanists, and so-called noble souls was a pale and marginal reflection in comparison. Unfortunately, it is in these terms (almost in the terms of what Easterners call "karma") that we must conceive the "community of destiny" invoked by some supporters of European unification. At the above-mentioned conference, one of the worthwhile contributions came from Francesco Coppola, who spoke about modern Europe's guilt complex and "dirty conscience" syndrome. How can we think of creating a basis for the defense of Europe against barbaric, anti-European forces and ideologies when the latter can be seen as the radical and mature development of trends and "diseases" that originated in Europe itself? This is the reason for the feeble immunity of the European world to the "leading civilizations" of our times—namely, the American and the Soviet-communist ones.

Thus, the problem of the spiritual foundation for an organically united Europe remains unresolved; any attempts of activist and revolutionary forces to bring about such a Europe lack a safe spiritual "rear guard," and leave behind themselves an unsecured and "mined" territory. This appears to be the case, unless we begin to wage a struggle inside Europe against all the evils that today appear at a macroscopic level (in all of their forms, whether acute or superficial) within all the non-European and anti-European powers. The requirement is to proceed to an inner detoxification, carried through as far as is possible, even at the highest price. For instance, besides the political and economic domains, how can we fail to recognize the degree to which Americanization has spread among the European masses in matters of customs, tastes, and fashion? This amounts to saying that the problem of the European attitude toward the modern world must be faced and dealt with in the "reactionary" and revolutionary-conservative terms mentioned in the first chapter of this book. To claim, however, that we should not ask militants what is their "ideological horizon"; that it will be enough if they do not collaborate with non-European powers; and that they should unite to fight for Europe in a common party, setting aside the problem of a clear, common worldview—all this would amount to confining this noble cause to the level of an irrational activism lacking a flag and a backbone; thus, even if the practical goal were achieved, divisions and struggles would soon ensue within the European bloc. In general, even if we were to admit that this was the proper way to achieve European unity (besides the fact that the premise for an organic and non-"communitarian" structure would be lacking), this Europe would not be the bearer of any particular ideal. This type of Europe would appear as another power bloc, alongside the Chinese, American, Russian, and even Afro-Asiatic: alongside or in opposition to them and without any differentiating, qualitative factor, since in the climate of "modern" civilization no such factor can be determinant.

Obviously, it would be a pure utopia to yearn to oppose in practical terms all the material aspects of modern civilization: among other things, this would involve surrendering the practical means that are necessary today for every defense and attack. However, it is always possible to establish a distance and a limit. It is possible to enclose that which is "modern" in a well-controlled material and "physical" domain, on the plane of mere means, and to superimpose upon it a higher order adequately upheld, in which revolutionary-conservative values are given unconditional acknowledgment. The Japan of yesterday demonstrated the possibility and the fecundity of a solution of this type. Only in that case could Europe represent something different, distinguish itself, and assume a new dignity among world powers. When it is claimed that European peoples today have a common culture and therefore one of the conditions already exists for unifying them in one nation, we should reply that, aside from the past and from what I have written before, this culture is by now increasingly shared not only by Europeans, but by a great part of the "civilized" world as well. This culture does not have frontiers. European contributions (through books, writers, artists, researchers, etc.) have been absorbed by non-European countries, and non-European contributions by European countries; such a general leveling (which is now extending also to lifestyles and tastes), together with the leveling that is furthered by science and technology, has been used as an argument by those who do not want a united Europe but rather a unified world, in a supernational organization or World Government. It is obvious that a united Europe could become spiritually differentiated and represent something different and unchanging (and even become a leader if the modern world were to enter a crisis in the future), only by dealing with this problem and by providing a serious solution.

Coming back to less general problems, at the beginning of this book I talked about the need to overcome the false dilemma of fascism and antifascism, a binomial in which everything that is not democracy, Marxism, and socialism is superficially characterized as "fascism." This can also be applied to the European ideal. It goes without saying that there cannot be compromises or "discussions" with all that is comprised in the formula "antifascism." The first European detoxification should concern this obsession with "antifascism," which is the catchphrase of the "crusade" that has left Europe in a pile of rubble. However, we cannot side either with those pro-European sympathizers who can only refer to what was attempted in Fascist Italy and Nazi Germany before the war, toward the creation of a new order. These groups fail to recognize that Fascism and National Socialism were movements and regimes in which different and even contrasting tendencies coexisted; their development in the right, positive, revolutionary-conservative sense could have occurred only if circumstances had allowed for an adequate, further development, which was stricken down by the war they ignited and by their ensuing defeat. This is how we should at least proceed to a precise distinction, if we want to draw reference points from those movements.

Besides doctrinal difficulties, which I have examined, a radical European action finds its major obstacle in the lack of something that could represent a starting point, a firm support, and a center of crystallization. Before 1945 we could at least witness the wonderful sight of the principle of a supernational European Army, and the legionary spirit of volunteers from many nations who, having been organized in several divisions, fought on the Eastern front against the Soviets; at that time the foundation was the Third Reich. Today the only concrete, though partial, European initiatives of various governments are taken on a mere economic plane, without any deep ideological and ideal counterpart. Those who are sensitive to the idea of a united Europe in a higher sense are only isolated individuals, and not only are they not supported, but also they are even opposed by their own countries; and much more so, let me add, if their necessary antidemocratic and anti-Marxist profession of faith is openly declared. In effect, a European action must proceed in parallel with the rebirth and the revolutionary-conservative reorganization of the individual European countries: but to recognize this also means to acknowledge the disheartening magnitude of the task ahead.

Despite this, we could suggest the idea of an Order, whose members would act in the various nations, doing what they can to promote an eventual European unity, even in such unfavorable conditions. The enthusiasm of young militants who conduct an active propaganda should be commended, but it is not enough. We should count on people with a specific qualification, who occupied or intended to occupy key positions in their own nations. What kind of men could be up to this task? Assuming bourgeois society and civilization as a reference point, it is necessary to win over to the cause and to recruit people who neither spiritually belong to the bourgeoisie nor are affected by it, or who are already beyond it. A first group should be composed of members of ancient European families that are still "standing" and who are valuable not only because of the name they carry, but also because of who they are, because of their personality. It is very difficult to find such men but there are some exceptions, and even during and after the last World War, some of these figures emerged. Sometimes it is a matter of awakening something in the blood that has not been entirely lost but still exists in a latent state. In these elements we would expect to find the presence of congenital, "racial" dispositions (*racial* in the elitist and non biological-racist sense of the term) that guarantee an action and a reaction according to a precise and secure style, free from theories and abstract principles, in a spontaneous and complete adherence to those values that every man of good birth considered obvious before the rise of the Third Estate and of what followed it.

In regard to a second and more numerous section of the Order, I have in mind men who correspond to the human type shaped here and there through selections and experiences of an essentially warrior character, and through certain disciplines. Existentially speaking, this type is well versed in the art of "demythologization": it recognizes as illusion and hypocrisy the entire tenacious legacy of the ideologies that have been employed as instruments, not to bring down this or that European nation, but to deal a deadly blow to the whole of Europe. These men harbor a healthy intolerance for any rhetoric; an indifference toward intellectualism and politicians' gimmicks; a realism of a higher type; the propensity for impersonal activity; and the capability of a precise and resolute commitment. In the past, in some elite fighting units, today among paratroopers and analogous corps (e.g., Marines and others), some disciplines and experiences favor the formation of this human type, which displays the same traits in various nations. A common way of being constitutes a potentially connective element, beyond nationalities. By winning over these elements to the European cause, we could constitute, with a "force at the ready," the most active cadres of such an Order. If direct and integrating communications were established between these two groups (which is not as difficult as it may first appear), the foundation would be laid. For these men, the most important concerns should be the European idea in terms of values and of worldview, followed by the Order and then by the nation.

Naturally, the personality of an authentic leader at the center and head of the Order is of the utmost importance. Unfortunately, no such person exists today: it would be dangerous and rash to see him in any of the figures who are currently working here and there, albeit with the best of intentions, selflessly and bravely, to form European groups. One has to consider here that no one could have detected in advance the potential of any of the men who later became leaders of great movements. Nevertheless, it is easy to see the great advantages in the case where such a man, in whom authority and status now became manifest, had been there from the beginning.

We do not need to repeat what the basic requirement is for such a European action to mature and bear any results. One must first get rid of the political class, which holds the power in almost all European countries in this time of interregnum and European slavery. This would be immediately possible if a sufficient mass of today's peoples could be reawakened from their stupefied and stultified condition that has been systematically created by the prevailing political-social ideas.

But the greatest difficulty for the true European idea is the deep crisis of the authority principle and the idea of the State. This will seem contradictory to many, because they believe the strengthening of that principle and that idea would bring in its wake a schismatic division and thus a rigid, anti-European pluralism. We have already shown why this is not at all the case, when we were speaking of the *Männerbünde* and indicating the higher level that characterizes the idea of a true State and its authority, in contrast to everything that is merely "folk" or "nation." For the individual, true political loyalty includes, besides a certain heroic readiness, a certain degree of transcendence, hence something not merely nature-bound. There is no break, but rather continuity when one crosses from the national level to the supernational: the selfsame inner readiness will be required as in the times of Indo-European origins and of the best feudal regimes, in which it was also a matter of the voluntary union of free powers, proud to belong to a higher order of things that did not oppress but rather embraced them. The real obstacles are only fanatical nationalism and the collapse of society and community.

In summary, let it be said that breaking through into more thoughtful minds is the idea that in the current state of affairs, the uniting of Europe into a single bloc is the indispensable prerequisite for its continuation in a form other than an empty geographical concept on the same materialistic level as that of the powers that seek to control the world. For all the reasons already explained, we know that this crisis involves a dual inner problem, if under these circumstances one hopes to establish a firm foundation, a deeper sense, and an organic character for a possible united Europe. On the one hand, an initiative in the sense of a spiritual and psychic detoxification must be taken against what is commonly known as "modern culture." On the other, there is the question of the kind of "metaphysics" that is capable, today, of supporting both a national and a supranational principle of true authority and legitimacy.

The dual problem can be translated into a dual imperative. It remains to be seen which and how many men, in spite of it all, still stand upright among so many ruins, in order that they may make this task their own.

Appendix

EVOLA'S *AUTODIFESA* (SELF-DEFENSE STATEMENT)

In April of 1951, Julius Evola was arrested in his residence at 197 Corso Vittorio Emmanuele in Rome by men of the Ufficio Politico della Questura (the political section of the Questura, the public prosecutor's office). The accusation was that he had been the "master," the "inspirer" with his "nebulous theories" of a group of young men who were accused in turn of having hatched organizations for clandestine struggle: the FAR [Fasci d'Azione Rivoluzionaria] and the neofascist-oriented Legione nera. Hence, they were all accused of "glorifying Fascism" *[apologia di Fascismo]* and of having "attempted to reconstitute the dissolved Fascist Party." Evola was held in the Regina Coeli prison until the trial, which took place in the Court of Assizes in Rome and lasted from early October until 20 November 1951. Evola was defended by Professor Francesco Carnelutti and fully acquitted. Evola's self-defense statement has been here translated from the Italian by Joscelyn Godwin.

Gentlemen of the Court:

The original accusation on which my arrest was based referred to Article 1 of Law no. 1546 of 1947: that together with others, I had promoted the revival of the dissolved Fascist Party under the guise of various organizations, particularly the one alleged to be behind the group of young men called "Imperium." It is not worth saying more than a few words about this accusation, which is devoid of any basis whatsoever.

Nothing, in fact, has been produced to my charge that would lead anyone to think that my relationships with these groups had developed in any way but on the purely intellectual and doctrinal level, concerning the doctrine of

287

the State, ethics, and the outlook on life. And as for these relationships, emphasized tendentiously and arbitrarily by the Questura, I must say that they have not been any more significant than those that I have had with various other groups: monarchical, independent, or nationalist, as for example E. M. Gray's group "Il Nazionale," or that of "Meridiano d'Italia" [connected to MSI, the Movimento Sociale Italiano]. Certainly I have felt particularly drawn toward these young men of Imperium for two reasons: first, because they insist on the necessity of an inward and spiritual revolution of the individual as the presupposition for political struggle—and [Enzo] Erra, the director of Imperium, indicated this in precise terms during his interrogation—and second, because among all the currents of the MSI, this group defended right-wing positions tied to spiritual and hierarchical values against the socialist tendency widely represented in that party.

I have been a complete stranger to secretly organized initiatives, nor has anyone ever spoken to me about them. As for a certain activism, I have often urged against furnishing arms to the adversary in that way, since no serious person thinks that there is any basis in Italy, given the international situation, for a real revolution or an antidemocratic coup d'état. I have not only written this in a letter that the Questura has confiscated (but which it has taken care not to produce), but also elsewhere: for instance, in an article for *Il Nazionale* entitled "Trarre partito dall'ostacolo" [Taking Advantage of the Obstacle]. There I said that the increased severity in antifascist repression intended by the new drafting of Scelba's law ought to encourage the salutary renunciation of external and fairly anachronistic forms of expression and activism, in favor of concentration on a serious doctrinal preparation.

In general—since there has been talk of being an "ideological accessory"—in none of my writings has there been any incitement, even indirect or involuntary, to terrorist or clandestine actions. The Questura's statement has tried to establish an absurd relationship between the constitution of the "Legione nera" and a point in my booklet *Orientamenti*, where it is said that the tragic character of our times demands a sort of "Legionairism." But I specify exactly what that means: legionairism not as an organization, but as a spirit, an inward attitude. Here are the exact words: "The attitude of him who can choose the hardest life, who is able to continue fighting even when he knows that the battle is materially lost, and who holds to the ancient precept that loyalty is mightier than fire" (*Orientamenti*, pp. 5–6). The same meaning is expressed further on (p. 22), speaking of the "man standing upright among the ruins." It concerns nothing other than an ethical, heroic, and spiritual attitude. Misunderstandings are not possible, and where they have occurred, I cannot take responsibility for them.

I have never encouraged the formation of parties—I deny the very concept of the party—or of subversive movements. This is how I indicate what is to be done (p. 6): "A silent revolution, proceeding in the depths, where the premises are created, first inwardly and in the individual, of that Order which, when the time is ripe, will also manifest externally, supplanting like lightning the forms and forces of a world of decadence and corruption." Permit me to cite two other passages. On page 5: "To get up again, to arise inwardly, to give oneself a form, to create an order and a direction within oneself," instead of "furthering the demagogy and materialism of the masses," taking a position—I say just that—"against those who can think only in terms of programs, organizational and partisan problems." On pp. 6–7: "In the face of a slovenly world, whose principles are 'Who'll make you do that?' or 'First the belly, then morality,' or again 'These aren't times that allow one the luxury to demonstrate character,' or finally 'I've got a family'—one can retort: 'We cannot be otherwise than we are: this is our life, this is our being.' Whatever of positive value that can be achieved today or tomorrow will not be thanks to the abilities of agitators or politicos, but through the natural prestige and recognition of men who are equal to it, and thereby become the guarantors for their ideas." After exhorting them to maintain this level of high ethical tension despite this whole ruined world, I am said to be—in the exact words of the Questura—a "malefic and shady character," instigator of fanatical youth!

I move on to the second accusation: that I have "glorified ideas proper to Fascism" in articles published in various numbers of the reviews *La Sfida*, *Imperium*, and in *Orientamenti*, as "several consecutive actions of a single criminal design."

In this regard I must first bring forward a very significant piece of data.

This crime was imputed to me only in a second phase: it did not figure in the accusation laid before me by the Public Prosecutor when he interrogated me. Obviously it was an expedient, a "strategic conversion," so as to ensure a "consolation prize" in case of the likely failure of the first and principal accusation. It is enough to look at the dates of the incriminating writings to be convinced of this: they date from six months to two years (!) before my arrest.

Orientamenti bears the date 1950, and appeared about a year before it. Not only that, but it is a compendium of articles already published elsewhere and reorganized at the invitation of a group that is not the same as Imperium, and which only served as a distribution network for the review of that name. How can it be that these "consecutive actions of a single criminal design" went unnoticed for such an improbably long time? There are only two possibilities. Either one must conclude that the political surveillance of the Press has a very singular rhythm and promptness; or else—the only sensible hypothesis—these writings have been selected out of a quantity of my other writings in the same spirit, including more recent ones, that have appeared in well-watched pages such as *Meridiano d'Italia, Rivolta Ideale, Lotta Politica*—selected not for their intrinsic contents, but for the sole fact of their having appeared in the pages of the Imperium group, thereby establishing my nonexistent implication in the presumed illegal organizational initiatives that are imputed to this group. Such a device must be transparent to any objective judiciary.

There is more. The original report of the Questura deals hardly at all with the presumed crime of "glorification" that I am supposed to have committed with these writings. Arrogating to itself the competence, the authority, and the function of judging in matters of high culture, of philosophy, of racial doctrine, and even going into the merits of what I say on Darwinism, on psychoanalysis, on existentialism, the report of the Political Office of the Questura seeks rather to denigrate my status as a writer, presenting me as a dilettante known only to little groups of esotericists—and it is comical to see how ignorant the compiler of this report is of what "esotericism" means!—who has deluded these young neofascists with his philosophical, magical, morbid theories (it even goes so far as to speak of *insania mentis!*), and must be responsible for their unconsidered actions.

Thus they stray into a field absolutely foreign to the material of the accusation (of which see Article 7). And although it is extremely antipathetic to have to speak about oneself, I feel obliged to make a short rectification of such a distorted caricature of myself.

If I were nothing but a dilettante and a fanatic, unknown outside the circles in question, may I ask why publishers of the first rank such as Laterza (the publisher of Croce), Bocca, and Hoepli should ever have printed various works of mine, some of them concerning racism? More than one of these works has been reprinted, and several have been translated into various foreign languages. One may also ask how I was ever invited to give courses of lectures at universities in Italy (Milan, Florence) and abroad (Halle, Hamburg), beside having been an invited speaker at foreign societies that are open only to the principal exponents of traditional and aristocratic European thought, such as the Herrenklub of Berlin, Countess Zichy's Cultural Association of Budapest, and the Prince Rohan's Kulturbund in Vienna?

That which has been described in terms of unbalanced, shady, and "magical" theories actually consists of systematic studies on metaphysics, on Orientalism, on ascesis, on the science of myths and symbols—studies, once again, that are also appreciated abroad. In this regard I will only mention that this very year, the publisher Luzac of London, Europe's most distinguished in this field, has published one of my works on Buddhism, *The Doctrine of Awakening*.

The statement of the Questura demands rectification of another point concerning racism. Always trying to place me in a compromising light, it presents me as a nazi-fascist fanatic, who in his lectures abroad has attacked Latinity and denigrated Italianity in favor of the Aryan-Germanic idea, causing alarm right up the Fascist hierarchy, following warnings from consulates.

All this is a misunderstanding derived from incompetence and deficient information.

It must be realized that in modern racial studies, "Aryan" and even "Nordic" do not in fact mean German; the term is synonymous with "Indo-European," and is correctly applied to a primordial, prehistoric race from which were derived the first creators of the Indian, Persian, Greek, and Roman civilizations, and of which the Germans are only the final adventitious branches. All this is shown in the clearest possible way in my works *Rivolta contro il mondo moderno* and *Sintesi di dottrina della razza*. The kind of racism I have defended, far from being an "extremism," belongs within the efforts I made, also in other fields, to rectify the ideas that were developing in a deviant direction in Fascism, as well as in National Socialism. Thus, I countered the racism that was materialistic and vulgarly anti-Semitic with a spiritual racism, introducing the concept of "race of the spirit" and developing an original doctrine on that basis. Moreover, I opposed the Aryan-Germanic ideal defended by Nazism with the Aryan-Roman ideal; I certainly attacked the confused idea of Latinity, not in favor of the Germanic idea but to exalt the concept of pure Romanity, conceived as a more august and original force than all that which is generically Latin.

That is not all. The attorney of the Questura seems unaware that the lectures he mentions, and whose title was significantly "The Aryan-Roman reawakening of Fascist Italy," were followed by others in various German cities, whose texts I have collected in Italian, extracted from *Rassegna Italiana*. Here I displayed what the ancient Classical and Roman idea had to offer for redirecting various ideas in vogue in Germany, and for raising them to a higher, spiritual level. It is possible that some Italian consul abroad, deficient in such studies, sent alarming reports. But as to the preoccupation that my racial theory is supposed to have caused right up the Fascist hierarchy, things stand very differently. After these lectures, Mussolini, on his personal initiative, wanted to speak to me to express his approval of my racial formulations, because he considered them useful for giving an independent, indeed superior, position to Italian thought vis-à-vis the Nazi ideology—on which the then chief of the Race Office, Dr. Luchini, could give precise testimony. And I must say that this recognition, made spontaneously by Mussolini to a non-Fascist—i.e., a non-party member, is one of the most gratifying memories of my life. In any case, I would say that the theory of race is only a subordinate and secondary chapter in the collection of ideas that I have defended, despite what some people believe.

Next, when the report of the Questura claims that for a certain period during Fascism I was "under surveillance" for personal motives obscurely mentioned—and, it adds, for magical activity!—there is not the slightest truth in that. It would be as well to remember, in cases of this sort, what people were obeyed in servile fashion by the Questura, whose officials were all enrolled in the Party, whereas I never was. As the affirmer of an independent way of thinking, as I will readily allow, I had devoted friends in Fascism, and also deadly enemies who tried to undermine me by every means, putting about all manner of rumors and slanders. Among those enemies were Starace and his henchmen, who even tried to use the Questura of the time, but with no results. And today it seems the Questura does not hesitate to exhume these old tales against me: used yesterday to make me appear antifascist, and today, on the contrary, to confirm the accusation of Fascism.

Why is there no reference, instead, to the fact that in 1930 the Political Office of the Questura passed an injunction on me for the suspension of the journal I edited, *La Torre*? And why was that? For "attacks against the Fascist squadristi." Naturally, it was not a matter of squadrism per se, but only of some unscrupulous types who used the excuse of Fascism and squadrism for all kinds of license, and who in order to take advantage of me, who was attacking them, being protected by Starace, even used the police.

I do not intend to present myself either as an antifascist or as a victim of Fascism. But all this should be duly recorded in order to reveal the methods that are being used against me.

Now that all that has been clarified, and all tendentious accretions removed, I pass to the question of fact, as to the accusation of having defended "ideas proper to Fascism," But here I find myself perplexed, because the accusation neither names the articles with which it is concerned, nor—as is common practice—indicates specific passages corresponding to the worst of the crime; nor, more generally speaking, does it indicate what these "ideas proper to Fascism" might be.

[At this point the Public Minister, Dr. Sangiorgi, declared that it was not a question of specific passages in Evola's works, but rather the general spirit of them. Regarding the categorization of "ideas proper to Fascism," he added that in his view they could refer to monocracy, to hierarchism, and to the concept of aristocracy or elitism. After all that had been put, on request, into the court record, Evola continued.]

Very well. As for monocracy, that is nothing but a different name for monarchy, in the original and not necessarily dynastic sense of the term. As for hierarchism, I will say at once that I defend the idea of hierarchy, not that of hierarchism. Once that is clear, I should say that if such are the terms of the accusation, I would be honored to see, seated at the same bench of accusation, such people as Aristotle, Plato, the Dante of *De Monarchia*, and so on up to Metternich and Bismarck. I reject the accusation of defending ideas proper to Fascism, because the expression "proper to" contained in Article 7 means "specific to"; means ideas that have not simply been present in Fascism, but ideas that can be found only in Fascism, and not elsewhere.

Now, in regard to myself this is absolutely not the case. I have defended, and I still defend, "fascist ideas," not inasmuch as they are "fascist" but in the measure that they revive ideas superior and anterior to Fascism. As such they belong to the heritage of the hierarchical, aristocratic, and traditional conception of the State, a conception having a universal character and maintained in Europe up to the French Revolution. In fact, the position that I have defended and continue to defend, as an independent man—because I have never been enrolled in any party, not in the PNF [Partito Nazionale Fascista], the PRF [Partito Repubblicano Fascista], or the MSI—should not be called "fascist" but traditional and counterrevolutionary. In the same spirit as a Metternich, a Bismarck, or the great Catholic philosophers of the principle of authority, De Maistre and Donoso Cortès, I reject all that which derives, directly or indirectly, from the French Revolution and which, in my opinion, has as its extreme consequence bolshevism; to which I counterpose the "world of Tradition." All this results in the clearest possible way from my fundamental work, delivered to the Court, *Rivolta contra il mondo moderno*, whose two parts are entitled precisely "The World of Tradition" and "Genesis and Face of the Modern World." In the preface I indicate that this book is the key to the proper comprehension of my specifically political writings; and the English critic McGregor speaks thus of the work, in his review of its second edition: "Rather than the masterpiece of the Italian Spengler, I would call this book the bulwark of the European aristocratic and traditional spirit." This position of mine is well known, and not in Italy alone. Also in a very recent book by the Swiss historian A. Mohler (*Die konservative Revolution*, Stuttgart, 1950, pp. 21, 241, 242), I have been honored to be placed beside Pareto, and considered as the principal Italian exponent of the so-called "conservative revolution."

Thus, in my view there is no cause to speak of a glorification of "ideas proper to Fascism." My principles are only those that, before the French Revolution, every well-born person considered sane and normal. I leave undetermined for today the dynastic and institutional question. However, all that I write, including the incriminated articles and *Orientamenti*, could be interpreted equally well as the defense of the pre-constitutional and traditional idea of monarchy and hierarchy: a defense that none of our laws criminalizes, because if Article 1 of the Emergency Laws has its counterpart in Article 2, which prohibits the reconstruction—at least by violent means—of the monarchy, Article 7 has no counterpart in a prohibition of the glorification of a "monarchical" ideology.

As to historical Fascism, if I have supported those aspects of it that can be justified within this order of ideas, I have combated the ideas in it that are more or less redolent of the materialistic political climate of recent times; and such criticisms of what is today commonly considered as Fascism are frequent in the very writings that are being proposed to incriminate me. I will limit myself to a few essential points.

1. I am opposed to totalitarianism, counterposing to it the ideal of an organic, differentiated State, and considering "fascist hierarchism" as a deviation. In *Orientamenti*, pp. 13–14, one reads that totalitarianism represents a wrong direction and the abortion of the need for a virile and organic political unity: "Hierarchy is not hierarchism—the latter an evil that is trying to flourish in a minor mode today—and the organic conception has nothing to do with sclerotic statolatry or a leveling centralization." I have taken an antitotalitarian position even more extensively and energetically in an article that I submit to the Court entitled "Stato organico e totalitarismo" [The Organic State and Totalitarianism], which appeared in *Lotta Politica*, the official organ of the MSI. I have defended the same thesis, transposed to the cultural plane, in the incriminated essay in *Imperium* (no. 2) where, criticizing the ideas of the writer Stending, I recognize with him that the evil from which modern culture is suffering is its fragmentation, due to the paralysis of a central, directive idea; but I oppose the totalitarian solution, in which there is not a spiritual, super-elevated, and transcendent principle, but rather the brutal political will to tyrannically enslave and unify the culture, of which we see the ultimate result in Sovietism.

2. A specifically Fascist conception was that of the so-called "ethical State" of Gentile. I have harsh words for it (*Orientamenti*, pp. 20–21).

3. Some like to depict Fascism as an "oblique tyranny." During that "tyranny" I never had to undergo a situation like the present one. As things stand in this regard, the axiom that I take from Tacitus is: "The supreme nobility of the rulers is not to be masters of slaves, but of lords who also love liberty in those who obey them" (p. 14).

4. Concerning the problem of sovereignty, I reject every demagogic, dictatorial solution. The true authority—as I say (p. 15)—cannot be that of "a tribune or chief of the people, holder of a simple, unformed spiritual power devoid of any chrism from above, resting his precarious prestige on the irrational energies of the masses." In so-called "Bonapartism" I see "one of the dark apparitions of Spengler's *Decline of the West*," and I recall the phrase of Carlyle on "the world of servants who want to be governed by a pseudo-hero" (pp. 12–13).

5. I have repeatedly attacked the idea of "socialization," which, as you know, was a watchword of the Fascism of the Salò Republic. I have not adhered to its doctrine (the Points of Verona), albeit approving the behavior of those who fought in the North on principles of honor and loyalty. In socialization I see Marxism in disguise, a demagogic tendency. On this, see *Orientamenti*, pp. 11–12, and more than a third of the incriminated article "Due intransigenze" [Two Intransigences] (*Imperium*, no. 4). The influence that I wanted to exert on the young men of the Imperium group and other youthful currents was, in fact, in the direction of a counter-position to the materialist and leftist tendencies present in the MSI.

6. The defense of the corporative idea should not constitute a crime, given that it is found in today's legal parties—e.g., the PNM [Partito Nazionale Monarchio] and the MSI—and even in some currents of political Catholicism. However, I criticize certain aspects, according to which Fascist corporativism was a simple bureaucratic superstructure that maintained classist dualism. To this I opposed an organic and anti-classist reconstruction of the economy within the unions themselves (pp. 12–13).

Last, a brief summary of the theses contained in the articles in *Imperium* no. 1 and in *La Sfida*.

The first of these simply recalls the meaning of the word *imperium* in its Roman origins: it was synonymous with *auctoritas* and with power derived from divine forces, from above. I then affirm that the crisis of the modern political world reflects the crisis of such a principle or power, and of the heroic values connected to it.

The article in *La Sfida* signed with the pseudonym "Arthos" and summarized in *Orientamenti* pp. 8–9 is based on Metternich's principle: "One does not negotiate with subversion." I take the theme from a saying of Engels: that the liberal revolution merely prepares for the communist one and works for the latter. I then say that just as the communists base their subversive radicalism on this conception, one should also start from it when trying to act in the opposite direction: i.e., in the counterrevolutionary direction of a true reconstruction, without making concessions to subversion.

No references to Fascism or to men belonging to it are to be found in either of these writings. That is all.

Having thus demonstrated that in the incriminated writings—just keeping to those and without referring to my other books, as scientific honesty would have demanded—I am against totalitarianism, against demagogic dictatorship, against the "ethical State," against every form of deconsecrated authority, against a "merely individual and formless power," against despotism—Tacitus's words—against socialization, even against a certain corporativism, I request that the matter should rest there and that the crime of "glorification" should be retracted.

In fact, the central ideas defended by me, as I have said, could appear in Fascism, but they are not "proper" to Fascism, as article no. 7 claims. What remains belongs essentially in the domain of ethics and the conception of life, and, as for politics, it comes down to an attitude of intransigence that is traditional, and if you wish "reactionary"; in a resolute stance against subversion, individualism, collectivism, demagogy, in whatever form it appears, against the world of politicians and men without character.

What the Court is called upon to decide in my case is this: is the climate in today's Italy such that declaring that one wants to hold oneself aloof from any partisan or organized activity, and defending such a position as a writer, on the doctrinal plane, warrants being brought before a tribunal as guilty of an "ideological crime"?

NOTES

Preface to the American Edition

1. Among these, however, many articles can also be found from the Fascist period that make generalizations in a manner which, for Evola, is astonishingly superficial. Moreover, they are prejudice-laden, polemical-emotional, and frequently spiteful. They deal mostly with the themes of Freemasonry, world conspiracies, and Judaism.

2. Edizioni di Ar, Padua, 2000.

3. See Dana Lloyd Thomas, "Il filogermanesimo di Julius Evola: le reazioni dello stato fascista" (The Germanophilia of Julius Evola: The Reactions of the Fascist State) in *Politica Romana* 4/1997, pp. 263–293.

4. Il Mulino, Bologna, 1990.

5. Ibid., p. 646.

6. Dana Lloyd Thomas, "Quando Evola fu degradato" (When Evola was Degraded) in *Il Borghese*, 24 March 1999, pp. 10–13.

7. See Francesco Germinari, *Razza del sangue, razza dello spirito: Julius Evola, l'antisemitismo e il nazionalsocialismo (1930–1945)* [Race of Blood, Race of Spirit: Julius Evola, Anti-Semitism, and National Socialism 1930–1945], Bollatti Boringhieri, Turin, 2001.

8. See H. T. Hansen, "Julius Evola und die deutsche konservative Revolution" (Julius Evola and the German Conservative Revolution) in *Criticón*, No. 158, April/May/June 1998, pp. 16–32. In general, this essay concerns the great importance that the so-called "Conservative Revolution" had for Evola, and goes into the contacts that he cultivated with some of its representatives.

9. A state structure based on the idea of an ascetic, disciplined ruling order. This conception was also dear to Evola and is a subject he repeatedly addresses in *Men among the Ruins*. (Editor's note)

10. Leopold Ziegler, *Briefe 1901–1958* (Letters 1901–1958), Kösel, Munich, 1963, p. 209.

11. The more precise documentary details can be found in my aforementioned study "Julius Evola und die deutsche konservative Revolution," pp. 25, 26.

12. The quote is from a secret report, presumably written by the Gestapo, entitled "Der Spannkreis, Gefahren und Auswirkungen" (The Spann Circle, Dangers and Consequences). Othmar Spann's representative, Dr. Walter Heinrich, is described on p. 5: "He is, like all followers of Spann, an emphatic opponent of racial thinking. From his assistant, Dr. Krautzberger, originates the remark, "If people would just read Rosenberg's *Mythus* then everyone might be cured of this nonsense."

13. Evola comments on this himself in *Il cammino del cinabro* (The Path of the Cinnabar), Scheiwiller, Milan, 1972, p. 138.

14. Ibid., p. 139

15. Christophe Boutin, *Politique et Tradition* (Julius Evola dans le siècle 1898–1974) [Politics and Tradition: Julius Evola in the Age of 1898–1974], Paris, 1992, pp. 241–243.

16. See Julius Evola, *Le Fascisme vu de droite* (French ed. of Fascism Viewed from the Right [see note 17]), "Avertissement du traducture," Puiseaux, 1993, p. 9.

17. *Il fascismo visto dalla Destra con note sul III Reich* (Fascism Viewed from the Right, with Remarks on the Third Reich), Rome, 1974, p. 214.

18. The phrase appears in German in the original Italian edition.

19. See his article "'Lâcher prise' et maîtrise sur le chemin du cinabre—A propos du livre de Jean-Paul Lippi sur Julius Evola" in *Politica Hermetica* ("Letting Go" and Mastery on the Path of the Cinnabar—Apropos the Book by Jean Paul Lippi about Julius Evola), 13 (1999), pp. 212–30.

20. See, for example, Maria Teresa Pichetto, *Alle radici dell'odio: Preziosi e Benigni antisemiti* (At the Roots of Hatred: Preziosi and Benigni, Anti-Semites), Franco Angeli, Milan, 1983.

21. In regard to this, see Gianfranco de Turris, "Nota del Curatore" in the fourth corrected edition of Julius Evola, *Rivolta contro il mondo moderno*

(Revolt Against the Modern World), Edizioni Mediterranee, Rome 1998, p. 12 f.

Men among the Ruins

1. *The Republic*, 592. Shorey trans., adapted.

2. See the excellent study by A. Mohler, *Die konservative Revolution in Deutschland, 1918–1932* (Stuttgart, 1950).

3. I have attempted to contribute to this endeavor of discerning between the positive and negative aspects of Fascism in my book *Il Fascismo: Saggio di una analisi critica dal punto di vista della Destra*. [Fascism: An Essay of Critical Analysis from the Point of View of the Right] (Rome: Volpe, 1970).

4. On this point, aside from the perspective adopted by the author, proper to some schools of sociology and of the history of religions, we could agree with H. Wagenvoort's *Roman Dynamism*, Oxford, 1947.

5. C. Schmitt, *Politische Theologie*, Munich/Leipzig, 1934 (English edition: *Political Theology*, Cambridge, Mass., 1985).

6. A specific instance of such intervention of the pure principle of sovereignty is that which corresponds to the previously mentioned situations [in chapter 1]; I am referring to those cases where, in order to preserve the traditional continuity, it is necessary to adopt new forms, which eventually may include a new right.

7. A literal translation of the German term *Männerbünde* (singular form: *Männerbund*) into English would be "men's societies." This, however, does not adequately capture any of the subtleties of the expression, or of what it originally referred to. Various translations into English have included "warrior societies," "warrior bands," and even "military confraternities"; all of them are somewhat lacking. For these reasons it has been left in the original German. (Editor's note)

8. The first to call attention to this political meaning of the *Männerbünde* was H. Schurtz in *Altersklassen und Männerbünde*, Berlin, 1902. See also, with due reservations, A. Van Gennep's *Les rites du passage*, Paris, 1909 (English edition: *The Rites of Passage*, Chicago, 1960).

9. Conversely, it is significant that sovereigns and heads of state were often attributed a *paternal* rather than maternal symbol.

10. V. Pareto, *Trattato di sociologia generale*, Florence, 1923, § 1713 (English edition: *The Mind and Society: A Treatise on General Sociology*, New York, 1935; repr. 1963).

11. G. Mosca, *Elementi di scienza politica*, Bari, 1947 [1896], II, ch. IV, 4, p. 121: "It often happens that those parties targeted by demagogical propaganda respond in kind by using similar tactics. Thus they, too, make promises that are impossible to keep, and adulate the masses, enticing their coarsest instincts and exploiting and stirring all their prejudices and greed whenever they hope to take advantage of them. This is an ignoble race in which those who willingly lie lower their intellectual level to the level of those who have been deceived, and thus, from a moral point of view, go even lower." (An English edition of Mosca's *Elementi . . .* was published as *The Ruling Class*, New York, 1939.)

12. There is a saying by Louis d'Estonteville, at the time of the Hundred Years War (which raged from the second quarter of the fourteenth to the third quarter of the fifteenth century) between France and England: "Wherever there is honor and loyalty, there alone is my country."

13. Goethe expressed the following principles of "organic philosophy," which may as well apply to the political domain: "The more imperfect the living being, the more the parts resemble each other and reproduce the image of the whole. The more the living being becomes perfect, the more the parts are dissimilar. When the parts look like each other, they are decreasingly subordinated to each other; the subordination of the organs characterizes a creature of superior order." In the political application of this principle, the parts are the single individuals, while the organic whole is the State.

14. Concerning the original background of the "natural right" and its corresponding *Weltanschauung* [worldview], see my *L'arco e la clava* [The Bow and the Club] (Milan: Scheiwiller, 1971), ch. 8.

15. O. Spann, *Gesellschaftslehre*, Munich, 1923, p.154.

16. Cf. Plato, *Republic*, 489c: "Everyone who needs to be governed should go to the door of the man who knows how to govern, rather than the ruler imploring his natural subjects to let themselves be ruled, if he is really good for anything." The principle of the *ascesis of power* is important: "Contrarily to those who currently rule in every city" (520d), it is said that "the true leaders hold office . . . because they know no equal or better men to

whom it could be transferred" (347c–d; trans. Shorey, adapted). Leopold
Ziegler has rightly remarked that he for whom power signifies climbing
and enrichment has thereby proved unworthy of it. He alone deserves
power who has separated the desire for it, the *libido dominandi* [yearning
for power], within himself.

17. In regard to the feudal system, Pareto remarks (*Trattato di sociologia generale*,
§ 1154): "It is ridiculous to think that the ancient feudal system was imposed in Europe through brute force: it was partially upheld out of feelings of mutual affection between classes, as can be observed in other parts
of the world where feudalism exists, such as Japan. . . ." In general, this
occurs in all the social institutions where a hierarchy exists "that ceases to
be spontaneous in virtue of being exclusively or mainly imposed by force
only when it is about to disappear and give birth to another. I said 'mainly'
because the mere tool of force is never lacking."

18. *Annals*, XVI, 20. This is echoed by G. B. Vico's words (*Scienza nuova*, II,
23): "Men first want bodily freedom, then spiritual freedom, i.e., freedom
of opinion, and equality with one other; after that they want to surpass
their equals, and finally to bring down their superiors." (*Editor's note:* We
have translated this quotation from the original Italian, but numerous
English editions of Vico's text exist—e.g., *The New Science of Giambattista
Vico*, New York, 1948.)

19. *Republic* 564 a, trans. Shorey.

20. A parallel phenomenon to the individualistic "wresting free" on the part
of the single individual is the predominance that wealth as paper currency
(i.e., "liquid wealth") has increasingly gained and the fact that the latter
has become increasingly rootless, labile, and nomadic (i.e., "mobile").
However, following this order of considerations would be too much of a
digression here.

21. Machiavelli (*The Prince*, XVIII) says what counts is *appearing* rather than
being, since appearances strike most people, while being is acknowledged
only by a few. A certain foreshadowing of the type of the popular leader is
found in Machiavelli's precept that the prince ought to rely more on the
people than on the "great ones" (i.e., on the "barons"), who would obviously not bow to his absolutism. Prior to Machiavelli, Philip the Fair had
consolidated his power by pursuing an antiaristocratic policy.

22. Julius Evola, *Revolt Against the Modern World*, trans. by Guido Stucco (Rochester, Vt.: Inner Traditions, 1996).

23. We may recall here the Aristotelian notion of social justice, which was understood not as an *equal* distribution of goods, but as a distribution based on the different dignity of the function and qualification of individuals and groups: thus, a fair economic *inequality*.

24. On this cf. Werner Sombart, *Il borghese*, Paris, 1926, p. 419 (original German edition, *Der Bourgeois*, 1913; English edition appeared as *The Quintessence of Capitalism: A Study of the History and Psychology of the Modern Businessman*, London, 1915).

25. Gentile went as far as describing communism as an "impatient corporativism." This amounted to saying that between the corporativism of the Fascist era (as he interpreted it) and communism there was allegedly no qualitative difference, because they were just two stages and views oriented in the same direction.

26. The problem must be framed essentially in these terms, for the proletariat in the old Marxist sense of the word is almost nonexistent today in the West: the former proletarian "workers" today often enjoy a higher economic status than that of the middle class.

27. *Will to Power*, § 764.

28. Concerning the civilizations of being and of becoming, see my *L'arco e la clava*, ch. 1.

29. See my *Teoria dell'Individuo Assoluto* [Theory of the Absolute Individual] (Turin: Bocca, 1927) and *Saggi sull'idealismo magico* [Essays on Magical Idealism] (Rome: Atanor, 1925).

30. It is necessary to point out that the spirit of Hegel's original philosophy was a type of *sanctioning process of pure reason*, so much so that Hegel, almost like Plato or the Eleatics, accused nature or reality of "impotence" wherever it did not conform to the sanctioned aprioristic rationality. The complete collapse of "ethical rationalism," in the historicist sense of a passive conformity of will and reality, of idea and fact, has occurred in Hegel's epigones, and especially in Gentile's "actualism."

31. While Gentile's philosophy is as distasteful (i.e., weak, presumptuous, and confused), as his paternalistic, authoritarian, and monopolizing attitudes

during the Fascist era, nevertheless we must ascribe to his merit as a man that he had the courage to remain on the side of Fascism even when he should have considered it to be "historically passé," as it ended on the losing side of the war.

32. For this order of ideas, see E. Momigliano, *Federico Barbarossa*, Milan, 1940.

33. The fact that the Church consecrated the League of Lombard Communes may be left aside: the same Church that upheld the Communes against the Emperor oppressed them in its own territory. The Church did not have Italian national concerns at heart, but only the defense of its hegemonic pretenses, in view of which it did not refrain from using any means available. The most flagrant example is to be found in the League of Cognac, where the Church sided with the House of France, the Protestants, and the Sultan in order to undermine the Empire, right at the time when the Turks, after conquering Constantinople, were threatening Europe, and Protestantism was growing in the heart of Europe.

34. This degree of Masonry of the Scottish Rite in some lodges is also called the degree of the Knight Templar and sometimes the formula "The Templars' Revenge" is associated with it. This shows a sinister distortion of what was once the spirit of Templarism and of the Ghibelline movement, which I have discussed in my book *The Mystery of the Grail*, trans. by Guido Stucco (Rochester, Vt.: Inner Traditions, 1996).

35. An English biographer of Metternich's, A. Cecil (*Metternich*, London, 1933), rightly shows that the idea of the Holy Alliance defended by Metternich (the *"bête noire"* of 1848 revolutionaries, who should rather be seen as the last great European man), represented the "ancient Roman and Latin idea of a system of supernational order and equilibrium." However, the vocations of Rome's natural heirs at that time had a different orientation.

36. We may also recall that the House of Savoy had attained regal dignity when, with a shameless turnaround, it separated itself from France and allied with Austria, on whose side fought Prince Eugen, a Savoian and one of the greatest military leaders of all time.

37. This very interesting document was published in the *Mercure de France*, in the October 1918 issue, pp. 547–551 (cited in H. Rollin, *L'apocalypse de notre temps*, Paris, 1930, p. 469). It is also interesting that, from a more practical point of view, Wilhelm II's project was a development of the Triple

Alliance not only in an anti-French, but also in an anti-English (according to the meaning of the secret agreement stipulated between Germany and Russia in Bjoerkoe) and an anti-American direction: the Triple League was also supposed to oppose the pan-American projects of the United States, which were threatening European commerce. The same instances reappeared in the period of the "Axis," though at a sensibly lower level.

38. It is significant that not long ago in both England and the United States there was no mandatory draft: the armed forces were made up of volunteers, who received a good pay. In this way the mercantile and bourgeois section of the nation had nothing to do with the profession and the discipline of arms.

39. Especially in my *Revolt Against the Modern World*.

40. In the Christian doctrine expounded by Saint Augustine (*De civitate dei*, XV, 5) a similar view concerning the just war is expressed in rather distinct terms: "While a good man is still on the way to perfection, one part of him can be at war with another; because of this rebellious element, two good men can be at war with each other. The fact is that in everyone, 'the flesh lusts against the spirit, and the spirit against the flesh.'"

41. In the ancient world there are several instances of States, from Rome to ancient China, in which the political and military element merged into the higher levels of the social hierarchy. This feature has remained in European monarchies in regard to the Sovereign, who usually, as the supreme political leader, also had the role of commander-in-chief.

42. In this spirit, in many traditional European States, government officials wore a uniform just as regular soldiers did.

43. Concerning Jünger's views, see my *L'"Operaio" nel pensiero di E. Jünger* [The "Worker" in the Thought of Ernst Jünger] (Rome: Volpe, 1974). It is significant that Jünger has not been a mere "writer" but also an officer, a volunteer in WWI, wounded many times, and the recipient, among other decorations, of the highest German Medal of Valor.

44. Protestantism may be set aside, since it has the character more of a mere religious confession built on an individualistic-social basis than of an organized tradition. Besides Roman Catholicism, we should consider the Greek Orthodox Church or Eastern Churches in general, but their jurisdiction

concerns people who fall outside the context of the problems discussed in this book.

45. Especially in *Revolt Against the Modern World* and *Maschera e volto dello spiritualismo contemporaneo* [Mask and True Face of Modern Spiritualism].

46. In this we had the typical case of those *Männerbünde* that embodied the political principle, as opposed to the physical-social principle I previously discussed. Concerning the Knights Templar, they had their own initiation and esoteric doctrine, reserved to higher degrees, which were not reducible to the mere Christian religiosity fostered by the Church. See Julius Evola, *The Mystery of the Grail*, trans. by Guido Stucco (Rochester, Vt.: Inner Traditions, 1997).

47. St. Paul wrote (Romans 13:2): *"Qui resistit potestati, Dei ordinationi resistit"* [Whoever leads resistance against the political powers, leads resistance against the order of God]. According to some theologians, not even an unjust political leader ceases to be God's representative, and thus he must be obeyed. Donoso Cortès wrote in his *Essay on Catholicism, Liberalism, and Socialism* (Italian ed.: Milan, 1854, p. 19 [English ed.: Philadelphia, 1862]): "The people, by not obeying the person of the prince as such, but God alone, expressed the highest and most glorious human prerogative, that of not submitting to anything else but the yoke of divine authority."

48. This relationship was destined to last for a long time in the States of the Greek Orthodox rite, namely in the Eastern Church that is directly connected to the tradition of the Byzantine Empire; in those States, the political leader is also the supreme leader of the religious community, which has a national character and is not subject, in matters of spiritual affairs, to an extra-State authority, such as the Roman curia, as is the case in Catholic countries.

49. In a traditional Catholic periodical, *Adveniat Regnum*, it has been claimed that the limited success that Traditionalism has enjoyed in Italy is due to the fact "tradition has been sought outside the Tradition." Obviously, Catholicism is here allegedly portrayed as "Tradition" with a capital T. If memory serves me, the sin of intellectual pride is one that is most stigmatized by Christians, and yet this sin is at the basis of such presumptions.

50. Concerning this movement see Julius Evola, *Cavalcare la tigre* [Riding the Tiger] (Milan: Scheiwiller, 1971): paragraph 17.

51. See my *L'arco e la clava*, ch. 7.

52. In relation to this, see ch. 14 of my *L'arco e la clava*, entitled "Intelligent Stupidity."

53. It may appear strange to our contemporaries that one of these principles was the rejection of what today goes by the name of "advertising," because the latter was regarded as an unfair means to undermine the competition, which should instead be defeated in an honest way, through the better quality of manufactured products.

54. Having mentioned this, we should recall that the development of communism in Russia has eliminated such illusions. Just as the soldiers' committees that were supposed to replace or integrate the High Command in the Army were quickly disposed of, an analogous thing happened in the economy. In the first euphoric and utopian phase of the communist revolution, capitalists and company managers were eliminated, and "factory committees" were instituted that enjoyed unlimited powers. This phase was destined to be followed by one in which the technical direction was monopolized by a minority; the workers' committees were left with only a consultative function and a competence in matters pertaining to work conditions, but also with the power of veto. In a third phase, this right appeared to be incompatible with the autonomy required by the technical-directive elite to coordinate the economic and productive processes in view of the various "plans" of the Russian economic reconstruction and corresponding interests, not only economic but political as well. Thus, the "control exercised by the workers," which was originally the slogan, ended up lacking any substantial reality. This will always necessarily be the case in the modern age.

55. C. Costamagna, *Discorso sulla socializzazione* [Discourse on Socialization], Rome, 1951.

56. It was Bismarck who first spoke of a "revolution from above" in an analogous order of ideas. Through the legislation of 1878, which was applied until 1890, Bismarck banned Marxist Social-Democracy, accused of plotting the subversion of the existing socio-political system and of breaking the social peace and the harmony between classes. Bismarck also made sure that Germany was the first European State to undertake preventative measures of public assistance for the working classes. It is significant that such measures were of little avail, clearly showing that Marxist subversion

did not pursue objective, positive goals of a social nature, but rather had declared subversive purposes. When discussing the "tactics and the strategy of global revolution," Lenin wrote that revolution must begin with economic demands (that is, with economic pretexts), and then shift to *political* demands.

57. Oswald Spengler has rightly written in his *Jahre der Entscheidung* (English edition: *The Hour of Decision*, New York, 1934): "The regulation of the economy is like the training of a racehorse by an expert rider; not the constriction of the living economic body into a type of corset and its transformation into a machine with buttons to be pushed." (*Editor's note:* We have newly translated this quotation from the original German.)

58. Disraeli's saying is found in his novel, *Sybil* (London, 1845); Malinsky's and De Poncins's observations have been outlined in their book entitled *La guerre occulte* [The Occult War] (Paris, 1936); while the last quote is found in Niet, *La Russie d'aujourd'hui* [The Russia of Today] (Paris, 1902).

59. *Dialogues aux enfers entre Montesquieu et Machiavel, ou la politique de Machiavel au XIX siècle, par un contemporain* [Dialogue in Hell between Montesquieu and Machiavelli, or the Politics of Machiavelli in the 19th Century, by a Contemporary], Brussels, 1864.

60. Hugo Wast, *Oro* [Gold] (Buenos Aires, 1935), p. 20. Ford's quotation is taken from an article published in the daily *The World* (February 17, 1921) and was developed in his famous work, *The International Jew*.

61. Concerning communism it is written: "The fact that we have been able to make Gentiles believe in such a wrong idea is the manifest proof of their shallow view of life compared to ours; the hope of our success is based on this."

62. An interesting detail is that Darwin was very privileged, in that he lived long enough to witness the triumph of his ideas and immediately found a great number of followers who developed and popularized his subversive ideas.

63. In its day I ran into a curious pamphlet that was published clandestinely in Paris in 1937: *La dernière perfidie de la race perfide: Hitler instrument d'Israël* [The Ultimate Perfidy of the Perfidious Race: Hitler, Instrument of Israel]. It claimed that the same Learned Elders of Zion employed Hitler's anti-

Semitism to provoke a global upheaval, which, in the end, would have ensured their goals by undermining the values of personality and freedom. We cannot deny that this text, which was published before World War II, although filled with errors and divagations, nevertheless reflected the feeling of something that is not entirely fantastic (as long as one discounts the reference to Israel and distinguishes the various influences, both positive and negative, that were at work in the Third Reich).

64. More commonly referred to now as the "New Age" movement. (Editor's note)

65. See *Revolt Against the Modern World*, part II ("Genesis and Face of the Modern World").

66. In this regard we can refer mainly to the researches of F. Altheim and E. Trautmann in their *Italien und die dorische Wanderung*, Amsterdam, 1940.

67. I am referring here to the meaning given by humanists to the term "Classical." To me, things are the opposite: I regard as "Classical" the prehumanistic and elementary original world, with less regard for the arts than for worldview and general lifestyle.

68. Besides, reactions against "Latinity"—understood as a factor of decadence and distortion in contrast to racial forces that are more genuine and valid— are not lacking in peoples who belong to the "Latin" group, for example in France.

69. Pareto, *Trattato generale di sociologia*, § 1856.

70. See my *L'arco e la clava*, ch. 13, entitled "Roman World, German World, and Northern Light," in which I took up and developed this order of ideas.

71. I have made a contribution to the development of the doctrine of race in a more than biological sense, emphasizing the concepts of races of the soul and of the spirit, beyond mere bodily attributes, in my *Sintesi di dottrina della razza* [Synthesis of a Doctrine of Race] (Milan: Hoepli, 1941). In Germany, L. F. Clauss has expounded similar views.

72. These elements of style were emphasized by H. F. K. Günther in his *Lebensgeschichte des romischen Volkes* (Pahl, 1957).

73. In one of my early works (*Imperialismo pagano*, Rome: Atanor, 1928) I mentioned a "Mediterranean tradition." What I meant by it was clarified in

later works of mine, such as *Revolt Against the Modern World*. The German edition of this book no longer contained this expression.

74. Talking about false myths, we should recall that the Italian philosopher Gioberti used to uphold the primacy of the Italian race due to the fact that according to him the latter was a "noble descendant of the Pelasgians." The truth is that the Pelasgians were degenerated archaic Mediterranean populations that had nothing to do with the successive creations of the Hellenic and Roman civilizations.

75. The most remarkable contribution to this idea was given by L. F. Clauss (cf. his *Rasse und Seele*, Munich, 1934). In what follows I will often refer to his typology, after integrating it with that of other authors. In these studies mention is often made of "Western man," more or less the equivalent to the "Mediterranean" type.

76. D'Annunzianism is one of the most characteristic phenomena of the "Mediterranean" style in regard to this particular trait. This is true when we consider not just an artistic component, but the overall style that Gabriele D'Annunzio exhibited in his life, even as a leader and a soldier.

77. V. Pareto, *Le mythe vertuiste* (Paris, 1911): "Many authors are mistaken [about the Roman spirit] because they fail to sufficiently distinguish three very different things: virtuousness, temperance, and dignity. The Romans ignored the first, held the second in great esteem, and even more so the third."

78. Cf., in this regard, my work *Cavalcare la tigre*.

79. J. Thiriart, *Un Empire de 400 millions d'hommes: l'Europe*, [Europe: An Empire of 400 Million] (Brussels, 1964). The book has also been published in Italy by Volpe.

80. U. Varange [pen name of Francis Parker Yockey], *Imperium*, London, 1948 (U.S. edition: New York, 1962). Unfortunately, this book mistakes "the empire" for one of those power blocs of a "Caesarian" character that Spengler had declared to be the final phenomenon of a period of *Zivilisation*, namely the twilight phase.

Books of Related Interest

INTRODUCTION TO MAGIC
Rituals and Practical Techniques for the Magus
by Julius Evola and the UR Group

THE HERMETIC TRADITION
Symbols and Teachings of the Royal Art
by Julius Evola

REVOLT AGAINST THE MODERN WORLD
Politics, Religion, and Social Order in the Kali Yuga
by Julius Evola

THE DOCTRINE OF AWAKENING
The Attainment of Self-Mastery According to the Earliest Buddhist Texts
by Julius Evola

THE OCCULT CONSPIRACY
Secret Societies—Their Influence and Power in World History
by Michael Howard

THE MYSTERY OF THE GRAIL
Initiation and Magic in the Quest for the Spirit
by Julius Evola

THE WAY OF HERMES
New Translations of *The Corpus Hermeticum* and
The Definitions of Hermes Trismegistus to Asclepius
*Translated by Clement Salaman, Dorine van Oyen,
William D. Wharton, and Jean-Pierre Mahé*

MEDITATIONS ON THE SOUL
Selected Letters of Marsilio Ficino

Inner Traditions • Bear & Company
P.O. Box 388
Rochester, VT 05767
1-800-246-8648
www.InnerTraditions.com

Or contact your local bookseller